Toward an
Old
Testament
Theology

Toward an Old Testament Theology

Walter C. Kaiser, Jr.

ZONDERVAN
PUBLISHING HOUSE

OF THE ZONDERVAN CORPORATION | GRAND RAPIDS, MICHIGAN 49506

Toward an Old Testament Theology

Copyright © 1978 by Walter C. Kaiser, Jr.

Fifth printing 1981

Library of Congress Cataloging in Publication Data

Kaiser, Walter C.
    Toward an Old Testament theology.

    Bibliography: p. 271
    Includes index.
    1. Bible. O.T.—Theology. I. Title.
BS1192.5.K3   230   78-865
ISBN 0-310-37100-7

Printed in the United States of America

To my wife, Marge

'att 'ālît 'al kullānâh (Proverbs 31:29b)

Contents

Preface

No aspect of Old Testament studies is more demanding than theology. The sheer magnitude and scope of this discipline have been enough to discourage most scholars from entering their contributions before the end of their academic careers was in sight.

Such caution should have settled the issue for this writer. However, the more I read the theologies of our day, the more restless I became. I felt some important options were being neglected in the contemporary dialog. This was especially true in the unsettled area of methodology and definition.

It is our contention that Old Testament theology functions best as a handmaiden to exegetical theology rather than in its traditional role of supplying data for systematic theology. The interpreter needs some way to readily obtain the theology that relates to the text he is investigating. This new role for biblical theology is presented in Part I. If our analysis proves true, it could supply the missing ingredient in the perplexing debate between a mere descriptive B.C. type of theology and an imposed normative type of A.D. theology. It is our contention that the writers themselves, by way of explicit reference, allusion, and inferred presumption cast their messages against the backdrop of an accumulated theology which they, their hearers, and now their readers must recollect if they are ever to capture the precise depth of the message they had originally intended. It is for this reason that we have sided with the diachronic method of Gerhard von Rad, for it will best serve the needs of exegesis and carry out the original vision of the discipline.

There was also another matter. The quest for the unity of the Old Testament's message as found in its present canonical shape is presumed by all in the name of the discipline—Old Testament theology, not theologies—but is almost universally conceded to be nonexistent. If the text is to be allowed to first speak for itself before our assessments are made, then we would vigorously like to propose that the element of the "promise" is that center which may be demonstrated from every era of the canon.

It is our hope that this work may be expanded and refined over the years as colleagues of all theological persuasions enter into conversation with this writer. We have deliberately entered into a wide and hopefully irenic dialog with scholars representing a wide ecclesiastical and theological spectrum in the hopes that the compliment might be returned by those who do not share this writer's evangelical stance. Of course, the work is addressed to more persons than the professionals of the discipline; it is also written with the needs of the pastor, college or university student, seminarian, and the serious student of the Old Testament in mind.

One more happy task remains. I must acknowledge the help of so many fine people who have aided this work. I am especially grateful for a spring sabbatical granted by the Board of Education of Trinity Evangelical Divinity School which allowed me to begin this project in 1975. A number of others have shared in typing this manuscript in some stage of its production: Georgette Sattler, Jenny Wiers, Donna Brown, and Jan Woods. But I owe most to my wife who was my greatest supporter and best helper. Therefore, I commend this work to the glory of God, grateful for His grace for all that has been accomplished in this text. May my readers also find it to be of benefit in their understanding and interpreting the theology of the Old Testament.

PART I
DEFINITION AND METHOD

Chapter 1

The Importance of Definition
and Methodology

Since 1933 biblical theology has held the place of honor in theological studies. Especially prominent during this era was an existential form of the discipline known as the Biblical Theology Movement. However, with the publication of Langdon B. Gilkey's now deservedly famous article entitled "Cosmology, Ontology, and the Travail of Biblical Language"[1] and James Barr's inaugural address "Revelation Through History in the Old Testament and Modern Thought,"[2] the "cracking of the walls"[3] of the new movement had begun. Both essays hit at the heart on the Biblical Theology Movement by exposing its divided stance of modernity and Scripture. As Gilkey put it, "Its world view or cosmology is modern while

---

[1]Langdon B. Gilkey, "Cosmology, Ontology, and the Travail of Biblical Language," *Journal of Religion* 41(1961): 194-205; also published in *Concordia Theological Monthly* 33(1962): 143-54.

[2]James Barr, "Revelation Through History in the Old Testament and Modern Thought," *Interpretation* 17(1963): 193-205; also published in *Princeton Seminary Bulletin* 56(1963). An expansion appears in Barr's book, *Old and New in Interpretation* (London: SCM, 1966), pp. 65-102.

[3]Brevard S. Childs, *Biblical Theology in Crisis* (Philadelphia: Westminster Press, 1970), p. 61.

its theological language is biblical and orthodox."[4] Consequently, biblical miracles and divine speeches were dispensed with so as not to offend modernity's achievements while biblical language and frequent reference to the "mighty acts of God" (a biblical but nonetheless convenient phrase which obviates the necessity of espousing miracles) were retained.

Certain questions had to be faced. In what sense(s) did God "act" in history? And what did these "acts" mean? Was the language of biblical theology merely an equivocation of terms, or was it to be understood analogically or univocally with the things to which it pointed?

Gilkey and Barr concluded that the Biblical Theology Movement, for all its then thirty years of activity, had remained within liberal categories; indeed, it had hardly surpassed Schleiermacher's brand of liberalism. Nevertheless, the search for a third alternative between the traditional conservative and the aggressive liberal positions was an honest attempt to retain what was generally agreed by all but the conservatives to be the assured results of source criticism.[5] This was to be done without degenerating into such sterile intellectualism that it left the local pastor without a preachable message. In its wake at least two influential American journals were established to help bridge this very gap: *Theology Today* in 1944[6] and *Interpretation* in 1947.[7] The contribution of these and similar journals along with the huge bibliography of monographs in this era was both impressive and often extremely helpful.

Nevertheless, just as Walther Eichrodt's two volume Old Testament theology in German had begun the "golden age" in 1933,[8] so Gerhard von Rad's double volume Old Testament theology[9] now

---

[4]Gilkey, *Concordia*, p. 143.

[5]This contest has never been conceded by either side. The most recent conservative critiques are: Kenneth Kitchen, *Ancient Orient and Old Testament* (Downers Grove, Ill.: InterVarsity Press, 1966); Gerhard Maier, *The End of the Historical-Critical Method* (St. Louis: Concordia, 1977).

[6]"Our Aims," *Theology Today* 1(1944): 3-11.

[7]Balmer H. Kelly, "In Retrospect," *Interpretation* 25(1971): 11-23.

[8]Actually, two monographs authored by E. König (1922) and J. Hämel (1931) and two important journal articles by C. Steuernagel (1925) and Otto Eissfeldt (1926) had preceded Eichrodt's work, but he was the one who set the pace and captured the scholar's attention in 1933. For one of the most extensive treatments of the history of OT biblical theology and an exhaustive bibliography, see Robert C. Denton, *Preface to Old Testament Theology*, rev. ed. (New York: Seabury Press, 1963). Bibliography updated with Wilfrid J. Harrington, *The Path of Biblical Theology* (London: Gill and MacMillan, 1963), pp. 405-17.

[9]Gerhard von Rad's two German vols. appeared in 1957 and 1960. The English translations came in 1962 and 1965.

* obviate – "anticipate + dispose of beforehand to make unnecessary."

appears destined to mark its climax and to portend its ominous
reversion to a history of Israel's religion type of study.

The genesis of this reversion could be seen when von Rad
answered the question of the *object* of a theology of the OT forth-
rightly: it was what Israel professed about Yahweh. These pro-
fessions were not statements of faith; they were *acts* by which the
people expressed their awareness of their relation to God. Accordingly, it was impossible to write a theology of the OT; now there
were *theologies* of the OT. Further, true factual history must be
separated from interpreted history which was the expression of Israel's faith as observed in such credos as Deuteronomy 25:5-10. In
this changing and doctored interpretation of history, von Rad asserted, biblical theology could find its object!

As if to demonstrate the fact that von Rad marked a theological
watershed, Roland de Vaux queried, "Is it possible to write a 'Theology of the Old Testament'?"[10] and Robert Martin-Achard surveyed
*"La Theologie de l'ancien testament apres les travaux de G. von
Rad."*[11] But all were agreed, a "crisis" had indeed arrived.

Some were even more dramatic. For example, Horace Hummel
boldly announced " 'Biblical Theology' is dead, and IOVC [*The
Interpreter's One-Volume Commentary on the Bible* (Nashville:
Abingdon, 1971)] is its witness."[12] J. Christiaan Beker,[13] Brevard S.
Childs,[14] B. W. Anderson,[15] and Hans-Joachin Kraus merely called it
a crisis.[16]

It was obvious by now that the post-von Rad era was indulging
itself in a large amount of self-analysis, and some real methodological problems had remained unsolved. What was not so clear was
whether it also signaled a new beginning, for the new decade
brought a whole new list of contributors (or were some of them
delayed entries in the older quest?).

There was an evangelical contribution from the Mennonite

---

[10]Roland de Vaux, *The Bible and the Ancient Near East,* trans. Damian
McHugh (London: Darton, Longman and Todd, 1971), pp. 49-62.

[11]Robert Martin-Achard, "La Theologie de l'ancien testament apres les travaux
de G. von Rad," *Etudes Theologiques et Religieuse* 47 (1972): 219-26.

[12]Horace Hummel, "A Second Rate Commentary [review article]," *Interpretation* 26(1972): 341.

[13]J. Christiaan Beker, "Biblical Theology in a Time of Confusion," *Theology
Today* 25(1968): 185-94.

[14]Childs, *Biblical Theology.*

[15]B. W. Anderson, "Crisis in Biblical Theology," *Theology Today* 28(1971):
321-27.

[16]Hans-Joachin Kraus, *Die Biblische Theologie: Ihre Geschichte und Prob-
lematik* (Neukirchener Verlag, 1970).

theologian Chester K. Lehman in 1971 entitled *Biblical Theology,* volume I, OT. The next year Walther Zimmerli, the German promise-fulfillment theologian, entered his *Grundriss der alttestamentlichen Theologie,* while Georg Fohrer, following his large *History of Israelite Religion* (German edition, 1969) and his studies in *Old Testament Theology and History* (German, 1969), contributed the *Theologische Grund-strukturen des alten Testaments* (1972). The Irish Catholic scholar W. J. Harrington published *The Path of Biblical Theology* in 1973, and the American Catholic John L. McKenzie added his *A Theology of the Old Testament* in 1974. To these major monographs must also be added the scores of journal articles that have continued to appear.

Therefore, it is only fair to ask, "Where are we now?" And we can answer that amidst all the confusion of the last decade, some things have become abundantly clear. In spite of its highest hopes, biblical theology has not been able to restate and reapply the *authority* of the Bible.[17] In fact, the Bible's authority has, if anything, diminished during this period rather than increased.[18] It has not fully avoided the sterility of source criticism on the one hand or the historicism of the history of religions on the other.[19] Nor has the force of philosophical theology been exchanged in every case for a methodology that refused to lay any a priori grids of any sort over the text. More recently, some have toyed with a "process theology" grid,[20] but there has always been a long list of potential philosophical suitors waiting in the wings of biblical theology.

If thirty years of history has taught anything, it has underscored the desperate need for a solution to the unresolved issues of the definition, method, and object of OT theology. Since its inception, these methodological and definitional problems have dogged the steps of every biblical theologian. The resolution of these issues, more than any other, would free the discipline from its periodic enslavement to reigning fads of philosophy and prevent its imminent capture by a revived historicism.

---

[17]James Barr, *The Bible in the Modern World* (London: SCM, 1973), pp. 1-12; also called "The Old Testament and the New Crisis of Biblical Authority," *Interpretation* 25(1971): 24-40.

[18]See the great efforts of John Bright, *The Authority of the Old Testament* (Nashville: Abingdon, 1967); Daniel Lys, *The Meaning of the Old Testament* (Nashville: Abingdon, 1967); and James D. Smart, *The Strange Silence of the Bible in the Church* (Philadelphia: Westminster Press, 1970), especially pp. 90-101.

[19]Pieter A. Verhoef, "Some Thoughts on the Present-Day Situation in Biblical Theology," *Westminster Theological Journal* 33(1970): 1-19.

[20]James Barr, "Trends in Biblical Theology," *Journal of Theological Studies* 25(1974): 267.

THE NATURE OF OLD TESTAMENT THEOLOGY

Eichrodt began the "golden age" with a well-deserved attack on the reigning historicism of his day. He asserted that "the essential inner coherence of the Old and New Testaments was reduced, so to speak, to a thin thread of historical connection and causal sequence between the two, with the result that an external causality . . . was substituted for a homogeneity that was real."[21] Thus the OT was reduced to a collection of detached periods with little or no unity.

But after one quarter of a century, Gerhard von Rad came almost full circle and adopted the very position that had originally prompted Eichrodt's rebuke. By separating the "kerygmatic" intention, or homiletical purposes, of the different writers of the OT from the facts of Israel's history, von Rad not only denied any *genuine* historical foundation for Israel's confession of faith in Yahweh, but he switched the subject of theological study from a focus on God's Word and work to the religious conceptions of the people of God. For von Rad, there was no necessity to ground the kerygma of belief on any historically objective reality, on any history as event. The Bible is not so much the source of the faith of OT men as it is the expression of their faith. Moreover, he opined that each historical epoch had a theology unique to itself with internal tensions, diversity, and contradictions to the theology of the other OT epochs. In fact, there was for him no synthesis in the mind of the biblical authors or in the texts, only a possible "tendency towards unification."[22] Historicism had returned! The OT possessed no central axis or continuity of a divine plan; rather, it contained a narration of the people's religious reading of their history, their attempt to make real and present older events and narratives.

The object and focus of the discipline's study was shifted from history as event and the Word as revelation to a history-of-religion approach. Meanwhile, von Rad criticized Eichrodt's structural type of theology for its failure to demonstrate that the covenant concept was indeed central to the whole OT canon. In this regard, von Rad's diachronic type of theology, which treated each successive epoch in the canon as an organizing framework for biblical theology, was closer to the object originally set for this discipline. The problem was not in the use of a historical sequence of epochs but in allowing

---

[21]Walther Eichrodt, *Theology of the Old Testament* (London: SCM, 1961), p. 30.

[22]Gerhard von Rad, *Old Testament Theology*, 2 vols. (London: Oliver and Boyd, 1962), 1:118.

this legitimate use of history to swallow up the total interests of the discipline.

Whenever the interests of history began to dominate, the discipline lapsed into the same sterility that it had sought to evade in 1933. It left untouched the question of normative theology. As James Barr argued, such theology had failed to provide any reasons or criteria for deciding what was to be taken as normative or authoritative in the OT or how this new norm could be the basis for all our theological decisions.[23]

But if von Rad was on the right track in a diachronic, longitudinal (long-cut) approach which paid attention to the chronological sequence of the OT and its message, Eichrodt was also partially correct when he observed that no theology was possible if there were not some constant or normative concepts throughout that history.

Where were these constant elements to be found? Unfortunately, in spite of all the disclaimers to the contrary, the imposition of theological conceptuality and even of theological categories derived from systematic or philosophical theology became common. When the historical-descriptive type of biblical theology (Gabler-Stendahl) yielded to a theological-normative type (Hoffmann-Eichrodt), an illegitimate jump in exegetical practice was always the result. Whereas the descriptive type stopped with what the text *meant,* those who urged that the reader of Scripture go on to find out what the text *means* to us today did so on the basis of a Kierkegaardian leap in epistemology and exegesis. The formulations of normativeness came from one's modern framework or from the ready-made formulations of systematic theology. The *then* of the ancient text suddenly became the *now* of the present reader's needs, with no one knowing how or by what process.

In such models modern faith and contemporary proclamation *(Geschichte* and kerygma) easily replaced history *(Historie)* and exegesis. And even on those other models where exegesis and history were involved, they tended to become an end in themselves, filled with archaic particulars and a fragmented totality. The greatest need, in that case, was to carry out the exegesis of the individual text in light of a total theology of the canon. But what was this whole theology of the canon like? Once again, the nagging insistence of this need to identify a normative pattern became apparent.

Such a question was not the invention of modernity. It had long since occurred to the ancient writers themselves. This quest for a

---

[23]Barr, *Bible in the Modern World,* p. 79.

center, a unifying conceptuality, was at the very heart of the concern of the receivers of the divine Word and the original participants in the sequence of events in the OT. For them the question of factualism was not as important as the question of meaning; after all, in many instances they were the actual parties to or participants in these very events described in the text. Significance and correlation of these facts with what they had known or failed to apprehend of all antecedent events or meanings with which this new event might now be connected were much more important. Therefore, their witness and record of all the interconnections and ways in which the activity and corresponding message was passed from one key figure, generation, country, crisis, and event to another must be of paramount interest in establishing the focus of our study. Should an inductive search of the OT record yield a constant pattern of progressive events, with meanings and teachings in which the recipients were made aware of each selected event's participation in a larger whole, then the path of the discipline's progress would have been set.

That would be the question: Did the progress of history involve relationships where each advance in word, event, and time was organically related to previous revelation? The answer, at least in principle, would be straightforward and direct. Such progress need not exclude organic relationships inasmuch as the OT record itself would frequently insist on making precisely these connections. Many will quarrel with the factualism or originality of these textual connectors by insisting that the "assured results" of source criticism have deleted most of them or exposed their secondary or tertiary status. Perhaps the best we could do for such readers (while evangelicals remain alienated [!] from theological discourse) is to urge that this liability (with its claims to "scientific" objectivity) be overcome (temporarily) by listening to *the canon* as a canonical witness to itself. For our part we believe all texts should be innocent of all charges of artificiality until they are proven guilty by clear external witnesses. The text should first be dealt with on its own terms. All editorial impositions designated by modernity (derived not from real sources—to which evangelicals have no objection—but rather deduced from broad philosophical and sociological impositions over the text) which can be credited with atomizing the text and deleting the connectors allegedly assigned to pious or misguided redactors must be excluded from the discipline until validated by evidence. Biblical theology will always remain an endangered species until the heavy-handed methodology of imaginary source criticism, history of tradition, and certain types of form criticism are arrested.

Such a protest cannot be facilely equated with a static concept of the development of the record. On the contrary, we insist that if the biblical record is allowed to speak its own intention first, it clearly indicates progress, growth, development, movement, irregular and sporadic revelations of meaning, and selections of events in the full flow of historical currents. We do agree with Père de Vaux that this history was not just homiletically useful; it had to be real history, or it was both unworthy of personal belief and liable to internal collapse from the sheer weight of its own contrivances. To borrow, with apologies, an old adage, some of the generations might have been fooled some of the time, but not all of the remnant of the people all of the time.

So there was real progress in revelation.[24] But such progress did not exclude either an organic relatedness or the possibility of realizing every now and again a full maturation of one or more points of revelation along this admitted route of growth. Neither history nor revelation proceeded at a prescriptively set uniform rate of maturation.

More often than not the growth was slow, delayed, or even dormant, only to burst forth after a long period in a new shoot off the main trunk. But such growth, as the writers of Scripture tell it, was always connected to the main trunk: an epigenetic growth, i.e., there was a growth of the record of events, meanings, and teachings as time went on around a fixed core that contributed life to the whole emerging mass.

Whether the event, meaning, or teaching was viewed as a seedling, trunk, branch, root, or leaf, it all participated in the vitality of the whole organism. As such, each part of the historical process was as qualitatively perfect as the whole even if some parts were severely limited either in their quantitative significance to the whole or in their duration. For example, some events, meanings, or teachings were deliberately given with a built-in statement of obsolescence that limited the range of its application to certain historic times. Such was the tabernacle legislation with its accompanying ceremony: it was a copy made according to the pattern shown to Moses on Mount Sinai (Exod. 25:9,40; 26:30; Num. 8:4). Hence its limitation.

Once in a while historical progress also allowed a full matura-

---

[24]James Orr dealt with this problem in his Lake Forest University lectures, "The Progressiveness of Revelation," *The Problem of the Old Testament* (London: Nisbet, 1909), pp. 433-78. The other man who responded to the works by John Henry Newman and Adolph Harnack on developmentalism was Robert Rainey, *Delivery and Development of Christian Doctrine* (Edinburgh: T. & T. Clark, 1974), pp. 35-73.

tion of an aspect of the record, and at those points the text amazes us with the way in which meaning and teaching outstrip experience and the times. Men and time were neither in control of the theologically significant, nor were they the measure of divine capability! Therefore, care must be exercised in this area lest a brand of theological positivism be allowed to spring up which would dictate what could or did happen in the progress of revelation. God remained sovereign Lord even in this realm. Consequently, the suddenness of the description of the Creation, the Fall of the first human couple, the universal extent of the Abrahamic promise, the priesthood of all Israel, or Isaiah's depiction of the new heaven and the new earth ought not to startle us and be judged as impossible. Only the embarrassment of an overly refined spirit of modernity would feel obliged by some prior commitment to a philosophical principle or to a sociology of knowledge to adjudge such textual claims as impossible even before they were found guilty on the grounds of accepted canons of evidence.

The nature of the theology of the OT as conceived here is not merely a theology which is in conformity with the whole Bible, but it is that theology described and contained *in* the Bible (subjective genitive) and consciously joined from era to era as the whole previously antecedent context becomes the base for the theology which followed in each era.

Its structure is historically arranged and its content is exegetically controlled. Its center and unified conceptuality is to be found in the textual descriptions, explanations, and connections.

THE METHOD OF OLD TESTAMENT THEOLOGY

Four main types of theologies have appeared in recent years.

1. The structural type describes the basic outline of OT thought and belief in units borrowed from systematic theology, sociology, or selected theological principles and then traces its relationship to secondary concepts (Eichrodt, Vriezen, van Imschoot).
2. The diachronic type sets forth the theology of the successive time periods and stratifications of Israelite history. Unfortunately, the emphasis fell on the successive traditions of the religious community's faith and experience (von Rad).
3. The lexicographic type limits its scope of investigation to a group(s) of biblical men and their special theological

9

vocabulary, e.g., the sages, the Elohist, the Priestly vocabulary, etc. Gerhard Kittel, ed., and G. W. Bromiley,
trans., *Theological Dictionary of the New Testament,* 9
vols. (Grand Rapids: Eerdmans, 1964-74); Peter F. Ellis,
The Yahwist: The Bible's First Theologian (Notre Dame:
Fides Publishers, 1968).

4. The biblical themes type presses its search beyond the
vocabulary of the single key term to encompass a whole
constellation of words around a key theme (John Bright,
The Kingdom of God; Paul and Elizabeth Achtemeier,
The Old Testament Roots of Our Faith).

The ambiguity of method is obvious; for while the structural
type emphasizes that a theology must represent the systematic for-
mulation of religious ideas, the diachronic type verges off in the
direction of a history-of-religions approach in its insistence that
biblical theology is a purely historic discipline which records impar-
tially the beliefs of the religious community without trying to assess
the bearing these events and thoughts might have had on permanent
normative religious truth. The other two types generally grappled
with the same basic issue, only on a much more limited scope of the
canon or range of biblical ideas.

But both of the chief contenders for the field of OT theology
presented major methodological problems for the kind of OT theology envisaged here. The structural type maps out a program of study
that is so close methodologically to systematic theology that one is
hard-pressed to discover the real usefulness of its mission other than
the heuristic value of seeing what a systematic theology of the OT
would look like. But how would that service the theological or
exegetical needs of the community of faith? And why cause all the
fuss about the awful imposition of the categories of Western
philosophy or those of the great ecclesiastical confessions of the
Christian church if the resulting structure is only a weak concatena-
tion of the relationship between God and man? In such a case,
biblical theology has no independent mission and makes a very
small contribution if any.

Likewise, the diachronic model verges off in the direction of the
history-of-religion approach. While it has supplied the new and
unique framework of the progress of event and thought through the
events of history, it has tended to settle for a presentation which was
purely descriptive in character. Thus, while biblical theology began
as a reaction against the barrenness of the history-of-Israelite-
religion approach, it seems now that due to the poverty of its own

10

methodology, it has been recaptured by this area of theology. However, this was not a necessary concomitant feature of the method as we hope to show later.

Is there, then, a distinctive methodology for this discipline? Or has all the toil of the last half century been for no real purpose? Is there an inner, persistent, distinctive, and characteristic theme or plan that would mark off the central concern for the OT? And would it aid the theological curriculum or even the general reader's appreciation of the text to have this plan laid out in its successive installments? Does all this amount to a system or a logic that builds within the Old Testament? And does this pattern give evidence that it expects additional events and meanings even beyond the range of its canonical writings? Even more crucial, can it be shown from the claims of the original participants in the events and thoughts of these OT texts that they were conscious of a continuing stream of events, meanings, and ideas which preceded them and that they felt themselves obligated to acknowledge some type of permanent, normative demands laid on their beliefs and actions? These are the hard, methodological problems which the past generation and ours have found difficult to answer, especially since this discipline was viewed as the synthesis of all the "assured results" of OT study over the past two centuries. Unfortunately, some of these results represented as great bondage to grids, systems, and philosophies as those the discipline had originally attempted to evade in 1933.

Our proposal is to distinguish sharply biblical theology's method from that of systematics or the history-of-religion. There is an inner center or plan to which each writer consciously contributed. A principle of selectivity is already evident and divinely determined by the rudimentary disclosure of the divine blessing-promise theme to all men everywhere as the canon opens in Genesis 1-11 and continues in Genesis 12-50. Rather than selecting that theological data which strikes our fancy or meets some current need, the text will already have set up priorities and preferences of its own. These nodal points can be identified, not on the basis of ecclesiastical or theological camps, but by such criteria as: (1) the critical placement of interpretive statements in the textual sequence; (2) the frequency of repetition of the ideas; (3) the recurrence of phrases or terms that begin to take on a technical status; (4) the resumption of themes where a forerunner had stopped often with a more extensive area of reference; (5) the use of categories of assertions previously used that easily lend themselves to a description of a new stage in the program of history; and (6) the organizing standard by which people, places, and ideas were marked for approval, contrast, inclusion, and future and present significance.

Not only must the job of selectivity be initiated and guided by textual controls set by the authorial truth-intentions of the writers of the OT, but these same men must also be closely followed in the evaluation of all theological conclusions drawn from these "selected" theological data.

If the value judgments, interpretations, and estimates which they placed on these key events and persons in the text be deleted, dismissed, neglected, or replaced with those of our own, we will need to blame no one but ourselves if the authority of the Bible seems to also have evaporated beneath our own best scholarly efforts. The truth of the matter, for better or for worse, is that these writers claim they were the recipients of divine revelation in the selection *and* evaluation of what was recorded. Consequently, all serious theologies will need to reckon with both aspects of this claim, not to speak of the claim itself to have received revelation.

To repeat then, in our proposed methodology, biblical theology draws its very structure of approach from the historic progression of the text and its theological selection and conclusions from those found in the canonical focus. Thereby it agrees in part with the historical and sequential emphasis of the diachronic type of OT theology and the normative emphasis of the structural type.

Yet it does more than merely synthesize or eclectically accept a new combination of what has been heretofore a set of antithetical methods. It deliberately attempts to derive its theology from the exegetical insights of canonical sections, whether it be a summarizing paragraph or chapter, a key teaching passage, a strategic event as evaluated in the context where it first appeared and in subsequent references in the canon, or a whole book or group of books which are so closely connected in theme, approach, or message as to provide an explicit unity.

Amidst all the multiplexity and variety of materials, events, and issues, it is our contention that there does exist an eye to this storm of activity. Such a starting point is *textually* supplied and *textually* confirmed as the canon's central hope, ubiquitous concern, and measure of what was theologically significant or normative. While the NT eventually referred to this focal point of the OT teaching as the promise, the OT knew it under a constellation of such words as promise, oath, blessing, rest, and seed. It was also known under such formulas as the tripartite saying: "I will be your God, you shall be My people, and I will dwell in the midst of you" or the redemptive self-assertion formula scattered in part or in full form 125 times throughout the OT: "I am the Lord your God who brought you up out of the Land of Egypt." It could also be seen as a divine plan in history which promised to bring a universal blessing through the agency of an unmerited, divine choice of a human offspring: "In thee shall all families of the earth be blessed" (Gen. 12:3).

So crucial is the passive rendering of Genesis 12:3 (also 18:18; 28:14—all niphal form verbs) that Bertil Albrektson[25] acknowledges that if the niphal form is passive here and not reflexive as most modern translations claim, then a clear reference to a divine plan by which Abraham is chosen to be God's instrument to reach all the nations of the earth is explicitly taught in the text. But, alas, he feels constrained to reject it on the basis that this formula appears in the hithpael form (usually a reflexive form) in Genesis 22:18 and 26:4: "Bless oneself."[26]

But a strong protest must be raised at this point for several exegetical reasons. First of all, in Genesis 12:2 the divine blessing already is said to be attached to Abraham's person: "And thou [or "it," referring either to Abraham's name or nation] shalt be a blessing." Hence, neither he nor the nation are merely to be a formula of blessing; neither will he merely bless himself! Instead, even apart from the controversial niphal of verse 3, Abraham is to be the medium and source of divine blessing. Such was his destined mission in the first set of promises of verse 2 before moving on to another and higher statement of purpose in verse 3.

All five passages in Genesis (both the niphal and hithpael forms of the verb "to bless") are treated in the Samaritan, Babylonian (Onkelos), Jerusalem (Pseudo-Jonathan) Targums as passives. Indeed, the harmonistic interpretation which insists on rendering three niphals by two hithpaels is also misinformed when it insists on a uniform reflexive meaning of the hithpael, for that is not true.[27] Thus it cannot be assumed so facilely that the sense of the hithpael is clear and therefore it should be made the basis of rendering the sense of the "disputed niphal." The sense of both of these stems changed under the pressure of polemical interest in Rashi, then Clericus, and now the greater majority of linguists and exegetes.

---

[25]Bertil Albrektson, *History and the Gods* (Lund, Sweden: C. W. K. Gleerup Fund, 1967), p. 79.

[26]For the hithpael form of this verb, see Psalm 72:17 and its parallelism in context, but note the LXX and Vulgate *passive* rendering.

[27]The most definitive discussion of this problem ever is O. T. Allis's "The Blessing of Abraham," *Princeton Theological Review* 25(1927): 263-98. See especially p. 281 where he lists these possible examples of a passive meaning for the hithpael: Genesis 37:35; Numbers 31:23; Deuteronomy 4:21; 23:9; 1 Samuel 3:14; 30:6; 1 Kings 2:26; Job 15:28; 30:16,17; Psalms 107:17,27; 119:52; Isaiah 30:29; Lamentations 4:1; Ezekiel 19:12; Daniel 12:10; Micah 6:16.

Meanwhile, O. T. Allis's linguistic challenge has stood unrefuted and even unacknowledged by contemporary scholars—the meaning is clearly passive and the implications for OT biblical theology are massive!

The focus of the record fell on the *content* of God's covenant which remained epigenetically constant, i.e., the accumulation of materials as time went on grew around a fixed core that contributed life to the whole emerging mass. This content was a given word of blessing and promise. It was a declaration guaranteed by a divine pledge that God would freely do or be something to a certain person(s) in Israel there and then and to later Jewish descendants in the future so that God might thereby do or be something for all men, nations, and nature, generally. The immediate effects of this word were divine blessings (happenings or arrival of persons) usually accompanied by a promissory declaration of a future work or completion of the series—a divine promise. Accordingly, men received the promise and waited for the promise all in one plan.

But in its composition, it contained such variegated interests as to include: (1) material blessings of all men and beasts; (2) a special seed to mankind; (3) a land for a chosen nation; (4) spiritual blessing for all the nations; (5) a national deliverance from bondage; (6) an enduring dynasty and kingdom that would one day embrace a universal dominion; (7) a forgiveness of sin, and on and on.

No principle foisted as an "abstract divining rod" over the text could be expected to yield so great a theological payload. Only a textually supplied claim could have pointed our attention to such a constellation of interconnected terms and contents as are found in this single plan of God—His promise. The progress of this doctrine can be historically measured and described. Further, it will include its own pattern for a permanent, normative standard by which to judge that day and all other days by a yardstick which claims to be divinely laid on the writer of Scripture and on all subsequent readers simultaneously.

THE SCOPE OF OLD TESTAMENT THEOLOGY

Inevitably the question of the limits of the discipline is raised. Should it include materials outside the OT canon? Should it attempt to include all the OT in all its detail, or can it develop some fair type of representative coverage that will present the interests of a total OT theology?

To the first query we contend that the scope of our study is properly restricted to the canonical books in the Jewish collection.

To add to our consideration the Apocrypha, Qumran materials, Nag Hammadi texts, and Rabbinical writings would seriously weaken the stated purpose of discussing the *wholeness* of biblical theology within a stream of revelation where the writers were consciously contributing under divine command to an existing record of divine revelation. The possibility of discovering the unity or center of the OT or its correlation with the NT would be gone forever, for the theme line would now be blurred by the intrusion of what would basically belong in the history of Israel's religion.

Even more determinative is the judgment of Christ Himself, for He decisively pointed to the Jewish collection of books as known in His day and affirmed that these were the ones that spoke of Him. Such a judgment ought to settle for believers and caution all other students of the discipline to restrict the scope of their "theological" studies to that canon. Meanwhile, of course, a history-of-religion approach will need to enlarge its area of studies to include all of the intertestamental literature in its purview.

The goal of a theology of the OT is not to laboriously enter into a discussion of every piece of information that bears on religious history or practice. Therefore, all mere historiographic, cultic, institutional, or archaeological studies ought to be relegated to other parts of the body of theology.

This is not to say that there is a "canon within the canon," as if it were the theologian's prerogative to give to some parts of the canon a preferential status while denigrating other parts by labeling them as secondary or less in status. True enough, the Bible, *la Biblia,* is a plural word pointing to the composite character of the books that go to make up the whole. But this external nomenclature cannot amount to evidence for a multiple canonicity.

Still less can the presence of a central theme or a material center which carries the main line and meaning of the narrative be used as a divisive tool to segregate levels of canonicity, authority, or revelatory value. Instead, if the center is indigenous to the text itself, its authentication should be realized in that it unites all of the supporting parts of the canon. The very development of artificially devised systems of bifurcating the text once again implies that the modern scholar/reader's sieve, through which all the biblical texts are sifted, is more accurate and dependable than the claims of the prophets or apostles who stood in the divine counsel and received what they recorded. In other words, what was denied to the biblical writers by modern readers, they now claim for their own sieves! No, the whole of the canonical text must be received on an equal level.

Therefore, all the text is equally important and comes to be judge of us, not we of it. But this is not to say that it is all important for the same reason. Not every text teaches doctrine. Nor does every text give ethical instruction; but the whole aggregate does lend itself to one unified totality with special surprise moments when the story line or the attached teaching received a terrific advance forward due to the significance of a new word or work of God. Hence, it is possible to have unity without uniformity, solidarity without static constancy. There was little, if any, sameness in form, character, degree, and regularity of occurrence of interdependence which produced a harmony of thought, purpose, and life.

Consequently, biblical theology need not repeat every single detail of the canon in order to be authentic and accurate. In fact, what would be the most preferable of theologies would be that method which could so synthesize what many refer to as the "disparate" details to the central theological structure of the canon as to bring out their own representative validity, distinctiveness, and theological contribution to the material and formal center of the Bible.

That it is possible to write a biblical theology of sorts on particular sections of a large book of the Bible (e.g., Isa. 40-66) or on a group of books belonging to a certain common historical stage of revelation is not denied either. However, such a sectional approach will always presume on the larger theological whole. That is, it will ultimately need to be informed by all the antecedent theology against which this small section may have been projected and especially on the whole theme of the canon. The accumulation of the total message was never far from most of the writers' minds as they chose the words or connected their experiences with what had been their religious and revelational heritage up to that point in time. Notice, this is not the usual Analogy of Faith procedure in which the NT or later theology is allowed to set the pace for earlier passages. On the contrary, it is what we will call the Analogy of Antecedent Scripture where chronologically antecedent canonical theology must be checked to see whether it informed the theology under investigation.

One other point needs to be made: OT theology is a legitimate and distinct discipline from NT theology. To be sure, OT theology is obliged to point to those connecting links with NT theology as NT theology is likewise obliged to trace its connecting roots to the OT. But because of the sheer enormity of handling thirty-nine books covering such a vast period of time, it would be better to package the one biblical theology under the two labels of the two testaments. Further, if, as we believe it can be successfully argued, biblical

16

theology is first and foremost an exegetical tool and not primarily an aid in the construction of systematic theology, then it will once again be more useful if the one biblical theology were published in two parts matching the two testaments. Thus, without standing aloof from either testament, it could be argued that the impact and usefulness of the theology would be greater if it were packaged separately.

THE MOTIVATION FOR OLD TESTAMENT THEOLOGY

The primary impulse in constructing any biblical theology is no longer a protest against systematic theology. That certain estrangement between the representatives of the two disciplines did exist in the past—though not necessarily—cannot be denied. But that was when the discipline was searching for a separate set of categories from those of systematics and when both disciplines were committed to espousing a normative approach to theology. Now with the rising fortunes of a purely descriptive approach to biblical theology and a closer approximation, if not an outright imitation, of the methods of the history-of-religion study, the need to distinguish between these two disciplines is even more urgent than in the former clash with systematic theology.

But given the original interest of biblical theology in the historical roots of the message as it developed and the balancing judgment which sought to identify the text's own collection of normative evaluations, the purpose and role of this new discipline should be stated in much more different terms than it is currently.

Rather than finding an overlap in the systematic or historical areas, we believe biblical theology is a twin tool of the exegete. Its most immediate application is in the area of hermeneutics. Here its contribution is neither competitive nor merely tolerated as an alternative approach to a similar body of material.

Its role is so distinctive that without it the exegetical task likewise falls into a historicism of a B.C. or first century A.D. description. Its message becomes time bound and locked up in the *then* of the event with very little to carry over to the *now* of the proclamation or application situation of the reader or listener.

Even if exegesis should avoid the historicist trap with such abominable practices as resorting to moralizing, allegorizing, psychologizing, reinterpreting, or spiritualizing the text after it has fulfilled its professional obligations by locating the text accurately in the writer's space and time situation, it could also fall into a linguistic dead-end approach where the exegete and interpreter concludes his work when the verbs are parsed, the unusual forms are identified, and connections with important cognate forms are noted. Important as this exercise is, it too cannot overcome a purely analytical result.

Meanwhile the text begs to be understood and set in a context of events and meanings. Historical studies will put the exegete in contact with the flow of events in space and time, and grammatical and syntactical analyses will identify the collection of ideas in the immediate section of period under investigation. But what discipline will put the exegete in touch with that which the writer of this single text found enduring and of special relevance to his day because of its explicit or implied allusions to the great acts and theological evaluations of the preceding revelation? It is precisely at this point that biblical theology will make its most distinctive and unrivaled contribution.

In every successful exegesis, there must be some means of identifying the center or core of the canon. When this distinctive pattern and family resemblance is located and collected from the fruit of a host of exegetical endeavors covering the whole OT canon, the exegete, interpreter, preacher, reader, and listener of individual pieces of text is enabled to hear God's normative Word.

Of course, the warning must be reissued once again against all premature impositions of assorted generalizations or allegedly heightened and contemporaneous meanings on the text. In no way could such a half-baked theologizing substitute for that diligent search for an internally derived principle of unity.

Such a claim must carry its own verification and justification. If it cannot demonstrate that its interests are precisely those raised in the progress of growth of these "centrally accredited norms," then they must be abandoned and the search begun all over again.

When the right center is located, however, the exegete's job may be completed after he has worked through the steps of the grammatical-historical-syntactical-cultural exegesis by adding the theological step.

Theological exegesis, when used with the grammatical-historical-syntactical-cultural steps, will employ the Analogy of Antecedent Scripture to aid the interpreter in making an authorized transfer from the *then* of the B.C. context of the OT to the *now* of the twentieth century. In contrast with the method used by systematic theology called the Analogy or Rule of Faith (which is a collection of the fundamental doctrines of the faith from the chief and most obvious chapters of Scripture without specially noting the time period in which they appeared or the like), the Analogy of Scripture strictly limits its use to that build-up of the core of the faith which temporally and historically *preceded* the text under investigation. While the Analogy or Rule of Faith is deductive and collects all materials regardless of its relative dating, the Analogy of Scripture is inductive and collects only those antecedent *contexts* which were in the Scripture writer's mind as he wrote this new passage as indicated by the same terminology, formulas, or events to which this context adds another in the series.

Depending on where the exegete is working in the canon, he will use the theology of the periods which preceded his text as they introduce analogous or identical topics, share key words, or raise similar theological interests. It is this theology which "informs"[28] the text and supplies the background and available message against which this new revelation was given.

Instead of using the NT or subsequent OT texts and ideas to interpret (or even worse yet, to reinterpret) the old material—an outright act of rebellion against the author and his claim to have received divine authority for what he reports and says—we urge the new biblical theologian to provide the exegete with a set of accumulating technical, theological terms, identifications of the key interpretive moments in the history of God's plan for man, and an appreciation for the range of concepts grouped around a unifying core—all of these according to their historical progression in time.

Likewise, expedients such as trying to bridge the B.C./A.D. gap by using the analogy of the human situation[29] or the method of re-presentation of the text in proclamation[30] to contemporize the message would be unnecessary.

Studied use of the results of biblical theology will mark out the abiding message as being grounded in historical specificity. Thus, exegesis will be the chief benefactor of this discipline's efforts while in a less direct way systematics will also wish to consult its results along with those of exegetical theology, the history of dogma, and philosophy of religion.

---

[28]John Bright, *Authority of the Old Testament* (Nashville: Abingdon, 1967), pp. 143,170.

[29]Lawrence E. Toombs, *The Old Testament in Christian Preaching* (Philadelphia: Westminster Press, 1961); idem, "The Problematic of Preaching from the Old Testament," *Interpretation* 23(1969): 302-14. Toombs said, "Insofar as we of the twentieth century share with ancient man in a common humanity, his evaluations of his situation are potentially relevant to our own," ibid., p. 303.

[30]Martin Noth, "The Re-Presentation of the Old Testament in Proclamation," *Essays on Old Testament Hermeneutics*, ed. Claus Westermann, 2nd ed. (Richmond: John Knox, 1969), pp. 76-88.

Chapter 2

The Identification of a
Canonical Theological Center

No discipline has struggled more valiantly to fulfill its basic mission but with such disappointing results as OT biblical theology. Inherent in its very name is the presumption that an inner unity which can bind the various OT themes, concepts, and books will be found. But, alas, to judge from the available literature, that inner unity or central concept appears to have remained hidden and perhaps buried beneath all the variegation and diversity of form and content in the OT.

THE ISSUES INVOLVED

Simply stated, the real problem is this: Does a key exist for an orderly and progressive arrangement of the subjects, themes, and teachings of the OT? And here is the most crucial and sensitive question of all: Were the writers of the OT consciously aware of such a key as they continued to add to the historical stream of revelation?

The answer to these questions will literally determine the destiny and direction of OT theology. If no such key can be demonstrated inductively from the text, and if the writers were not deliberately writing out of such an awareness, then we shall have to be

20

content with talking about the different theologies of the OT. Consequently, the idea of an OT theology as such must be permanently abandoned. Not only would it be necessary to acknowledge that there was no unity to be found in the OT, but the search for the legitimate and authoritative lines of continuity with the NT would need to be abandoned as well.

Of course, this latter eventuality will not come as a surprise to some, for already they have decided that this state of affairs does exist. Thus, while retaining the traditional terminology of OT theology, the focus of most OT theologies shifted from unity to variety, from developing lines of continuity to competing trends of diversity. That is also the judgment of Rudolf Smend. In an important essay in which he surveys the last 150 years of OT theology, he begins by saying, "The confidence with which one has postulated the existence of a center *(Mitte)* of the Old Testament, has steadily become less and less."[1]

Even the very terms by which we referred to this phenomena remained elusive. Most referred approximately to a central core of events and/or meanings in the OT which provided some type of unifying center for the welter of detail. Georg Fohrer spoke of a *"Mittelpunkt"*[2] while Rudolf Smend, as we have already noted, chose *"Mitte"* and Günter Klein used *"Zentralbegriff."*[3] Other terms have included "central concept,"[4] "focal point," "essential root idea," or "underlying idea."[5]

In spite of the terminological variations, a similar note is sounded in all these terms. Perhaps the word "center" is the most useful, but it also has certain drawbacks. It does stress the desire traditionally located in OT theology of identifying the integrating points in the entirety of the testament, but that word does not indicate any linear historical building of materials within that center. Hence, there still is a need for some term that has both a dynamic aspect of the growth of revelation yet contains a unifying point of reference to it. So far, such a term has not suggested itself;

---

[1]Rudolf Smend, "Die Mitte des Alten Testaments," *Theologische Studien* 101(1970): 7.

[2]Georg Fohrer, "Der Mittelpunkt einer Theologie des AT," *Theologische Zeitschrift* 24(1968): 161-72.

[3]Günter Klein, "Reich Gottes' als biblischer Zentralbegriff," *Evangelische Theologie* 30(1970): 642-70.

[4]Walther Eichrodt, *Theology of the Old Testament* (London: SCM, 1961), pp. 13-16.

[5]Th. C. Vriezen, *An Outline of Old Testament Theology*, 2nd ed. (Newton, Mass.: Charles T. Branford Co., 1970), p. 150.

nevertheless, the idea is clear enough from the several terms which approximate the concept from different angles.

Various analogies have also been suggested for this unifying but developing concept. One epigenetical concept uses the relation of the seed acorn to the full-grown oak tree. Just so, the central idea matures as revelation progresses into the NT era. Another analogy uses the successive folds of a road map. Again the emphasis is on unity with plenty of provision for expansion and development. Only this kind of dual emphasis will simultaneously respond to the demands of a *theology* of the OT (with its implied unity) and the requirements of a revelation in *history* (with its contribution of development, progress, and enlargement).

THE CURRENT RELUCTANCE TO ADOPT A CENTER

Traditionally, it has been commonplace among biblical theologians to find the justified warning against the all-too-prevalent temptation to impose one's own philosophical grid or theological framework over the testament. Such externally formulated structures cannot, of course, adequately serve as a key to the systematic ordering of the content of the OT. The procedure is to be faulted both on methodological and on theological grounds.

The problem in methodology is that it denies the priority of the results of careful exegesis. Instead of inductively deriving one's center from the testament, a grid foreign to the form and content of the text is slipped hastily and often carelessly over the material, resulting in the obstruction of the text's own point of view; and large amounts of intractable material are left dangling outside the imposed system.

When one joins to this fact the further complication that all alien grids fail to reproduce or share in any derived authority which could have been borrowed from the text had the form of its presentation more closely approximated that of the very text it was investigating, the theological problem has been faced. The writers of the text claimed to possess the divine intentionality in their selectivity and interpretation of what was recorded. Consequently, if biblical theology does not aim at reproducing the author's truth-intentions in its general theological shape and content, then that generation of interpreters will necessarily suffer a corresponding loss of authority from that word and a demise of confidence from their theological descendants.

But can such a center be identified from the texts themselves? For some, this may just be a further example of another modern "abstract divining rod" by which the OT is forced to yield some pleasant (or even not-so-pleasant) theological payload. It is one thing to wholeheartedly condemn all attempts to impose a key or system over the OT, but it is another to *inductively* derive such a core from the testament itself. This is precisely where most OT theologies have been wrecked. In an attempt to steer between the Charybdis of chronological ordering of the canon (which, as we have seen, often sadly resulted in nothing more than a purely descriptive treatment) and the Scylla of a topical arrangement (which also unfortunately simply adopted the categories of philosophy, systematic theology, or some system of covenants and dispensations), it frequently has suffered shipwreck on one or the other extreme. How can a discipline which by name and definition searches for the pattern, plan, person, and meaning of the record settle for a purely descriptive classification of the information and facts in the text? If this discipline is merely a descriptive science, should it be called "theology"? Should not the definition of biblical theology be closely linked with the *nature* of the Bible?[6] On the other hand, how could it take normative categories *ab extra* from systematics and use these to unfold the pattern of meanings according to the canon's own way of saying things? Must not the particular purpose of every narrative and proposition in the Bible be understood first in the light that it contributes to the whole or total purpose and message?

But does a fair reading of the text lead one to such alleged single purpose? Ever since the second half of the eighteenth century, men of the Enlightenment and their intellectual descendants have found themselves compelled as men making decisions in research to press the case for the Scripture's multiplicity, variegation, and diversity. By and large, no internal coherence was possible since, in their estimation, the observed tensions amounted to contradictions. The same opinion continues to the present moment even in NT theology.[7]

More recently in OT studies, the prestigious voices of G. Ernest Wright and Gerhard von Rad have added their weight to a rising chorus that has decided that there is no unifying center to the OT. G. E. Wright rules out any single theme on the grounds that it would not be "sufficiently comprehensive to include within it all the vari-

---

[6]A. A. Anderson, "Old Testament Theology and Its Methods," *Promise and Fulfillment,* ed. F. F. Bruce (Edinburgh: T. & T. Clark, 1963), p. 8.

[7]E. Käsemann, "The Problem of a New Testament Theology," *New Testament Studies* 19(1973): 242; W. G. Kümmel, *The Theology of the New Testament* (Nashville: Abingdon, 1973), pp. 15-17.

ety of viewpoint."[8] Von Rad, no less definite, asserts that the OT "has no focal point such as is found in the New."[9] Interestingly enough, as already noted above, even the NT assurance has collapsed and also followed the lead of the OT field.

Gerhard Hasel has also joined in this denial saying that the biblical theologian "cannot and must not use a concept, fundamental idea, or formula as a principle for the systematic ordering and arranging of the OT kerygmatic message and as a key that determines from the start how he will present the content of the OT testimony."[10] However, he does freely acknowledge that "the final aim of OT theology is to demonstrate whether or not there is an inner unity that binds together the various theologies and longitudinal themes, concepts, and motifs"[11] even though it is a "hidden inner unity."[12]

Still, the issue must be pressed: Is the unity all that opaque? Were the authors of Scripture merely diffident or even ignorant of any divine master plan behind the course of human events, authorial selectivity of what was to be included or excluded, and the claims for supramundane evaluations of what was recorded? Immediately, some will protest that this prematurely raises the dogmatic consideration as to whether God did, as a matter of fact, reveal Himself in human writings. And we concede the point that this could be construed in that light. However, we wish only to establish at this point that the writers *claimed* (whether we concur here or not is not the issue) that they felt themselves to be under a divine imperative. They were under a holy obligation to speak what was often contrary to their own personal interests and wishes (cf. Jeremiah's agony of soul in this regard); but speak they must.

What is more, not only does a fair representation of their claim attribute the content and selection of what they record to God, but it contains numerous patent and latent references to an accumulation of both promises and threats and persons, and programs which

---

[8]G. Ernest Wright, "The Theological Study of the Bible," *Interpreter's One Volume Commentary on the Bible* (Nashville: Abingdon, 1970), p. 983.

[9]Gerhard von Rad, *Old Testament Theology*, 2 vols. (London: Oliver and Boyd, 1962), 2:362.

[10]Gerhard Hasel, *Old Testament Theology: Basic Issues in the Current Debate* (Grand Rapids: Eerdmans, 1972), p. 62. See also his study, "The Problem of the Center in the Old Testament Theology Debate," *Zeitschrift für die Alttestamentliche Wissenschaft* 86(1974): 65-82.

[11]Hasel, *Old Testament*, p. 93. Page H. Kelley came to the same conclusion: "The search for a unifying theme should be regarded as a valid one, else the Old Testament would be reduced to a collection of unrelated literary fragments," "Israel's Tabernacling God," *Review and Expositor* 67(1970): 486.

[12]Hasel, *Old Testament*, p. 93.

preceded them. Further, they claim to be both in a direct succession to these earlier words and contributors in their further development of both the fulfillment and the enlarged promise for the future!

What, then, was the medium through which these claims were made known, and why has the scholarly community all of a sudden soured on the feasibility of finding such a unity if such a claim was consciously transmitted as argued here? Could such a recorded biblical history be the source of theological meaning and unification?

HISTORY AS THE MEDIUM OF MEANING

Up until the decade of the seventies, the principle which was held with greatest reverence among most biblical theologians was that history was the chief medium of divine revelation in the OT.[13] What could be known of God was to be known primarily through history.

By this choice, OT theologians could, so they hoped, set off by way of contrast Israel's uniqueness from the neighboring peoples of the ancient Near East which invested the natural world with myriads of divine powers. They could also, if all went according to their expectations, bypass *the embarrassment of the classical view* that claimed revelation was to be located in the words of Scripture.[14]

Surprising as it may seem, it was not until 1967 that the basis for the oft-repeated assurance that history was the chief—indeed almost the only—medium of divine revelation was finally subjected to a thorough analysis in the light of the Bible's claims as over against those of the comparative material from the ancient Near East. It was Bertil Albrektson who did this in his book *History and the Gods*. To be sure, James Barr had already delivered a vigorous challenge to this new axiom of biblical theology in his 1962 inaugural address,[15] claiming that verbal revelation had just as much a right to occupy the center of the theological stage as did history. It was only apologetically more convenient to quietly delete the propositional part of the biblical record from public attention, complained Barr. Even apart from this important neglect of the Bible's own system of meanings, it turned out that revelation was not centered in real history after all,

---

[13]G. E. Wright, *The God Who Acts: Biblical Theology as Recital* (London: SCM, 1952), p. 13; Vriezen, *Outline*, p. 189.

[14]J. Baillie, The *Idea of Revelation in Recent Thought* (New York: Columbia University Press, 1956), p. 62ff.

[15]James Barr, "Revelation Through History in the Old Testament and Modern Thought," *Interpretation* 17(1963): 193-205.

i.e., events as they "actually" or "really" happened. Instead, the arena of God's action in scholarly reconstruction resulted in something less real than events which occur in space and time; but, as if to compensate for that loss, we were assured that they were "kerygmatically" more useful!

It was von Rad, more than anyone else, who sharpened a contrast between the two versions of Israel's history. For him, there were "no *bruta facta* at all [in the OT]; we have history only in the form of interpretation, only in reflection."[16] Now there were two types of history: the one obtained from the reconstructions of the modern historico-critical method, the other from Israel's credal confessions supplied from the traditio-historical method. The former yielded the "critically assured minimum" while the second tended "towards a theological maximum."[17]

In this dichotomy, the old ghost of Immanuel Kant was still haunting academia. Von Rad, like his predecessor in 1926, Eissfeldt,[18] had managed to divide reality into two parts: there was the phenomenal world of the past (available to us from historico-critical research), and there was the noumenal world of faith. Israel's faith, like biblical theology, was to have as its object, not the real acts of God in real history, but that which the people of ancient times confessed to have happened in spite of modern critical doubts about its factual status. These credal confessions (e.g., Deut. 26:16-19) about a minimal number of alleged events in Israel's past redemption were reenacted in the cult; and as such, the "re-telling" of these events constituted at once the kerygma and a theological interpretation of the OT. Handled in this way, this second version of Israel's history was naturally subject to various forms of adaptation, reinterpretation, reflection, and even actualization.[19]

In the meantime, another group of scholars was contending just as vigorously for the other alternative: faith in the historical events

---

[16]Gerhard von Rad, "Antwort auf Conzelmanns Fragen," *Evangelische Theologie* 24(1964): 393; *Old Testament Theology*, 2:416, as cited by Gerhard F. Hasel, "The Problem of History in Old Testament Theology," *Andrews University Seminary Studies* 8(1970): 29, to whom I am indebted in several places in this section for his fine analysis. He, in turn, acknowledged the incisive analysis of Martin Honecker, "Zum Verständnis der Geschichte in Gerhard von Rad's Theologie des Alten Testament," *Evangelische Theologie* 23(1963); cf. Hasel, *Old Testament*, chap. II.

[17]Von Rad, *Theology*, 1:108.

[18]Otto Eissfeldt, "Israelitisch-jüdische Religions-geschichte und alttestamentliche Theologie," *Zeitschrift für die Alttestamentliche Wissenschaft* 44(1926): 1ff.

[19]Hasel, "Problem," p. 34, for documentation in von Rad.

reconstructed by source criticism. Franz Hesse[20] rejected von Rad's case for making the confessional level of history the object of faith. How could such erroneous history be the object of real faith? he queried. Faith must rest on what happened, he concluded, and only modern historico-criticism can tell us what actually took place and did not take place in the OT tradition.

But which historico-critical theory? There were at least three available: the so-called Baltimore School of William Foxwell Albright and John Bright; the A. Alt and Martin Noth axis; and G. E. Mendenhall of the University of Michigan. Especially critical were the assessments of these three schools of the "historical minimum" of the prepatriarchal through the conquest eras. There was no scientific history of Israel to be had—especially on the basis of the premises found in the historico-critical method.

Roland de Vaux also vigorously disagreed with von Rad's locating the object of Israel's faith and ours in a subjective and often fallible estimate of history. His challenge was direct: either the interpretation of history offered is true and originates from God, or it is not worthy of Israel's faith and ours. Further, such a view not only is unworthy of our attention, it is devastating in that it attacks the foundation of all faith: "the truthfulness of God."[21]

De Vaux's solution, like Wolfhart Pannenberg's argument, is to stress the "internal" or "intrinsic" connection[22] or unity of events and their meanings.[23] For de Vaux, the connection was in the God who ordered both the events and interpretations. Pannenberg, on the other hand, stressed the "context" of the original happening with its accompanying interpretation.

To the extent that these two men insisted on the legitimacy and the necessity that the connection of history and its canonical significance be the proper starting point for biblical theology, we concur. It was precisely this original unity of the historical events with their attached meanings in the text which provided the possibility for overcoming the post-Kantian dualism and the positivistic tendencies of modern historiography. Not only had new canons of history and historiography which were antithetical in their premises to the whole Christian faith appeared, but a tyranny of the particular (in its

---

[20]Cited by Hasel, *Old Testament*, pp. 31-34.

[21]Roland de Vaux, *The Bible and the Ancient Near East,* trans. Damian McHugh (London: Darton, Longman and Todd, 1971), p. 57.

[22]Ibid., p. 58.

[23]Wolfhart Pannenberg, "The Revelation of God in Jesus Christ," *Theology as History: New Frontiers in Theology* 3(1967): 127.

isolation from the whole) had also arisen as a supporting pre-occupation.

Events, facts, or statements were viewed in their individuality, uniqueness, and separation from their contribution to the totality or the multiplicity of the whole context or situation. Even if the event was retained in its wholeness (which was rare), the attached words were neatly cut off from the happening.

It was here, more than anywhere else, that the unity of the Bible was lost. Rather than starting with the organization and plan claimed by the canonical writers themselves, a principle of natural development or of a Hegelian dialectic was laid over the texts. When the results turned out to be disappointingly sterile in theology—even to the most resolute of all of the modern historiographers—the resulting vacuum was filled with new categories of "history," existentialism, or secularity.

Unless biblical theology is freed from the tyranny of the particular and the shackles of an imposed philosophical-historiographical grid of modernity which takes precedence over the text, no hope remains for any theology of the OT. Neither the so-called scientifically assured minimum nor the theologically devised maximum will take us anywhere. Both systems, whether in the name of objectivity or of faith, vaunt themselves over the texts which have a deserved right, whether it is among those claiming inspiration or not, to be first heard on their own terms and in their own canonical and contextual wholeness. Then when any measuring devices of truth, factualism or validity of interpretation are applied (as they must) to the *total* contexts (which is another must), they should not be those which provincially reflect the parochial interests of a generation which has an axe to grind for *or* against any special outlook on life. Instead, all criteria should approach the issue in a similar fashion to the American system of jurisprudence: a text is innocent until proven guilty by known data provided by sources whose truthfulness on those points can be demonstrated or which share the same general area of contemporaneity as the texts under investigation and whose performance record of producing reliable data has been good.

Given this approach, history can again be consulted in the wholeness of its context of the times and the context of its attached interpretation. In this way, history can conceivably again be a medium of meaning along with unity of its context.

Did biblical history exhibit a divine plan then? Or must we once again sink into generalities about the importance of history without the benefit of a good inductive study of the terminology or pattern of thought claimed by the texts?

Fortunately, Bertil Albrektson has made a preliminary study of the Hebrew terms connected with a divine plan in history.[24] In his survey he found that there were ten passages where *'ēṣâh* (usually translated "counsel," "advice," but also meaning in these passages "purpose" or "plan") was used in a nominal verbal form. They are Psalms 33:10-11; 106:13; Proverbs 19:21; Isaiah 5:19; 14:24-27; 19:17; 25:1; 46:10; Jeremiah 49:20; 50:45; and Micah 4:12. In two other passages, *maḥªšāḇâh* ("thought," "purpose") is used for the divine plan: Jeremiah 29:11; 51:29.

In addition to these two terms, two more are added by Albrektson. They are *mᵉzimmâh* ("a hostile plan") in Job 42:2; Jeremiah 23:20; 30:24; 51:11 and *derek* ("way," "path") in Psalm 103:7; cf. Exodus 33:13; Deuteronomy 32:4; Psalm 18:31; Isaiah 55:8-9; 58:2.

When Albrektson completed this survey, he disappointingly concluded that he found no single divine intention as would demonstrate that God has a fixed plan for the history of Israel and/or the nations from one end of time to the other. For him, the words are imprecise and wide ranging in that they refer to a number of divine intentions but not to one single plan. What is more, distribution of the passages is rather limited since they seem to group themselves around Jeremiah, Isaiah, Micah, and the Psalms.[25]

Now we agree in part; most of these passages are an expression of an individual application of God's intention to a particular situation in Israel or the nations. But how can such a disclaimer be made for a text like Micah 4:12? Does not the prophet clearly state that the pagan nations do not know Yahweh's *thoughts;* they do not understand His *plan?* Is this not in the context of a plan which involves many nations simultaneously? Likewise, in Psalm 33:10 the "counsel [plan] of the nations" is set in juxtaposition to Yahweh's plan which "stands forever" and "from generation to generation" (v. 11). Surely this type of speaking commits the writer to claiming that God does have some long-range planning which counters the moves and planning of the total world community.

Perhaps the greatest weakness of Albrektson's line of argumentation is that it adheres too closely to a lexicographical approach. While he does acknowledge that the *matter* could still be present even when the *word* for a plan was not, he does not discuss one of the grandest claims of all made in Isaiah 40 and the following chapters. The divine challenge repeatedly comes: "Who is like Me?

---

[24]Albrektson, *History and the Gods,* pp. 68-77.
[25]Ibid., pp. 76-77.

Who declared it from the beginning so that we might know, or ahead of time so that we might say, he was right!" (Isa. 40:25; 41:26-28; 42:9; 44:7-8,26-28; 45:21; 46:10-11; 48:3-6).

Even more important is the connection between the claim of God to have already announced, long before anything happened, the course of events from start to finish and the fact that all this was in accordance with His "plan" and "purpose." The context which obviously and explicitly unites these two themes is Isaiah 46:9-11: "I am God . . . who declares the end from the beginning . . . who says, My *plan* shall stand, also, I will accomplish all My *purpose* [note singular 'purpose'] . . . I have formulated it, indeed, I will accomplish it." God is willing to stake, as it were, His whole character and claim to be the one unique God on the fact that He is able to speak and declare the future. The pagan's god can do neither. Furthermore, God's announcements are not random ad lib comments on this or that, here and there. They follow a premeditated plan which encompasses the start and finish of the parts and the whole! All will take place as He has said.

Such talk, apart from any considerations of a unified center for OT theology, takes us back to the original obstacle for most modern biblical scholars: prediction! Indeed, Albrektson verges on saying as much when he introduces the key verse in Genesis 12:3. For him the choice is clear: Does Yahweh here survey past history from the aspect of the achieved result where "all nations of the earth bless *themselves*"? Or does Yahweh project a divine plan for events yet to come all within a universalistic framework where "all the nations of the earth *shall* be blessed?"[26] The issue revolves around the translation of the crucial word *nibᵉrᵉkû*. We concur: the results of this study cannot be of a small interest to the whole progress of OT theology.

Now we have already anticipated this point by arguing in the last chapter that the passive sense is not only possible ("all nations shall be blessed") but is the required translation which fits the single truth-intention of the author. Albrektson freely conceded that if the passive translation were correct—and he recognized it did carry a great deal of contemporary support from O. Procksch, S. R. Driver, G. von Rad, and H. W. Wolff—then the passage did claim that God had a plan in which Abraham was selected as His instrument of divine blessing and by which He would reach all the nations of the earth.[27]

However, many interpreters assume that the reflexive transla-

---

[26]Ibid., p. 78.
[27]Ibid., p. 79.

tion ("all nations shall bless themselves") is to be preferred since the same message as the passive usages of Genesis 12:3; 18:18; 28:14 is given in the hithpael form of the verb in 22:18 and 26:4. The known hithpael, so it is argued, will set the range of meanings for the disputed niphal. But such a procedure is contested here. In addition to the linguistic arguments in chapter 1, it is of more than passing interest that we note also the passive rendering of the Septuagint text and that of Acts 2:25 and Galatians 3:8, which follow the Septuagint. Furthermore, Genesis 12:2 had said that "he" (i.e., Abraham or "it," the nation) "would be a blessing"; it was left to verse 3 to say to whom and how.

Perhaps the most balanced assessment of Genesis 12:2-3 is to be found in C. von Orelli's work on prophecy and God's kingdom.

First of all (vv. 2,3) the divine blessing is attached to Abraham's person, of whom it is said expressly *weh^{e}yēh b^{e}rākâh* ["and he shall be a blessing"] which by no means signifies merely that he himself will be blessed (Hitzig), or that his name will be a formula of blessing, but extols him as the medium and source of divine blessing (cf. Prov. 11:25: *nephesh b^{e}rākâh*, a soul that finds pleasure in blessing, from which accordingly, streams of blessing flow). How Abraham himself, in virtue of his special relation to God, was a mediator of blessing to those about him, is shown in Gen. 20:7; that his people in the same way were to convey the divine blessing, the dispensation of God's grace to the whole world, see in Isa. 19:24; Zech. 8:13. In the present passage the import of the brief saying is expounded in verse 3, according to which God's relation to men depends on their attitude to Abraham (cf. 20:7), and the Lord will deal well with those who wish well to him and do homage to the divine grace revealing itself in him; and, on the other hand, will make him feel His displeasure who despises and scorns one whom God has blessed. The singular number here is significant. It can only be single-handed sinners who so misunderstand one who is a source of blessing to all about him, as to condemn and hate him, *and in him his God.* The world, as a whole, will not withhold homage, and will therefore enjoy the benefit of this source of blessing . . . We are certainly of the opinion that the niphal here [v. 3] must have a *meaning of its own, distinct from the hithpael* (so also Tuch, G. Baur, Hengstenberg, Keil, Kautzsch, etc.). In distinction from the piel (48:20) and hithpael, it expresses more the *objective experience* of the divine blessing. Only, even where the hithpael is used, the significant position of the word at the end of the promise requires even there more than a mere ceremonial honour is meant. The distinction therefore is not material. The act of blessing is no mere formality, for which reason also the name of God or of a man used in it is of high importance. The former shows *from whom* the highest good is to be expected, the latter *in whom* it is to be found, and through whose mediation it may be attained. Therefore it is not something trifling that is affirmed, even in the reflexive sense. Not merely will Abraham's good fortune be proverbial throughout the world, but all nations of the earth will see that in Abraham the highest good is to be found; and thus *he will be the priestly mediator of salvation between God and the world*, since Abraham's blessing will bring to those farthest off the knowledge of the true God, and in praying for such blessing they will use the name of Abraham who prevailed with God. They would not do the latter [pray for blessing] (hithpael), *unless the blessing and virtue of his person and name* had been attested to them (niphal) [italics ours].[28]

It is not for us to protest over either the text's universalism so early in the history of revelation or over the announced futurity of its development. Only philosophical and historico-critical biases could subvert the obvious intention of the author on both of these scores. Again, let us take the text on its own terms and assume it is innocent until *proven* guilty. Nothing in the text implies that Genesis 12:2-3 and its parallels are "retrojections" from the days of blessing under David and Solomon as H. Gunkel, W. Wolff, and others would have it. On the contrary, David himself expressed surprise and confused delight when he was told that he and his sons were to stand in a direct line with this earlier blessing (2 Sam. 7:18-20). In his prayer of response, he referred to the promise given to the patriarchs and repeated in Deuteronomy so as to show that this was already accepted as part of the ancient word of revelation. It was not a contemporary "retrojection" or reevaluation of the faith of the ancient fathers!

Therefore, we respectfully submit that just where Albrektson finally turned down the possibility that there might be a unifying plan of God which governed history and the string of authorial estimates as to what these things meant, there the plan of God was revealed. It was the plan, not only for history, but for all of biblical theology.

CANONICAL PRECEDENCE FOR A CENTER

OT theologians have missed the only way for safe passage through these treacherous waters. That way must be an *inductively* derived theme, key, or organizing pattern which the successive writers of the OT overtly recognized and consciously supplemented in the progressive unfolding of events and interpretation in the OT. If amidst all the variety and multiplexity of the text there does, as we

---

[28]C. von Orelli, *The Old Testament Prophecy of the Consummation of God's Kingdom Traced in Its Historical Development*, trans. J. J. Banks (Edinburgh: T. & T. Clark, 1889), pp. 107-8.

contend, exist an eye to this storm of activity, it must be *textually* demonstrated that it is the canon's own "starting point" and *textually* reconfirmed in the canon's united witness that it is its own ubiquitous concern, central hope, and constant measure of what was theologically significant or normative!

Such a textually derived center, what the NT eventually was to call the "promise" *(epangelia)*, was known in the OT under a constellation of terms. The earliest such expression was "blessing." It was God's first gift to the fish, fowl (Gen. 1:22), and then to mankind (v. 28).

For men, it involved more than the divine gift of proliferation and "dominion-having." The same word also marked the immediacy whereby all the nations of the earth could prosper spiritually through the mediatorship of Abraham and his seed: this, too, was part of the "blessing." Obviously, pride of place must be given to this term as the first to signify the plan of God.

But there were other terms. McCurley[29] counted over thirty examples where the verb *dibber* (usually translated "to speak") meant "to promise." The promised items included (1) the land (Exod. 12:25; Deut. 9:28; 12:20; 19:8; 27:3; Josh. 23:5,10); (2) blessing (Deut. 1:11; 15:6); (3) multiplication of God's possession, Israel (Deut. 6:3; 26:18); (4) rest (Josh. 22:4; 1 Kings 8:56); (5) all good things (Josh. 23:15); and (6) a Davidic dynasty and throne (2 Sam. 7:28; 1 Kings 2:24; 8:20,24-25; 1 Chron. 17:26; 2 Chron. 6:15-16; Jer. 33:14). Also note the noun *dābār* ("promise") in 1 Kings 8:56 and Psalm 105:42.

To these "promises" God added His "pledge" or "oath," thus making the immediate word of blessing and the future word of promise doubly secure. Men now had the divine word and a divine oath on top of that word (see Gen. 22; 26:3; Deut. 8:7; 1 Chron. 16:15-18; Ps. 105:9; Jer. 11:5).[30]

The case for this inductively derived center is even more wide-ranging than the lexicographical or vocabulary approach traced so far. It also embraced several epitomizing formulae which summarized that central action of God in a succinct phrase or two. Such was what we have called the tripartite formula of the promise. This formula became the great hallmark of all biblical theology in both testaments. The first part of the formula was given in Genesis 17:7-8 and 28:21, viz., "I will be a God to you and to your descendants after

[29]Foster R. McCurley, Jr., "The Christian and the Old Testament Promise," *Lutheran Quarterly* 22 (1970): 401-10, esp. p. 402, n. 2.

[30]Gene M. Tucker, "Covenant Forms and Contract Forms," *Vetus Testamentum* 15(1965): esp. pp. 487-503, for the use of "oath" with promise.

you." When Israel approached the eve of nationhood, again God repeated this word and added a second part, "I will take you for My people" (Exod. 6:7). Thus Israel became God's "son," His "firstborn" (Exod. 4:22), "a distinctive treasure" (Exod. 19:5-6). Finally, the third part was added in Exodus 29:45-46 in connection with the construction of the tabernacle: "I will dwell in the midst of you." There it was: "I will be your God; you shall be My people, and I will dwell in the midst of you." It was to be repeated in part or in full in Leviticus 11:45; 22:33; 25:38; 26:12,44,45; Numbers 15:41; Deuteronomy 4:20; 29:12-13; et. al. Later it appeared in Jeremiah 7:23; 11:4; 24:7; 30:22; 31:1,33; 32:38; Ezekiel 11:20; 14:11; 36:28; 37:27; Zechariah 8:8; 13:9; and in the NT in 2 Corinthians 6:16 and Revelation 21:3-7.

Another formula, found in Genesis 15:7, "I am Yahweh who brought you out of Ur of the Chaldeans," was matched by an even greater work of redemption: "I am the Lord your God who brought you out of the land of Egypt" (found almost 125 times in the OT). Still another formula of self-prediction was, "I am the God of Abraham, Isaac, and Jacob." All such formulae stress a continuity between the past, present, and future. They are parts of God's single ongoing plan.

As the record progressed, an accumulation of various metaphors and technical terms began to emerge. Many of these focused around the Davidic descendant. He was the "Seed," "Branch," "Servant," "Stone," "Root," "Lion," etc.[31] More often than not, the text had a backward glance to previous contexts which contained parts of the same metaphors and technical terms.

Nevertheless, neither the vocabulary nor the formulae and technical terms by themselves would make the case for a unified plan to the entirety of the OT progress of theology. The accent must ultimately fall where it fell for the writers themselves—on a network of interlocking moments in history made significant because of their content, free allusions to one another, and their organic unity. The focus of the record fell on the *content* and *recipients* of God's numerous covenants. The content remained epigenetically constant, i.e., there was a growth—even a sporadic growth from some points of view—as time went on around a fixed core that contributed vitality and meaning to the whole emerging mass. The content was a divine "blessing," a "given word," a "declaration," a "pledge," or "oath"

---

[31]Dennis C. Duling, "The Promise to David and Their Entrance into Christianity—Nailing Down a Likely Hypothesis," *New Testament Studies* 20(1974): 55-77.

that God Himself would freely do or be something for all men, nations, and nature, generally.

Consequently, the revelatory event and/or declaration was frequently an immediate "blessing" as well as a promissory "word" or "pledge" that God would work in the future or had already worked in some given event or situation. God had done so in a way that significance had been given to man's present history and by this, simultaneously to future generations, also.

KEY OLD TESTAMENT PASSAGES ON THE PROMISE

The two pivotal characters were, no doubt, Abraham and David. Their respective covenants are initially recorded in Genesis 12:1-3 and 2 Samuel 7:11-16 (cf. 1 Chron. 17:10-14). The Abrahamic promise and blessing immediately captured the attention of that original audience, as it did all subsequent readers, by the exalted nature of its content and the sheer repetition of its provision in Genesis 12-50. Likewise, the Davidic promise became the bright hope in most of the writing prophets and the chronicler.

Perhaps it is not too much to point also to a prophetic consensus on the "New covenant" announced most prominently in Jeremiah 31:31-34. If one takes into account the dozen-and-a-half references to the same covenant elsewhere in Jeremiah and the other prophets under such rubrics as the "everlasting covenant," the "new heart and new spirit," "covenant of peace," or just "My covenant," then the expectation of a new work of God along the lines of the Abrahamic-Davidic covenant is broadly based.[32] As if to underline the importance already placed in the New covenant, Hebrews 8 and 10 quote it, and it becomes the longest OT passage quoted in the NT.

Here, it would appear, the modern consensus ends. But any faithful discussion of the canon's own view of things would necessarily include a discussion of key passages or central moments in the history of revelation as indicated by the writers of Scripture. Especially of seminal importance are Genesis 3:15; 9:25-27; and 12:1-3.

Genesis 3:15

There can be no doubt that this passage was intended as a pivotal interpretation on the first human crisis. Far beyond God's cursing "the serpent" (always with the article and thus, no doubt,

---

[32]Walter C. Kaiser, Jr., "The Old Promise and the New Covenant: Jeremiah 31:34," *Journal of Evangelical Theological Society* 15(1972): 14, nn. 14-17.

referring to a title) "above"[33] all cattle and all the beasts of the field and consigning his fate to "on your belly you shall go" and "dust shall you eat"[34] was the divinely implanted hostility: "I will put enmity"—an enmity between the serpent and the woman—"between your seed and her seed." Then comes the most important but also the most disputed passage of all: "He [not 'it'] shall crush to pieces your head, and you shall crush His [not 'its'] heel."

Now clearly the pronoun translated "he" or "it" ("she" in one translation!) is a masculine singular independent personal pronoun in Hebrew. But the problem comes from the fact that Hebrew employs a grammatical gender agreeing with its masculine antecedent, "seed" *(zera')* whereas English employs the natural gender. The contention, therefore, is that the only proper translation of Hebrew *hû'* would be "it" or "they." That is the question then: Are the "seed" and "he" collective, or is either singular?

The question, we contend, is misdirected, especially if the divine intention deliberately wished to designate the collective notion which included a personal unity in a single person who was to obtain victory for the whole group he represented. That such an interpretation is not a Christian retrojection from a NT *pesher* or midrash can be seen in the pre-Christian Septuagint translation of the Hebrew Scriptures. The Greek boldly used the masculine independent pronoun *autos*, which failed to agree with the Greek neuter antecedent "seed" *(sperma)*. R. A. Martin, in a brilliant note on this phenomena, concluded that of the 103 times where the Hebrew masculine pronoun is used in Genesis, "in none of the instances where the translator has translated literally does he do violence to agreement in Greek between the pronoun and its antecedent, except here in Genesis 3:15."[35] Far from being a mere coincidence or some sort of oversight, Martin argues that the quality of the Greek translation of the Pentateuch is much more carefully done in comparison to

---

[33]Hebrew *min* is a particle of distinction and eminence, not a partitive ("any of the cattle"); rather, it is the comparative form ("above the cattle"). In this curse, "the serpent" is distinguished from other divine creations, viz., the animals, and marked off for greater rebuke. The same particle is seen in Judges 5:24: "Blessed above women" *(minnāšîm)*—blessed like no other woman (cf. Deut. 33:24).

[34]A reference not to the diet and locomotion of "the serpent" but of his humiliation and subjugation (cf. Ps. 72:9; Isa. 49:23; Mic. 7:17). Creeping on the belly, i.e., the posture of the serpent, came to be regarded as contemptible (Gen. 49:17; Job 20:14,16; Ps. 140:3; Isa. 59:5). Also, "to eat dust" equaled "to descend to the grave" in Descent of Ishtar 5:8; also, note Amarna E.A. 100:36. Consider that God had already made "creeping things" in His creation and had pronounced them "good."

[35]R. A. Martin, "The Earliest Messianic Interpretation of Genesis 3:15," *Journal of Biblical Literature* 84(1965): 427.

other books or sections. What is more important, in other instances where the same type of choice between literalness and agreement of the antecedent and its pronoun occurred in Genesis, the translator declined the opportunity to translate literally (as he did in Gen. 3:15). Instead, he freely used the necessary feminine or neuter pronoun—even when the Hebrew pronoun required a masculine— to agree with its grammatical antecedent. That makes the LXX choice to break this rule in Genesis 3:15 extremely impressive— especially when one considers the fact that the LXX was a third or second century B.C. translation.

But what of the Hebrew author's intention? The case for a singular unity of the collective group of descendants is strengthened by the singular suffix which refers to the seed's head, *hû' yᵉšûpkā rō'š:* "He shall crush *your* [sg.] head." Further, if we understand the author's phrase in Genesis 4:1, Eve thought she had just such a deliverer when she bore Cain. Said she, "I have gotten a man, *even the Lord.*" The Hebrew reads *'et YHWH.* Translating the particle as "with" doesn't make too much sense. Hence it must be a record, even as Luther seems to argue in his translation, of the mistaken hope of Eve that she had received immediate relief from her punishment with the birth of Cain.

Whatever the decision on Genesis 4:1 brings (and it is by no means decisive), it was plain from the subsequent history of revelation to Shem, Abraham, Isaac, Jacob, and their descendants that a representative child continued to be both God's visible guarantee for the present and a pledge for the future. Also, he was representative of the interests and spiritual and material fortunes of the whole lot who were joined to him.

Genesis 9:25-27

We find the following comments of von Orelli[36] on this passage full of honest exegetical sense. Since our generation has for the most part lost contact with such exegetical methodology, we shall quote extensively from several sections of his treatment:

> Instead of blessing Shem himself, the aged father [Noah], with prophetic glance at Shem's future salvation blesses (... in the sense of praising ... [when] it has God for its object ...) Yahveh, the God of Shem, whom he sees in intimate union with Shem. The oracle of blessing is thus turned into praise of Him who is the source of blessing, and has proved Himself such. Shem's highest happiness is that he has this God for his God. Here, for the first time, as Luther notes, we find the genitival combination common

---

[36]C. von Orelli, *Old Testament Prophecy*, p. 98ff.

afterwards: *God of a man, nation,* etc. For when humanity parts into different branches, the universal Deity also is specialized. To one portion of humanity the true, living God stands in a relation of mutual possession . . .

But the second hemistich *weyiškōn be'āhºlê šēm* ["And he shall dwell in the tents of Shem"] is difficult. The chief question in dispute is, who is to be considered the subject of *yiškōn* ["dwell"]. Among moderns, von Hoffmann, Baumgarten, H. Schultz, after the example of Onkelos and other Jewish expositors, and also Theodoret, have taken *God* as the subject, which would give an attractive and highly significant sense: Japhet gains the wide world, but Shem's distinction consists in this, that God dwells in his midst. *Šākēn* is used specially of the dwelling of God (Num. 35:34). By the later Jewish theologians, His gracious presence is called directly the *Šekînâh*, a reminiscence of Onkelos. Nor is there any weight in the objection usually urged against this interpretation, that the parallelism requires Japhet as the subject in this verse since Shem has been dismissed in the preceding one; for, just as the curse on Canaan recurs, so the blessing on Shem may recur, and we should thus obtain the pleasing arrangement: 1. Curse on Canaan; 2. Blessing of firstborn Shem and its antithesis in the curse of Canaan; 3. The second blessing on the middle brother, with reminiscences of the higher blessing on the first and the curse on the third.

At this point, von Orelli falters in our judgment. He continues:

Nevertheless, the majority of ancient and modern expositors give up the reference of ["dwell"] to God, as it seems to us rightly. For it cannot be denied that in the first hemistich the emphasis lies on the repeated *ypt* ["Japhet" and "enlarge"], not on Elohim, on which account the harmony of style is best preserved by referring what follows to Japhet. An antithetical relation of the two clauses *(but He will dwell)* would of necessity have been noted in the language used. More especially we should expect to find the name Yahveh, seeing that God dwells in Shem's tents as Yahveh. The plural designation of place would also be strange, since God elsewhere always dwells in his [tent]; yet this might perhaps be explained by the indefinite generality of the oracle.

However, von Orelli, for all the propriety of these excellent questions, is also now in an exegetical impasse, for what could it mean to have Japhet dwelling in Shem's tents? He struggled with the options in this manner:

But supposing Japhet to be taken as the subject, his dwelling "in the tents of Shem" makes no less difficulty. Some, not without anti-Jewish tendency, have after Justin M. (c Tryp. 139) understood a hostile occupation of the Shemitic country, which would introduce a quite incomprehensible infringement of Shem's birthright-blessing . . . The dwelling of this race in the tents of the former seems to give the impression, if not of conquest, still of a crowding inconvenient to both in strange contrast with the ["enlargement"]. The use of the phrase to denote peaceful, hospitable relation cannot be proved ... Nor does the uniform refrain, in which the *lamo*, ["to him," or "*his* slave"] was to be taken as a singular, favour any reference to Shem in this phrase.

Finally, von Orelli considers J. D. Michaelis's handling of *Shem* as an appellative: "*renowned* tents" instead of "tents of Shem." But this von Orelli also rejects because of the ambiguity it would cause with the use of the proper name in the preceding verse. He weakly concludes, after beginning so well, that Hebrew proverbs are fond of assonance, hence the "God of Shem" and "the tents of Shem" echo very similar sounds in Hebrew!

On balance, of the two options for the subject of "dwell," it would seem preferable to take the subject of the previous stich: Elohim. This is the most logical grammatical position to take. Certainly Japhet as subject makes very little sense at all, and the use of *Shem* as an appellative appears as a desperation move. The objections raised to this view have all been anticipated by what von Orelli had said prior to listing his objections except for his expectation that Yahweh should have been the subject of "dwell" and not Elohim. But in defense of Elohim, we can only note that the full revelation of the "tabernacling" or "dwelling" and the disclosure of the nature or character of Elohim as Yahweh had to wait for the Mosaic revelation of Exodus 6 and 29.

Genesis 12:1-3

Since we have already discussed the content and the importance of that disputed phrase "in you all the nations of the earth shall be blessed," we might simply add here that the word has an obvious resumptive quality about it. The "seed" is still at the center of its focus while it adds many new features. The fact that it is repeated and renewed so frequently in Genesis 13,15,17,22,24,26, and 28 also constitutes another reason why OT theologians should find it to be of great significance.

The passages of 2 Samuel 7 and Jeremiah 31 will be discussed later on, but for now the rudimentary points that go into the making up of the single plan of God have been made. The divine promise pointed to a seed, a race, a family, a man, a land, and a blessing of universal proportions—all guaranteed, according to Genesis 17, as being everlasting and eternal. In that purpose resides the single plan of God. In that single plan lies a capability of embracing as much variety and variegation as the progress of revelation and history can engender. In that unity of goal and method unfolded a march of events which the writers described and in a series of interconnected interpretations they likewise boldly announced God's normative views on those events for that generation and those to come.

Chapter 3

The Development of an Outline
for Old Testament Theology

An adequate treatment of the conceptual groupings of OT theology necessitates an awareness of the sequence of historical events in the life of Israel. Israel's theology—and ours—is rooted in history. Thus Hebrews 1:1-2 continued that sequence when it affirmed that "God, who in many and various ways had spoken to our fathers in the past by the prophets, had in these last days spoken to us in His Son."

Contrary to the prestigious opinion of Gerhard von Rad and his school, the OT did reflect on Israel's history according to a pre-announced principle of selectivity.[1] That principle by which historical incidents were included or rejected was the consistent prophetic statement: "Thus says the Lord."

This was far from being a mere syncretistic assimilator of traditions which mechanically or charismatically collated existing traditions and interpreted them in the light of the present day. Rather, there was a single principle, a single understanding of all revelation, which sorted things out for writers. It was God's revealed "promise"

---

[1]Gerhard von Rad, *Old Testament Theology*, 2 vols. (London: Oliver and Boyd, 1962), 1:116ff.

in which He would be the hope of all men and effect divine work of universal implications.

Such a stress is not that of a fideistic imposition on the text of a later Christian faith nor the result of a scientifically assured minimum from destructive types of historical and literary criticism. It is rather the claim of the canon itself as it now exists.

Moreover, a definite order of key events and meanings become the repeated subject of numerous sections in the Psalms (136,105,78) and the prophets (Jer. 2; Ezek. 16,20,23). Beginning either with Creation or the call of Abraham, the narrative usually followed the same pattern of selectivity and emphasis.

The main substance of those events specially selected and interpreted by the writers of the OT could also be recorded in short summaries which Gerhard von Rad designated as an early Israelite Credo—Deuteronomy 26:5-9:

> A wandering Aramean was my father; he went down with a few people into Egypt and there he became a nation, great, mighty, and populous. But the Egyptians treated us harshly, they afflicted us, and laid hard toil upon us. Then we cried to Jahweh, the God of our fathers, and Jahweh heard us, and saw our affliction, our toil, and oppression. And Jahweh brought us out of Egypt with a mighty hand and an outstretched arm, with great terror, with signs and wonders, and brought us to this place and gave us this land, a land flowing with milk and honey.[2]

Similarly, Joshua 24:2-13 rehearsed much the same history in a form which took on legal status as the citizens of Israel together served as "witnesses against themselves" (v. 22) as to the truthfulness and significance of this historical sequence of events (cf. v. 27).

Therein lies the inner unity to Israel's history and theology. It was more than a "strong tendency towards unification";[3] it was a fact of life and the life of the faithful. It was strung out on the washline of history, but it contained accompanying conceptual motifs which the writers claimed were not of their own invention but of God's devising. His was the sole right to interpret, set values, see significances, and to point out meanings for the times and the future.

But what of this historical sequence? How shall the events be grouped? Is there a conceptual convention which can be borrowed from systematics for organizing OT theology? And if there is a method of study which best suits the needs of a new responsible type of exegetical theology which carefully marks the writer's use of language first in the light of his inherited set of terms and concepts

---

[2]Ibid., p. 122.
[3]Ibid., p. 118.

from Scripture antecedent to his day, what are its division points in history? These questions we seek to answer.

THE HISTORIC PERIODS OF OLD TESTAMENT THEOLOGY

Just as the NT apostles and their epistles were in many ways the interpreters of the Acts and Gospels, so OT theology could likewise begin with the prophets for much the same reason. However, even for the phenomenon of biblical prophecy, there was the ever-present reality of Israel's history. All of God's previous saving activity had to be acknowledged and confessed before one could see more steadily and more holistically the further revelation of God. Therefore, we must start where God began: in history—real history—with its attendant geography, men, and events.

Prolegomena to the Promise: Prepatriarchal Era

The Abrahamic covenant is first given in Genesis 12:1-3. It marks the beginning of both God's election of the man by whom He would deliver the whole world if men would believe and also of Israel's history and theology.

Abraham did, of course, occupy a central place in the climax of revelation. But one must not trade off the moments that led to it as being insignificant or even nonexistent. The text moves from the wideness of all creation to the provincialism and strictures resulting from the successive sins of mankind. Yet it also moves from the threefold plight of man as a result of the Fall, the Flood, and the founding of Babel to the universality of God's new provision of salvation to all men through Abraham's seed.

Furthermore, the key word and concept is the repeated "blessing" of God—a "blessing" existent in only an embryonic state at first but interconnected with subsequent blessings and words of promise from the hands of a gracious and loving God. At first it is the "blessing" of the created order. Then it is the blessing of family and nation in Adam and Noah. The climax came in the fivefold blessing to Abraham in Genesis 12:1-3 which included material and spiritual blessings.

In the sense, then, of being a word before a word, of running ahead in germinative form, these blessings of the revelation in Genesis 1-11 could be called a prolegomena to the promise.

The spirit of modernity has found serious objections to treating Genesis 1-11 in a straightforward way. However, we believe such objections are poorly grounded and inadequately defended. Our own stance has been to treat the records for what they claim to be until they are proven otherwise by artifacts, epigraphs, or related evidential facts.[4]

Provisions in the Promise: Patriarchal Era

So significant was this era that God announced Himself as the "God of the patriarchs" (i.e., "fathers"), or the "God of Abraham, Isaac, and Jacob." Moreover, the patriarchs were regarded as "prophets" (Gen. 20:7; Ps. 105:15). Apparently this was because they personally received the word of God. Frequently the word of the Lord "came" to them directly (Gen. 12:1; 13:14; 21:12; 22:1) or the Lord "appeared" to them in a vision (12:7; 15:1; 17:1; 18:1) or in the personage of the Angel of the Lord (22:11,15).

The lifetimes of Abraham, Isaac, and Jacob form another distinct time in the flow of history. These three privileged recipients of revelation saw, experienced, and heard as much as or more in their combined two centuries of life than all those who lived in the preceding millennia! Consequently, we may safely mark off Genesis 12-50 as our second historic period in the unfolding of OT theology just as was done by later generations who had the written Scripture record.

People of the Promise: Mosaic Era

A son (Gen. 3:15) born to a Semite (Gen. 11:10-27) named Abraham was to be used to form a people and eventually a separate nation. Such a call to nationhood meant that "holiness," or separation unto God, was not an optional feature. Therefore, both concepts were to receive major attention in this era of revelation.

Israel was then called a "kingdom of priests and an holy nation" (Exod. 19:6). Lovingly, God outlined the moral, ceremonial, and civil means of accomplishing such a high calling. It would come in the primary act of the Exodus with God's gracious deliverance of Israel from Egypt, Israel's subsequent obedience of faith to the Ten Commandments, the theology of the tabernacle and sacrifices, and the likes of the covenant code (Exod. 21-23) for civil government.

All the discussion about being a new people of God was elaborated from Exodus 1-40; Leviticus 1-27; and Numbers 1-36. During this whole era, God's prophet was Moses—a prophet who had no equal among mankind (Num. 12:6-8). Indeed, Moses was the pattern for that great Prophet who was to come, the Messiah (Deut. 18:15,18).

---

[4]See our study, "The Literary Form of Genesis 1-11," *New Perspectives on the Old Testament*, ed. J. B. Payne (Waco, Texas: Word, 1970), pp. 48-65.

Place of the Promise: Premonarchical Era

One of the parts of the promise of God that received a full enactment in the events of history and on the pages of Scripture was the conquest of the land of Canaan. The promise of the land as a place where God would cause His *name* to *rest* was by this time already six centuries old. The ancient word given to Abraham was now to receive at least a seminal fulfillment. Therefore Deuteronomy with its concern about this place of rest (12:8-11) and the book of Joshua with its description of the conquest of that land are clearly joined in concept and act.

But do we have a clear unit of history which can be set off as sharply as the patriarchal or Mosaic eras were by Scripture's own claims? And should this history extend through the period of the Judges to include the theology of the ark-of-the-covenant-of-God narratives in 1 Samuel 4-7? These questions do not admit any decisive conclusions—the times became so distorted and all appeared to be in such flux due to the moral declension of man and the sparsity of the revelation of God. Indeed, the word of God did become "rare" in those days when God spoke to Samuel (1 Sam. 3:1). Consequently, the lines of demarcation are not as sharply drawn even though the central themes of theology and the key events are historically well-recorded.

Our plan, then, is to allow for an overlap during this period of the conquest and occupation of the land. This overlap is between the theme of the place of rest and the emerging demand for a king to rule a nation tired of its experiment with theocracy as it had been practiced by a rebellious nation. At best, the premonarchical era was a time of transition.

However, the history of Joshua, Judges, and even Samuel and Kings was assessed from the viewpoint of the moral standard of Deuteronomy. And its chief connecting points were easily discerned: Deuteronomy 28,31; Joshua 1,12,24; Judges 2; 1 Samuel 12; 2 Samuel 12; 1 Kings 8; and 2 Kings 17. These significant moments in the history of revelation of this period are usually conceded by most biblical theologians today.

King of the Promise: Davidic Era

What Genesis 12:1-3 was to the patriarchal era, 2 Samuel 7 is to the times of David. The forty years of David's reign compare in length to the Mosaic era, but their importance for generations to come defies comparison.

As a prelude to the history of this period, the early signs of regal aspirations in Gideon's son Abimelech, the peoples' request for a king during the judgeship of Samuel (1 Sam. 8-10), and even the reign of Saul prepare us negatively for the grand reign of David (1 Sam. 11–2 Sam. 24; I Kings 1-2; and royal Davidic psalms like Pss. 2,110,132,145).

History and theology combined to emphasize the themes of a continuing royal dynasty and a perpetual kingdom with a rule and realm that would become universal in extent and influence. Yet each of these regal motifs was painstakingly connected to ideas and words from an earlier time: a "seed," a "name" which "dwelt" in a place of "rest," a "blessing" to all mankind, and a "king" who now ruled over a kingdom which would last forever.

Life in the Promise: Sapiential Era

Solomon's forty years were marked by the erection of the temple and by another flurry of divine revelation. In part, this period is much like the premonarchical times in that it too is partially transitional in nature. Yet it also had its own distinctive character as well.

No period of time is more difficult to relate to the whole of a continuing OT theology than that of the wisdom literature of this era found in Proverbs, Ecclesiastes, Song of Songs, and the Wisdom Psalms. Nevertheless, as the Mosaic law presumed and built upon patriarchal promise, so Solomonic wisdom likewise presupposed both Abrahamic-Davidic promise and Mosaic law.

The key concept of the sapiential era was "the fear of the Lord"—an idea already begun in the patriarchal era as the *response* of believing faith (Gen. 22:12; 42:18; Job 1:1,8-9; 2:3). It was this connecting link that tied the promise and the law into the beauty and fullness of all of man's living in the here and now. The temporal became more than a mere existence; living could now be meaningful, enjoyable, and unified with eternal values and commitments.

Day of the Promise: Ninth Century

The "Day of the Promise" is the first of five great prophetic eras, each with their own basic emphases ranging from the division of the kingdom in 931 B.C. to the postexilic situation.

Now that David's "house" and Solomon's temple had been established, the subjects of each of the multifaceted promises had reached a provisional plateau in their development. God's future ruler was now visible in the line of David and God's personal presence in the midst of his worshiping subjects was dramatized in the temple.

Accordingly, the prophets could now turn their focus on God's world-wide plan and kingdom. Alas, however, Israel's sin also

46

claimed much of the prophets' attention. Nevertheless, mingled with these words of judgment were the persistently inserted bright prospects of another day when God's everlasting realm and rule, as announced so long ago, would receive its fullest realization.

Many place Joel and Obadiah in the ninth century as the earliest of the writing prophets. While Obadiah could be placed at any of three different times in Judah's history, the best would probably be in the reign of Jehoram (853-841 B.C.), when Edom revolted against Judah along with the Arabians and Philistines (2 Kings 8:20-22; 2 Chron. 21:8-10,16-17).[5]

Likewise, Joel is usually dated in the reign of Joash of Judah (835-796 B.C.) because there is no mention of Assyria, Babylon, or Persia among the long list of Israel's enemies—presumably because they were not yet on the historical scene.[6] If this reign be the general time period, then the book must come early in the reign, say from 835-820, while the godly high priest Jehoiada acted as advisor to the youthful King Joash.

Regardless of Joel's and Obadiah's final dating, their theology is clear: it is the day of the Lord. A day is coming in which Yahweh will vindicate Himself by such great works of salvation and judgment that all men will instantaneously recognize these works as divine in their cause. At that time, God will complete what all the prophets anticipated and the believing remnant had hoped for.

Joel's locust plague and Obadiah's concern over Edom's lack of brotherly love were occasions for God's ancient word of promise to be renewed and enlarged.

Servant of the Promise: Eighth Century

The quintessence of OT theology reached its peak during the eighth century. It included the works of such prophets as Jonah, Hosea, Amos, Isaiah, and Micah. Graciously, each was sent a decade or so in advance of the threatened judgment on Damascus, capital of Syria, which fell in 732 B.C., and Samaria, the capital of the northern ten tribes of Israel, which fell in 722 B.C.

Nothing can adequately describe the dizzy heights each of these prophets attained in his writings. Indeed, "To whom shall we liken our God? and to what shall we compare Him?" queried Isaiah of his

---

[5]The other options are: (1) during Ahaz's reign (743-715 B.C.); (2) when Edom invaded Judah (2 Chron. 28:16-18); and (3) during the fall of Jerusalem under Nebuchadnezzar in 586 B.C. (2 Kings 25:1-21; 2 Chron. 36:15-20).

[6]However, it is puzzling why the Arameans of Damascus are not mentioned also since they put Joash under heavy tribute *late* in his reign (2 Kings 12:17-18; 2 Chron. 24:23-24).

day and ours (Isa. 40:18). Similarly, Micah asked, "Who is a pardoning God like Thee?" (Mic. 7:18). And Amos announced pointedly that God would "raise up the fallen hut of David" again (Amos 9:11).

But dominating the whole era was that magnificent mini-OT theology of Isaiah 40-66 with its key personage the Servant of the Lord from the seed of Abraham and David.

Renewal of the Promise: Seventh Century

At the close of the seventh century came another succession of writing prophets: Zephaniah, Habakkuk, Nahum, and Jeremiah. Again Nahum warned (as had Jonah more than a century earlier) of the imminent destruction that would come on the Assyrian city of Nineveh (which did come in 611 B.C.). The other three prophets likewise warned Judah's capital, Jerusalem, which was hit in 606, 598, and finally fell in 586 B.C. If only men would repent, they could save themselves from the horrors and realities of impending desolation.

Nevertheless, the bleak gloom was not the only word for Judah; there was the joyous prospect of a renewed covenant for a believing remnant. Jeremiah entitled it God's "New covenant" and built around it a program for the rejuvenation of all men, nations, and nature in his little book of comfort (Jer. 30-33). And for Zephaniah there was more light on that coming day of the Lord. In the meantime, Habakkuk thundered out his solution to his own moments of despair and doubt: the just would live by faith.

Yet the ancient themes were also clearly and prominently present in this new advance. The lines of continuity stretched out especially to those days when the tripartite formula first heard by the patriarchs and Moses would be a total reality: "I will be your God, you shall be My people and I will dwell in the midst of you." So it was to be then and in the future.

Kingdom of the Promise: Exilic Times

Ezekiel and Daniel, while living in Babylonian Exile, continued to sharpen even more clearly how it was that the coming "Good Shepherd" would one day reign over a reunited twelve-tribed Israel in Canaan. Yes, the Son of man would come with the clouds of heaven and would be given a dominion, glory, and kingdom wherein all people, nations, and languages would serve Him. His dominion would be an everlasting dominion which would not pass away, and His kingdom would be such that would not be destroyed. Earthly kingdoms would come and go, but His would never succumb.

In this regal note these two exiled prophets led Israel into the sixth century and new day for all mankind. The scope and majesty of what had been so anciently promised to Abraham and David was staggering.

Triumph of the Promise: Postexilic Times

Together, the histories of Ezra-Nehemiah, Esther, Chronicles, and the prophecies of Haggai, Zechariah, and Malachi make up the final note of revelation in the OT canon.

They move from the despondency of conditions in Israel after their return from the seventy years of Babylonian Exile to the complete triumph of God's person, word, and work. What seemed to be small and insignificant to them in a day like 520 B.C. was directly connected in glory and durability with God's final wrap-up of history. Was the rebuilt temple small and insignificant in their eyes? Yet it was *that* very temple whose glory would be even greater than the Solomonic temple. No work done at the urging of God's prophets could be regarded solely on empirical grounds. There was the larger connection of the part to the whole of God's total finale in history. Men must now look up, believe, and work. Their King was coming, riding on a donkey, bringing salvation (Zech. 9:9). He would even go forth and fight all the nations of the earth, which one final day would gather to do battle against Jerusalem (Zech. 14).

And as if to reestablish the validity of the roots of this messianic vision of the kingdom of God on earth, the chronicler used Israel's past history to show the normality of this vision after the pattern of the Davidic "house" and the Solomonic temple and worship.

So the history of Israel lengthened, but the seminal roots of her theology remained intact as the plant grew into a fully developed tree with each new growth.

THE KEY ITEMS IN EACH HISTORIC PERIOD

The situation is just what Patrick Fairbairn assessed it to be:

> In this outline, which we present, chiefly because of the happy manner in which it connects together the beginning and the end, and exhibits the analogy that subsists between God's method of working in nature and in grace, only some of the more obvious links are noticed. When the matter is looked at more closely, far more is discovered of the progressive unfolding of the first promise and the interconnection between it and subsequent prophecies and of these again with each other.[7]

---

[7]Patrick Fairbairn, *The Interpretation of Prophecy*, 2nd ed. (Edinburgh: T. & T. Clark, 1856), p. 185.

So the first of God's word of blessing-promise in the Creation was followed by that embryonic word in Eden given to the woman's seed: there would be a victorious Seed over a sniping seed of Satan. Before we reach the time of Abraham, this word is enlarged in the benediction of Noah on Shem to a whole race or a line in whose tents God would dwell. Hence, the key items in this prepatriarchal time were "blessing," "seed," and a race in the midst of whom God "dwelt."

The patriarchs also freely received God's benediction in an heir ("seed"), an inheritance ("land"), and a heritage ("all the nations of the earth shall be blessed"—the gospel according to Gal. 3:8).

The Mosaic era at first stressed Israel as God's "son," His "firstborn." With the Exodus, God called the Israelites jointly into being "a royal priesthood and a holy nation" to Him. Subordinate to this high election to privilege was an election to service. Israel was to be holy and clean. The former meant she was to be totally and entirely separated unto God body, soul, and life. The latter called her to be prepared and fit for the worship of God. Adequate instruction in proper morality was linked to God's abiding character and His work in the Exodus. Likewise, provision for restoration to divine favor in case of any human failure to meet that moral standard was given in the sacrificial system.

The themes of the premonarchical era revolve around the "rest" of God, Spirit of God, ark of the covenant, and the injunction to love, fear, and serve God with all of one's heart, soul, strength, and mind.

For David, it was a dynasty ("a house"), a "throne," and a "kingdom." For Solomon it was the "fear of God" as the beginning of wisdom, living, knowing, and acting. As the palace was the symbol of the former era of the monarchy, especially under the glorious days of David, so the temple and the house built by wisdom were the marks of the Solomonic era.

The prophets then took up in sequence the themes of the day of the Lord, the Servant of the Lord, the New covenant, the kingdom of God, and the triumph of God's plan.

But it all belonged to one plan. As Carl Paul Caspari summarized it:

> The Old Testament prophets form a regular succession; they are members of an unbroken continuous chain ... When, therefore, the Spirit of God came upon a prophet and irresistibly impelled him to prophesy (Amos 3:8), it naturally happened first, that here and there, sometimes more sometimes less, he clothed what the Spirit imparted to him in words of one or other of the prophets he had heard or read—the words of his prophetical forerunner thus

cleaving to his memory and forming part of the materials of utterance of which the Spirit availed himself; and second, that the later prophet attached himself to the prophetical views of the earlier, and in the power of the prophetic Spirit . . . either confirmed them anew by a fresh promulgation, or expanded and completed them.[8]

And so it could be said for the whole OT canon.

THE PROVISION FOR UNIQUE ITEMS

Not everything was a bland repetition nor a recasting in a new situation of the words of one or more of the writer's forerunners. There was, to again use Caspari's words, "a fresh promulgation" which developed almost completely new areas of thought in that single plan of God's promise.

While each of these fresh branches of teaching was frequently linked by historical antecedents or by way of response to the accumulated canon up to that point, often they were so startling in their novelty as to threaten later attempts at tracing their continuity with the existing canon. The best example of this is, no doubt, the wisdom literature. It was so disparate and diverse from the revelation which claimed to precede it that many to the present day still cannot see any connection at all. Consequently, it can be used as a sure sign of a unique and innovative item if some are willing to conclude that it is a novel, unattached oddity.

Second only to wisdom literature is the law and its placement alongside the Abrahamic-Davidic promise. But again, the text insists on its points of continuity, especially with the patriarchal era. But the massiveness of original revelation which develops what it means to be a people of God is staggering. It too must go down as being another key instance of a major new item in the revelation of God's single plan. In fact, it is so new that most again question its continuity rather than its innovative abilities.

But more should be listed here than wisdom and law. On the one hand, there was the constant narrowing and making more specific of what the ultimate fulfillment was to be. It was a sort of election within the election, i.e., a man David from a tribe of Judah, from a nation Israel, from a race of Semites, from the seed of a woman. On the other hand there was a constant expansion and completion of the nascent projections in event, thought, and expression. In this process there was a constant lifting of the technical terms, hopes, and concepts of the writer's forerunners as he con-

---

[8]As cited by Fairbairn, ibid., p. 199.

tinued the unbroken, continuous chain in the emerging details of the plan of God: His promise. But each writer added to the theme. The writers of the OT were more than mere parrots. They were participants in a long line of revelation, true, but they were also recipients of additional revelation *par excellence*.

THE RESULTING OUTLINE

The resulting shape that emerges for OT theology with its "long-cut" diachronic base and normative implications for exegetical theology or expository preaching is as follows:

I. Prolegomena to the Promise: Prepatriarchal Era
   A. Word of Creation
   B. Word of Blessing
   C. First Word of Promise: A Seed
   D. Second Word of Promise: The God of Shem
   E. Third Word of Promise: A Blessing to All the Nations

II. Provisions in the Promise: Patriarchal Era
   A. Word of Revelation
   B. Word of Promise
      1. An Heir
      2. An Inheritance
      3. A Heritage
   C. Word of Assurance
   D. Ruler of Promise
   E. God of Promise

III. People of the Promise: Mosaic Era
   A. My Son, My Firstborn
   B. My People, My Possession
   C. Kingly Priests
   D. An Holy Nation
   E. The Law of God
   F. The Tabernacling God

IV. Place of the Promise: Premonarchical Era
   A. Inheritance of the Land
   B. Rest in the Land
   C. Chosen Place in the Land
   D. Name Dwelling in the Land
   E. Conquest of the Land

  F. Prophetic History in the Land
    1. Repentance and Blessing
    2. Predictive Word and Fulfilled Event
    3. A Prophet like Moses

 V. King of the Promise: Davidic Era
  A. A Promised King
    1. A Usurping Ruler
    2. A Rejected Ruler
    3. An Anointed Ruler
  B. A Promised Dynasty
    1. A House
    2. A Seed
    3. A Kingdom
    4. A Son of God
  C. A Charter for Humanity
  D. A Promised Kingdom
    1. The Ark and the Kingdom
    2. The Royal Psalms and the Kingdom
    3. The Succession Narrative and the Kingdom

 VI. Life in the Promise: Sapiential Era
  A. The Fear of the Lord
  B. Life in the Lord
  C. Integration of Life and Truth in the Lord
  D. Wisdom from the Lord
  E. Eudaemonism and the Lord

 VII. Day of the Promise: Ninth Century
  A. The Prophets and the Promise
  B. The Promise in the Ninth Century
  C. Edom and the Promise: Obadiah
  D. The Day of the Lord: Joel

 VIII. Servant of the Promise: Eighth Century
  A. Rebuilding David's Fallen Hut: Amos
  B. Freely Loving Israel: Hosea
  C. Mission to the Gentiles: Jonah
  D. Ruler of Israel: Micah
  E. The Promise Theologian: Isaiah

 IX. Renewal of the Promise: Seventh Century
  A. Mission to Gentiles Revisited: Nahum
  B. The Day of the Lord: Zephaniah

C. The Just Shall Live by Faith: Habakkuk
D. The Word of the Lord: Jeremiah

X. Kingdom of the Promise: Exilic Times
   A. The Good Shepherd's Reign: Ezekiel
   B. The Promised Kingdom's Success: Daniel

XI. Triumph of the Promise: Postexilic Times
   A. God's Signet Ring: Haggai
   B. God's Conquering Hero: Zechariah
   C. God's Messenger of the Covenant: Malachi
   D. The Kingdom Is the Lord's: Chronicles, Ezra-Nehemiah, Esther

Chapter 4

The Connections Across Historical Epochs of Emerging Themes in Old Testament Theology

Whenever biblical theologians have identified some key terms or category as a theological center for organizing the developing theology of either or both testaments (as we have also done here), immediately they are confronted with the mass of diverse emphases in Scripture. For some, it is more than a diversity of subject matter. The multiplicity of ideas amounts to nothing less than contradictions and reversals of opinion between the successive writers of Scripture. Even when the text is treated fairly in its final canonical shape,[1] the

---

[1]We shall avoid the discussion that belongs to OT introduction or to the history of Israelite religion, viz., the process in the formation of that text, the results of literary criticism, and traditio-historical criticism. Suffice it here to say that evangelicals do believe in and utilize higher criticism, form criticism, etc. What they cannot agree with is the use of imaginary or hypothetical sources (Chronicles and Kings refer to many *real* sources, cf. Luke 1:1-4) and philosophical or sociological presuppositions which cannot stand the test when applied to epigraphical materials uncovered by the archaeologists of comparable age, style, and character as the biblical texts since the antiquity and authorship of many of the excavated texts are secure on other grounds! Cf. W. C. Kaiser, Jr., "The Present State of Old Testament Studies," *Journal of Evangelical Theological Society* 18(1975): 69-79.

issue of diversity still remains; and the goal of reaching a unified theology appears hopelessly impossible.

Nevertheless, even after the more prejudicial evaluations have been cared for by an objective type of higher criticism, four key tension points remain as symbols of the fact that the OT appears to contain a variety of viewpoints rather than a single integrated theme. If bridges could be built across these high walls, perhaps there would be hope for the whole project of writing an OT theology with a central focal point. The four crucial connections are:

1. Prepatriarchal "Blessing" and Patriarchal "Promise"
2. Patriarchal "Promise" and Mosaic "Law"
3. Premonarchical "Deuteronomism" and Davidic "Promise"
4. Sapiential "Creation Theology" and Prophetic "Promise"

No matter whatever else needs to be done by way of prolegomena to biblical theology, the varying emphases of these eras will need to preempt any other discussion. A plausible solution to these admittedly tricky connections would contribute a major portion to the type of OT theology attempted here.

PREPATRIARCHAL "BLESSING" AND PATRIARCHAL "PROMISE"

There seems to be little doubt that the key motif of the creation narratives was the "blessing" of God on the creatures of the sea and air (Gen. 1:22) and on man and woman (v. 28). Nor was the explanation of that blessing difficult either; it was both a *capacity* and a *result*, to summarize Pedersen.[2] God's creation was to be prolific and bountiful on the earth.

This divine blessing was continued in Genesis 5:2 and after the Flood in Genesis 9:1. But blessing was present even apart from the use of the word "to bless" or the formula: "And God blessed them saying, 'Be fruitful and multiply and fill the earth.' " As Claus Westermann correctly argued, blessing is implied in what he called the *Heilsschilderung* ("portrayal of salvation").[3] It is our contention that

---

[2]Johannes Pedersen, *Israel: Its Life and Culture* (New York: Oxford University Press, 1926-40), p. 182.

[3]Claus Westermann, "The Way of Promise Through the Old Testament," *The Old Testament and Christian Faith*, ed. Bernhard W. Anderson (New York: Harper & Row, 1963), pp. 208-9.

such *Heilsschilderungen* are also present in prepatriarchal passages such as Genesis 3:15 and 9:27. Thus blessing is found in concept, formula, and divine acts.

The obvious link between Genesis 1-11 and the patriarchal era is one that the text itself makes in its fivefold repetition of the "blessing" given to Abraham in Genesis 12:1-3. Both Zimmerli[4] and Blythin[5] noted this association of "blessing" with the theme of "promise" in the patriarchal record. However, they did not carry back their observations to Genesis 1-11 as we have, nor did they notice that this emphasis fell just where the two epochs met in the canon: Genesis 12:1ff. The earlier epoch had ended with the query: What now could be done for the nations at large who were more and more alienated from God who had made them and blessed them with such proliferation? And the answer was in the form of another blessing. God introduced a Semite by the name of Abraham. In him all the families of the earth would find blessing. Indeed, the verb "to bless" appears 82 times in the patriarchal narratives. Thus the verbal and conceptual transition was smooth, continuous, and intentional.

But there is more. The blessing was pointedly continued from father to son in varying situations, e.g., Isaac was blessed because of his father (Gen. 26:24). Even the formula of blessing observed in the creation narratives appeared again: "I am El Shaddai, be fruitful and multiply! A nation and a community of nations shall come from you" (Gen. 35:11).

Connected with the concept of "blessing" was the idea of being successful in a venture or being made prosperous by God. The verb *ṣālaḥ (hiṣlîaḥ)*, "make prosperous, bring success," was used in Genesis 24:21,40,42,56 in parallelism with *bārak*, "to bless" (Gen. 24:1,27,31). It was God's indication that His favor was upon the patriarchs—everything they attempted succeeded. Consequently, we feel confident in associating these two concepts of "blessing" and "promise" across the two eras. While there exists no distinctive Hebrew verb or noun for "promise," the root *bārak* in the intensive form of the Hebrew verb served admirably well for the time being. Meanwhile, God continued to announce His acts of future deliverance even as He graciously supplied mankind and all of creation with the capacity and results of success right then and there.

Both promise and blessing were so closely intertwined that

---

[4]Walther Zimmerli, "Promise and Fulfillment," *Essays on Old Testament Hermeneutics*, ed. Claus Westermann, 2nd ed. (Richmond: John Knox, 1969), pp. 90-93.
[5]Islwyn Blythin, "The Patriarchs and the Promise," *Scottish Journal of Theology* 21(1968): 72.

many scholars began to look for ways to segregate their origins and concerns. But there has never been a secure demonstration of their dichotomization, much less a scholarly consensus. On the basis of the results of traditio-historical criticism, scholars (beginning with Albrecht Alt) have alleged that each patriarch originally had his own separate clan god: "The Shield of Abraham," "The Fear [or 'Kinsman' as W. F. Albright wanted it] of Isaac," and "The Mighty One of Jacob." For Alt, "the choosing of Abraham and his descendants [had] originally nothing to do with Yahweh and his choosing of Israel, but [went] back to the religion of the gods of the Father."[6] Thus there were two choosings (the patriarchs and Israel) and several gods (the three "clan gods" of the patriarchs and Israel's Yahweh). Likewise, linked to these divine choosings were the promises of these gods which invariably focused on two matters: the increase of the patriarchs' posterity and their possession of the land of Canaan. But again, Alt divides the whole and awards the patriarchs the first promise and declares the second an editorial retrojection back to patriarchal times subsequent to Israel's entry into the land.[7]

While Martin Noth[8] asserted that both the promise of land and the promise of progeny were very old, he did, however, assign to Jacob and not Abraham the greater prominence in this era. Likewise von Rad[9] agreed. For him the twofold promise was very old and went back to the time of the patriarchs. Only the later Israelite understanding of the promise of land was different from what the patriarchs understood it to be. For them, explained von Rad, it had an immediate and direct fulfillment as they settled in the land; but it later came to mean a final return under Joshua after a departure from the land.

Nevertheless, a deep tendency still persisted in modern scholarship to associate "blessing" passages solely with the concerns of progeny and wealth—perhaps this was even a vestigial rudiment of Canaanite society and religion—while "promise" passages focused on concern for the land.[10]

But neither the promise nor the blessing were syncretistically

[6]Albrecht Alt, "The God of the Fathers," *Essays on Old Testament History and Religion*, trans. R. A. Wilson (Garden City, N.Y.: Doubleday, 1968), p. 82.

[7]Ibid., pp. 83-84.

[8]Martin Noth, *A History of Pentateuchal Traditions*, trans. B. W. Anderson (Englewood Cliffs, N.J.: Prentice-Hall, 1972), pp. 54-58,79-115,147-56.

[9]Gerhard von Rad, *Old Testament Theology*, 2 vols. (London: Oliver and Boyd, 1962), 1:168ff.

[10]See for example Blythin, "Patriarchs," p. 70.

created ad hoc out of the cultural experiences or imitations of other religions surrounding Israel. The repeated claim of the patriarchs was that the promises were given by divine revelations, revelations which generally began with *'āmar YHWH* or *wayyo'mer YHWH* (Gen. 12:1; 13:14; 18:13; 31:3). Neither were these blessings, as it was alleged, individual and immediate while in contradistinction the promises were corporate and future in nature. Rather, together the blessing-promises were addressed to those descendants of the present and future in the whole line of believers who had a historical representative individual (e.g., Abraham, Isaac, Jacob) as an earnest, or token, of what God would do in the immediate and distant future. Yet all the descendants were corporately included in the blessing and promise. All attempts to divide blessing-promise expose the artificiality and subjectivity of these schemes, for the text in its present canonical shape shouts "no" to every such artiface.

Hence we conclude that the generous word of God was realized in His "blessing" to man in both eras: "Be fruitful and multiply and fill the earth" (Gen. 1:28; 9:1,7; 12:1-3; 35:11) and in His promise and the various portrayals of salvation *(Heilsschilderungen)* in both eras, also: a seed, race, land, blessing to all nations, kings, etc. (Gen. 3:15; 9:27; 12:2-3; 15; 17). Some scholarly protestations to the contrary only prove the general reliability of this link.

PATRIARCHAL "PROMISE" AND MOSAIC "LAW"

Even more serious was the disjuncture that appeared between law and promise. Here some believed that even the apostle Paul and the writer of Hebrews could be cited among the detractors to the unity of law and promise, if not the sheer facts of the OT text itself. But the connections once again were so clear at several points that the patriarchal materials were unfairly suspected of receiving more retrojections of material from that grandest moment of them all—the moment of nation-making at the deliverance from Egypt.

Take, for example, the formula of self-prediction or self-revelation found in Exodus 20:2 (and about 125 times in the rest of the OT): "I am Yahweh thy God, who brought you out of the land of Egypt." A similar formula existed in Genesis 15:7: "I am Yahweh who brought you out of Ur of the Chaldeans." They were too similar in form, it was alleged, to be independent of each other. So what type of dependence was assigned? The priority of Exodus 20:2! But why not the reverse pattern—especially since the text claimed that pattern? Cannot a text be innocent until proven guilty? Or must we always presume since it is religious or early in time it is suspect?

Likewise the indications of a divine epiphany and the aspects of awe and dread that surrounded Abraham's reception of the covenant in Genesis 15:17 similarly greeted Israel when the covenant was delivered from Sinai in Exodus 19:18. The smoke, fire pot, and flaming torch of Genesis 15 were matched by the smoke, kiln, and fire of Exodus 19. The texts read:

> And it came to pass that when the sun went down and it was dark, behold, a smoking fire pot and a flaming torch passed between the pieces.   —Genesis 15:17

> And mount Sinai was wrapped altogether in smoke because Yahweh descended on it in fire; and the smoke thereof ascended like the smoke of a kiln.   —Exodus 19:18

Likewise the patriarchal phrase "the God of my/thy father" continued into the Mosaic age. In God's call of Moses, He said:

> I am the God of thy father, the God of Abraham, the God of Isaac, and the God of Jacob. And Moses hid his face, for he was afraid to look on God.   —Exodus 3:6

When Israel was delivered from Pharaoh, the people sang:

> Yahweh is my strength and my song,
> and He has become my salvation.
> This is my God, and I will praise Him;
> The God of my father, and I will exalt Him.
> —Exodus 15:2

And prior to Moses' meeting with his father-in-law, Jethro, his son Eliezer is named with this explanation that followed his name:

> For the God of my father was my help
> and delivered me from the sword of Pharaoh.
> —Exodus 18:4

One need only compare the same formula in Genesis 26:24; 28:13; and 32:10.

What God did at the Exodus was directly related—to take the present canon's claim—to God's remembering His covenant with Abraham, Isaac, and Jacob (Exod. 2:24; 3:13,15-16; 4:5; 6:3,5,8). The promise of the land became more prominent for the moment—He had sworn to give it to the fathers (Exod. 6:4,8; 13:5,11; 32:13; 33:1; Num. 10:29; 11:12; 14:23; 32:11). But the other elements of the ancient "blessing" were also evident: Exodus 1:7,9 has a sevenfold stress (to count the expressions) on the amazing and rapid increase of Israel to the chagrin of the Egyptians. Moreover, there was the "firstborn," God's "son," in Exodus 4:22, who continued the theme of

60

the "seed" as well. Thus the writer of Exodus saw fulfillment of parts of the ancient promise of blessing delivered to the patriarchs. The covenant had not been forgotten.

But the continuity of the narrative itself was not the problem troubling most theologians. It was the nature of the materials in the two covenants. Sinai imposed commands, demands, and obligations whereas the Genesis materials seemed to reflect the gifts of blessing and promise. That was the troublesome contrast. How could the two covenants be related in content?

In a widely received study of the literary structure of the Hexateuch, Gerhard von Rad[11] pointed to the credo of Deuteronomy 26:5-9—and similar credos such as Joshua 24:16-18—with its confession restricted to the patriarchal beginnings, the oppression in Egypt, the deliverance from Egypt, and the wilderness wanderings and entrance into Canaan as the heart of the first six books of the canon. The most striking feature is that the events of Sinai, indeed the heart of the Pentateuch, are not included in the credo. Von Rad drew the conclusion, then, that the Sinai events belonged to a separate—even if it were old—tradition and a separate history unconnected to the Exodus or wilderness experience. Only later during the Exile did the so-called Yahwist dare to link law and gospel. Otherwise, Sinai was a cultic legend of doubtful historicity and an intrusion which separated the Kadesh materials in Exodus 17 from their continuation in Numbers 10.

However, there was a strong voice of dissent.[12] Most significant of all was the clear association of the Exodus with Sinai in Exodus 19:3-8 and 20:2-17. In fact, if the total context of two of the credo passages were considered (much less the total context of Deuteronomy 26), they, too, linked the deliverance from Egypt with an appeal to accede to the demands of the Sinaitic covenant—Joshua 24 and 1 Samuel 12.[13] Consequently, Sinai must not be cut off from the history or theology of the Exodus or the promise.

But the problem still remained. How were the demands of Exodus 20–Numbers 10 to be integrated, if at all, with the blessings of promises of the preceding ages? Perhaps an approach might best

---

[11]Gerhard von Rad, *The Problem of the Hexateuch and Other Essays,* trans. E. W. T. Dicksen (New York: McGraw-Hill Co., 1966), pp. 1-26.

[12]See the summary of these views in Herbert B. Huffmon, "The Exodus, Sinai, and the Credo," *Catholic Biblical Quarterly* 27(1965): 102-3, nn. 6-10.

[13]Joshua 24:25 refers to statutes, ordinances, and witnesses (vv. 22,27) and oaths of acceptance (vv. 16,21); so argued J. A. Thompson, "The Cultic Credo and the Sinai Tradition," *The Reformed Theological Review* 27(1968): 53-64.

be made by noting the connection in the patriarchal era between command, promise, and blessing. The command form came in both as an imperative and a prohibition. According to P. V. Premsagar[14] the list from Genesis would read as follows:

12:1	"Go from your own country"
13:14	"Lift up your eyes and look"
15:1	"Do not be afraid"
15:9	"Bring me a heifer"
17:1	"Walk before me and be perfect"
22:2	"Take your son, your only son . . . and go"
26:2	"Do not go down to Egypt, but stay in this country"
26:24	"Fear not"
31:3	"Go back to the land of your fathers"
35:11	"Be fruitful and multiply."

Here, however, command preceded promise and blessing. At Sinai it was an implication and a natural response to the grace of God manifested in the promise, especially the portrayal of salvation in the Exodus itself. For Abraham obedience was not a condition of the covenant. Yet the duty of obedience was particularly stressed in Genesis 22:18 and 26:5: "Because you have obeyed My voice . . . and kept My charge, My commandments, My statutes, and My laws." So it was as Hebrews 11:8 put it: "By faith Abraham . . . obeyed." Faith had to be joined to works to demonstrate its effectiveness and authenticity.

Let it also be affirmed that if the promise was a gift from God, so was the law likewise regarded. The psalmists celebrated this point of view (Pss. 1:2; 19:7-11; 40:8; 119). Moses expressed this, too, when he asked Israel rhetorically, "What nation has God so near to them as the Lord your God?" or "What nation has statutes and judgments so righteous as all this law which I set before you this day?" (Deut. 4:7-8). Israel's response was repeated three times: "All that the Lord has spoken we will do" (Exod. 19:8; 24:3,7). Rather than rebuking them for "rashly" accepting so stringent terms when promise and blessing were available, the Lord responded:

> They have spoken well all that they said. Would that they always had such a mind to fear Me and to observe all My commandments so that it might be well with them and with their children forever!
> —Deuteronomy 5:28-29

Finally, promise did not oppose God's law for the following reasons: (1) Both the promise and the law were initiated by the same

---

[14]P. V. Premsagar, "Theology of Promise in the Patriarchal Narratives," *Indian Journal of Theology* 23(1974): 121.

covenant-making God; (2) Far from being a legalistic code or a hypothetical means of earning one's salvation, the law was a means of maintaining fellowship with Yahweh—not the grounds of establishing it; (3) The same law that demanded a standard of holy living equal to the character of God Himself also made provision for failure under that law by forgiveness and atonement of sin; and (4) The context of every and any demand of the law was the atmosphere of grace: "I am the Lord your God who brought you out of Egypt." This is an event which even the patriarch Abraham was vaguely aware of from Genesis 15:13-14: "Your descendants will be aliens living in a land that is not theirs . . . slaves . . . held in oppression for 400 years . . . after which they shall come out with great possessions." Naturally some will disregard this as a later harmonizing detail projected back to smooth out the transition, but the text must remain innocent until proven guilty by better criteria than the subjective imposition of value judgments. Such objections, in lieu of any proof, merely prove that the stumbling block, found not only in prophetic literature but elsewhere, continues to be the biblical claim to be able to predict events before they take place.

PREMONARCHICAL "DEUTERONOMISM" AND DAVIDIC "PROMISE"

The central text for the Davidic period is 2 Samuel 7. But rather than coming as a brand-new interruption in the history of revelation, it carefully rehearsed the old affirmations made in the promise and at Sinai and gave them a continuing significance in David's administration. Some of these features in 2 Samuel 7 were:

9: "I will make you a great *name*" (Gen. 12:2, et al.)
10: "I will appoint a *place* for Israel and plant them" (Gen. 15:18; Deut. 11:24f.)
12: "I will set up your *seed* after you" (Gen. 17:7-10,19)
14: "He will be *My son*" (Exod. 4:22)
23-24: "I will be to you for a God and you shall be to Me for a people" (Gen. 17:7-8; 28:21; Exod. 6:7; 29:45; Lev. 11:45; 22:33; 25:38; 26:12,44,45; Num. 15:41; Deut. 4:20; 29:12-13, et al.—two parts of the tripartite formula).

Even the same peculiar plural Hebrew verb in 2 Samuel 7:23 was a clear allusion to the identical question in Deuteronomy 4:7-8: "Who is like thy people, like Israel, one nation in the earth . . . whom Elohim *have gone?*" Thus the Davidic covenant tended to absorb the older promises made to Israel.

But how does the Davidic blessing of 2 Samuel 7 fit—if at

all—the theology of the "deuteronomistic historian"? The deuteronomistic type of materials usually included injunctions about "keeping" God's "statutes, commandments, and judgments," walking "in the ways of Yahweh," and doing "that which is right in the eyes of Yahweh," "with all your heart and all your soul." Most biblical scholars now agree with the conclusion formulated in 1943 by Martin Noth:[15] The OT books of Deuteronomy, Joshua, Judges, Samuel, and Kings evidence an astonishingly unified design. The standard or norm for judging Israel's history during the conquest, settlement of the land, the judges, monarchy, and divided monarchy was Deuteronomy 5-30 to which Deuteronomy 1-4 was added as a later introduction.[16]

The structure of this unified history breathed the hopes and threats of Deuteronomy. It emerged especially in the editorial comments on the selected historical events and personages or in well-placed speeches by the leading actors of that history: Joshua 1:11-15; Joshua 23; 1 Samuel 12; 1 Kings 8:14-61. Often the writer interposed his own assessment where he did not have a speech to summarize the theology of the times, e.g., Joshua 12; Judges 2:11-23; and 2 Kings 17:7-23.

Surprisingly enough, Noth did not select 2 Samuel 7 as a major articulation of deuteronomic thought. Even von Rad tended to treat the history of David in a separate way, claiming that it was "noticeably free from deuteronomistic additions."[17] He introduced what could have widened into another chasm. He suggested that there were originally two separate blocks of tradition which only in their final incorporation in these books worked into a kind of fusion: the Sinai/Mosaic tradition and the Mount Zion/Davidic tradition.[18]

Neither of these wedges reflected accurately the balance of focus of this section. Dennis J. McCarthy[19] adequately demonstrated

---

[15]Martin Noth, *Überlieferungsgeschichtliche Studien I, Die samme Inden und bearbeitenden Geschichtswerke im Alten Testament*, (Tübingen: Max Niemeyer Verlag, 1943). Whether the entire deuteronomistic work represents the time of the Exile is doubtful, but we leave that question to OT introductions to settle since it will not adversely affect our theological inquiries here.

[16]The unity of Deuteronomy as a second millennium work is now correctly defended on the basis of striking similarities in form between Deuteronomy and second millennium vassal treaties, e.g., Hittite treaties, cf. Meredith Kline, *Treaty of the Great King* (Grand Rapids: Eerdmans, 1963).

[17]Gerhard von Rad, *Studies in Deuteronomy* (Chicago: H. Regnery Co., 1953), p. 86.

[18]Von Rad, *Theology*, 1:334ff.

[19]Dennis J. McCarthy, "Second Samuel 7 and the Structure of the Deuteronomic History," *Journal of Biblical Literature* 84(1965): 131-38.

that 2 Samuel 7 did function as another one of the key moments in the history of Israel as theologically reflected in Deuteronomy through Kings. Deuteronomy did more than merely supply the norm for history in his view; it set a pattern for subsequent literary relationships.

According to McCarthy's fine analysis, three key passages schematically set forth programmatic statements (Deut. 31, Josh. 23, 2 Sam. 7) and six subsequent passages showed how they either worked or failed (two passages going with each of the three programmatic patterns): (Josh. 1,12; Judg. 2, 1 Sam. 12; and 1 Kings 8, 2 Kings 17). Only the assignment of the centrality of 2 Samuel 7 need be added to this refinement of Noth's view.

We believe each of the separate emphases of this history—whether it be word-fulfillment,[20] repentance,[21] and observance of the commandments and statutes of the Lord as the key to long life in the land—can be harmonized in one promise. Adding to such a continuum is the clear identification of the Zion/David themes and the Sinai/Moses materials in both Deuteronomy and the Joshua–Kings sequence by Ernest W. Nicholson.[22]

In repeating Nicholson's evidence, we would only reverse the flow of influence; it went from Deuteronomy to David rather than the opposite thesis he developed. Our reason is plain: the canonical shape of the message demands it and has priority until substantial evidence is found to the contrary. These themes may be tabulated as follows:

1. The obligation of David and all kings to follow the *"law of Moses"* (1 Kings 2:1ff.; 9:4f.).
2. The frequent appeal by Davidic kings to Israel's election, Exodus, and gift of the promised *land* (1 Kings 8:16,20f.,34,36,53; cf. Deut. 17:17f.).
3. The constant recognition of Jerusalem as "the *place* where Yahweh has chosen" (1 Kings 8:16,44,48; 11:13,32; 14:21; 2 Kings 21:7; 23:27; cf. Deut. 12).
4. The importance of "name-theology" ("I will cause My *name* to *dwell* there") for the significance of Jerusalem (1 Kings 8:29; 14:21; 2 Kings 21:7; 23:27; cf. Deut. 12).

---

[20]Von Rad, *Studies*, p. 78; *Theology* 1:339f.

[21]Hans Walter Wolff, "The Kerygma of the Deuteronomic Historical Work," *The Vitality of Old Testament Traditions*, coauthored by Walter Brueggeman and H. W. Wolff (Atlanta: Knox Press, 1975), pp. 83-100.

[22]Ernest W. Nicholson, *Deuteronomy and Tradition* (Philadelphia: Fortress Press, 1967), pp. 107-118.

5. The confidence that Yahweh's word would not "fail" (Josh. 21:45; 23:14; 2 Kings 10:10; cf. Deut. 13:1-5 or 18:15ff.).
6. The constant appearance of prophets (e.g., Nathan, Ahijah the Shilonite, Jehu son of Hanani, Elijah, Elisha) who spoke the unfailing word of the Lord but also taught Israel and Judah "to keep My commandments and My statutes in accordance with all the law which I commanded your fathers and which I sent to you by My servants the prophets" (2 Kings 17:13).

To this list we would add the most significant of all:

7. The promised "rest" of Deuteronomy and Joshua and David's measure of realization of that rest (Josh. 21:43-45; 2 Sam. 7:1,11; 1 Kings 5:4; cf. Deut. 12:8-11).

Clearly, both law and promise were included in this history. In fact, an element of conditionality is raised even in 2 Samuel 7:11-16 and 1 Kings 2:4 as it was already in Deuteronomy 17:18f. The promise was indeed secure, and the Davidic line through which the promise was to come was sure; but whether David and his sons were transmitters or also personal participants in these benefits as realized in their times was not secure, only their life of faith and obedience could determine that.

Thus we conclude that there was neither anomaly nor divergency of theology in the Davidic and historical narratives of the earlier prophetical books of Joshua, Judges, Samuel, and Kings. They originated in the environment of the Mosaic addresses of Deuteronomy, proceeded as Noth and others indicated in the key speeches of Joshua 1,12,23; Judges 2; 1 Samuel 12; and reached a climax in 2 Samuel 7 and its responses in 1 Kings 8 and 2 Kings 17.[23]

SAPIENTIAL "CREATION THEOLOGY" AND PROPHETIC "PROMISE"

For some the most intransigent of all connections is that of wisdom theology and the rest of OT theology. It is so highly individualistic and with so few linking concepts, terms, or formulas with either antecedent or subsequent theology of Israel that most despair of ever unifying it into the rest of OT theology.

---

[23]See the fine summaries of Carl Graesser, Jr. "The Message of the Deuteronomic Historian," *Concordia Theological Monthly* 39(1968): 542-51.

Nevertheless, we believe the key appeared already in Genesis 22:12 as the attitude of a life of faith in Abraham: he "feared God." Such was also the style of living manifested in Joseph (Gen. 42:18), Job (1:1,8-9; 2:3), and the midwives for the Hebrews in the Egyptian bondage (Exod. 1:15-21). The expression "to fear the Lord God" continued in Exodus 14:31; 20:20; Leviticus 19:14,32; 25:17; Deuteronomy 4:10; 5:26; 6:2,13,24; 8:6; 10:12,20; 13:4; 14:23; 17:19; 28:58; 31:12-13.

In one wisdom book, "the fear of the Lord" quickly assumed the position of motto: "The fear of the Lord is the beginning *(rē'šît)* of knowledge, but fools despise wisdom and instruction" (Prov. 1:7). Such a healthy fear prolonged life and yielded the fullness of life (Prov. 10:27; 14:27; 19:23; 22:4) even as the Mosaic law yielded the same fruit from faith, i.e., life (Lev. 18:5). Thus a "path," or as it is said today, a life style, was provided by this attitude of reverence and trust (Prov. 2:19; 5:6; 10:17; 13:14; 15:24). It became a veritable "tree of life" (Prov. 3:18; 11:30; 13:12; 15:4).

To fear God was "to turn away from evil." If announced positively, then, fearing the Lord was turning to God in a life of faith and trust. Only by such a commitment could one be enabled by the God who created the world to enjoy the otherwise mundane activities of eating, drinking, and earning a living. The wholeness of life, its patterns of meaning, its integration of faith, knowledge, and actions, and its significance were then realized (Eccl. 3:11,14; 5:7; 8:12; 12:13). Otherwise man remained bankrupt and unable to make it all "fit."

The fear of the Lord also was linked with the acquisition of wisdom (Prov. 1:7,29; 2:5; 8:13; 15:33). Since wisdom was a characteristic of God, it was His to share with all who came into a special relationship with Him. Indeed, by wisdom He had created the world (Prov. 3:19-20; 8:22-31); now He would share out of that same wisdom with all who feared Him.

But what of wisdom's relationship to the theology that follows it in the writing prophet's era? If the fear-of-the-Lord theme had its inception in the patriarchal theology and continued into Mosaic times, did it continue beyond? Indeed it did! It supplied so many of the concepts used by some of the prophets[24] and had such a strong prophetic savor about it that some scholars, without sufficient war-

---

[24]J. L. Crenshaw, "The Influence of the Wise upon Amos: The Doxologies of Amos and Job 5:9-16, 9:5-10," *Zeitschrift für die alttestamentliche Wissenschaft* 79(1967): 42-57.

rant, labeled the concept of wisdom and the fear of the Lord a prophetic reinterpretation of wisdom.[25]

Many of the prophetic techniques, images, or patterns were common to the wise men: the x + 1 pattern of Amos, "for three . . . yea four" (Amos 1:3,6,9,11,13 et al.); the rhetorical questions centered on natural phenomena (6:12); the cause and effect sequence (3:3-8); the woe oracles (5:18; 6:1); Isaiah's use of the vine allegory (Isa. 5) and the parable of the farmer (28:23-29); Jeremiah's use of the phrase "to take disciplining" *(mûsār,* Jer. 2:30; 5:3; 7:28; 17:23; 32:33; 35:13); and Ezekiel's emphasis on individual punishment (Ezek. 18:1ff.; also Jer. 31:29-30).[26]

But the place where the promise doctrine of the prophets and wisdom were most directly linked was in the sevenfold spirit prediction of Immanuel in Isaiah 11:1-2.[27] This "Shoot" *(hōṭer)* out of the "root" *(gēzaʻ)* of Jesse, David's father, and "Branch" *(nēṣer)* was to have:

"the Spirit of wisdom and understanding,
the Spirit of counsel and might,
the Spirit of knowledge and of the fear of the Lord."

As far back as 2 Samuel 14,16, and 20, wisdom was presented as a political virtue. Kings and rulers needed it if they were to rule a people or towns (Prov. 8:14-16). But wisdom also belonged to the character of God and originated in the fear of Him. Therefore, when Isaiah 11:1-10 prophesied that the future government of a Davidic descendant would possess this political virtue of "wisdom" *(hokmâh)* along with the other wisdom themes of "understanding" *(bînâh),* "counsel" *(ʻēṣâh),* "might" *(geḇûrâh),* "knowledge" *(daʻaṯ),* and the "fear of the Lord" *(yirʼaṯ YHWH)*—"His delight is in the fear of the Lord"—the connection is more than accidental. It is deliberate!

We conclude, then, that it is possible to discern the biblical writers themselves making the connections between the various

---

[25]William McKane, *Proverbs* (Philadelphia: Westminster Press, 1970), p. 348. Also Norman Habel, "The Symbolism of Wisdom in Proverbs 1-9," *Interpretation* 26(1972): 144, n. 24; pp. 143-49.

[26]For these and other examples, see J. Lindblom, "Wisdom in the Old Testament Prophets," *Wisdom in Israel and in the Ancient Near East,* eds. M. Noth and D. Winton Thomas (Leiden: E. J. Brill, 1955), pp. 202f.; David A. Hubbard, "The Wisdom Movement and Israel's Covenant Faith," *Tyndale Bulletin* 17(1966): 8-10.

[27]This connection is suggested by A. von Roon, "The Relation Between Christ and the Wisdom of God According to Paul," *Novum Testamentum* 16(1974): 207,212.

blocks of material and sections of Israel's history. Often the linkage was made in a critical speech, pronouncement, or in a repeated refrain that undergirds a whole section. Thus there were major items of continuity; but there were new items associated with familiar reference to the repeated blessing and promise of a seed, a land, a world-wide blessing, a rest, a king, a dynasty, and a God dwelling with His people.

All could be embraced, however, under the one comprehensive blessing called the promise. Such a category was sufficient to encompass a great variety of biblical books, themes, and concepts. In spite of an almost universal chorus to the contrary, the mass of data is neither intractable nor impossible. It does yield up a single theology with a deliberate plan of God. Furthermore, Scripture presents its own key of organization. The OT does possess its own canonical inner unity which binds together the various emphases and longitudinal themes. This is not a hidden inner unity. It lies open and ready for all: The Promise of God.

PART II
MATERIALS FOR AN
OLD TESTAMENT THEOLOGY

Chapter 5

Prolegomena to the Promise:
Prepatriarchal Era

The hallmark of Genesis 1-11 is to be found in the Edenic, Noachic, and Abrahamic "blessing." With the announcement of God's promise to *bless* all created beings in the beginning of the prepatriarchal narrative (1:22,28), at strategic points in the course of its narrative (5:2; 9:1), and at its conclusion (12:1-3), the theme, unity, and perimeters of the theology of Genesis 1-11 are secure.

Unfortunately, this block of biblical materials has rarely been treated in its unified contribution to theology. All too often theologians have restricted their attention, as Claus Westermann observed,[1] to a discussion of Creation, the Fall, and man's personal sin before God. However, the canonical shape of the message as we have it in Genesis 1-11 asks of the interpreter much more than those meager results. Man is placed before God in the Fall, but he is likewise located in a society and in the state according to chapters 4 and 6. Moreover, man was the recipient of much more than his life and successive curses.

---

[1]Claus Westermann, *Creation*, trans. J. J. Scullion (Philadelphia: Fortress Press, 1974), pp. 17-31. His analysis of Genesis 1-11 agrees at several points with conclusions we had already reached independently.

The pattern of events in all eleven chapters is too closely inter-woven to be left aside by the exegete or theologian. Structurally they exhibit the juxtaposition of God's gift of blessing with man's revolt. The divine word of blessing initiates every type of increase and legitimate dominion; it follows the central tragedy of the section— the Flood—and concludes the section in the blessing of the gospel itself. Man's revolt, on the other hand, is evident primarily in the three catastrophies of the Fall, the Flood, and the destruction of the tower of Babel. Here too the divine word is present; only it is a word of judgment and not of blessing.

But even this triple rhythm of blessing and curse, hope and doom, did not exhaust the basic structure and theology of the text in its wholeness. God's goal for history, while marked by the insertions of His word at critically important junctures, was opposed by man's continual rejection of these divine blessings in the areas of the family (4:1-16), cultural achievements (vv. 17-24), a doctrine of work (2:15), the development of the human race (5; 10; 11:10-32), and the state (6:1-6).

The double line of man's failure and God's special word of grace or blessing can be represented in this way:

Man's Failure		God's Blessing
1. The Fall (Gen. 3)	→	a. Promise of a Seed (Gen. 3:15)
2. The Flood (Gen. 6-8)	→	b. Promise of God's dwelling in Shem's tents (Gen. 9:25-27)
3. The Scattering (Gen. 11)	→	c. Promise of world-wide blessing (Gen. 12:1-3).

WORD OF CREATION

But as the theology of this section began, so did the world—by the divine word of a personal, communicating God. Ten times the text reiterates this lead-off statement: "And God said" (Gen. 1:3,6,9,11,14,20,24,26,29; 2:18). Creation, then, is depicted as the result of the dynamic word of God. To call forth the world in direct response to His word was to act as Jesus of Nazareth did when in response to His word men were healed. Said the centurion, "Only speak the word, and my servant will be healed" (Matt. 8:8). So the word was likewise spoken here, and the world came into being. This theological affirmation appears later in the psalms:

By the word of the Lord the heavens were made
  and all their hosts by the breath of His mouth . . .
He spoke, and it came into being;
  He commanded, and it stood forth.
—Psalm 33:6,9

Whether secondary causes were also thereby set into motion in effecting the result cannot be determined from the text. Every time the text would seem to imply a mediate creation (i.e., where the existing materials or forces of nature might be authorized or endowed by God to do the work of carrying out the creation order—the three instances being: "Let the earth bring forth" [Gen. 1:11]; "Let the waters bring forth" [v. 20]; "Let the earth bring forth" [v. 24]), the next verse in two of the three instances (vv. 21,25) attributes the same things, which appeared to be immediately authorized to effect the new work directly to God. Only Genesis 1:11 might be an exception to representing God's work as immediate creation since verse 12 continues that same way of speaking. However, that may be all it was: a way of highlighting the recipient (the earth or the waters) of the forthcoming benefits of God.

On the whole, however, the method of creation was as clear as its source: it was God who created, and He did it by His word. But word-creation stressed more than method. It also emphasized that creation was in accordance with God's prior knowledge of the world, for He spoke what He had previously thought of and planned. Likewise His purposeful design and predetermined function of all things was underscored since He often *named* what He created. Thus the essence and purpose of His creation was outlined from its inception. And if He named these things, He then *owned* them, for one only names what He owns or is given jurisdiction over.

Often the discussion of the time of creation consumes more time and energy than it should. Theology generally is disinterested in this discussion. However, the decision over whether Genesis 1-2 reports an absolute beginning or a relative beginning is central to its concern. Recently, many modern translations have prefered a "when . . . then" construction for Genesis 1:1-3: "When God created, . . . the earth being without form, . . . then God said."

While on some grammatical grounds such a construction is possible, there are strong arguments against such an analysis. Both the Hebrew Masoretic punctuation and those Greek transliterations of the Hebrew text into Greek letters show convincingly that there was quite a respectable history of interpretation which took the first word, *b^{e}rēšît*, as an absolute noun, "in the beginning," rather than as a Hebrew construct noun, "in beginning of creating."[2] Therefore,

---

[2]See for further support and additional arguments, E. J. Young, *Studies in Genesis* (Nutley, N.J.: Presbyterian and Reformed Publishing House, 1964), pp. 1-14. See also the fine article by Gerhard F. Hasel, "Recent Translations of Genesis 1:1: A Critical Look," *The Bible Translator* 22(1971): 154-67.

Genesis 1:1 commits itself to the absolute beginning of everything ("heaven and the earth") outside of God.

The use of the verb *bārā'*, "create" (Gen. 1:1,21,27; 2:3-4; 5:1-2; 6:7), does not appear to be as determinative for an absolute beginning as some might expect it to be. While the verb is indeed restricted to God as its sole subject, is never used with any agency of material, and is rendered by the strongest Greek verb for create *(ktizō)* in the LXX, it also appears in parallel usage to two other words in the creation narrative: *'āśâh*, "to make, do" (Gen. 1:26-27; cf. also its later parallels in Isa. 41:20; 45:18), and *yāṣar*, "to form, mold" (Gen. 2:7; cf. its later usage in Isa. 43:1; 45:18; Amos 4:13). In Isaiah 45:18 all three verbs appear in parallelism, thus disallowing any major distinctive between them:

Thus says the Lord,
Who created *(bārā')* the heavens, He is God!
Who formed *(yāṣar)* the earth
and made *('āśâh)* it
He established *(kûn)* it
He did not create *(bārā')* it a chaos
He formed *(yāṣar)* it to be inhabited.
I am the Lord, there is no one else.

To be sure, "create" does appear at the outset of the creative order (Gen. 1:1), at the first appearance of life (v. 21), and with the designation that man is made in the image of God (v. 27). But this cannot be used to support the untenable view of mechanistic evolution with three divine interruptions, as it were, at the creation of matter, the creation of life, and the creation of the *imago Dei*. The preceding evidence of parallel usage of creation verbs sees to that.

We conclude, then, that God initiated the creation process out of nothing but His word. More detailed statements will need to wait until Hebrews 11:3 states a doctrine of *ex nihilo*, "out of nothing," in definitive terms.

The "days" of creation climax in the creation of man and woman. They were the chief interest of our writer. For in typical style observed throughout the whole work on Genesis, he quickly traced the entire picture caring for those details which were only of passing interest first before he treated in detail the subject or persons which concerned him most. Adam and Eve both were made on the sixth day, but the duration of that "day" *(yôm)* and the details of how they were created are detailed in Genesis 2:4ff. By now the reader is aware of the author's elasticity in his use of the word "day": it shares the same range of meaning as is known in modern English. It is equal to daylight (1:5); our calendar days which make up the year (v. 14); and the whole span of creation, or as we would say, the *day* of the horse and buggy (2:4).

The sixth creative period of time must have lasted more than twenty-four hours, for Adam grew lonely for a companion (Gen. 2:20). Surely this took more than an afternoon's idle thought! Moreover, he busied himself with the task of naming the animals as his loneliness continued to build. Finally, God created a woman, and it was still that sixth "day."

Through the influence mainly of Augustine, the early church— up until the middle of the nineteenth century—held the majority view that there had been three creative "days" before the calendar type of days were created on the fourth day (Gen. 1:14). Thus the usage urged here is not a modern backward projection to an antiquated text that needed to be rescued from embarrassment. It was the clear teaching of the text itself.

Some of the details of what followed the divine word of Genesis 1:26 are now supplied in 2:4ff. Adam was not "alive" (*nepeš ḥayyâh*, literally, but inaccurately, "living soul") until God had taken some of the dust of the ground, shaped it, and breathed into it the breath of life. Now to be sure, there are anthropomorphic expressions here, but they are figures of God's direct activity. Man's vitality was a direct gift from God, for prior to that he was not "alive"—that much is certain!

Eve too was "built" (*bānâh*) by God, yet in such a way that her propinquity to Adam was assured. She was to be "bone of [his] bone and flesh of [his] flesh" (Gen. 2:23). Together they originated from the hand of God. Man was so linked to the soil that as his fortunes went, so did the fortunes of nature; and woman was likewise linked to man, for she was "taken from man."

Both, however, shared equally in the highest gift given to any of the orders of creation: the image of God. Male and female shared alike and equally in this highest mark yet set on creation. Only later in NT terms will the definitional content of this image become clear (e.g., knowledge, Col. 3:10; righteousness and holiness, Eph. 4:24). In the Genesis record, the precise content of the image is less specific. We see it expressed in concepts such as the possibility of fellowship and communication with God, the exercise of responsible dominion and leadership over the creation owned by God, and the fact that in some way unspecified as yet, God is the prototype of which man and woman are merely copies, replicas (*ṣelem*, "carved or hewn statue or copy") and facsimilies (*dᵉmût*, "likeness").[3]

WORD OF BLESSING

The word of creation was followed by a word of blessing. Accordingly, all creatures of sea and air were endowed with reproductive capabilities and given a divine mission:

> God blessed them by saying:
> "Be fruitful and multiply
> and fill the waters of the seas;
> and let the birds multiply on the earth."
> —Genesis 1:22

This part of the blessing mankind shares with the created order mentioned in verse 22, but an additional part of our blessing appears to stem decidedly from the gift of the image of God. Almost identical terms are used in verses 26 and 28 to amplify one part of the image that was foremost in the mind of God when He so graciously benefited that first couple; they were to subdue and have dominion over all creation (v. 28).

Of course, the divine mission to "subdue" (*kābaš*) and to "dominate" (*rādâh*) was no license for mankind to abuse the creative orders. Man was not to be a bully and a law to himself. He was only to be God's viceroy and therefore accountable to Him. Creation was to benefit man, but man was to benefit God!

Once more the divine word of blessing came: "God blessed the seventh day and sanctified it because on it [He] ceased (*šābat*) from all His work which He had done in creation" (Gen. 2:3). The day is called the Sabbath (*šabbāt*) because it was the day commemorating God's cessation (*šābat*) of His work. In this way He put a division between His work of creation and all subsequent work (usually termed providence). Thus history has the first of three great divine markers found in revelation: (1) the Sabbath; (2) the "it is finished" of Psalm 22:31; John 19:30 (the division between redemption promised and redemption accomplished); and (3) "it is done" of Revelation 21:6 (the division between history and eternity!).

Thus God made the seventh "day" holy as a perpetual memorial to the completion of the entire universe and all that was in it. His

---

[3]The literature on the image of God is huge. Some of the more representative but recent contributions are: D. J. A. Clines, "The Image of God in Man," *Tyndale Bulletin* 19(1968): 55-103; James Barr, "The Image of God in the Book of Genesis— A Study in Terminology," *Bulletin of John Ryland's Library* 51(1968): 11-26.

"rest" was to be symbolic for man both in his own rhythm of work and cessation from labor as well as for his eternal hopes. So decisive was this ending that the writer also abruptly "stops" his narration of events; he does not conclude with the expected: "And there was evening and there was morning, a seventh day."

All had been completed. Everything had been done. It was all "good"; in fact, it was all "very good" (Gen. 1:31). Every function, every being, and every blessing necessary to carrying out life and its joys were now in hand. But this was all an untested goodness.

FIRST WORD OF PROMISE: SEED

To test man's obedience and free decision to follow his creator, God placed the tree of the knowledge of good and evil in the garden of Eden with a prohibition that Adam and Eve were not to eat its fruit. As such, the tree contained no magical enzymes or vitamins; it simply stood for the possibility of man's rebellion against the simple word of God. In eating the fruit, mankind would personally "know," i.e., experientially taste, the opposite side of all the good they currently experienced. The totality of experience—both good and bad—would be in their repertoire of sensations.

Another factor must be added before the theology of the Fall can be understood. The serpent *(hannāḥāš)*, that creature who was "more subtle than the beasts of field" (Gen. 3:1), was also present in the garden. The craftiness and subtlety of the serpent was comparably greater than any of the beasts of the field.[4]

Most know that the NT identified this serpent with Satan: "God of peace will soon crush Satan under your feet" (Rom. 16:20); "The great dragon was thrown down, that ancient serpent, who is called the Devil and Satan, the deceiver of the whole world" (Rev. 12:9; 20:2); "The serpent deceived Eve by his cunning . . . for Satan disguises himself as an angel of light" (2 Cor. 11:3,14). But few recognize that he is treated as such in these passages as well.

Satan's form and shape are no more implied by his appellation serpent than by the name dragon. Nor is the curse on him determinative for setting his morphology. Genesis 3:14 only asserts that his conquest was so secure that "on his belly he would go" (cf. Gen.

---

[4]The Hebrew *mikkōl* can be taken in Genesis 3:1,14 as a partitive—"*any* of the beasts of the field" or as a comparative "than the beasts of the field." But in 3:14 all agree the same construction must be comparative. Context also dictates in favor of our rendering. See Paul Haupt, "The Curse on the Serpent," *Journal of Biblical Literature* 35(1916): 155-62.

49:17; Job 20:14,16; Ps. 140:3; Isa. 59:5; Mic. 7:17). Also, his contemptible station and abject humility were so real that he would lick the dust, or as we say today, "bite the dust." Both phrases were oriental pictures from the ancient Near East of vanquished mortals: they laid face down prostrate before the conquering monarchs often forming nothing more than a footstool for his throne.[5] Reptiles do not, of course, eat dirt for food; but Satan would taste defeat as a result of his part in the temptation. Also observe carefully that God had already created "creepers" in Genesis 1:24 and had pronounced them "good" (v. 25)!

The serpent consistently spoke on his own behalf in the dialog with the woman; he was not a surrogate for someone else. He was party to what God had said; in fact, he knew the possible alternatives and eventualities from his own knowledge. To the woman, he was a person and not one of the animals, for she did express surprise at being addressed by him. She was, however, offended by the distorted narrowness which he attributed to God and the limited freedom of the first couple. It was grossly unfair to attribute to God the fact that they were denied the privilege of eating from any of the trees of the garden.

Deception worked its trick, however, and the woman succumbed to the heavy pressure and cunning argumentation of the tempter himself. Adam also disobeyed, but on less strenuous grounds than those laid upon the woman. Thus the first tragedy of failure of three selected by the writer for theological reflection set the scene for a new word of divine blessing. If any was to come from any place, it would be from God.

It was a prophetic word of judgment and deliverance addressed to the serpent (Gen. 3:14-15), the woman (v. 16), and the man (vv. 17-19). The reason for the curse was stated in each case: (1) Satan beguiled the woman; (2) the woman listened to the serpent; and (3) the man listened to the woman—no one listened to God!

Consequently the ground would feel the effects of man's Fall. It would bring forth thorns and thistles as well as man's sweat. Meanwhile children would be born with pain, and a woman's "turning" (*tᵉšûqâh*), not "desire," to her husband would result in the fact that he would "rule over" (*māšal*) her. The serpent, for his part, would face the disgrace of certain defeat.

But in the midst of the heavy dirge of gloom and rebuke came God's surprising word of prophetic hope (Gen. 3:15). A divinely

---

[5]Cf. the Amarna Tablets, E.A. 100:36; Psalm 72:9; Isaiah 49:23; Micah 7:17.

instigated hostility ("I will put enmity") between the person of the serpent and the woman, between his "seed" and her "seed," climaxes with the triumphant appearance of a "he"—no doubt a representative person of the woman's seed. He would deliver a lethal blow to the head of Satan while the best the serpent would be able or even permitted to do would be to nip the heel of this male descendant.

Who this male descendant was to be was not immediately revealed. Perhaps Eve thought Cain was that one. She named her son Cain saying she had "gotten a man, even the Lord" (Gen. 4:1); at least, that is one way of rendering the enigmatic phrase. Regardless of how it is to be interpreted, she was mistaken; and the biblical text only records her longings and perhaps hints at the clear understanding she had of Genesis 3:15.

But God had not been silent. He had spoken, and His word prophesied of another day when a complete reversal of the serpent's temporary coup would happen as a result of the one who had spoken so authoritatively.

Furthermore, the blessing God had promised to mankind did continue. The genealogy of the ten most significant men in the antediluvian period recorded in Genesis 5 was one evidence of that blessing. They were "fruitful" and they did "multiply" just as Genesis 5:2 reaffirmed that word saying, "Male and female He created them and He blessed them." And so they had "sons and daughters."

Mankind was blessed in the fields (Gen. 4:1-2) and in cultural advances, also (vv. 17-22). Moreover, the selection of the twenty men leading up to Abraham plotted the progress of that "seed" promised to Eve as well as the agents of that blessing for their contemporaries.

Meanwhile the theme of judgment continued to mark the record. There was another notice of banishment from the immediate presence of the Lord. Just as Adam and Eve had been sent forth in Genesis 3:23-24 from the Garden of Eden, so Cain, the murderer of his brother Abel, was condemned to be "a fugitive and wanderer on the earth" (4:12-16).

So intimate had that sense of presence been that when offerings were brought to the Lord, it was the Lord Himself who first inspected the man (Gen. 4:4-5) and then the offering. God valued the heart condition of the offerer more than the gift he brought. Thus it was that jealousy broke out in the institution of the family, resulting in murder and the necessary imposition of the theme of judgment.

79

SECOND WORD OF PROMISE: THE GOD OF SHEM

The earth's second crisis came with the subversion of the institution of the state as it led an unruly populace in the practice of evil. Already a proud Lamech had begun to distort the purpose of government with his boastful tyranny and polygamy (Gen. 4:23-24). He was not to be challenged or rebuked by anyone. If Cain would be avenged by God sevenfold, then Lamech would be avenged seventy-seven times.

In the midst of the blessing of God—"men began to multiply on the face of the earth" (Gen. 6:1)—came the heaping up of evil. The rulers of the day, having adopted for themselves the Near Eastern titulary of "sons of God,"[6] autocratically began to multiply as many wives for themselves as they pleased. Their lust for a "name," i.e., a reputation (v. 4), led them to compound their excesses and abuse the purposes of their office.

In exasperation God gave up on mankind. His Spirit would not always continue to strive with men (Gen. 6:3). Such "mighty men" (v. 4), or aristocrats *(n^{e}pilîm gibborîm)* must be halted in their wickedness. The hearts of men and women were filled continually with evil. Once again the theme of expulsion will come, only in a much more tragic and final way: God would blot man from the face of the earth (v. 7).

"But Noah found grace in the eyes of the Lord" (Gen. 6:8), for he was "a righteous man, blameless in his generation" (v. 9). Thus the earth's second greatest time of need, according to this text, was to be relieved as it had been in Genesis 3:15 with an enactment of the salvation of God. There was a righteous remnant—not by accident or by any means of partiality. Noah's father, Lamech, found in Noah— at the time of his birth—the comfort that his work in the earth previously cursed by the Lord would now be lightened with Noah's help (5:29). The reference to Genesis 3:17 is patent, and the unity of this section to chapters 3-4 is clear.

The wickedness forcing the hand of God was not an inevitable fate alloted to all men now that the Fall was a *fait accompli*. There had been righteous men. Consider Enoch. "He walked with God" for 300 years, not as a hermit in isolation, but as a man raising a family of sons and daughters (Gen. 5:22). So pleased was God with his life of obedience and faith that "he was not" on earth any longer; God "took him" (v. 24). The text handles so easily the issue of mortal man

---

[6]Meredith Kline, "Divine Kingship and Genesis 6:1-4," *Westminster Theological Journal* 24(1961-62): 187-204.

being ushered into the very presence of God that we are amazed that no further explanation or caveat follows. Did Enoch's translation serve as a paradigmatic model for OT men until further revelation filled in the hiatus of information? The revelation of that fact would always be available if men wanted to ponder its implications.

Noah was of that stock. He found grace in the eyes of the Lord. Noah was "righteous before God in [his] generation" (Gen. 7:1). Instructed by God, he built an ark. Thus he and his family experienced the salvation of God while judgment came on the rest of mankind.

The divine blessing, "Be fruitful and multiply and fill the earth," was again repeated; this time to Noah, his wife, his sons, their wives, and every living thing on the earth, in the air, and on the sea (Gen. 8:17; 9:1,7). Here God added His special covenant with nature. He would maintain "seedtime, harvest, cold, heat, summer, winter, day, and night" without interruption as long as the earth remained (8:22). The contents of these promises formed an "everlasting covenant between God and every living creature of all flesh" (9:8,11,16) as signified by the rainbow in the sky. Along with this note of God's blessing was His explicit refusal "to never again curse (*gallēl*) the ground for the sake of man" (8:21), a reminder of a similar curse on the ground in Genesis 3:17. Likewise the reference to the "imaginations of [man's] heart" (*yēṣer lēḇ*) in 8:21 recalled a similar phrase using the same word (*yēṣer*) in Genesis 6:5. Given the repeated appearance of such features, it may be confidently asserted that the structural unity stretched from Genesis 1-11.[7]

The word of judgment and salvation reached its highest point in the aftermath of the earth's second crisis. It came through Noah after he learned what his son Ham had done to him while he was sleeping off the effects of his wine.

The structure of Genesis 9:25-27 is a heptastich which is divided into three parts by the repeated refrain of Canaan's servitude, a son of guilty Ham:

> And he said,
>> Cursed be Canaan;
>> A servant of servants will he be to his brothers.
>> —verse 25

---

[7]See the informative discussion of R. Rendtorff, "Genesis 8:21 und die Urgeschichte des Yahwisten," *Kirche und Dogma* 7(1961): 69-81, as cited by W. M. Clark, "The Flood and the Structure of the Prepatriarchal History," *Zeitschrift für die alttestamentliche Wissenschaft* 83(1971): 205-10. Rendtorff argued that the age of curse and primeval history both concluded in Genesis 8:21. As Clark pointed out, Genesis 9:25f. does raise the curse again, but it is of limited application to Canaan, and it is followed by an immediate blessing.

And he said,
  Blessed be the Lord God of Shem;
  Let Canaan be a slave to him.
                    —verse 26

God will enlarge Japhet,
  But He will dwell in the tents of Shem;
  Let Canaan be a slave to him.
                    —verse 27

Now the key issue is this: Who is the subject of the verb "he will dwell" in Genesis 9:27? We concur with the judgment of the Targum of Onkelos, Philo, Maimonides, Rashi, Aben Ezra, Theodoret, Baumgarten, and Delitzsch that the subject is "God." Our reasons are these: (1) the subject of the previous clause is presumed to continue into the next clause where the subject is unexpressed; (2) the use of the indirect object of the previous line as subject ("Japhet") would require strong contextual reasons for doing so; (3) the context of the next several chapters designates Shem as the first in honor of blessings; and (4) the Hebrew phrase $w^e yi\check{s}k\bar{o}n\ b^e'oh^ol\hat{e}$ $\check{s}\bar{e}m$, "and he will dwell in the tents of Shem," hardly makes sense if attributed to Japhet, for Japhet had already been granted the blessing of expansion.

The plan of the whole prophecy appears to devote the first strophe only to Canaan, the second to Shem and Canaan, and the third to all three brothers. On balance, then, the best option is to regard God as promising to Shem a special blessing. He would dwell with the Semitic peoples. The word for "dwell" is related to the later concept of Mosaic theology of the Shekinah glory of God wherein the presence of God over the tabernacle was evidenced by the pillar of cloud by day and the pillar of fire by night. Hence, the man Shem would be the one through whom the "seed" promised earlier would now come. Had not God said, "Blessed be the Lord God of Shem" (Gen. 9:26)? And why did He use this distinctive form of address? Could it be that the blessing and indwelling were linked? And could it be that they were God's next provision to earth's latest crisis?

THIRD WORD OF PROMISE:
A BLESSING TO ALL THE NATIONS

The third and final crisis to hit the earth during this period of mixed blessing and curse was the concerted effort put forth by the human race to organize and preserve their unity around some architectural symbol. As they put it, "Let us make a reputation [literally, 'name'] for ourselves, lest we be scattered abroad on the face of the whole earth" (Gen. 11:4).[8]

Even though the blessing of God continued to be realized in their multiplication (Gen. 11:10-32) and their filling the earth with some seventy nations (10:1-32), the thoughts of their hearts were again directed away from the glory of God or His provisions. The judgment of God came in the double form of the confounding of their speech and the scattering of the peoples over the face of the earth. But again the sin-curse theme was closely matched with a divine grace-blessing theme.

Instead of uniting men around an ethno-political project aimed at the glorification of man and his abilities to meet the needs of a disparate community of nations, God provided His word of blessing once again. It was a word that climaxed every blessing pronounced in the prepatriarchal narrative. Five times over Genesis 12:1-3 repeated the word "blessing." Nor was it any surprise that it was a word directed to one of Shem's descendants (cf. 9:27), Abraham. He was himself to be blessed; yet he was thereby to be a blessing to all the nations of the world. What the nations could not attain on their own organization and goals would now be given to them in grace.

The number of people included in "all the families of the earth" (*mišpᵉḥōṭ hā"ᵈāmâh*) is the same as the list of nations in Genesis 10. Had not Genesis 10:32 concluded, "These are the families of the sons of Noah" (*mišpᵉḥōṭ bᵉnê Nōaḥ*)? The promise, then, was universal and limited in its participation only by the response of faith—even as it was so limited for Abraham's participation.

Thus earth's third crisis was again resolved with the gracious word of the same God who dealt justly with sin. We conclude that the theology of this section is a unified development bracketed and advanced by the free word of God. It commences in a word of creative power; it concludes in a word of promise.

The debacles of man's first disobedience, the tyrannical distortion of political power, and the haughty aspiration of unity on a humanistic basis led to the judgment of the Fall, the Flood, and the dispersion of mankind. The theological factors found in each crisis which perpetrated the judgment of God were the thoughts, imaginations, and plans of an evil heart (Gen. 3:5-6; 6:5; 8:21; 9:22; 11:4). But God's salvific word was equal to every default. Alongside the sin-judgment themes came a new word about a seed (3:15), a race among whom God would dwell (9:27), and the blessing of the good news offered to every nation on the face of the earth (12:3).

---

[8]Samuel Noah Kramer, "The 'Babel of Tongues': A Sumerian Version," *Journal of American Oriental Society* 88(1968): 108-11.

Chapter 6

Provisions in the Promise:
Patriarchal Era

A new departure in the divine revelation commenced with Genesis 12. In this new era there was a succession of individuals who now served as God's appointed means of extending His word of blessing to all mankind. Under God's election for service and His call to personal and world-wide blessing, Abraham, Isaac, and Jacob became hallmarks of a new phase in the accumlated divine blessing.

WORD OF REVELATION

The emerging prominence assigned to the divine word in the prepatriarchal era did not diminish in the patriarchal times; instead, it increased. In fact, it may be noted as one of the distinctive features of Genesis 12-50, for repeatedly the patriarchs were presented as the frequent and immediate recipients of various forms of divine revelation.[1] It is not surprising, then, that the record should treat them as "prophets" (Gen. 20:7; and later in Ps. 105:15), men who had immediate access to the word and ear of the living God.

---

[1]P. V. Premsagar, "Theology of Promise in the Patriarchal Narratives," *Indian Journal of Theology* 23(1974): 114.

At crucial junctures in their history, God addressed these men directly in spoken words (Gen. 12:1,4; 13:14; 15:1; 21:12; 22:1) with the introductory formula of "The word of the Lord came to him" or "The Lord said to him." Therefore it was not only Moses to whom God spoke clearly "mouth to mouth" (Num. 12:6-8) but also Abraham, Isaac, and Jacob.

Even more startling was the fact that the Lord Himself appeared (lit., "let Himself be seen" [*wayyērā'*]) by these men in what has subsequently been called a theophany (Gen. 18:1). The reality of the living God's presence underscored the importance and authenticity of His words of promise, comfort, and direction. These appearances, also known as epiphanies, brought man, God, and His purposes for men and women into a very close nexus. All three patriarchs experienced the impact of God's presence on their lives (12:7; 17:1, 18:1; 26:2-5,24; 35:1,7,9). Each appearance of God marked a major development in the progress of revelation as well as in the lives of these men. There He would again "bless" the men, rename them, or send them on a mission which carried with it major consequences for the patriarchs if not for the whole scheme of theology to follow.

Coupled with these theophanies was the manifestation of "the Angel of the Lord" (Gen. 16:7).[2] The identity of this particular Angel appears to be more than just an angelic messenger from God. So frequently He received the respect, worship, and honor reserved only for God; yet He was consistently distinguished from God. His role and appearance are even more obvious in the period of the judges; however, there was no scarcity of references in this period either (16:7-11; 21:17; 22:11-18; 24:7,40; 31:11,13; 32:24-30; 48:15-16). Thus He carried an identity with God; yet He was also sent from Him! To say that the patriarchs regarded Him as equivalent to a Christophany would probably be to claim too much. One thing for sure, He was not the invisible God. And He acted and talked as the Lord. There the matter apparently rested until revelation clarified the enigma.

God also spoke during this era through dreams (*ḥᵃlôm*, Gen. 20:3; 31:10-11,24; 37:5-10; 40:5-16; 41:1-32) and visions (*maḥᵃzeh*, *mar'ōṯ*—15:1; 46:2). The vision was a distinct mode of communicating new knowledge to Abraham in a dramatic setting in which he was aware of a complete panorama of detail (chap. 15). Jacob, likewise, experienced a similar vision urging him to go down to Egypt (chap. 46). Dreams, however, were more widely distributed to

---

[2]See Aubrey R. Johnson, *The One and the Many in the Israelite Conception of God* (Cardiff: University of Wales Press, 1961), pp. 28-33.

persons such as the Philistine king Abimelech, Jacob's uncle Laban, the jailed Egyptian butler and baker, Pharaoh, and the young
inexperienced Joseph. In all such instances the emphasis was on the
dream as dream; its interpretation or revelation was not always an
integral part of this form of God's address to men and nations.

WORD OF PROMISE

What a premium this era placed on the innovative and beneficial
character of that word! Indeed, from the very outset of Genesis
12-50, the accent fell on God's word of blessing and promise. To
Abraham this one promise appeared in four stages of development.
They are to be found in Genesis 12:1-3; 13:14-16; 15:4-21; and
17:4-16 (perhaps 22:15-18 could be added, also).

The content of this promise was basically threefold: a seed, a
land, and a blessing to all the nations of the earth. If one could select
an emphasis in this series, pride of place would go to the last item.
On five separate occasions the patriarchs were designated as a blessing for all nations: Abraham in Genesis 12:3; 18:18; and 22:17-18;
Isaac in 26:3-4; and Jacob in 28:13-14. Indeed, world-wide blessing
was the whole purpose of the very first statement of the promise in
12:2-3.

Even before any technical vocabulary about entering into a
covenant appeared, God promised to enter into a relationship with
Abraham and thereby to be and to do something for Abraham that
would benefit both him and all the nations of the earth. The writer
presented Genesis 12:2-3 as the substance of that word of blessing
and promise.

First there were three short clauses addressed to Abraham alone
using the Hebrew cohortative form of the verb.

1. "I will make you a great nation."
2. "I will bless you."
3. "I will make your name great."

The third one states something that is almost certainly filled with
irony. The quest for a "name," that is to say "renown," "reputation,"
and even "superiority," had been the driving ambition of those
tyrannical kings called "sons of God" in Genesis 6:1-4 and the
architects of the Tower of Babel in Genesis 11:4. Now God Himself
would donate to one man on His own grounds what others had so
selfishly sought but failed to attain.

Moreover, the significance of this third clause and the previous
two becomes clear for the first time when the next clause is added to

the previous three. No doubt it is to be taken as a result clause. It states the divine purpose and intention for benefiting Abraham so generously: "So that [or in order that] it [or you] may be a blessing" (Gen. 12:2). The Hebrew simply reads *weh^eyēh b^erākâh.* Consequently a preliminary goal has been reached in this newly announced relationship. Abraham is to be a great nation, be personally blessed, and receive a great name "*so that* [he] might be a blessing."

But to whom? And how was Abraham to be a blessing? Those questions appear to be answered in the next three clauses. First, the Lord added two more promises in Genesis 12:3, again using the Hebrew cohortative for its verbs.[3]

4. "I will bless those who bless you."
5. "I will curse those who curse you."

Not only did God thereby continue the promise, but He introduced a whole class of people who would respond variously to Abraham. Only then was the grand finale reached. This time the Hebrew verb shifts suddenly to the "perfect tense"[4] in what again can only be a result clause: "So that in you all the nations of the earth shall be blessed."

What a vast sweep was now included in what might have been so trite and so personal an exchange between a single individual and his God! Of course, most competent commentators remain skeptical about the passive rendering of the niphal form of the Hebrew verb,[5] but they fail to see that already the previous result clause had stated as much without specifying exactly to whom Abraham was to be a blessing. The text is so clearly a response to the needs of the swarming multitudes listed in the table of nations (Gen. 10) and the multiplication of Shem's line (chap. 11) that it easily could be classified as one of the first great world-wide missionary texts of Scripture.

Thus far the emphasis was on God's word of blessing. There was a deliberate attempt to connect this new phase of theology with the prepatriarchal emphasis. Five times God had promised His blessing

---

[3]E. Kautzsch, *Genesius' Hebrew Grammar* (Oxford: Clarendon Press, 1909), p. 325, says that cohortative following the imperative expresses either result or intention. Intention fits here very well.

[4]I am indebted to H. C. Leupold, *Exposition of Genesis,* 2 vols. (Grand Rapids: Baker Book House, 1968), 1:411-14, for many of the observations in this analysis of Genesis 12:2-3.

[5]See our discussion in the introduction and especially our reference to O. T. Allis's article on "The Blessing of Abraham" which contained an irrefutable linguistic case on the passive rendering of this niphal. No one to this day has attempted a response to his evidence.

in the short space of two verses, but Abraham was to be the focus of attention: he was to be a great nation, he was to have a great name, and he was to be blessed by God and by all men. There was no direct reference as yet in Genesis 12:1-3 to a seed or an indwelling in the tents of Abraham as was promised in Genesis 1-11. Nor was there a reference as yet to a covenant (*bᵉrît*) which God would "cut" (*kārat*—15:18), "give" (*nātan*—17:2), "establish" (*hēqîm*—17:7,19,21), or "swear" to (*nišbaʿ*—22:16). As the references show, that was to come later in God's disclosures. Just now it was a relationship with a man which served as a basis for blessing the peoples of the earth. Interestingly enough, the actual realization of a promise such as nationhood would have to wait for several centuries until Israel was delivered from Egypt.

An Heir

When Yahweh appeared to Abraham after the patriarch had arrived at Shechem, that ancient word about a "seed" was again revived and now directed to Abraham (Gen. 12:7). From there on the importance of this gift of a child who would inherit the promises and blessings became one of the dominant themes in the patriarchal narrative. It appeared in 12:7; 13:15,16 (bis); 15:13; 16:10; 17:7,8,9,10,13,16,19; 21:12; 22:17 (bis), 18; 24:7; 26:3,4 (ter), 24; 28:13,14 (bis); 32:12; 35:12; 48:3,4.

Eve had been promised both a "seed" and a male individual— apparently from that "seed." Now the progress of revelation with greater specification elaborated on both the corporate and representative aspects of this promised "seed." It was to encompass so great a number that, in hyperbolic fashion, they would rival the stars of heaven and the sands on the seashore. But this seed would also be another "son"—born at first to Abraham, when all hope of his ever having children was lost, and then born to his son Isaac and to Isaac's son Jacob.

A line of successive representative sons of the patriarchs who were regarded as one with the whole group they represented matched the seminal idea already advocated in Genesis 3:15. Furthermore, in the concept of "seed" were the two aspects of the seed as a future *benefit* and the seed as the present *beneficiaries* of God's temporal and spiritual gifts. Consequently, "seed" was always a collective singular noun; never did it appear as a plural noun (e.g., as in "sons"). Thereby the "seed" was marked as a unit, yet with a flexibility of reference: now to the one person, now to the many descendants of that family. This interchange of reference with its implied corporate solidarity was more than a cultural phenomena or an accident of careless editing; it was part and parcel of its doctrinal intention.

The drama of the possible obstacles and frustrations that could have permanently blocked the divine intention here made up a large part of the historical record in this era. Barrenness seemed to plague doggedly all three wives of the patriarchs: Sarah (Gen. 16:1; 17:15-21); Rebekah (25:21); and Rachel (30:1). Old age was another threat in Abraham's case (17:17; 18:11-13). Egyptian and Philistine monarchs nearly stole the wives away from the patriarchs because of each husband's fearful lying (12:10-20; 20:1-18; 26:1-11). Added to this were the ravaging effects of famine (12:10), filial hostility (32:7-8), and the slaughter of infants conducted by Pharaoh (Exod. 1:22). But through it all the meaning was precisely as God put the question to Sarah: "Is anything too miraculous ['wonderful' or 'difficult,' Heb.—*h^{a}yippālē'*] for the Lord?" (Gen. 18:14).

Not even Abraham's attempt to preserve this seed was to count, for the whole life of this child (and each one that followed him) was entirely a gift of God. Therefore when God "tested" *(nissâh)* Abraham's faith by asking him to sacrifice his only son—yes, the very one on whom the whole plan and promise of God rested—he did not demur (Gen. 22:1-10). He feared God (v. 12) and believed that God would "provide" (vv. 8,14—*yir'eh*) so that he *and the lad* would be able to rejoin the party waiting at the base of Mount Moriah (v. 5).

Isaac also was more than a mere foil. He too had a deep stake in what was happening. Yet he learned obedience and trust in this same Lord. Later in his life, when Isaac had selected Esau to receive his blessing, and when everything humanly possible of going wrong was taking place as sons, mother, and father plotted as to whom would be the marked heir to carry the line of the "seed," again Isaac learned that the calling and election of God were not of human intellect or work. God made His selection of His heir apart from the tragic and ridiculous human attempts to upstage the divine plan and free gift.

An Inheritance

The promise of the land of Canaan to Abraham, Isaac, Jacob, and their seed ran through these narratives as the second of the three key themes (Gen. 12:7; 13:15,17; 15:7-8,18; 17:8; 24:7; 26:3-5 [pl. "lands"]; 28:13-14; 35:12; 48:4; 50:24). Genesis 15:18 described the borders of this land as extending "from the river of Egypt to the Euphrates." Genesis 17:1-8 emphasized that the land was to be an "everlasting possession." And Genesis 15:1-21 explained that the patriarch would possess the promised word about the land, but he would merely taste some of the reality of being personally in the land, for the full reality would be delayed until the "fourth generation" when "the iniquity of the Amorites [was] complete" (v. 16).

From the very first moment of God's call to Abraham, He had spoken of this "land" or "country" to which He was sending him (Gen. 12:1). As stated in the earlier chapters, Albrecht Alt was wrong in rejecting the promise of land as being an authentic part of the patriarchal promise. Likewise, Gerhard von Rad had no basis for denying that the entrance into the land by the twelve tribes was not exactly the same vision held by the patriarchs. Only Martin Noth allowed both the land promise and the promise of a seed to be part of the patriarchal religion. Faithfulness to the message of the text in the canonical shape as it has now come down to us demands that both promises be treated as equally authentic and necessary parts of God's message to the patriarchs.

The solemnizing of this offer of land took place in the so-called covenant of pieces (Gen. 15:7-21). Acting on the instructions given by Yahweh, Abraham took various sacrificial animals and divided them into two. After sunset "a smoking furnace and a flaming torch passed between the pieces" (v. 17), and Yahweh made a covenant to give to Abraham and his seed the whole land.

Such a material or temporal blessing was not to be torn apart from the spiritual aspects of God's great promise. Nor was it to be spiritualized or transmuted into some type of heavenly Canaan of which the earthly Canaan was only a model. The text was emphatic, especially chapter 17, that this covenant was to be eternal. However, already in Genesis 13:15 the offer of the land in its entirety was given to Abraham "forever." And when Abraham was ninety-nine years old, this promise was made into "an everlasting covenant" (*bᵉrît ʿôlām*—17:7,13,19) and the land was to be for an "everlasting possession" (*ᵃḥuzzat ʿôlām*—17:8; also 48:4). The word *ʿôlām*, "everlasting," must add something more to the noun it went with, for in the case of covenant there was already a strong idea of perpetuity.[6]

The ancestral promises were fulfilled in the later settlement of the land under Joshua. This, in turn, became a token or pledge of the complete land grant yet to come in the future even as the earlier occupations were simultaneously recognized as "expositions, con-

---

[6]See the somewhat unsatisfactory studies of E. Jenni, "Das Wort *ʿôlām* in AT," *Zeitschrift für die alttestamentliche Wissenschaft* 84(1952): 197-248; idem, "Time," *Interpreter's Dictionary of the Bible*, 4 vols. (Nashville: Abingdon, 1964), IV:644; James Barr, *Biblical Words for Time* (Naperville: Allensons, 1962), p. 69, n. 1.

firmations, and expansions of the promise."[7] Thus even Joshua's settlement of the land did not exhaust the promise of this land as a place chosen by Yahweh for His people. For just as the promise of a son had been enlarged to include in that sonship all the patriarch's descendants, so there was an "overspill" here as well in the land promise.

A Heritage

The third and climactic element in the promise was that Abraham and each successive son of promise were to be the source of blessing; indeed, they were to be the touchstone of blessing to all other peoples. All nations of the earth should be blessed by them, for each was the mediator of life to the nations (of Abraham—12:3; 18:18; 22:17-18; of Isaac—26:3-4; and of Jacob—28:13-14).

The apostle Paul would later point to this phrase and declare that it was the same "gospel" he preached. Simply put, the good news was "in [the promised seed] all the nations of the earth shall be blessed" (Gal. 3:8). Thus the embryo of God's good news could be reduced to the linchpin word "blessing." The one who was blessed was now himself to effect blessing of universal proportions. In contrast to the nations who sought a "name" for themselves, God made Abraham a great name *so that* he might be the means of blessing all the nations.

But it might be asked, How were the nations to receive this blessing mediated by Abraham or any of his successive sons? The method must be the same as it was for Abraham. It was by faith: "He believed the Lord, and he added it up for him as righteousness" (Gen. 15:6).

The literal rendering of Genesis 15:6 is simply he believed in Yahweh *(he'emîn baYHWH)*. This, of course, was more than a vague intellectual assent to a supreme deity in general. The object of his faith was to be found in the content of the total promise. As such, pride of place may be given to the oldest, most ancient, and most central part of that promise: the person of the man of promise signified by that male descendant who was to come from the seed (3:15). Indeed, when God first met Abraham, the issue of progeny was not specifically included but inferred (12:1-3), for the first clause promised to make Abraham into a great nation. His trust, then, was in the Lord—but particularly in the Lord who had promised.

---

[7]Jürgen Moltmann, *Theology of Hope* (New York: Harper & Row, 1965), p. 105.

Once again let us repeat von Orelli's summation of this connection between Abraham and the faith of the nations.

> How Abraham himself, in virtue of his special relation to God, was a mediator of blessing to those about him, is shown in Gen. xx.7; that his people in the same way were to convey the divine blessing, the dispensation of God's grace to the whole world, see in Isa. xix.24; Zech. viii.13. In the present passage the import of the brief saying is expounded in [Gen. 12:]3, according to which God's relation to men depends on their attitude to Abraham (cf. xx.7), and the Lord will deal well with those who wish well to him and do homage to the divine grace revealing itself in him; and on the other hand, will make him feel His displeasure who despises and scorns one whom God has blessed. The singular number here is significant. It can only be single hardened sinners who so misunderstand one who is a source of blessing to all about him, as to condemn and hate him, and in him his God. The world, as a whole, will not withhold homage, and will therefore enjoy the benefit of this source of blessing. The latter is implied in the final words [of 12:3] which puts the crown on the promise. ... But whether the subjective act of homage or the objective act of divine blessing lies in the niphal ["be blessed"], exegetes are not agreed. That one involves the other follows, however, from the preceding words.[8]

Since the verb to "believe" in Genesis 15:6 is the Hebrew hiphil form of the verb *'āman* (cf. English "amen"), Geerhardus Vos pointed to the "causative-productive sense"[9] of the verb and to the preposition. Both, in his judgment, showed that faith had its source and its object in the personal Yahweh. For Abraham, it meant he had to renounce all his human efforts to secure the promise and depend on the same divine person who spoke of the future to work in the present and the future to accomplish what He said He would do. Thus Abraham possessed the promises of God as yet unrealized when he possessed the God of the promises and His trustworthy word.

Some will object to an unconditional construction being laid over the Abrahamic promises. Five passages are often cited as

---

[8]C. von Orelli, *The Old Testament Prophecy of the Consummation of God's Kingdom Traced in Its Historical Development*, trans. J. J. Banks (Edinburgh: T. & T. Clark, 1889), p. 107.

[9]Geerhardus Vos, *Biblical Theology* (Grand Rapids: Eerdmans, 1954), p. 98. Gerhard von Rad, *Old Testament Theology*, 2 vols. (London: Oliver and Boyd, 1962), 1:171, stressed that the object of faith was "something in the future," God's "plan for history (Gen. xv. 5)," and this is what Abraham believed and " 'made himself secure' in."

examples of stipulations placed on Abraham: Genesis 12:1; 17:1,9-14; 22:16; 26:5.

The first is the imperative, "Get thee out from your country, your kindred, and your father's house to a land I will show you" (Gen. 12:1). This imperative is followed by two imperfects and then a series of cohortative imperfects in verses 2-3. But does such a command amount to a formal condition on the divine intention to bless? While admitting that there is a certain conditional element present, Cleon Rogers correctly demonstrated that the accent of the passage was on the cohortatives which emphasized intentionality rather than obligation and that this type of construction occurs in Genesis 45:18 (where the stress was on what Joseph intended to do for his brothers) or Genesis 30:28 (what Laban intended to do for Jacob) and Genesis 27:3; 1 Samuel 14:12; 28:22; 2 Samuel 14:7.[10] The summons to "go," then, was an invitation to receive the gift of promise by faith.[11]

Genesis 17:1-2 would appear at first to impose another condition: "Walk before Me and be blameless and I will make My covenant between Me and thee." Once more the sequence was two imperatives followed by two cohortative imperfects. Therefore, what was true of 12:1-3 is applicable here also. Furthermore, the promise had already been repeated several times prior to this time in 12:1-3,7; 13:14-17; 15:7-21; and 16:10. Consequently, some expositors have argued that the force of the verb translated "I will make" *(weʾettenâh)* does not mean "to set up" but "to put into force" or "make operative the one that is in force."[12] The identical argument would apply for 17:9-14 where circumcision might, at first blush, seem like another condition on the promise. But verse 11 completely settled the argument: circumcision was only a "sign" of the covenant, not its condition.

The last two passages are more difficult. In Genesis 22:16-18 Abraham was told, "Because *(kî yaʿan ʾašer)* you have done this [been willing to offer your son] . . . , I will bless you . . . because *(ʿēqeb ʾašer)* you obeyed My voice." In Genesis 26:5 the blessing is repeated to Isaac "because *(ʿēqeb ʾašer)* Abraham obeyed My voice

---

[10]Cleon L. Rogers, Jr., "The Covenant with Abraham and its Historical Setting," *Bibliotheca Sacra* 127(1970): 252 and n. 61.

[11]Hans Walter Wolff also agrees; Walter Brueggemann and Hans Walter Wolff, "The Kerygma of the Yahwist," *The Vitality of Old Testament Traditions* (Atlanta: Knox Press, 1975), p. 47.

[12]Leupold, *Genesis*, 1:514; C. F. Keil and F. Delitzsch, *Biblical Commentary on the Old Testament*, 25 vols. (Grand Rapids: Eerdmans, n.d.), 1:223.

and kept My charge, My commandments, My statutes, and My laws." In our judgment, the conditionality was not attached to the promise but only to the participants who would benefit from these abiding promises. If the condition of faith was not evident, then the patriarch would become a mere transmitter of the blessing without personally inheriting any of its gifts directly. Such faith must be evident also in an obedience that sprang from faith. Certainly the promise was not initiated in either chapter 22 or 26; that had long since been settled. But each chapter did have a sensitive moment of testing or transition. Further, the election of God had been with a purpose of not only blessing Abraham and the nation (18:18) but also with a purpose of charging him and his household to "maintain the way of the Lord by doing righteousness and justice in order that (*l*^{e}*ma'an*) the Lord might bring on Abraham what He has promised him" (v. 19).

The connection is undeniable. The duty of obedience (law, if you wish) was intimately tied up with promise as a desired sequel. Therefore, the transition to the coming time of Mosaic law should not be all that difficult for any who had really adequately listened to the full revelation of the promise in the patriarchal era.

WORD OF ASSURANCE

Throughout the patriarchal narratives one more theme rang out as another part of the blessing of the promise. It was simply God's pledge: "I will be with you."

Actually, the first time God's presence with men was explicitly mentioned was where the writer commented that God was "with" (*'et*) Hagar's son Ishmael (Gen. 21:20). Then it appeared as a word in the Philistine mouths of Abimelech and Phicol to Abraham: "God is with (*'im*) you in all that you do" (21:22) and later to Isaac: "We can certainly see that the Lord is with (*'im*) you" (26:28).

Out of 104 examples of this formula of the divine presence employing the two Hebrew prepositions translated "with" (*'et* and *'im*) in the OT, 14 examples appear in the Isaac and Jacob narratives of God's assurance.[13] God appeared to Isaac with the comforting words, "Fear not, for I am with (*'ēt*) you" (26:24). Or as He said it in an earlier appearance, "Sojourn in this land, I will be with (*'im*) you"

---

[13]Horst D. Preuss, " *'eth, 'im*," *Theological Dictionary of the Old Testament*, eds. G. J. Botterweck and H. Ringgren; trans. John T. Willis (Grand Rapids: Eerdmans, 1974–) 1:449-63, especially 456.

(26:3). For Jacob, it was a dream of a ladder with God's assurance as he set out for Haran: "Behold, I am with *('im)* you" (28:15).

To this Jacob vowed, "If God will be with *('im)* me, and will protect me in the way I go, . . . then the Lord will be my God" (Gen. 28:20-21). Again, when Jacob was about to return to Canaan, the Lord repeated His earlier promise: "I will be with *('im)* you" (31:3). Accordingly, Jacob repeated to Laban that the Lord had indeed been with *('im)* him (31:5; 35:3). Jacob's son, Joseph, likewise experienced that same divine presence of God (39:2,3,21,23).[14] As Jacob had been favored and blessed by the God who knew of his problems with a scheming Laban, so Joseph was likewise rescued and blessed by the same Lord who followed his changing situation in Egypt.

Yahweh's active presence manifested His character, power, and ability to fulfill the repeated word of promise. It was preeminently a word of personal relationship. The divine presence, of course, had been felt by Abraham before the words were put into a promise-theology formula. For example, the victory Abraham won over Chedorlaomer in Genesis 14:13-24 was an illustration of this fact even if the word was not present. Similarly, so was the intimacy of Abraham's cross-examination of God over His justice in dealing with Sodom and Gomorrah (18:23-33); the Judge of the whole earth would do what was right. Had He not been Abraham's "shield" and "exceeding great reward" (15:1)?

Abraham received the first part of what was to become the oft-repeated tripartite formula of the promise. For now, it was the divine promise: "I will be a God to you and to your seed" (Gen. 17:7). The sovereign God of all the universe would now condescend and call Himself the God of Abraham and his seed. Therein lies the essence of their personal relationship. No wonder James remarked that Abraham was "called the Friend of God" (James 2:23). Their relationship was one of love (18:19), action (19:29), and blessing in all that Abraham did (21:22).

RULER OF PROMISE

As the blessing Abraham received in Genesis 12:1-3; 15; and 17 was transferred to Isaac in 26:3-6 and then to Jacob in a dream at Bethel in 28:13-14 and especially at Paddan-Aram (35:9-12; cf. 46:1-4), so Judah, the fourth son of the patriarch, received it from Jacob's blessing in 49:8-12.

---

[14]Charles T. Fritsch, "God Was With Him: A Theological Study of the Joseph Narrative," *Interpretation* 9(1955): 21-34.

True, Joseph did receive a double portion in the inheritance since his two sons were in a sense adopted by Jacob (cf. *bᵉ kōrāt* of 1 Chron. 5:1), but Judah became the "leader" *(nāgîd)* among his brethren. The oldest son, Reuben, lost his birthright because he dishonored his father's marriage bed (Gen. 35:22). Simeon and Levi, Jacob's second and third sons, were bypassed because of their outrageous revenge on the Shechemites (34:13-29). So the mantle of leadership fell to Judah.

As Isaac had blessed Jacob in Genesis 27:29, so Jacob now transmitted the same supremacy over his brothers to Judah in 49:8. His prowess would make him a princely tribe, and he would maintain his superiority over his foes. His emblem would be the regal lion. To him are given the scepter *(šēbet)* and the ruler's staff *(mᵉhōqēq—49:10).*

But what is the meaning of the phrase "until Shiloh comes" *('ad kî yābō' šîlōh)?* Again, the opinion of von Orelli merits careful attention:

> The context on one hand, the oldest authorities in respect of reading on the other, conduct us to our translation. *Šᵉlloh* was the reading handed down from antiquity, and the LXX rendered this neutrally: *heōs 'ean 'elthē ta apokeimena autō* [until there come the things stored up for him]. Instead of this abstract neuter subject we take the personal subject dominating everywhere here and render: *until he come into that which belongs to him,* therefore *into his own,* his possession described on the sequel. Cf. especially the blessing of Moses on Judah, Deut. xxxiii. 7: *wᵉ'el 'ammô tᵉbî' ennû* ["to his people bring him"]. As champion of the other tribes, he will display untiring energy until he has won his territory without curtailment; and then not merely will the tribes of Israel do homage to him but other nations also will bow to his rule.[15]

Of the last phrase of Genesis 49:10, viz., "he shall take to him the peoples" *(wᵉlô yiqqᵉhat 'ammîm),* he continued:

> [peoples] cannot apply to the Israelites merely, . . . but must refer to the more general national rule, which according to xxvii. 29 is part of Jacob's heritage, and will be Judah's special portion.[16]

For Ezekiel or later Jewish and Christian interpreters to regard this as another addition to the doctrine of the seed to come is

---

[15]Von Orelli, *Prophecy,* pp. 121-22. The Lucianic and Origenic recensions of the LXX read *heōs an elthē apokeitai,* "until he, to whom it is reserved, comes."

[16]Ibid. See W. Gesenius, *Hebraisches und Aramaisches Handworterbuch,* 17th ed., F. Buhl, ed. (Leipzig, 1921), p. 596ᵇ. He concluded that *'ammim* is never used of Israel exclusively; it refers to all peoples or people outside Israel.

therefore not unwarranted. Neither was Ezekiel's allusion in 21:27, "until He comes whose right it is, to Him I will give it," out of bounds either.[17] The Man of promise would be overwhelmingly successful; He would reign over all the peoples of the earth because it was His right and destiny so to do. Furthermore, He would originate from the tribe of Judah in Israel!

GOD OF PROMISE

In the patriarchal narratives, there was a series of names for God. He was El Olam, "the Everlasting God" (Gen. 21:33); El Elyon, "the Most High God" (14:18-20,22), or Yahweh Yireh, "Yahweh will provide" (22:14). But the most frequent and important name was El Shaddai, usually translated "God Almighty" (17:1; 28:3; 35:11; 43:14; 48:3; cf. also 49:25—'*et* Shaddai).

In the book of Job, El Shaddai is used some thirty times beginning with Job 5:17. This is not unexpected, for the prologue and epilogue of that book have such clear credentials for placing the events of Job in the patriarchal era. Some of these indicators are: (1) the wealth of Job puts him in the class of such big cattle owners (Job 1:3,10) as was true also of Isaac (Gen. 26:13-14; cf. 30:29-30); (2) his officiating at sacrifices on behalf of his children (Job 1:5; 42:8) can likewise only be compared to the patriarchal or prepatriarchal age; (3) the currency in use (*q*ᵉ*śîtâh*—Job 42:11) is the same as mentioned in Jacob's time (Gen. 33:19; cf. Josh. 24:32); (4) the longevity of Job (over 140 years, or five generations, Job. 42:16) is comparable to Joseph's 110 years and three generations (Gen. 50:23); and (5) Job's death (42:17) is described in exactly the same terms as that of Abraham (25:8) and Isaac (35:29).

Regardless of what scholars ultimately decide the meaning of

---

[17]For further study, cf. W. L. Moran, "Genesis 49:10 and its use in Ezekiel 21:32," *Biblica* 39(1958): 405-25. He would vocalize "Shiloh" as *šay* and *lôh* and change *yābô'* to the hiphil *yûbā'*, "until tribute is brought to him and his is the obedience of the people." Moran rightly rejects the reading *šilu(m)* as an alleged Akkadian cognate meaning "Prince, ruler, king" (which does not occur in Akkadian, 405-409) and the reading of the City Shiloh (which is never spelled *šylh* in Hebrew, 410-11), but he also rejects *šello* (409-10,14-16) because the unexpressed subject cannot be "the staff" or "the septer" since this ruins the parallelism. (Orelli, of course, took the personal subject dominating the whole section.) Further, it should have been written *šellô hô'* and *še* as a relative pronoun is very improbable since that is a feature of the northern dialect. (In response to these last two problems, we call attention to the parallel between *welô* and *šiloh* in the two parallel lines and to the use of *še* in contexts not necessarily northern or late.)

Shaddai is (whether "nourisher" or "God of the Mountain"),[18] the pattern of usage is clear in the six patriarchal references and most of Job's more than thirty references. This name stressed the might and power of God; thus the LXX rendered it in Job as *ho pantokrátōr*, the "All-Ruler" or "Almighty." As Gerhardus Vos stated it,[19] El Shaddai emphasized the supernatural work of His grace. As He overpowered nature and forced her to forward His plan of salvation, El Shaddai indicated God's ability to master nature. Thereby it linked together His work in Creation and now His overpowering work in history to effect His plan.

Outside of these six references in Genesis and the thirty-one references in Job, this divine name appears three other places in the Pentateuch (Exod. 6:3; Num. 24:4,16), four times in the Prophets (Isa. 13:6; Joel 1:15; Ezek. 1:24; 10:5), and in Psalms (68:15 [Heb.]; 91:1) and Ruth (1:20-21). Together they fit the general tenor of the name and its use in the patriarchal era; God is omnipotent and a great Sovereign who can and will act on behalf of those whom He loves and who are called according to His purpose and plan.

Thus the theology of this section was intertwined around that *word* from on high, its *blessing* to a chosen seed, and the *assurance* of the divine presence that guaranteed the certainty of the promised heir, inheritance, and heritage or even the present success of the patriarchs. It was all God's word of encouragement.

So blessed were these men that their benefits overflowed to their neighbors. Hence Laban claimed that he was blessed of Yahweh on account of his proximity to Jacob (Gen. 30:27,30). In the same way Pharaoh was blessed because of his proximity to Joseph (39:5).

Perhaps this same concept of physical proximity was involved in the act of communicating blessing from father to son as H. Mowvley suggested.[20] Rather than locating the root for the verb to bless *(brk)* as Gesenius did in the root *prq*, "to break," i.e., the bending of or breaking of one's knees when homage or thanks is given, he followed J. Pedersen, von Rad, and Procksch who translate the verb *bārak* as "to place on the knees of." (Joseph may have placed his

---

[18]From Ugaritic *ţdy*, "mountains," or from *šd*, "breast"; contrast *šd*, "field."

[19]Vos, *Theology*, pp. 95-96. He noted the connection in Isaiah 13:6 and Joel 1:15 between shaddai and the Hebrew verb *šādad*, "to overpower, destroy." Cf. Frank M. Cross, "Yahweh and the God of the Patriarchs," *Harvard Theological Review* 55(1962): 244-50.

[20]H. Mowvley, "The Concept and Content of 'Blessing' in the Old Testament," *Bible Translator* 16(1965): 74-80.

children on Jacob's knees—Genesis 48.) Thus Isaac touched and kissed Jacob as he imparted his blessing to him (Gen. 27:27). So Laban kissed his grandchildren and blessed them (31:55). Likewise, the one who wrestled with Jacob touched the hollow of his thigh (32:25-32).

Just as important as the act, however, was the word of blessing itself. The blessing was many things: a prediction, the gift itself resulting from blessing (Gen. 33:11), a capacity given by God to ensure the fulfillment of the promise (17:16; 24:60), the reward of prosperity (15:1), the peace of the Lord (26:29), and nothing less than the presence of God Himself (26:3,28).[21]

The patriarchs' confidence that they survived death, even if the actual method or means was left undiscussed, appeared with the other blessings of the age. Abraham believed that the almighty God could effect the deliverance of his son from death itself in Genesis 22. He had as much a right to this view as Gilgamesh had for his friend Enkidu or the myth of Tammuz had for dead vegetation. Therefore, the patriarchal text always carefully distinguished the fact that each patriarch was "gathered to his people" from the act of burial in the "grave" (Gen. 25:8-9; 35:29; 37:35; 49:29,31,33). Neither was their relationship to God or His continuing association with them canceled after death, for He repeatedly identified Himself, the living personal God, as the "God of Abraham, Isaac, and Jacob" (Exod. 3:6; cf. Mark 12:26; Luke 20:37).[22] No wonder the psalmist confidently expressed the fact that men continued to enjoy fellowship with God beyond the grave (Pss. 16:10; 49:15; 73:24). Likewise, Job argued in 14:14 that man enjoyed the same prospect of "sprouting forth" again as did the felled tree (Job. 14:7).[23]

---

[21]Ibid., pp. 78-79.

[22]For fuller discussion, see James Orr, *Christian View of God and the World,* appendix to lecture V (Grand Rapids: Eerdmans, 1947), pp. 200-210; Patrick Fairbairn, *The Typology of Scripture,* 2 vols. (Grand Rapids: Zondervan, 1963), 1:343-59.

[23]See our full discussion in the chapter on wisdom theology.

Chapter 7

People of the Promise:
Mosaic Era

In spite of the four hundred years of silence which separated the patriarchal times from the Mosaic era, the theology hardly missed a beat. For example, the brief review of Jacob's family concluded in Exodus 1:7 with seven words deliberately piled one on the other. These evidenced the fulfillment of God's promise that Jacob's seed had indeed been "fruitful," "increased greatly," "multiplied," and "grown exceeding strong." It was a clear allusion to the blessing promised in Genesis 1:28 and 35:11.

But the seed was now more than a mere family; it was a people, a nation. There lies the new distinction for this era. And their experience of the gracious acts of God was more than a collection of personal interventions for selected individuals. Here, as their confession, God's acts would be reaffirmed by the whole nation: "Yahweh delivered His people from Egypt." Nevertheless, it all would be traced back to the same comforting assurance: "I will be with you," for that was God's name and character. His name was "I am," i.e., Yahweh, the God who would be dynamically, effectively present when He was needed and when men called on Him.

The loyal love and dependable grace of this covenant-making God to His promises dominated the transition between these ages.

He had heard Israel's groanings in Egypt, and His interest in them and action on their behalf were summed up as a "remembering" of His covenant with Abraham, Isaac, and Jacob (Exod. 2:24). The God of the deliverance was one and the same as "the God of your fathers" (3:13); "the God of Abraham, the God of Isaac, and the God of Jacob" (vv. 15-16).

Previously, God had appeared to Abraham, Isaac, and Jacob in the character and nature of El Shaddai; but now He would manifest Himself as Yahweh (Exod. 6:3) by delivering Israel and leading her into the land He had sworn to give to the patriarchs (6:8; 33:1). Again, all this divine activity could be subsumed under one concept: it was a "remembering" of His covenant (6:5).

Hence the author of Exodus connected the patriarchs and the Exodus periods directly; for him the Sinaitic covenant was theologically and historically a continuation of the Abrahamic promise. Rather than treating Egypt and Sinai as an interruption to the previous promises, their needs became a new opportunity for another manifestation of God's divine loyalty to His oft-repeated promise.

MY SON, MY FIRSTBORN

Jacob's twelve sons and Joseph's two children multiplied until they became a great nation during the Egyptian bondage. After four hundred and thirty years of slavery (Exod. 12:40), the sons of Jacob had had enough; they cried out to God for help.

Help came in the person of Moses and in the miraculous interventions and words of the Lord. Moses' first act as the newly appointed spokesman for the living God was categorically to command Pharaoh, "Israel is my firstborn son: ... Let my son go" (Exod. 4:22-23). Yahweh was now to be seen as a "Father" by what He did: He brought Israel into being as a nation; He fostered the nation and led it. That is what fatherhood was all about. So Moses would reason in his final speech to Israel: "Is not [the Lord] your Father, who created you, who made you, and established you?" (Deut. 32:6).

The text pointedly used the singular for the whole community of Israel collectively. When the OT referred to individual Israelites, it used the plural (e.g., "You are sons of the Lord your God" [Deut. 14:1]). But the individual Israelite was also a "son of God" precisely because he was a member of the chosen people.

While it is true that it was commonplace in the ancient Near East for monarchs to claim that they were sons of one god or another—and especially true in Egypt where the Pharaoh was thought to be derived from sexual union between the god and the queen—Israel carefully avoided any idea of divine sonship. Yet when God used the designation "my firstborn son," it was not a mindless epithet or a poetic indulgence. It was an integral part of God's call and His deliverance of Israel from Egypt.

Israel's sonship expressed a relationship:[1] Israel was the son of Yahweh but not merely in the sense of a *citizen* of a nation, a *member* of a craftsman's guild, or a *disciple* of a teacher. Hebrew *ben*, "son," can be understood in varying contexts in all of these senses. Here, however, it was a familial relationship: a people who made up the family of God. Israel was not a family in an adopted sense or a mere ethnic, political, or social unity. Rather, it was a family formed, saved, and guarded by God the "Father" of this family.

As true sons, Israel must imitate its Father in activity. Everything the Father is, the son should aspire to be (e.g., "Be ye holy as I am" [Lev. 19:2], *passim*). The son, on his part, must respect the wishes of the Father and show his respect and gratitude by doing what his Father commands him to do. The Father, on the other hand, would demonstrate His love in His tender and loyal dealings with His son.

The title "firstborn" (*bᵉkôr*), on the other hand, usually meant the first child to be born (e.g., Gen. 25:25) or to open the womb (e.g., Exod. 13:2). In the transferred sense, as used here, it denoted "first in rank," "first in preeminence." As such it bestowed special rights and honors of inheritance and favor on its recipients.

The rights of primogeniture were superseded when another son was designated as "firstborn." What had previously rested on position was now removed and grounded in grace. So it was with Jacob who was renamed Israel. Esau was the first in position of actual birth, then Jacob (Gen. 25:25-26); but it was Jacob who received God's favor and the surprise of being called His "firstborn." Likewise Ephraim was Joseph's second child, but Jeremiah recognized him as God's "firstborn" (Jer. 31:9).

The importance of both the meaning and the concepts of collective solidarity in the terms "My son" and "My firstborn" are not always appreciated by readers and theologians of the OT. "Seed" is a collective term which first appeared in Genesis 3:15 as a representative person for both the whole group identified with him and the ultimate or final representative person who was to come. "My son" and "My firstborn" likewise functioned in the same dual capacity.

---

[1]I am indebted to Dennis McCarthy for many of the insights here: "Israel, My Firstborn Son," *The Way* 5(1965): pp. 183-91.

They were collective terms which represented and included that *one* who was to come and the *many* who already believed on him.

Readers of the NT should not be surprised, then, when the same terms were used of Jesus the Messiah. He, too, was addressed by what had become, by then, technical terms. He, too, was delivered out of Egypt and was given the same familial term "my son" (Matt. 2:15; cf. Hos. 11:1). Moreover, He was God's "firstborn," *prōtotokos* (Rom. 8:29; Col. 1:15,18; Heb. 1:6; Rev. 1:5). And the title *prōtotokoi* He shared with all believers just as it was true of all Israel in the OT (Heb. 12:23). The continuity of terms, identities, and meanings throughout both testaments is more than a mere accident. It is a remarkable evidence of a single-planned program and a unified single people of God.

MY PEOPLE, MY POSSESSION

Israel was more than a family or God's son; Israel had also become a *gôy*, a "nation" (Exod. 19:6). This fact first became evident when the Lord told Moses at the burning bush, "I have seen the affliction of My people who are in Egypt" (3:7). This title Moses repeated to Pharaoh in God's categorical demand: "Let My people go" (Exod. 5:1; 7:14; 8:1,20; 9:1; 10:3). To be called a "people" (*'am*)[2] meant that they were an ethnic social group with enough numerical strength and enough unity to be regarded as a corporate whole. Yet they were so intimately linked to Yahweh that He called them "My people."

Yahweh's loyalty to His people became evident in the events of the plagues, the Exodus, and the wilderness journey. Israel was to be released from servitude to Pharaoh so that she might serve the Lord. However, when the Egyptian monarch consistently refused to yield to Yahweh's demands, His power (called the "finger of God" in Exodus 8:19; [cf. Exod. 31:18; Ps. 8:3; Luke 11:20]) was unleashed in increasing degrees of severity against Pharaoh, his people, and their lands and goods.

But the objective was never mere punishment as a requital for Pharaoh's obstinacy. The plagues had a salvific purpose for *both* Israel and Egypt. They were to convince Pharaoh that Yahweh indeed had spoken and had to be feared and obeyed; Israel had no choice and neither did the Egyptians.

Was this God chauvinistic and unfairly partial to Israel to the

---

[2]Contrast our conclusions with those of Richard Deutsch, "The Biblical Concept of the 'People of God,'" *Southeast Asia Journal of Theology* 13(1972): 4-12.

detriment of the Egyptians' economy? Not so again! The text insisted that His plagues also had an evangelistic appeal to the Egyptians. Each catastrophe was invoked so "that you [Egyptians] might know that I am the Lord in the midst of the earth" (Exod. 8:22); "that [you] might know that there is none like Me in all the earth" (9:14; cf. 8:10); "to show [you God's] power so that [His] name might be declared throughout all the earth" (9:16); and "that [you] might know that all the earth belongs to the Lord . . . [and that you might] fear the Lord God" (vv. 29-30).

Egypt's gods were no gods at all. Only Yahweh was God; and He was such in all the earth, not just in the patriarchs' territory of Haran or Canaan. His name and power had to be published throughout the whole earth so that all nations of the earth might "fear Him," i.e., "believe Him." And so some Egyptians did. Some of Pharaoh's servants "feared the word of Yahweh" (Exod. 9:20) and did as Moses commanded. No doubt that is the explanation for the "mixed multitude" that left Egypt with Israel (12:38). It included those Gentiles who had come "to know," i.e., to experience personally, the Lord God of all the earth.

Even after the miraculous deliverance was accomplished on the evening of the Passover, many Egyptians still clung adamantly to their reckless course of direct confrontation with this incomparably great God. Patiently, the divine offer of grace remained open as they pursued Israel as she crossed the sea. They must "know that I am the Lord" (Exod. 14:4) even when that God had received praise and glory from Israel for His mighty victory over Pharaoh, his chariots, and his horsemen (v. 18).

The effect on Israel was overwhelming. After she saw what God had finally done against the impervious Egyptians, they "feared the Lord and believed in the Lord and in His servant Moses" (Exod. 14:31). Together they sang:

> Thy right hand, O Lord,
> is glorious in power.
> Thy right hand, O Lord,
> shatters the enemy.
> —Exodus 15:6

> Who is like thee, O Lord, among the gods?
> Who is like thee, majestic in holiness,
> Terrible in glorious deeds, doing miracles?
> —Exodus 15:11

All Israel's freedom was owed to the loyal love (*hesed*—Exod. 15:13) Yahweh had for His people. Other peoples heard and trembled, but God's people whom He had purchased *(qānâh*—15:16) saw the "salvation of the Lord" *(yᵉšûʿaṭ YHWH*—14:13). Human manipulation was clearly excluded; it was God's "deliverance" (3:8; 6:6). He was Israel's "kinsman-redeemer" *(gōʾel*—6:6) who with miracles and an "outstretched arm" took them and called them "My people" (v. 7).

The meaning of this event had been set forth in the ceremony of the Passover held on Israel's last night in Egypt. That rite was to be celebrated annually along with the accredited explanation supplied in Exodus 13:14-16. You must say, went the explanation to later generations, that "the Lord slew all the firstborn in Egypt, both the firstborn of man and cattle. Therefore I sacrifice to the Lord all the males that first open the womb; but all the firstborn of my sons I redeem *(pādâh)*" (v. 15).

Thus Israel was constituted a "people." In fact, Exodus 12:3 called her a "congregation" *(ʿēdâh)* for the first time as she began to prepare for the Passover meal in each family. Abraham had become numerous; indeed, he had now become a great nation, and God's two great redemptive acts of the Passover and the Exodus had underscored the reality of this new fulfillment.

Most surprising of all was Israel's status as God's "choice or treasured possession" *(sᵉgûllâh*—Exod. 19:5). But what made Israel so valuable and what exactly did the phrase mean? The meaning of this special term was elucidated by Moshe Greenberg who pointed to its Akkadian equivalent *sikiltum*[3] and by C. Virolleaud who noted Ugaritic *sglt*, which he translated "proprieté."[4] The basic root of this term was *sakālu*, "to set aside a thing or a property." It was the opposite of real property, e.g., real estate, which could not be moved. God's *sᵉgûllâh*, on the other hand, was his *moveable* treasure. Israel's value, then, came from God's love and affection which He had set on her. She became His property.

Later in Deuteronomy, Israel was also called "holy" *(qādôš)* as well as a "treasured possession." But these passages were always linked with the concept of the "people" *(ʿam*—Deut. 7:6; 14:2; 26:18,19; also without *sᵉgûllâh*—14:21; 28:9); thus the same point was preserved. Israel was to be God's distinct treasure set aside for a marked purpose.

With this we have a fourth new term to refer to Israel's standing

---

[3]Moshe Greenberg, "Hebrew *sᵉgûllā*: Akkadian *sikiltu*," *Journal of American Oriental Society* 71(1951): 172ff.

[4]As cited by Moshe Weinfeld, "The Covenant of Grant in Old Testament and Ancient Near East," *Journal of American Oriental Society* 90(1970): 195, n. 103.

before a God who had chosen and called her, not individually, but collectively, which gives the complete meaning of peoplehood and nationhood. The whole concept could be reduced to a single phrase: "I will take you to Myself for a people" (Exod. 6:7). That affirmation became the second part of the tripartite formula: "I will be your God and you shall be My people." Only the third part was lacking now: "And I will dwell in the midst of you." That would come momentarily.

But who was this God and who could be compared to Him (Exod. 15:11)? Moses and Miriam had celebrated the answer on the occasion of the Red Sea deliverance in a song which magnified God's incomparable greatness. His deliverance from Egypt (15:1-12), which also signaled His future help in their pending entrance into Canaan (vv. 13-18), made His undisputed sovereignty over man, nations, and nature most clear: "The Lord will reign forever and ever" (v. 18).

Few passages are more pivotal for the discussion of God's name[5] and character than Exodus 6:2-8. The distinction between His appearance to the patriarchs as El Shaddai and His present manifestation to Moses as Yahweh (YHWH) has continued to be a source of scholarly debate and conjecture. Certainly the patriarchs were not without a knowledge of the name "Yahweh," for it did occur in the Genesis record well over one hundred times. What Exodus 6:3 stressed was the two niphal reflexive verbs, *wā'erā'* ("I showed Myself") and *nôda'tî* ("I did not make Myself known") and the Hebrew preposition *b^e* ("by") before El Shaddai and by implication before Yahweh.

This preposition, known as a *beth essentiae,* is to be translated "as" and means that "God showed Himself to Abraham, to Isaac, and to Jacob *in the character of* (i.e., with the accompanying attributes of the name of) El Shaddai; but *in the character of My name* Yahweh I did not make Myself known to them." The name, then, revealed the character, qualities, attributes, and essence of the person so designated.

Such an analysis of Exodus 6:3 may be confirmed by an examination of 3:13. When God promised to go with Moses when he stood before Pharaoh and the people, Moses queried, "Suppose the people ask, '*What* is the name of this God who will lead us out of Egypt?' What shall I say then?"

---

[5]See W. C. Kaiser, Jr., "Name," *Zondervan Pictorial Encyclopedia of the Bible,* 5 vols. (Grand Rapids: Zondervan, 1975), 4:364.

As Martin Buber[6] and others have noted, the interrogative "what?" *(mâh)* is to be distinguished from "who?" *(mî)*. The latter only asked for the title or designation of a person while *mâh*, especially when connected with the word "name," sought out the qualities, character, powers, and abilities resident in that name.

Thus, the answer came back bluntly. His name was "I am the God who will be there" (Exod. 3:14). It was not so much an ontological designation or a static notion of being (e.g., "I am that I am"); it was rather a promise of a dynamic, active *presence*. As God had revealed Himself in His supernatural control over nature for the patriarchs, now Moses and Yahweh's son, Israel, would know His presence in a day-by-day experience as it never was known before. Later on in Deuteronomy, this will develop into a whole name-theology. The name came to represent the presence of God Himself instead of merely experiencing the effects of His presence on nature.

KINGLY PRIESTS

This uniquely owned, treasured possession was destined to be a royal priesthood composed of the entire congregation. Israel, the first-born of the nations, was given the status of sonship, delivered from Egypt as if they had been borne along on eagles' wings, and made ministers on behalf of themselves and the nations. This mediatorial role was announced in Exodus 19:3-6:

Thus shall you say to the house of Jacob,
and you shall declare to the sons of Israel,
You have seen what I did to the Egyptians,
And that I bore you on eagles' wings,
and brought you to Myself;
And now if you will listen attentively to My voice,
And keep My covenant
You will be My treasured possession above all peoples,
though the whole earth is Mine;
Yes, you will become for Me kingly priests and a holy nation.

The entire world belonged to the Lord; yet in the midst of the nations He had placed Israel. To her He had given a special task. Few have captured the meaning of this text better than Charles A. Briggs:

We have a further unfolding of the second Messianic prophecy

---

[6]Martin Buber, *Kingship of God* (New York: Harper & Row, 1967), pp. 104-6, 189-90; also, J. A. Motyer, *The Revelation of the Divine Name* (London: Tyndale, 1956), pp. 3-31.

[Gen. 9:27] in that the dwelling of God in the tents of Shem becomes the reign of God as the King of the kingdom of Israel.

> The kingdom of God is a kingdom of priests, a holy nation. It has a sacred ministry of priesthood, as well as sovereignty with reference to the nations of the world. As holy, the Israelites are the subjects of their holy King, and as priests they represent Him and mediate for Him with the nations. Thus the third feature of the Abrahamic covenant is unfolded. As the essential thing to Abraham had been the promised seed, as the essential thing to Jacob had been the promised land, so now, when Israel had become a nation, separating itself from the Egyptians, and entering into independent national relations to the various nations of the world, the essential thing became the relation which they were to assume on the one side to God their king, and on the other to the nations, and indeed first of all the positive side of that relation. This is represented in our promise: as a ministry of royalty and priesthood. They are a kingdom of priests, a kingdom and a priesthood combined in the unity of the conception, royal priests or priest kings.[7]

Briggs noted that the term "kingdom of priests" *(mamleket kōhᵃnîm)* was more a compound noun than it was a construct relation of the genitive case. In fact, the terms were so closely combined in their unity that Israel was to be at once priest-kings and also royal priests. It was to be true of everyone in the nation as a whole just as all had been included in sonship.[8]

Recently, William Moran[9] has convincingly argued that "kingdom of priests" is not a synonym for a "holy nation." It was a separate entity. Further, *mamleket* occasionally meant "king" (1 Kings 18:10; Isa. 60:11-12; Jer. 27:7-8; Hag. 2:22), especially in prose passages such as Exodus 19.

For Moran, the style of the passage was remarkably personal. It began in verse 3 "to the sons of Israel" *(liḇᵉnê yiśrā'ēl)* and concluded in verse 6 "to the sons of Israel" *('el bᵉnê yiśrā'ēl)*. In the message addressed to the people, verses 4-6, the first and last clauses, were introduced by the emphatic "you" *('attem)*. Other repetitions of references to persons stressed the deep personal address in the

---

[7]Charles Augustus Briggs, *Messianic Prophecy* (New York: Charles Scribner's Sons, 1889), p. 102.

[8]Ibid., pp. 102-3, n. 2.

[9]William L. Moran, "A Kingdom of Priests," *The Bible in Current Catholic Thought*, ed. John L. McKenzie (New York: Herder & Herder, 1962), pp. 7-20, esp. 14-16. See some mild revisions of Moran in Brevard S. Childs, *The Book of Exodus* (Philadelphia: Westminster Press, 1974), p. 367; yet cf. p. 342, n. 6 and p. 374, n. 6.

covenant of Exodus 19:3-6: "you" *('eṭkem, bis)*, "to me" *(lî, ter)*, and alliteration "though all belongs to me" *(kî lî kol,* K-L-K-L).

The distinctive nature and special status given to this nation, God's personal possession, *sᵉgûllâh*, was wrapped up in their universal priesthood. They were to be mediators of God's grace to the nations of the earth even as in Abraham "all the nations of the earth were to be blessed."

Unfortunately for the people, they declined the privilege of being a national priesthood in preference to representation under Moses and Aaron (Exod. 19:16-25; 20:18-21). Therefore the original purpose of God was delayed (not scrapped or defeated forever) until NT times when the priesthood of all believers was again proclaimed (1 Peter 2:9; Rev. 1:6; 5:10). Nevertheless, Israel's role of being the agents chosen by God to minister to the needs of the nations was not rescinded.

The people keenly felt the magnificence and holiness of Yahweh's presence in the thunder of His voice and in the lightning effect of His presence that left the natural world in seismographic convulsions. Thus they begged Moses to approach God on their behalf and receive His communications for them. So Moses became the first Levite to represent the people.[10] Later, by divine authority, Moses consecrated Aaron and his sons to function at the altar (Exod. 28:1). Other jobs connected with the sanctuary and the cult were given to the whole tribe of Levi after they had proved their faithfulness during the golden calf incident (Exod. 32:25-29).

Still, the whole scene had been an unprecedented event in the annals of men. Of the original encounter with God at Sinai, Moses queried the people in Deuteronomy 4:32-37:

> Did any people ever hear the voice of God speaking out of the midst of fire, as you have heard, and still live? . . .
>
> Out of heaven He let you [all] hear His voice . . . and on earth He let you [all] see His great fire . . . because He loved [you].

But now God's voice was heard by Moses; and the mediatorial work for Israel must now be performed by the priests, Aaron and his sons, and the Levites. The representative nature of the Levitical priesthood was made even more graphic in Numbers 3:12-13. For every first-born son in each Israelite family, a Levite was consecrated to God in lieu of the death of that first-born son. Rather than

---

[10]Note, however, that there apparently had been priests prior to this new provision (Exod. 19:22,24).

completing the implied logical consequences of the death and sacrifice to the Lord of every first-born thing to show Yahweh's ownership over the whole earth, this legislation halted that inference in the case of first-born from men and women. In their case God was pleased to provide the Levites as substitutes. Likewise, the high priest represented all the people, for he bore the names of all the tribes of Israel on his breastplate as he went into the sanctuary (Exod. 28:29).

This priesthood was given to Aaron in a "perpetual statute" (Exod. 29:9) and renewed again to Phinehas (Num. 25:13). It is important to notice that the office, the priest*hood,* was eternally secured, not the particular individuals or family. Thus it did not suffer abrogation when it later passed temporarily from Phinehas's descendants to Ithamar's line. The conclusion, once again, is the same: the promise remained permanent but the participation in the blessings depended on the individual's spiritual condition.

A HOLY NATION

Yet another title was given to Israel in Exodus 19:6. There was to be a nation but not like the ordinary run of nations that did not know God. Israel was to be a holy nation. But this promise was to be linked with the people's response and preparation for the theophany. Such requirements were a "test" according to Exodus 20:20:

Do not fear: for God has come to prove you,
and that the fear of Him may be before your
eyes that you may not sin.

Was this covenant a deliberate change from the promissory covenant of the patriarchs to a conditional covenant in which "obedience was the absolute condition of blessing"?[11] Was God displeased with the response of the people who pledged, "All that the Lord has spoken we will do" (Exod. 19:8; 24:3,7)? Could this be interpreted as a "step downward" and a "mistake" tantamount to "rejecting God's gracious dealings with them"?[12] What was the relationship of the "if" statements (Exod. 19:5; Lev. 26:3ff.; Deut.

---

[11]James Freemen Rand, "Old Testament Fellowship with God," *Bibliotheca Sacra* 109(1952): 153. Note C. I. Scofield, *Scofield Reference Bible* (New York: Oxford University Press, 1909), p. 20: "The Dispensation of Promise ended when Israel rashly accepted the law (Exod. 19:8)."

[12]Rand, "Fellowship," p. 155.

11:13ff.; 28:1) and the command "You shall walk in the way which the Lord your God has commanded you that *(lema'an)* you may live and that *(we)* it may go well with you and that *(we)* you may live long in the land which you shall possess" (Deut. 5:33)?

The contrast implied in these questions was too sharp for the text. If the alleged obligatory nature of this covenant should prove to be the new grounds for establishing a relationship with the covenantal God, then it should prove possible to demonstrate that the same logic can be applied to the conditional statements noticed in the chapter on patriarchal theology.[13]

The "if" is admittedly conditional. But conditional to what? It was a condition, in this context, to Israel's distinctive position among all the peoples of the earth, to her mediatorial role and her status as a holy nation. In short, it could qualify, hamper, or negate Israel's experience of sanctification and ministry to others; but it hardly could effect her election, salvation, or present and future inheritance of the ancient promise. She must obey God's voice and heed His covenant, *not* "in order to" *(lema'an*—purpose clause) live and have things go well for her, *but* "with the result that" *(lema'an*—result clause)[14] she will experience authentic living and things going well for her (Deut. 5:33).

Israel was to be separate and holy; she was to be separate and as no other people on the face of the earth. As an elect or called people now being formed into a nation under God, holiness was not an optional feature. Israel had to be holy, for her God, Yahweh, was holy (Lev. 20:26; 22:31-33). As such, they could not be consecrated any further to any thing or person (27:26) or enter into any rival relationships (18:2-5).

Eternal life or living in the benefits of the promise was not now conditioned by a new law of obedience.[15] Nor did Leviticus 18:5 make it so when it said, "Do this and you shall live in them." Andrew A. Bonar was wrong when he commented on this verse:

> But if, as most think, we are to take, in this place, the word [sic] "*live in them*," as meaning "eternal life to be got by them," the scope of the passage is, that so excellent are God's laws, and every

---

[13]See Genesis 18:17ff.; 22:18; 26:5.

[14]This Hebrew particle is used to indicate inevitable consequence as well as purpose; see S. R. Driver, *A Treatise on the Use of Tenses in Hebrew*, 4th ed. (Oxford: Clarendon Press, 1906), p. 200.

[15]For parts of the following argument and further details see W. C. Kaiser, Jr., "Leviticus and Paul: 'Do This and You Shall Live' (Eternally?)," *Journal of Evangelical Theological Society* 14(1971): 19-28.

special minute detail of these laws, that *if a man were to keep these always and perfectly,* the very keeping would be eternal life to him. And the quotations in Rom. 10:5, and Gal. 3:12 would seem to determine this to be the true and only sense here (italics his).[16]

But this view misses the following points:

1. Leviticus 18 begins and ends (vv. 2,20) with the theological setting of "I am the Lord your God." Thus law-keeping here was Israel's sanctification and the grand evidence that the Lord was indeed her God already.
2. Instead of imitating the customs of the surrounding pagans, Israel's happy privilege would be to manifest the *life already begun* in faith by her observance of God's laws.
3. "Those things" which Israel was to do were the Lord's statutes and judgments which were sharply contrasted with the customs and ordinances of the Egyptians and Canaanites.
4. The same point made in Leviticus 18:5 will be made by Moses later on in Deuteronomy 16:20 and by Ezekiel in Ezekiel 20:11. G. A. Cooke summarized it succinctly:

> The ancient mind fastened on the outward acts revealing the inward state. While the modern mind goes directly to the internal condition.[17]

Patrick Fairbairn was of a similar mind:

> Neither Moses nor Ezekiel, it is obvious, meant that the life spoken of, which comprehends whatever is really excellent and good, was to be *acquired* by means of such conformity to the enactments of heaven; for life in that sense already was theirs ... Doing these things, they lived in them; because life thus had its due exercise and nourishment and was in a condition to enjoy the manifold privileges and blessings secured in the covenant. And the very same thing may be said of the precepts and ordinances of the [NT] gospel: a man lives after the higher life of faith only insofar as he walks in

---

[16]Andrew A. Bonar, *A Commentary on Leviticus* (1846; reprinted ed., London: Banner of Truth Trust, 1966), pp. 329-30. So also agrees Charles L. Feinberg, *The Prophecy of Ezekiel* (Chicago: Moody Press, 1969), p. 110: "Obedience would have brought life physically and spiritually, temporally and eternally (see Deut. 4:40; 5:16)."

[17]G. A. Cooke, *The Book of Ezekiel,* I.C.C. (Edinburgh: T. & T. Clark, 1967), p. 199.

conformity with these; for though he gets life by a simple act of faith in Christ, he cannot exercise, maintain and enjoy it but in connection with the institutions and requirements of the gospel (italic his).[18]

5. One of the ways of "doing" the law was to recognize the imperfection of one's life and thus to make a sacrifice for the atonement of one's sins. Thus Leviticus 18:5 was not a hypothetical offer of eternal life as a reward for perfect law-keeping. The law itself assumed and provided for lawbreakers in the great sacrificial system which was a part of that covenant of law!

6. Furthermore, the people had not spoken "rashly" in saying in Exodus 19:5, "All that the Lord says, we will do." On the contrary, the Lord had spoken in glowing terms of approval in Deuteronomy 5:28-29: "Oh that there were such an heart in them that they would fear Me and keep all My commandments always" (cf. 18:18).[19]

Let it be noted well that *even* the Sinaitic covenant was initiated by Yahweh's love, mercy, and grace (Deut. 4:37; 7:7-9; 10:15, *passim*). When Israel broke the law of God, she no more forfeited her inheritance to the promise and her certain transmission of the promise to her children than did the patriarchs or the Davidic royal line later. Even Israel's involvement in the golden calf incident did not end God's faithfulness (Exod. 32). It only highlighted the necessity of obedience for those who claimed to have experienced the grace of God's deliverance in the Exodus and the truth that the Lord God is "merciful and gracious, slow to anger, and abounding in steadfast love and faithfulness" (Exod. 34:6).

---

[18]Patrick Fairbairn, *An Exposition of Ezekiel* (Evansville: Sovereign Grace Publishers, 1960), pp. 215-16.

[19]Note also J. Oliver Buswell, *A Systematic Theology of the Christian Religion*, (Grand Rapids: Zondervan, 1962), p. 313: "The words, *en autē* [Rom. 10:5] and the corresponding words in Galatians 3:12, *en autois*, where the same Old Testament passage [Lev. 18:5] is quoted, should not be construed as instrumental, but as locative, indicating the sphere or horizon of life of a godly man ... Moses is obviously describing not the means of attaining eternal life, but the horizon within which an earthly godly life ought to be lived." The *New Scofield Reference Bible*, E. Schuyler English et al., eds. (New York: Oxford University Press, 1969), p. 95, now says, "The 'if' of v. 5 is the essence of law" and hence "the fundamental reason why 'the law made nothing perfect' (Heb. 7:18-19; cp. Rom. 8:3)." We believe this still misses the point. Even the added observation about the order is not correct either: "To Abraham the promise preceded the requirement; at Sinai the requirement preceded the promise. In the New Covenant the Abrahamic order is followed (see Heb. 8:8-12)."

THE LAW OF GOD

No formula appeared with greater insistence in this period of time than "I am Yahweh" or "I am Yahweh your God" (Lev. 18:5,30; 19:2,4,10,12,14,16,18,25,28,30,31,32,34,37; 20:7,8,24,26, *passim*). And that was the basis for any and all demands laid on Israel. Her Lord was Yahweh, the God who was dynamically present. What is more, He was holy; therefore, Israel had no choice in the matter of good and evil if she were to enjoy the constant fellowship of one whose very character did not and would not tolerate evil.

To aid the young nation recently released by centuries of bondage into the privileges and responsibilities of freedom, God gave His law. This single law had three aspects or parts: the moral law, the civil law, and the ceremonial law.[20]

The Moral Law

The context of God's moral demands was twofold: "I am Yahweh your God," and "I brought you out of the land of Egypt, out of the house of slavery" (Exod. 20:2). Consequently, the standard of moral measurement in deciding what was right or wrong, good or evil, was fixed in the unwavering and impeccably holy character of Yahweh, Israel's God. His nature, attributes, character, and qualities provided the measuring stick for all ethical decision. But there was, by the same token, an environment of grace—the free loving act of deliverance from Egypt. Israel did not need to keep the law in order to be released from Egypt. On the contrary, since she was so dramatically redeemed, the lever of obligation could not be easily rejected by Israel.

Should anyone doubt that grace was in the foreground of the law, let him carefully ponder the sequence of the Exodus, the journey to Sinai, God's graciousness to Israel during the wanderings, and His forgiveness of the idolatrous and sexually distracted golden calf cultists.

The form of the moral law as found mainly in the Ten Commandments (Exod. 20:2-17; Deut. 5:6-21) was overwhelmingly negative. However, this had nothing to do with either the tone or aim of that law. It was simply easier to express a believer's restrictions in a few words, for his freedom was so vast. Besides, all

---

[20]For a defense of God's single law having "heavier or weightier" parts to it, see W. C. Kaiser, Jr., "The Weightier and Lighter Matters of the Law: Moses, Jesus, and Paul," *Current Issues in Biblical and Patristic Interpretation: Studies in Honor of Merrill C. Tenney,* ed. G. F. Hawthorne (Grand Rapids: Eerdmans, 1975), pp. 176-92.

morality is double sided anyway—every moral act is at one and the same time a refraining from a contrary mode of action and the adoption of its opposite. It would make no difference if that law were stated negatively or positively. Further, when an evil was prohibited, as for example murder, that law was not fulfilled when men merely abstained from violently snatching away the lives of their fellow humans. It was only "kept" when men and women did all that was in their power to aid their neighbors' lives. Human life was viewed as valuable since mankind was made in the image of God, and thus life was based on the character of God. Therefore, human life must be preserved and enhanced—both! Nor could one refuse to do either, i.e., to refuse to preserve or to seek to improve the life of his neighbors. Inactivity in the moral realm could never be a fulfilling of the law; that would be equivalent to a state of death. More was required of Israel than merely refraining from doing anything forbidden.

The Decalogue did, however, contain three positive statements: "I am the Lord your God" (Exod. 20:2); "Remember the Sabbath day" (v. 8); and "Honor your father and your mother" (v. 12). To each of these three statements having nonfinite verbal forms the other seven negative statements were in turn subordinated.[21] These three positive injunctions introduced three spheres of man's responsibility:

1. Man's relationship to his God (Exod. 20:2-7)
2. Man's relationship to worship (vv. 8-11)
3. Man's relationship to society (vv. 12-17).

In the first sphere of responsibility, man was told to love God with a proper internal and external veneration for His person and work. The second sphere declared God's sovereignty over man's time while the third spelled out the sanctity of life, marriage, property, truth, and internal desire.[22]

The Ceremonial Law

The same law that made such high demands on mankind also provided in the event that there was a failure to reach those standards an elaborate sacrificial system. But that was only one of the

---

[21]J. J. Owens, "Law and Love in Deuteronomy," *Review and Expositor* 61(1964): 274-83.

[22]For further detail, see W. C. Kaiser, Jr., "Decalogue," *Baker's Dictionary of Christian Ethics*, ed. C. F. H. Henry (Grand Rapids: Baker Book House, 1973), pp. 165-67.

three strands belonging to the ceremonial law. One had to take note of the tabernacle with its theology of the "tabernacling" God (see later for a development of this point) and the theology of uncleanness and purification.

To begin with the last first, it must be insisted that the "unclean" was not equated in the writer's mind with that which was dirty or forbidden. The teaching of this section of Scripture was *not* that cleanliness was next to godliness. That may be all well and good, but the word of the text was cleanness, not cleanliness.

Simply put, cleanness meant the worshiper was *qualified* to meet Yahweh; "unclean" signified that he lacked the necessary qualifications to come before the Lord. This doctrine was closely aligned with the teaching of holiness: "Be ye holy" urged the text repeatedly, for "I the Lord your God am Holy." Similarly, holiness in its positive aspect was a *wholeness:* a life entirely dedicated to God and set apart for His use.

Many of the basic actions of life left one unclean. Some of these acts often were unavoidable—such as caring for the dead or giving birth—but which nonetheless rendered one unclean. Instead of using this word as his rubric to teach hygiene or sanitary standards, Moses used it to fix in the worshipers' minds the "otherness" in being and morality of God as compared to men.

Had not God told Moses to remove his sandals from his feet because the ground on which he stood was holy? And why so? Wasn't Moses' inner heart attitude sufficient preparation for a proper meeting with God? Obviously not! Proper preparation for worship also led to external acts that involved the whole person and not just his heart. While pride of place is to be given to a repentant and open heart, mankind still must take a holistic view when preparation was being made to meet God. He was radically different from men in general.

But lawbreakers were not left without remedy. Fellowship with God was conditioned only on faith in Himself and what He had promised; if broken by sin, it was rectified by God's forgiveness on the basis of a ransom as ordained by God. The principle was "The life of the flesh is in the blood, and I have given it to you on the altar to make atonement for your souls" (Lev. 17:11). Hence the means of dealing with sin was provided for by God Himself in the system of sacrifices.

Not all the sacrifices addressed the problem of the disruption of fellowship between God and man. Some, like the peace or fellowship offerings, were rich times of sharing with one another the gifts of God in His presence. But others, like the whole-burnt offering, sin offerings, or guilt offering, were specifically provided for the hiatus caused by sin's damaging effects.

Forgiveness was not and could not be cheap just as human forgiveness necessitated that someone pay if the reality of forgiveness were ever to be more than a cliché. In the same way divine forgiveness would necessitate the same. And that payment was wrapped up in the theology of atonement (Hebrew root *kpr*).

Now there are four basic Hebrew words using *kpr:* a "lion," a "village," to "caulk" or smear a ship with pitch as in Noah's ark, and "to ransom by a substitute." It is this fourth root of *kpr*, *kipper*, that interests us here.

Some argued that the fourth word was related to the third, "to caulk," and to Near Eastern cognate words meaning "to cover." But Hebrew usage dictated differently. The noun form clearly indicated that a substitute of one kind or another was always meant (e.g., Exod. 21:30; 30:12; Num. 35:31-32; Ps. 49:8; Isa. 43:3-4).[23] Thus the denominative verb likewise meant "to deliver or ransom someone by a substitute." Man, by his sin against God, owed his very life as a forfeit to God; but God had provided that animals' lives should serve for the time being until the God-man could later give His life as the only proper and final substitute.

How many sins could be atoned by such a system in Israel? All sins of weakness or rashness were capable of being atoned whether they were done knowingly or unwittingly. Leviticus specifically affirmed that the trespass offering was for sins such as lying, theft, fraud, perjury, or debauchery (Lev. 6:1-7). And on the great day of Atonement (Yom Kippur), "all" the sins of "all" Israel of "all" who had truly repented ("afflicted their souls" [Lev. 16:16,21,29,31] were forgiven. Indeed the most persistent phrase in the Levitical sacrificial instructions was the assurance: "And he shall be forgiven" (Lev. 1:4; 4:20,26,31,35; 5:10,16; 16:20-22). Therefore, the old but false distinction between witting, i.e., "sins done with a high hand," and unwitting, i.e., as it was explained, sins done in ignorance of what the law said on the matter, was unwarranted. The unwitting sins (*bišᵉgāgâh*), or better still, sins "in error," involved all sin which sprang from the weakness of flesh and blood. But the sin of Numbers

---

[23]Leon Morris, *The Apostolic Preaching of the Cross* (Grand Rapids: Eerdmans, 1955), pp. 160-78 and J. Hermann, "Kipper and Kopper," *Theological Dictionary of the New Testament*, 9 vols., Gerhard Kittel, ed., and G. W. Bromiley, trans. (Grand Rapids: Eerdmans, 1965), 3:303-10. Hermann concluded by saying, "It would be useless to deny that the idea of substitution is present to some degree," p. 310.

15:27-36, the sin of a "high hand" (*b*e*yād rāmâh*), was plainly that of rebellion against God and His Word. So Numbers 15:30-31 explained, "He blasphemed the Lord ... because he has regarded with contempt the word of the Lord." This is what the NT calls blasphemy against the Holy Spirit or the unpardonable sin. It was high treason and revolt against God with the upraised, clenched fist: a picket against heaven! But this was not to be put in the same class as sins of murder, adultery, or the like. Treason or blasphemy against God was much more serious. Rather, it attacked God Himself.

If all sins, except the unpardonable revolt against God, were forgivable, what part did the sacrifices play and how efficacious were they? Subjectively, they were most effective.[24] The sinner did receive complete relief. His sins were forgiven on the basis of the word of a faithful God and the God-approved substitute. Of course, the efficacy did also depend on the internal state of the sinner's heart (Lev. 16:29,31; and later, Ps. 50:10-13; Prov. 21:27; Isa. 1:11-14; Jer. 6:20; 7:21; Hos. 5:6; 6:6; Amos 5:25; Mic. 6:6-7). And he did get relief from the penalty and memory of his sins. On the day of Atonement there were two goats to indicate two parts of the same act—one goat slain as the substitute so that sins might be forgiven and the other goat led away ("*a*z—"goat"—*'āzal*—"to lead away"— Lev. 16:26) to picture the fact that those same sins were forgotten in the sense that God remembered them against Israel no more.

Nevertheless, man's sin was not objectively cared for as yet. The blood of bulls and goats could never take away or remove sin, and neither did the OT claim it did (Heb. 10:4)! These were substituted animals, not people; hence, they could only be symbols of that real sacrifice yet to come. Thus in the meantime there was a "passing by" (*parēsis*—Rom. 3:25) of the sins of the OT on the basis of God's declared Word until He would later provide His own final substitute who was a true man, yet one who had not sinned.

The Civil Law

As far as theology is concerned, this aspect of God's law was a mere application of the moral law to selected parts of the community's life, especially where tensions were likely to develop in that day. True justice and holiness on the part of the judges and rulers was to be measured by the demands of the Decalogue. Accordingly,

---

[24]I was greatly aided in my understanding of parts of this argument by Hobart Freeman, "The Problem of Efficacy of Old Testament Sacrifices," *Bulletin of Evangelical Theological Society* 5(1962): 73-79.

the civil law illustrated its practice in the various cases or situations which confronted the leadership during the Mosaic era.

THE TABERNACLING GOD

The single most important fact in the experience of this new nation of Israel was that God had come to "tabernacle" *(šākan)*, or "dwell," in her midst. Nowhere was this stated more clearly than in Exodus 29:43-46 where in connection with the tabernacle it was announced:

> There [at the entrance] I will meet with the sons of Israel, and it shall be sanctified by My glory. I will consecrate the tent of meeting and the altar . . . I will dwell ("tabernacle") among the sons of Israel, and I will be their God. And they shall know that I am the Lord their God who brought them out of the land of Egypt, that I might dwell among them: I am the Lord their God.

Now the triad was complete. One of the most frequently repeated formulas of the promise would be:

> I will be your [their] God;
> You [they] shall be My people.
> And I will dwell in the midst of you [them].

In its very first announcement, the dwelling of God was connected with the tabernacle. In fact, one of the names of the tent-sanctuary of God was *miškān*, which clearly was related to the verb *šākan*, "to tent, dwell, tabernacle." Ordinarily Hebrew preferred to speak of a permanent dwelling as *yāšab*, "to sit, dwell," and so it did whenever it spoke of Yahweh dwelling in heaven. But as Frank Cross pointed out, invariably when the text pointed to Yahweh's presence dwelling with men on earth, or in the tabernacle and later in the temple, the verb was *šākan*.[25] Thus, it would appear, even as Cross suggested, that these two verbs contrasted the divine transcendence *(yāšab)* with divine immanence. And in the case of the tabernacle, it was the place where He would take up His temporary abode. A new sense of the "closeness" and active presence of God was to be Israel's.

The only exception to this distinction was to be found in the use of *yāšab* and its derivatives to express the fact that God was "en-

---

[25]Frank M. Cross, Jr., "The Priestly Tabernacle," *The Biblical Archaeologist Reader*, eds. David N. Freedman and G. Ernest Wright (Garden City, N.Y.: Anchor Books, 1961), pp. 225-27.

throned," or sat on the throne,[26] especially in the use of this verb in connection with the central piece of furniture in the tabernacle: "He who is enthroned on the Cherubim" (1 Sam. 4:4; 2 Sam. 6:2; 1 Chron. 13:6; Ps. 99:1; Isa. 37:16). The ark of the covenant of God with its mercy seat, or place of atonement, overspread by the two cherubim was the most intimate of all the expressions of God's nearness to His people. Exodus 25:22 commented:

> There I will meet you and from above the mercy seat, from between the two cherubim that are upon the ark of the covenant, I will speak with you of all that I will give you in commandment for the people of Israel.

The theology of the tabernacle was to be formed in the purpose statement of Exodus 25:8: "Make a tabernacle that I might dwell (*šākan*) among them."[27] But its central feature both in the theology of atonement and in the theology of the divine presence was the ark of the covenant of God.

Yahweh's divine presence was so central and significant in the Mosaic era that four other forms are used to speak of it: the "face," "appearance," or "presence" of the Lord (*pānîm*); His "glory" (*kābôd*); the "angel of the Lord" (*mal'ak YHWH*); and His "name" (*šēm*). The passage that connects most of these divine presence themes is Exodus 33.[28] There Moses had asked God to show him His "glory" (v. 18) so that he might be assured that God's "face," i.e., "presence" (vv. 14-15) was indeed going before him. To this request God acceded by causing all His "goodness" to pass before Moses, and there God proclaimed in front of Moses the "name" Yahweh (v. 19). Protected by the "hand" of God while he waited "in the cleft of the rock," the reality of God's presence was verified by Moses as he saw the "aftereffects" ("my back," *'ahōrāy*) of the radiance (glory) of God's presence after it had passed in front of him (vv. 21-23).

Of the angel that would accompany Israel, the promise had been equally clear. Exodus 23:20-21 declared:

---

[26]Ibid., p. 226.

[27]See for further details, R. E. Clements, *God and Temple: The Presence of God in Israel's Worship* (Philadelphia: Fortress Press, 1965), pp. 35ff. and Gerhard von Rad, *Old Testament Theology*, 2 vols. (London: Oliver and Boyd, 1962), 1:234-36. He argues that God's permanent dwelling was attached to the ark while the *mô'ēd*, "meeting of God," was connected with the tent.

[28]Page H. Kelley, "Israel's Tabernacling God," *Review and Expositor* 67(1970): 488-89.

Behold, I send an angel before thee, to keep thee in the way, and to bring thee into the place I have prepared. Beware of him, and obey his voice. Provoke him not, for he will not pardon your transgressions: for My name is in him.

He was that same one mentioned in Exodus 32:34 as "My angel [which] shall go before you." If the name—i.e., the character, nature, or attributes—of God was "*in* him," could He be less than the nonincarnate Word tabernacling among them? Indeed, God's presence was with Israel, and He would give her "rest" (Exod. 33:14). To such a promise as this, God signed His name, as it were, in Exodus 29:46: "I am the Lord."

The theology of those days revolved around three dominating concepts: redemption (from Egypt), morality, and worship. As Bernard Ramm put it:

Redeemed man is called to morality; moral man is called to worship. The redeemed man shows his repentance in the quality of his moral life; he shows his gratitude in his worship.[29]

---

[29]Bernard Ramm, *His Way Out* (Glendale, Calif.: Regal Books, 1974), p. 148.

Chapter 8

Place of Promise:
Premonarchical Era

The spirit and the theology of Deuteronomy extended far beyond the confines of the closing days of the Mosaic era or even the contents of a single work. Deuteronomy served as an introduction to most, if not all, of the former or earlier prophets: Joshua, Judges, Samuel, Kings. The thesis of Martin Noth, already referred to in chapter 4, regarded Deuteronomy to 2 Kings as an original work which attempted to write a history of Israel from Moses to the Exile and interpret it from the vantage point of theology. This interpretation was one of the most insightful contributions to OT studies in this century. Whether it was all the work of one author who wrote most of Joshua-2 Kings after the shadows of the fall of Samaria in 721 B.C. and fall of Jerusalem in 586 B.C. had passed is another matter. But of the basic theological motivation and general prophetic tone of these books there can be very little debate.

The close relationship between Deuteronomy and the books of Joshua through 2 Kings, which scholars delight in calling the work of the deuteronomic historian, can be seen everywhere. Foremost among these similarities is the deuteronomic phraseology which Moshe Weinfeld[1] has listed in great detail.

In addition to the influence of language and style, Deuteronomy has also contributed the basic theological tradition. According to Gordon J. Wenham,[2] the books of Deuteronomy and Joshua are bound together theologically by five *leitmotifs:* (1) the holy war of conquest; (2) the distribution of the land; (3) the unity of all Israel; (4) Joshua as the successor of Moses; and (5) the covenant. Each of these five themes appeared in the first chapter of Joshua: holy war (vv. 2,5,9,11,14); the land (vv. 3-4,15); the unity of Israel (vv. 12-16); the role of Joshua (vv. 1-2,5,17); and the covenant (vv. 3,7-8,13,17-18).[3]

Yet there is more. In these books the Abrahamic-Davidic covenant tradition will be linked with the Sinaitic-Mosaic covenant. For example, David and his successor recognized their obligation to obey the "law of Moses," to keep the statutes, commandments, and ordinances of God written there, that they might prosper in all that they did and be established (1 Kings 2:1-4; 9:4-5). In fact, Solomon freely appealed to God's ancient work in the Exodus and the promised gift of the land to that generation (1 Kings 8:16,20,34,36,53).

But one of the most immediate concerns that linked the patriarchal and Mosaic traditions with the earlier prophets of Joshua–2 Kings was the frequent reference made to the *place* which Yahweh would choose or already had chosen for His name to dwell. Closely tied with this concept was the theme of the "rest," the "inheritance," which was to be Israel's possession when she entered the land. These two emphases emerge as the two dominant theological themes of the premonarchical era.

However, the theology of the earlier prophets is more than just a collection of deuteronomic themes. For these earlier prophets (what others call the deuteronomic history of Joshua–Judges–Samuel–Kings), there were, as Dennis J. McCarthy has pointed out,[4] three programmatic statements which dominated both the history and theology from the Exodus to the Exile: Deuteronomy 31, Joshua 23,

---

[1]Moshe Weinfeld, *Deuteronomy and the Deuteronomic School* (Oxford: Clarendon Press, 1972), appendix A, pp. 320-59. See also the list of S. R. Driver, *A Critical and Exegetical Commentary on Deuteronomy* (New York: Charles Scribner's Sons, 1916), pp. lxxviii-lxxxiv.

[2]Gordon J. Wenham, "The Deuteronomic Theology of the Book of Joshua," *Journal of Biblical Literature* 90(1971): 140-48.

[3]Ibid., p. 141.

[4]Dennis J McCarthy, "II Samuel 7 and the Structure of the Deuteronomic History," *Journal of Biblical Literature* 84(1965): 131-38.

and 2 Samuel 7. These three passages came from three of the most emotionally charged moments in the history of Israel: The swan song of Moses (Deut. 31), the last speech of Joshua (Josh. 23), and the unexpected divine announcement made to David when he was contemplating the construction of the house of God (2 Sam. 7). These key statements underscored the prophetic emphasis in the mouths of God's spokesmen for the most crucial moments in the history and the theology of Israel. However, six other passages followed up these three programmatic statements with well-placed speeches by the leading actors in that history (Josh. 1:11-15; 1 Sam. 12; 1 Kings 8:14-61) or the writer's own assessment and summary of the times (Josh. 12; Judg. 2:11-23; 2 Kings 17:7-23). Actually, two passages were matched with each of the three programmatic texts. The resulting pattern was as follows:

I. Deuteronomy 31
   A. Joshua 1
   B. Joshua 12
II. Joshua 23
   A. Judges 2:11-23
   B. 1 Samuel 12
III. 2 Samuel 7
   A. 1 Kings 8
   B. 2 Kings 17

While this structure will aid us in understanding the overall theological plan in the earlier prophets (Joshua-2 Kings), it cannot form the total progress of theology for all of Israel's subsequent history from the Exodus to the Exile—too much would be neglected, e.g., wisdom theology and the latter prophets. Neither does its adoption here detract from the theme already discovered in prepatriarchal, patriarchal, or Mosaic eras. The theme of both swan songs by two of Israel's greatest leaders, Moses and Joshua, centered on the momentary fulfillment of that anciently announced promise: a land, a rest, and a place chosen by Yahweh (Deut. 31:2-3,5,7,11,20,23; Josh. 23:1,4,5,13,15). These three features dominated the transition from the Mosaic era to the premonarchical era.

INHERITANCE OF THE LAND

Sixty-nine times the writer of Deuteronomy repeated the pledge that Israel would one day "possess" and "inherit" the land promised to her. Sporadically he explicitly linked this pledge to the word that Abraham, Isaac, and Jacob had received (Deut. 1:8; 6:10,18; 7:8; 34:4). Thus Israel was forced to relate the impending conquest of Canaan under Joshua to the promise of God and not to any feelings of national superiority.

The land of Canaan and the people of Israel alike were called the "inheritance *(naḥªlâh)* of Yahweh" (1 Sam. 26:19; 2 Sam. 21:3; 1 Kings 8:36) or His "possession" *(ªḥuzzâh,* Josh. 22:19; *yªruššâh,* 2 Chron. 20:11). Ever since Exodus 19:5 had called Israel Yahweh's "treasured possession" *(sªgûllâh),*[5] they had become a "treasured people" out of all the peoples of the earth (Deut. 7:6; 14:2; 26:18) and a "people of inheritance" *('am naḥªlâh,* Deut. 9:26,29; 32:8-9; 1 Kings 8:51,53; 2 Kings 21:14).[6] Thus Israel became the promised people, and Canaan became the promised land.

In Deuteronomy the land became the special area of focus. Repeatedly in some twenty-five references the land was called a gift from Yahweh (Deut. 1:20,25; 2:29; 3:20; 4:40; 5:16, *passim*). And this gift was the same land that was promised to the "fathers" (Deut. 1:8,35; 6:10,18,23; 7:13; 8:1; 9:5; 10:11; 11:9,21; 19:8; 26:3,15; 28:11; 30:20; 31:7,20-21,23; 34:4). Why von Rad would confuse the issue and say that since the land belongs to Yahweh, "it is now quite clear that this notion is of a totally different order from that of the promise of the land to the early patriarchs" is hard to understand.[7] His line of argument does not stand up to the blunt claims of the text. Surely the fact that Yahweh is the true owner of the land is no mark of syncretism with features from Canaanite religion. While Baal may have been regarded as the Lord of the land and the giver of all blessings in pagan Canaanite religion, Yahweh was Lord of all the earth—His creative word, to use a fine von Rad phrase, had settled

---

[5]The English AV "peculiar" derives from Latin *peculiaris* and that from *peculium,* a technical term meaning private property which a child or a slave was permitted to possess. At Alalakh, the cognate *sikiltu* is the "treasured possession" of the god. I am endebted to J. A. Thompson for this material, *Deuteronomy* (Downers Grove, Ill.: InterVarsity Press, 1975), pp. 74-75, n. 1.

[6]Cf. J. Hermann, "*Naḥªlâh* and *Nâḥal* in the Old Testament," *Theological Dictionary of the New Testament,* 9 vols., Gerhard Kittel, ed., and G. W. Bromiley, trans. (Grand Rapids: Eerdmans, 1965), 3:769-76. Also Patrick D. Miller, Jr., "The Gift of God: The Deuteronomic Theology of the Land," *Interpretation* 22(1969): 451-61.

[7]Gerhard von Rad, "The Promised Land and Yahweh's Land in the Hexateuch," *The Problem of the Hexateuch and Other Essays,* trans. E. W. Truemen Dicken (New York: McGraw-Hill, 1966), p. 88; idem, *Old Testament Theology,* 2 vols. (London: Oliver and Boyd, 1962), 1:296-301.

that issue. Consequently there were not two viewpoints on the inheritance of the land. It can only be Israel's because it was first Yahweh's land and His to give to whomever He pleased for however long He pleased. Had not Deuteronomy begun with the same observation about some of the previous inhabitants of Transjordania? The Emim, Horites, and Zamzummim had been dispossessed and destroyed by the Lord (Deut. 2:9,12,21) and their lands had been divinely given to Moab, Edom, and Ammon just as Israel had similarly received Canaan from His hands. The comparison with Israel is made in that very context: "As Israel did to the land of their possession which the Lord gave to them" (Deut. 2:12).

It is agreed that Leviticus 25:23 did say, "The land is Mine [says Yahweh]; you are only strangers and sojourners with Me." But was that at cross-purposes with the promise made to the patriarchs that they would possess the land? Never in Israel's history did she ever own outright the land, earth, or soil in our sense of the word; it was always granted to her by Yahweh as a fief in which she could cultivate and live on it as long as she served Him. But this land, like the whole earth, belonged to the Lord—and so did the abundance that was in it and the people who lived on it. That was the lesson taught to Pharaoh in the repeated plagues ("That you might know that the earth is the Lord's" [Exod. 9:29]) and to Job ("Whatever is under the whole heaven is mine" [41:11]) and later in Psalm 24:1 and in that great commentary on the Davidic covenant, Psalm 89:11.

Von Rad was likewise too concerned over the fact that the word "inheritance" *(naḥᵃlâh)* was persistently used to denote tribal lands, but that nowhere in the Hexateuch was the total land called Yahweh's "inheritance."[8] But there were examples of its use with the whole land. J. Hermann[9] noted that it was Joshua's job to lead Israel in taking the whole land as an "inheritance," or in the verbal form, "to inherit" it (Deut. 1:38; 3:28; 31:7; Josh. 1:6—hiphil form of verb *nāḥal).* Of course, the emphasis of the hour was on each tribe. They had to be separately satisfied and do their part to receive their "share" *(ḥeḇel—*Josh. 17:5,14; 19:9), "portion" *(ḥēleq—*Deut. 10:9; 12:21; 14:27; 18:1; Josh. 18:5,7,9; 19:9), or "lot" *(gôrāl—*Josh. 14:2; 15:11; 16:1; 17:1; 18:11; 19:1,10,17,24,32,40,51).

Previous to this the patriarchs had only possessed a small part of that land, a burial place, as an earnest of the fulfillment that was to come. Thus in a real sense, Canaan was the "land of their sojourn-

---

[8]Ibid., pp. 82,86.
[9]Hermann, *"Naḥᵃlâh,"* p. 771.

ing" (Gen. 17:8; 28:4; 36:7; 37:1; 47:1; Exod. 6:4). The patriarchs possessed mainly the promise but not the total reality itself.

The land was a gift, but Israel had to "possess" *(yāraš)* it; thus the reception of the gift had a corresponding action, a military action. Both of these notions, as Miller[10] pointed out, were located side by side in the expression "the land which Yahweh gives you to possess" (Deut. 3:19; 5:31; 12:1; 15:4; 19:2,14; 25:19). Divine sovereignty and human responsibility were complementary ideas rather than antithetic pairs.

What God gave could only be called a "good land" (Deut. 1:25,35; 3:25; 4:21-22; 6:18; 8:7,10; 9:6; 11:17) just as His work in creation had received His word of approbation. It was "a land flowing with milk and honey" (Deut. 11:9; 26:9,15; 27:3; 31:20).[11] In every way the promised inheritance was a delightful gift—owned by Yahweh and leased to Israel in partial fulfillment of His word of promise. In this land Israel was to be blessed (Deut. 15:4; 23:20; 28:8; 30:16), but special emphasis was placed on the blessing of the ground (28:8). Thus God's "blessing" again became one of the connecting concepts which united the theology of the earlier periods with that of the premonarchical era.

REST IN THE LAND

One of the new provisions added to the expanding revelation of the promise theme was the provision of "rest" for Israel.[12] So special was this rest that Yahweh would call it *His rest* (Ps. 95:11; Isa. 66:1). It was precisely this aspect of the promise theme which provided a

---

[10] Miller, *"Gift,"* p. 454.

[11] J. A. Thompson, *Deuteronomy*, pp. 120-21, noted that this same phrase appears in the Egyptian Tale of Sinuhe (*ANET*, 18-25, lines 80-90), four times in Exodus (3:8,17; 13:5; 33:3), Leviticus (20:24), four times in Numbers (13:27; 14:8; 16:13,14), five times in Deuteronomy (see above).

[12] For a development of the ideas in this section see W. C. Kaiser, Jr., "The Promise Theme and the Theology of Rest," *Bibliotheca Sacra* 130(1973): 135-50. Also see Gerhard von Rad, "There Remains a Rest For the People of God: An Investigation of a Biblical Conception," *Hexateuch and Essays*, pp. 94-102. A New Testament approach to the problem is E. Käsemann, *Das Wandernde Gottesvolk* (Göttingen: Vandenhoeck and Ruprecht, 1957); J. Frankowski, "Requies, Bonum Promissum populi Die in VT et in Judaismo (Heb. 3:1-4:11)," *Verbum Domini* 43(1965): 124-49; O. Hofius, *Katapausis: Die Vorstellung vom Endzeitlichen Ruheort im Hebräerbrief* (Tübingen: J. C. B. Mohr, 1970); David Darnell, "Rebellion, Rest and the Word of God: An Exegetical Study of Hebrews 3:1-4:13" (Ph. D. diss., Duke University, 1974); and Elmer H. Dyck, "A Theology of Rest" (M.A. diss., Trinity Evangelical Divinity School, 1975).

key link between the end of the book of Numbers and the time of David: the two texts at opposite ends of the time period being Deuteronomy 12:9-10 and 2 Samuel 7:1,11.

Nowhere in the patriarchal promises did "rest" *(m^enûhâh)* appear as one of God's future blessings to the fathers or Israel. But when it first appeared in Deuteronomy 12:9, one gathers that it might already have been known in the tradition of the people:

> For you have not as yet come to the resting place *(m^enûhâh)* and to the inheritance *(nah^alâh)* which Yahweh your God is giving to you.

Yet it must be noted that Moses had been promised "rest" *(nûah)* as early as Exodus 33:14 when he led Israel out of Egypt. Later in Deuteronomy 3:20, Moses again promised that "rest" *(nûah)* would shortly come to all his fellow countrymen when they possessed the land of Canaan. Both of these words were cognates of the Deuteronomy 12:9 term. Indeed, the Hebrew root *nûah*, "to rest," supplied the majority of words for the concept of rest. Whenever the hiphil stem of this root was followed by the preposition *l^e*, "to, for," plus a person or group, it usually assumed a technical status. Thus in some twenty instances of *hēniah l^e*, it was a place granted by the Lord (Exod. 33:14; Deut. 3:20; Josh. 1:13,15; 22:4; 2 Chron. 14:5); a peace and respite from enemies round about (Deut. 12:10; 25:19; Josh. 21:44; 23:1; 2 Sam. 7:1,11; 1 Kings 5:18 [5:4]; 1 Chron. 22:9,18; 23:25; 2 Chron. 14:6; 15:15; 20:30; 32:22 [probable reading?]); or a cessation of sorrow and toil in the future (Isa. 14:3; 28:12).

The noun *m^enûhâh*, "resting place" or "rest," came to assume technical status as well. In Jacob's blessing of Issachar, the portion of land given to him was called a "resting place" (Gen. 49:15). So far as we can see, this usage was not as yet technical. But the strong associations of a geographical, spatial, and material "rest" in subsequent texts like Deuteronomy 12:9; 1 Kings 8:56; 1 Chronicles 22:9; Isaiah 28:12; and Micah 2:10 cannot be denied. This "rest" was a "place" where Yahweh would "plant" His people where they could live without being disturbed any more.

Yet there was more to this "rest" than geography. Rest was where the presence of God stopped (in the wilderness wanderings—Num. 10:33) or where He dwelt (1 Chron. 28:2; Ps. 132:8,14; Isa. 66:1). No doubt it was for this reason that David stressed the aspect of belief and trust as the basis of entering into that rest in Psalm 95:11. The condition was not an automatic one.

For the time being, "rest" would signify the quality of living in the land of inheritance when it was occupied. Yahweh Himself would give Israel rest in the land (Deut. 3:20; 12:10; 25:19). So Joshua 21:44-45 summarized the promise and its reality:

> The Lord gave them *rest* on every side just as He had sworn to their fathers. Not one of all their enemies had withstood them, for the Lord had given all their enemies into their power. Not one of all the good promises which the Lord had made to the house of Israel failed; all had come to pass.

But this only yielded a conundrum. If Joshua had fulfilled the promised rest, what was 2 Samuel 7:1,11 claiming, coming as it did from a later time? And how could Solomon, later still, be called a "man of rest" (1 Chron. 22:9; 1 Kings 8:56)? How, also, are we to understand the spiritual and material aspects of rest? The resolution of these matters can be found in the OT view of fulfillment. Specially named generations received their share of the completion of the single plan of God. This at once served as a partial confirmation of God's longstanding word and a contemporaneous installment on the fulfillment. This, in turn, simultaneously functioned as a means of connecting that word to its ultimate or climactic fulfillment since these periodic installment type of fulfillments were generically part and parcel with that ultimate event. Thus there was a single meaning in the mind of the author even though he might know of or experience multiple fulfillments of that single meaning! The promise was not to be thought of as having been given its final effect even in the aspect of the land.[13] Hence rest was more than entry and division of the land to all the tribes; it was also to be a final condition which pervaded the land. Thus after Israel entered the land, she was warned that she would only enjoy the quality of life God had intended for her if she continually obeyed His commandments (Deut. 4:10; 12:1; 31:13). The extent of Israel's possession of the land was likewise important before the promise could be said to have been completely fulfilled.

That was the way Stephen also put it in his speech in Acts 7:4-5:

> God removed him from there into this land . . .
> Yet He gave him no inheritance in it, . . .
> but promised to give it to him as a possession
> and to his descendants.

The emphasis of Joshua 21:43-45 was still on the promised word which had not failed Israel, nor would it. But whether Israel would

---

[13]In a different connection, see von Rad, *Theology*, 2:383.

retain her privilege of remaining in the land was another matter. She had to choose between life and death, good and evil. To choose life and the good was to "obey" one command which summarized all the others: Love the Lord your God. The presence of the conditional "if" did not pave the way for a "declension from grace into law"[14] any more than it did for the patriarchs or the generation of Moses, much less the Davidic covenant to come! Therefore the promise of the inheritance of God's rest was protected even in the event of subsequent sins by the recipient's descendants. Rest was no blank check in which future generations could slide by God's standards on their fathers' laurels. This promise was to be theirs only if they would appropriate it by faith—that was the spiritual and immediate benefit of "rest."

In its final fulfillment, the God of rest—whose house of "rest" (*menûḥâh*) contained the ark of the covenant of the Lord and His footstool (1 Chron. 28:2) built by the "man of rest" to whom God had given respite from all his enemies (1 Chron. 22:9)—would again take up His rest in His temple in the future messianic era (Ps. 132:14; cf. 2 Chron. 14:6), in "that day" "when the Lord extends His hand a second time to recover the remnant of His people" (Isa. 11:11). It is in this context that a series of psalms (93-100)—variously designated as "Apocalyptic Psalms," "Theocratic Psalms" (Delitzsch), "Millennial Psalms" (Thorluck), "Songs of the Millennium" (Binnie), "Group of Millennial Psalms" (Herder), "Second Advent Psalms" (Rawlinson), "Enthronement Psalms" (Mowinckel), or "Royal Psalms" (Perowne)—where the Lord is depicted as King reigning over all peoples and lands (Pss. 93:1; 96:10; 99:1), that Psalm 95 raised the offer of entering into God's rest again. For the psalmist, that ancient offer of rest was ultimately tied up with the events of the second advent. Every other rest, apparently, was only an "earnest," down payment, on the final Sabbath rest yet to come in the second advent.[15]

CHOSEN PLACE IN THE LAND

One of the most hotly debated phrases in the theology of Deuteronomy is the so-called centralization of sacrificial worship at one single sanctuary in Jerusalem. Indeed, this plank was the starting point and keystone from all other deductions made in the Wellhau-

---

[14]As suggested by von Rad, "Promised Land," *Hexateuch and Essays,* p. 91.
[15]See W. C. Kaiser, "Promise Theme," pp. 142-43. See also our discussion of Hebrews 3:7-4:13 on pp. 145-49 in that same article.

sian system of literary criticism.[16] The claim was that the cultic requirements of Deuteronomy were a clear advance over the altar law of the Sinaitic "Book of the Covenant":

An altar of earth you shall make for Me
and shall sacrifice on it your burnt offerings,
your peace offerings, your sheep and your oxen.
In every place where I cause My name to be remembered
I will come to you and bless you.
—Exodus 20:24

That is to say, the Sinaitic law limited the use of sacrifices only to those places sanctified by the divine presence—those places where God had appointed that His name should be remembered because He had met with His representative or people at that spot.

But was Deuteronomy reversing these Sinaitic directions when it ordered Israel to seek the Lord:

In the place [site] which the Yahweh will choose to put His name there (Deut. 12:5,11,21; 14:23-24; 15:20; 16:2,6,11; 26:2)

or

The place which Yahweh shall choose (Deut. 12:14,18,26; 14:25; 16:7,15-16; 17:8,10; 18:6; 31:11; Josh. 9:27)?

Both the laws of Deuteronomy and Exodus insisted that the place of sacrifice must be appointed and chosen by the Lord, not by man. Sacrifices may not be offered "in every place that you see" (Deut. 12:13).[17]

And when the context of Deuteronomy 12 is investigated, the contrast is not between many Yahweh altars and one such altar but between those altars erected to other gods whose names are to be destroyed and that "place" where Yahweh's name shall abide (vv. 2-5). Thus, instead of revoking the Sinaitic legislation, Deuteronomy built on it. We again hear of a "place" *(māqôm)* where Yahweh will "cause His name to be remembered" (or "dwell"), where sacrifices and offerings may be made, and where blessing will result.[18]

Scholarly attention, however, has focused on the article and number of the noun in the expression "the place" in Deuteronomy

---

[16]J. Wellhausen, *Prolegomena to the History of Israel*, trans. J. S. Black and A. Menzies (Edinburgh: T. & T. Clark, 1885), p. 368.

[17]*Kol hammāqôm;* (cf. Gen. 20:13; Deut. 11:24; Josh. 1:3), M. H. Segal, *The Pentateuch: Its Composition and Its Authorship* (Jerusalem: Magnes Press, 1967), p. 87, n. 17.

[18]As argued by G. T. Manley, *The Book of the Law* (London: Tyndale Press, 1957), p. 132.

12:5,14. Oestreicher argued that the article was distributive and not restrictive and the lack of an article in the expression "in one of your tribes" (v. 14) was to be given a general meaning due to an analogous expression in the fugitive slave in Deuteronomy 23:16[17].[19] Thus the translation of Deuteronomy 12:14 would be:

In every place which Yahweh shall choose in any of your tribes.

The singular number on the expression "the place" would denote a class and not a single locality even as it did in Deuteronomy 23:16.

E. W. Nicholson disagreed with this analogy, however. The subject of the Deuteronomy 23:16 law was a *class* of people, viz., runaway slaves seeking asylum, while the subject of the Deuteronomy 12:5-7 law was Yahweh. Further, the singular number on "place" is strange if the writer meant to say "in the places which Yahweh shall choose in your tribes."[20] Nicholson's counter arguments to Oestreicher are probably correct. But this still does not support a centralization hypothesis. The subject was not over one Yahweh altar versus many Yahweh altars—nothing is said on that topic. It is only about Yahweh's intention to put His name in an as yet unnamed place after the people arrive in Canaan. In fact Deuteronomy 27:1-8 with its injunction to build an altar on Mount Ebal raises a fatal flaw to the centralized altar theory. "It manifestly commands that which the law is supposed to forbid and, to make matters worse, uses the very words of Exodus xx.24 which Deuteronomy is supposed to revoke."[21]

At most, Deuteronomy taught that Yahweh would select a site in Canaan after He had helped Israel to "inherit" the land and to find "rest" (Deut. 12:10-11) in much the same way as He had done in the past. He would "make His name dwell" in the place of His election. This promise joined the Immanuel and Shekinah-glory theology of the patriarchal and Mosaic eras. And just as God had elected one man out of all humanity, viz., Abraham, and one tribe out of the twelve sons of Jacob, viz., Judah, so now He would choose one place

---

[19]Th. Oestreicher, "Dtn xii.13f. im Licht von Dtn xxiii.16f.," *Zeitschrift für alttestamentliche Wissenschaft* 43(1925): 246-49. Deuteronomy 23:16 would read, "He [the slave] shall dwell with you *in any place* which he shall choose within any of your gates" [italics mine].

[20]E. W. Nicholson, *Deuteronomy and Tradition* (Philadelphia: Fortress Press, 1967), pp. 53-54. Cf. p. 53, n. 1 for list of those challenging his exegesis. To this add Manley, *Book*.

[21]Manley, ibid., p. 134; cf. also James Orr, *The Problem of the Old Testament* (London: J. Nisbet & Co., 1909), pp. 174-80; Gordon J. Wenham, "Deuteronomy and the Central Sanctuary," *Tyndale Bulletin* 22(1971): 103-18, esp. 110-14.

in one of the tribes in which His name would dwell. There He would take up His dwelling (12:5), and there Israel would come to worship Him. It would function in many ways as the tabernacle had done for so long.

NAME DWELLING IN THE LAND

There are three other theologically important expressions which are connected with the "place" promise. They are phrases where Yahweh promises:

1. "To make his name dwell *(šākan)* there" (Deut. 12:11; 14:23; 16:2,6,11; 26:2).
2. "To put *(śîm)* His name there" (Deut. 12:5,21; 14:24; 1 Kings 9:3; 11:36; 14:21; 2 Kings 21:4,7; 2 Chron. 6:20; 33:7).
3. "That My name might be there" (1 Kings 8:16,29; 2 Kings 23:27).

Too much is made of this material when some, following von Rad, make this "name-theology" a replacement for the older "glory-theology" in that no longer is Yahweh Himself present at the ark of the covenant but only His name is now present.[22] Von Rad himself noted, however, that the "name" was present already in Exodus 20:24 and Exodus 31. The "name" here, as in the antecedent theology, stood for the total being, character, and nature just as name was used in the prohibition given at Sinai about taking the *name* of the Lord God in vain. Roland de Vaux could not agree with von Rad either. These three phrases meant "to claim ownership."[23] While it is true that God's "holy habitation" *(mᵉʿôn qōḏeš*—Deut. 26:15) and His "dwelling place" *(mᵉkôn šeḇeṯ*—1 Kings 8:30,39,43,49) is in heaven, the latter expression is also found in the Song of the Sea (Exod. 15:17) in parallelism with the "sanctuary" of the Lord.

The point seems to be that God is transcendent in that His permanent abode *(yšḇ, šḇṯ)* is in heaven; yet He is immanent in that He dwells *(škn)* on the earth (Exod. 25:8; 29:45; Lev. 26:11; Num. 16:3) in His glory, angel, name, and now in a "place" that He will yet elect (Deut. 12:5). There is no evidence that Deuteronomy or Moses rejected in any way this so-called dialectical conception of the divine abode. Heaven is not the exclusive dwelling place of God—He may "sit" or "be enthroned" there, but He also "tabernacled" on

---

[22]Gerhard von Rad, *Studies in Deuteronomy* (Chicago: Henry Regnery Co., 1953), pp. 38-44.

[23]As cited by Weinfeld, *Deuteronomy*, p. 194, n. 2.

earth as well. And Deuteronomy added to the list of His manifestations of Himself to Israel—the *place* where He will cause His *name* (His person) to dwell. What God owned He now openly possessed by having His name "put" on it or "called over" it.

CONQUEST OF THE LAND

Yahweh was known as a "Man of war" after His celebrated victory at the Red Sea (Exod. 15:3). Even before there was a king to lead her, the Lord went out at the head of Israel's army (Judg. 5:5,13,20,23). And the rules for such wars were given in explicit legal enactments in Deuteronomy:

1. The laws of battle (20:1-15)
2. The laws on beautiful captive women (21:10-14)
3. The destruction of Canaanite sanctuaries (12:1-4)
4. The extermination of previous inhabitants (20:16-20)
5. The purification for battle (23:9-14)
6. The war with Amalek (25:17-19).

These laws were illustrated in Joshua 1-11 where four full-length descriptions of this type of war were detailed:

1. Conquest of Jericho (Josh. 6)
2. Second attack on Ai (Josh. 8)
3. Southern campaign (Josh. 10)
4. Northern campaign (Josh. 11).

Two other descriptions recorded Israel's failure to conduct this type of war:

1. First attack on Ai (Josh. 7)
2. Unapproved treaty with the Gibeonites (Josh. 9).

Such wars have been named "holy wars" by Gerhard von Rad.[24] They were in actuality "Yahweh's wars" (1 Sam. 18:18; 25:28); therefore, such battles were not to be initiated by any leader or group without consulting the Lord first (1 Sam. 28:5-6; 30:7-8; 2 Sam. 5:19,22,23). After Israel had been assured by Yahweh that the anticipated battle was His own, then the trumpets were sounded and the cry went up: "Yahweh has delivered the enemy into our hands"

---

[24]Von Rad, *Studies*, pp. 45-59; idem, *Der heilige Krieg im alten Israel* (Zurich: Zwingli Verlag, 1951); Gordon J. Wenham, "The Deuteronomic Theology of the Book of Joshua," *Journal of Biblical Literature* 90(1971): 141-42.

(Judg. 3:27; 6:3; 7:15; 1 Sam. 13:3). The war began with Yahweh's promise of success and an exhortation to fight valiantly. Israel must only trust and not be afraid (Josh. 1:6,9; 6:2; 8:1; 10:8; 11:6). The men were then "consecrated" to the Lord, for their mission set them apart from all mundane activity (1 Sam. 21:6; 2 Sam. 11:11). Yahweh went before the army and dwelt in the camp (Deut. 23:14; Judg. 4:14) and "fought" on behalf of Israel (Deut. 1:30). The military leader of the army, though often specially endowed with powers, was ultimately dependent on the Lord, for He could save by few or by many (Judg. 7:2ff.; 1 Sam. 13:15ff.). This is vividly brought out by Joshua's vision of the "commander of the Lord" who stood with sword in hand ready for action (Josh. 5:13-15). At the climax of the battle, Yahweh sent terror or panic *(mᵉhûmâh, hāmam)* into the hearts of the enemy which brought about their overthrow (Josh. 10:10; Judg. 4:15; 1 Sam. 5:11; 7:10, *passim*).

In this type of warfare, spoils were not to be taken by anyone, for everything in this war was under "ban" *(hērem = hāram,* "to utterly destroy"—Deut. 20:17; 2:34; 3:6; 7:2). It was the exclusive property of the Lord; therefore, it was to be totally devoted to destruction (Josh. 6:17-27; 1 Sam. 15:3). What could not be burned, such as silver, gold, or iron, was to be placed in the sanctuary of God. The "ban" was just the opposite of a voluntary whole-burnt offering in which the offerer willingly gave up the entire animal in an act of total submission (Lev. 1; cf. Rom. 12:1-2). Here, after much divine long-suffering and waiting, God called for everything that belonged to Him in the first place—life, possessions, valuables—as an involuntary whole-burnt offering. Thus more was involved than mere destruction; it was a "religious punishment" which signified "the separation from the profane sphere and deliverance into the power of God."[25] As God had predicted to Abraham, He would wait "until the iniquity of the Amorite" was "complete" (Gen. 15:16). And so He did—six hundred years! Now Joshua was fulfilling that word.

The theology of this type of conquest emphasized the pattern of the priority of the divine command and the fidelity to which that divine word was carried out. When men were responsibly obedient, then God was sovereignly present; e.g., in Israel's southern campaign: "The Lord threw down great stones from heaven" (Josh.

---

[25]Johannes Bauer, "Ban," *Sacramentum Verbi* (New York: Herder & Herder, 1970), 1:55. Cf. also G. R. Driver, "Hebrew Homonyms," *Vetus Testamentum Supplements* 16(1967): 56-59, who sees two roots behind *hērem: hrm,* Akkadian *haramu,* "to cut off, separate," and *hrm,* Arabic *harama,* "prohibited, declared illicit."

10:11), for "the Lord fought for Israel" (v. 14). But when Israel "did not ask direction from the Lord" (Josh. 9:14), or when she attempted to attack Ai when Achan's personal sin of stealing from God those things in Jericho "dedicated to destruction" had left a cloud of moral pollution over *all* the people (7:11,13,19), the results were catastrophic and disgraceful.

PROPHETIC HISTORY IN THE LAND

Beyond the fulfillment of the Abrahamic promise of the land with its anticipated conquest, distribution, rest, and place for the name of God to dwell was another major theological element in Deuteronomy and the earlier prophets. It was the structure found in Joshua to 2 Kings and mentioned earlier in this chapter. In the case of the book of Judges, the meaning and significance of the narratives was to be found in a familiar cycle of apostasy, punishment, repentance, divine compassion, a deliverer, and a period of rest in the land. This cycle was first stated in Judges 2:11-3:6, but subsequently it served as an outline for the experiences of several generations. The most significant theological point was, as Carl Graesser, Jr., has observed,[26] that the phrases, concepts, and theological emphases were those of the book of Deuteronomy. Compare:

Judges 2:11 with Deuteronomy 4:25; 6:3
Judges 2:12 with Deuteronomy 4:25; 6:14
Judges 2:14 with Deuteronomy 6:15

The impact of Deuteronomy on Judges 2:11-14 was just as heavy as it had been on Joshua 1:2-9 where, according to Graesser, "more than fifty percent" of that speech could "be reproduced verbatim from verses in Deuteronomy."[27] Compare:

Joshua 1:2 with Deuteronomy 5:31
Joshua 1:3-4 with Deuteronomy 11:24
Joshua 1:5 with Deuteronomy 11:25; 31:6
Joshua 1:6 with Deuteronomy 31:23

---

[26]Carl Graesser, Jr., "The Message of the Deuteronomic Historian," *Concordia Theological Monthly* 39(1968): 544, n. 10. For a complete list of "deuteronomic" language, see S. R. Driver, *Introduction to the Literature of the Old Testament* (New York: Meridian Books, 1956), pp. 99-102. Also see Weinfeld, *Deuteronomy*, app. A, pp. 320-59 and S. R. Driver, *Commentary on Deuteronomy* (New York: Charles Scribner's Sons, 1916), lxxviii-lxxxiv.

[27]Ibid., p. 545, n. 19.

Joshua 1:7-8 with Deuteronomy 5:32
Joshua 1:9 with Deuteronomy 31:6

But what was the key or organizing concept that made this history more than just a dreary report of constant failure? What use was there in detailing these narratives for those days much less future generations? We believe Hans W. Wolff has correctly identified that lost piece of theology in the doctrine of repentance.[28]

Repentance and Blessing

"As long as Joshua lived," began Judges 2:7 on an ominous note, "the people served the Lord." However, from there on the story was the same: "They did evil in the sight of the Lord, . . . and departed from Yahweh . . . and followed other gods . . . [whereupon] the anger of the Lord was hot against Israel . . . and He sold them into the clutches of their enemies round about" (Judg. 2:11-12,14). Then "they cried to Yahweh" (Judg. 3:9; 4:3; cf. also 1 Sam. 12:19)—and there it was. Misery would finally find a voice and in her despair, Israel would "return" (*šûb*) to the Lord.

The basis for this injunction was to be found in Deuteronomy 30:1-10. Three times the catchword "to return" was repeated (vv. 2,8,10). "If you will turn back to Yahweh your God with all your heart and with all your soul," then God would again bless His people.

The earliest prophetic use of the term to "repent," to "return" to the Lord, appears in 1 Samuel 7:3.

> If you are returning (*šābîm*) to Yahweh with all your heart, then remove the foreign gods and Ashtaroth from your midst and direct your heart to Yahweh and serve Him alone so that He may rescue you out of the hand of the Philistines.

Wolff found 1 Kings 8:46ff. "the most impressive connection" with Deuteronomy 30:1-10—especially the rare phrase "to take something to heart" (*hēšîb 'el lēb*—Deut. 30:1b and 1 Kings 8:47a; cf. also 1 Sam. 7:3). Twice during his dedicatory prayer for the temple, Solomon prayed that God would be merciful to Israel if she "repented" and "turned" to Him (1 Kings 8:46-53).

Likewise 2 Kings 17:13 summarized the message "by all prophets and seers of Israel and Judah." It was simply "repent" (*šubû*):

---

[28]Hans Walter Wolff, "The Kerygma of the Deuteronomic Historical Work," *The Vitality of Old Testament Traditions*, coauthored by Walter Brueggemann and Hans W. Wolff (Atlanta: John Knox Press, 1975), pp. 83-100.

> Turn back *(šubû)* from your evil ways and observe My command-
> ments and statutes strictly according to the instruction which I
> gave to your fathers and which I sent to you by My servants the
> prophets.

The same word could also be used as the highest accolade given
to any Israelite king. Of King Josiah it was said in 2 Kings 23:25:

> There never had been a king like him who turned *(šāb)* to Yahweh
> with all his heart and with all his soul and with all his strength
> wholly in accordance with the instruction of Moses: and after him
> there arose no one like him.

He was faithful to the Davidic type; yet he was also faithful to the
Sinaitic commandment as well. There was no duality here. It was
one and the same thing. In fact, so markedly different in morality
and religion were the lives of the kings of Israel and Judah that
David and Jeroboam became standards of piety and impiety respectively. Every northern king was condemned because he "walked in
all the way of Jeroboam the son of Nebat and in the sin which he
made Israel to sin" (1 Kings 14:16; 15:26,30,34; 16:26; 22:52; 2 Kings
3:3; 10:29,31; 13:2,6; 14:24; 15:9,18,24,28; 23:15; also cf. 1 Kings
12:30; 13:34; 2 Kings 17:21-22). Of any good king of Judah it was
said, "He walked before Me as David his father walked" (1 Kings
3:3,14; 11:4,6,33,38; 14:8; 15:3,5,11; 2 Kings 14:3; 16:2; 18:3; 22:2).
   Out of all the kings of Israel and Judah only Hezekiah and
Josiah are commended unconditionally while six others—Asa,
Jehoshaphat, Jehoash, Amaziah, Uzziah, and Jotham—received a
qualified commendation. Consistently the others scorned the commandments and proudly refused to repent.
   Repentance was the basis for any new work of God after a time
of failure. And the result of that repentance was the "good" *(tôb)*
God would do to them. It is Walter Brueggemann[29] who pointed to
this theme of "goodness" as a parallel to Wolff's "repentance"
theme. For him the theme was a covenantal term. To speak "well" or
"rightly" *(tôb)* in all that they said (Deut. 5:28; 18:17) was for Israel
to honor a formal treaty or covenant obligation (cf. the only two other
instances, 1 Sam. 12:23; 1 Kings 8:36; and perhaps 2 Kings 20:3).[30]
   But in a larger sense, Israel was also the recipient of "good." As
such, "good" functioned as a synonym for *šālôm*, "peace" in its most
comprehensive and most holistic sense, observed Brueggemann,

---

[29]Walter Brueggemann, "The Kerygma of the Deuteronomic Historian," *Interpretation* 22(1968): 387-402.
   [30]Ibid., p. 389, nn. 6,7 refer to Aramaic treaties where *tôb* occurs.

while in Deuteronomy 30:15 "good" was a synonym for "life."[31]
Thus every "blessing" (an old theological term by this time) was
included in the good life which included life itself (Deut. 5:16,33;
6:18,24); longevity (4:40; 5:16; 22:7); the land (5:16,33; 6:18); and
the increase and multiplication of one's family (6:3). Israel was to
"obey" in order that Yahweh might do her "good" (12:25,28; 19:13;
22:7).

In the very text that Wolff found his programmatic threefold call
to "repent" (Deut. 30:2,8,10), Brueggemann found two divine offers
to make Israel "more prosperous *(ṭôḇ)* and numerous than [her]
fathers" (vv. 5,9). This goodness surpassed mere description and
moved into the category of promises and confession. The land given
to Israel was a "good land" (Deut. 8:7-10), for Israel would *"bless* the
Lord [her] God for the *good* land He had given [her]" (note also the
word of promise about the land in Deut. 1:8,25; 6:10,18).

The same word of goodness and blessing could be seen in the
Davidic house which did the "good" which Saul refused to do (1
Sam. 16:16; 20:7,12,31). Yet David was able to do the "good" because Yahweh granted it to him: "And when the Lord has dealt *well*
with my lord" (1 Sam. 25:31; cf. 1 Kings 8:66). Thus the key promise
to David in 2 Samuel 7:28, which was to "endure" (eight times in
that chapter there is the adverb "forever"), was called His *"good*
[word] to [His] servant." Everything related to the well-being of
David's realm could be summarized in this word "good" (2 Sam.
2:6).

Thus "repentance" has a counter theme: Israel was offered the
blessing, promise, and assurance of God. This balance prevented the
theologian, as Brueggemann correctly commented, from finding in
Deuteronomy only law, obedience, judgment, curse, and repentance; there were likewise the faithfulness and blessing of God to a
covenant and a word from which He does not renege.[32]

Predictive Word and Fulfilled Event

The prophetic historians especially found God's word "good."
His words were fulfilled in history—"Not one good word of all that
He had promised to the house of Israel had failed; all had come to
pass" (Josh. 21:45; 23:14; 1 Kings 8:56; 2 Kings 10:10). For that word
was not an "empty" *(rēq)* word or a word "void" of power (Deut.
32:47); once it was uttered, it reached its goal.

---

[31]Ibid., p. 391.
[32]Ibid., p. 38.

Such a series of "good" words uttered by the prophets could be made into another whole framework for another aspect of the single plan of God that embraced these days of entering into the promised inheritance, rest, and place where He would put His name. It was Gerhard von Rad[33] who pointed out this thread of prophecy and fulfillment throughout the prophetic historians. Each divine word of prediction spoken by the prophets had its corresponding historical event. His list included:

Word of Creation

Promise:	Topic:	Fulfillment:
2 Samuel 7:13	Solomon, the temple builder	1 Kings 8:20
1 Kings 11:29-36	Division of the kingdom	1 Kings 12:15
1 Kings 13:1-3	Josiah's pollution of Bethel altar	2 Kings 23:16-18
1 Kings 14:6-16	Uprooting of Jeroboam's kingdom	1 Kings 15:29
1 Kings 16:1-4	Uprooting of Baasha's kingdom	1 Kings 16:12
Joshua 6:26	Curse on rebuilding of Jericho	1 Kings 16:34
1 Kings 22:17	Death of Ahab in battle	1 King 22:35-38
1 Kings 21:21	Judgment on Ahab and his family	1 Kings 21:27-29; 2 Kings 9:7
2 Kings 1:6	Sick Ahaziah will die	2 Kings 1:17
2 Kings 21:10-16	Manasseh's sins will bring disaster	2 Kings 23:26; 24:2
2 Kings 22:15-20	Josiah will escape impending evil days	2 Kings 23:29-30.

This theology of history accented the priority of God's creative word. The northern ten tribes had their doom sealed with the apostasy of Jeroboam (1 Kings 14:16). Yet because of Yahweh's word of promise to David, Judah continued to live on (1 Kings 11:13,32,36). Yahweh wanted to leave "a light in Jerusalem" (1 Kings 15:4)—an obvious allusion to the Davidic house and promise (2 Sam. 21:17; Ps. 132:17; cf. 2 Sam. 14:7).

While David spoke this word to his son Solomon, "May Yahweh establish His word . . . there shall not fail a man to sit on the throne of Israel" (1 Kings 2:4), Solomon realized the fulfillment of that blessing in his own life (1 Kings 8:20,25), which Yahweh also confirmed to Solomon directly (1 Kings 9:5). Later on, Isaiah (55:3) reflected back on it and called this "good" word the "sure mercies of David" *(ḥasᵉdê Dāwid)*. Thus, the ancient words of blessing and promise were still being renewed, enlarged, and fulfilled. As von Rad put it, the prophets changed "the gears of history with a word of God."[34]

---

[33]Von Rad, *Studies*, pp. 74-91.
[34]Von Rad, *Theology*, 1:342.

A *Prophet Like Moses*

Every reference made to the promised seed throughout the prepatriarchal, patriarchal, and Mosaic eras had been generic in character; they portrayed the future redemption as the "seed" of the woman, the race of Shem, the "seed" of Abraham, the tribe of Judah, and the kingdom of Israel. But when Moses predicted in Deuteronomy 18:15-19 that Yahweh had said to him, "A prophet will I raise up for them, from the midst of their brethren, like you," the question now was: Did He mean a simple singular "prophet," a collective, or a generic idea? And was this "prophet" another messianic figure?

From the context one might, at first reading, only expect an individual prophet coming from Israel and compared with Moses. However, the prophetic office was not transmitted to Moses' successors like the Davidic line was. Rather, Moses' ministry and person were outside the usual class of prophets, for he had been placed over all God's house (Num. 12:7). He also had fulfilled the priestly functions before the Aaronic priesthood had been inaugurated (Exod. 24:4-8). Furthermore, each of the parallel offices of "judge" (Deut. 17:8-13), "king" (vv. 14-20), and "priest" (18:1-8) were collective and generic, not individual in the immediate context.

Thus we conclude that this promise is also generic. Moses recognized that his work was incomplete; yet he could see another prophet in view who unlike himself would complete the ministry of instruction and revelation of God. This coming prophet would be (1) an Israelite, "of thy brethren" (Deut. 18:15,18); (2) "like" Moses (vv. 15,18); and (3) authorized to declare the word of God with authority (vv. 18-19). Such an expectation was common knowledge even before the days of Jesus. Philip found Nathaniel and announced, "We have found Him of whom Moses in the Law and the Prophets did write" (John 1:45). Likewise the Samaritan woman concluded that Jesus was that "prophet" (4:19,29); and the multitude near the Sea of Galilee exclaimed, "This is truly the prophet that should come into the world" (6:14). Peter likewise quoted our passage in his temple address and applied it to Jesus (Acts 3:22-26), as did Stephen (7:37).

Summary

The key to the theology of this period remained the inheritance of the land and the "rest" into which Israel entered by faith. Furthermore, in that very "place" Yahweh would cause His name to dwell. And Israel's history would be marked by the "good" if she would "repent" and receive the "good" prophetic word sent from God at those crucial junctures in her history.

The internal structure for the narration of how Israel succeeded or failed to fully enter into that "rest" is found in the prophetic history with its programmatic statements and its evaluative comments put in the mouths of key speakers. In this sequence, it was the word of God through His messengers that led the way. The people followed in obedience or repentance—or in total collapse. Yet the promise of God continued to survive in David's house regardless of ineptitude present on every hand.

Chapter 9

King of the Promise:
Davidic Era

God's promise to David in 2 Samuel 7 has to be among the most brilliant moments in the history of salvation. It is matched in importance and prestige only by the promise made to Abraham in Genesis 12 and later to all Israel and Judah in Jeremiah's New covenant (Jer. 31:31-34). Therefore, this forty year segment out of the narratives of the prophetic historians (Joshua to 2 Kings) merits an extended and separate treatment even though it finds its basic location in the works of the earlier prophets.

However, there is more textual material to consider than a mere chapter as 2 Samuel 7 or its later commentaries such as Psalm 89. In our diachronic treatment of theology and in our desire to have biblical theology act as a basic aid primarily to exegetical theology rather than systematic theology, we will need to include the following in the Davidic era: (1) what scholars have referred to since Leonhard Rost[1] as the "succession narrative" (2 Sam. 9-20 and 1 Kings 1-2; i.e., the remaining history of David from the end of 1 Sam. 16-31 and from 2 Sam. 1-8; 21-24) and (2) the royal psalms

---

[1]Leonhard Rost, *Die Überlieferung von der Thronnach-folge Davids* (Stuttgart: W. Kohlhammer Verlag, 1926).

(Pss. 2,18,20,21,45,72,89,101,110,132,144:1-11). Likewise since David and the ark were so intimately united in much of their theology, this chapter will also consider (3) the "history of the ark" (1 Sam. 4:1-7:2) and that momentous experience in David's life when he moved the ark to Jerusalem (2 Sam. 6).

A PROMISED KING

Deuteronomy 17:14-20 had carefully specified the following:

> When you come to the land which the Lord your God is giving you and you possess it and dwell in it and then say, I will set a king over me, like all the nations that are round about me; you may indeed set as king over you him whom the Lord will choose. One from the midst of your brethren you will set as king over you.
> — Verse 14

Therefore kingship, as such, was not outside the plan of God. It had only to wait for the proper time and God's selection. Up to this point, Israel's government had been what Josephus had labeled a "theocracy"[2] in which the sovereignty and power belonged to God. Had not Israel also sung at the Exodus, "The Lord will reign for ever and ever" (Exod. 15:18)? But when would the promised kingship be set up under the theocracy?

A Usurping Ruler

In the interim, there were several false starts. Gideon had received the offer to "rule over" (*māšal*) the men of Israel after his stunning victory over Midian (Judg. 8:22). Not only was he to be their ruler, but the offer was an offer of a hereditary rulership: "You, your son, and your grandson also." To all this Gideon declined unconditionally and asserted instead the principle, "The Lord will rule over you" (v.23).

Gideon's son, however, was not that reluctant. After his father's death, Abimelek became king of Shechem (Judg. 9:15-18). This usurper (for so he would be if Yahweh were the real king), son of Gideon's maidservant, took a new name. Martin Buber[3] had argued that "to appoint a name" is never used in connection with giving a name to a child at birth; rather, it is consistently the verb "to call." This expression means "to give a new name" (cf. 2 Kings 17:34; Neh.

---

[2]Flavius Josephus, *Against Apion*, 2. 16. 164-66.

[3]Martin Buber, *Kingship of God*, 3d ed., rev. and enl., trans. Richard Sheimann (New York: Harper & Row, 1967), p. 74.

9:7). If Gideon renamed his son, then he probably did so on the occasion of his rejection of the kingly office, declaring instead that God his father was his king; hence, *Abi*, "my father," is *melek*, "king." But the expression in Judges 8:31 can also be translated, "They appointed him," or even, "He appointed for himself," the name "my father [before me] was—really—a king!"

The irony is clearly brought out in Judges 9:6 where the root *mālak*, "to be king, to reign," appears two times: "And they kinged 'father-king' as king." The whole experiment ended in tragedy for Abimelek and his "kingdom."

A Rejected Ruler

Neither was Samuel's generation any wiser when they also prematurely demanded a king (1 Sam. 8:4-6) on the false assumption that God was powerless to help them now that Samuel had grown old and his sons were morally corrupt (vv.1-3). It too was a rejection of Yahweh's kingship (8:7; 10:19). The whole situation grieved Samuel to no end (8:6).

Samuel's opposition appears at first to be strange in light of the promise of Deuteronomy 17:14-20 where directions had been given on how to act in the event that the people should desire a king. But Samuel's opposition, as was true of Yahweh as well, was a condemnation of the people's spirit and motives for requesting a king: they wished to be "like all the nations" in having a king (8:5,20). It was also a tacit statement of disbelief in the power and presence of God: they wanted a king to go before them and fight their battles (v. 20).

Graciously, God yielded to the people's requests after Samuel had done everything he could to make them aware of the responsibilities of being under a king (1 Sam. 8:10-19). They got what they had asked for: Saul. And Saul accomplished the task appointed him by God:

> He shall save My people from the hand of the Philistines; for I have seen the affliction of My people because their cry has come up to Me.
> —1 Samuel 9:16 cf. 10:1

So it was. Wherever Saul turned his hand, so mightily was the power of God on him as a Spirit-filled leader that he emerged victorious against every nation he fought (1 Sam. 14:47; cf. 2 Sam. 1:17-27 in David's lament). Saul also rooted out all kinds of superstition and the occult forbidden by Mosaic law (1 Sam. 28:9) and even seemed to be careful about such Levitical matters of detail as the eating of blood (14:34). He was "God's chosen" (10:24) and "anointed" (10:1).

145

But what of the perpetuity of that reign? Nowhere had Saul, or Samuel for that matter, been promised that the offer was a hereditary rule; yet 1 Samuel 13:13-14 showed that the possibility had been there nonetheless:

> The Lord would have established your kingdom over Israel forever. But now your kingdom shall not continue: the Lord has sought out a man after His own heart; and the Lord has appointed him to be a leader over His people because you have not kept what the Lord commanded you.

There would have been nothing unusual about this had not the promise of a ruler coming from the tribe of Judah already been given, but indeed it had in Genesis 49:10. The symbols of that office, a scepter and a ruler's staff, would not depart from Judah until the one to whom they legitimately belonged came. How then was the Lord able to offer Saul an everlasting kingdom—especially since he was from the tribe of Benjamin? There is no doubt that Israel was to have a king one day, for that had been made plain in Numbers 24:17 and Deuteronomy- 17:14. And Israel could have made several false—even premature—starts. But here the Lord Himself said to Saul, in retrospect, that the kingdom could have been an everlasting kingdom—there is the difficulty.

The solution to this conundrum was not to be found in an allegedly treasonous act of Samuel who, contrary to what Scripture claimed, was supposed to have single-handedly deposed Saul and chosen David instead. Nor could this particular issue be resolved by blaming the people alone with electing a king after their own heart (1 Sam. 12:13), for Saul was also the one whom "Yahweh had chosen" (9:16; 10:1,24; 12:13). It was Patrick Fairbairn who came closest to solving this issue:

> After the people had been solemnly admonished of their guilt in requesting the appointment of a king on *their* worldly principles, they were allowed to raise one of their number to the throne...
> And to render the divine purpose in this respect manifest to all who had eyes to see and ears to hear, the Lord allowed the choice first to fall on one who—as representative of the people's earthly wisdom and prowess—was little disposed to rule in humble subordination to the will and authority of Heaven and was therefore supplanted by another who should act as God's representative, and bear distinctively the name of His servant.[4]

---

[4]Patrick Fairbairn, *The Typology of Scripture*, 2 vols. (Grand Rapids: Zondervan, 1963), 1:121-22.

Thus the lesson was designedly allowed by God to show men that God alone was the supreme King, and any government had to function under His authority. Hence the lot temporarily fell to Benjamin (10:20) rather than Judah. Saul was incomparable[5] to all others because only he, to the exclusion of all others, was God's man according to Samuel (v. 24). His stature (v. 23) was a sign, but his divine election was what really made him incomparable.

Whether God might have given to Saul the "kingdom," later known as the northern ten tribes which subsequently broke away and were given to Jeroboam, and kept only "one tribe" (note Judah and Benjamin were here regarded as *one* tribe!) for David His servant that He might always have a "lamp" in Jerusalem, the city where God had chosen to place His name (1 Kings 11:33-37), is ultimately unknown.[6] One thing is known, Ephraim had always had a chip on her shoulder and was ready to challenge or secede from the rest of the tribes at the slightest provocation all during the era of the judges (Judg. 8:1; 12:1). Consequently, a rift had been in the making for a long time. But it does suggest what might have been involved for Saul had he continued in obedience to God.

The permitted monarchy was—even as foreseen in Deuteronomy 17:14-20—to be bound by certain restrictions. The people were not to appoint anyone who was not chosen by God, and the king was not to do his own will and pleasure; he was to rule according to the law of God. Thus Israel still had a theocracy of sorts where the king merely reigned as a viceroy of Yahweh, the heavenly Sovereign.

It is commonplace in recent scholarship to divide the narratives on the institution of the monarchy into two basic sources: one favorable to the monarchy (1 Sam. 9:1-10; 11:1-11,15; 13:2-14:46) and the other later and deuteronomistic and antimonarchical in its outlook (1 Sam. 7:3-8:22; 10:17-27; 12:1-25). More recently, Hans-Jochen Boecker[7] has shown that it is too simplistic to label 1 Samuel 8 and 12 as antimonarchical. These passages do give a more conditional acceptance of kingship as an institution from God, but that was

---

[5]For a discussion of this formula of incomparability, see C. J. Labuschagne, *The Incomparability of Yahweh in the Old Testament* (Leiden: E. J. Brill, 1966), pp. 9-10.

[6]J. Barton Payne, "Saul and the Changing Will of God," *Bibliotheca Sacra* 129 (1972): 321-25. He distinguishes between God's permissive will and His directive will in allowing Saul to be the first king, but he failed to directly link Genesis 49:10 and 1 Samuel 13:13*b* to this discussion.

[7]As cited by Bruce C. Birch, "The Choosing of Saul at Mizpah," *Catholic Biblical Quarterly* 37(1975): 447-48, n. 4.

mainly because the monarchy carried with it the greater danger of apostasy.

These chapters were no more antimonarchical than Jotham's fable of Judges 9:7-21 was. According to Eugene H. Maly's[8] careful analysis, this fable contained a caricature of Abimelek, the would-be king, and a figurative description of the impending destruction that awaited the Shechemites. The worthlessness of the bramble's (Abimelek's) rule and the prediction of the fire coming forth from the bramble to destroy the Shechemites was no general condemnation of kingship itself; rather, its criticism was directed at those who were foolish enough to look to such protection as this and at the worthless king himself. Again, the focus was on the response of men, not on the institution itself.

An Anointed Ruler

When Saul was rejected, the Lord looked for a "man after His own heart" (1 Sam. 13:14); and David, the son of Jesse, was His selection. He was first anointed by the prophet Samuel (1 Sam. 16:13); then he was anointed as king of Judah (2 Sam. 2:4); and the final anointing was over all Israel (2 Sam. 5:3). Even as Saul had ten times been called the "anointed of the Lord" (*māšîaḥ YHWH*, 1 Sam. 24:6[7],10[11]; 26:9,11,16,23; 2 Sam. 1:14,16), so now David is "anointed" and "the Spirit of the Lord came mightily on [him] from that day forward" (1 Sam. 16:13). He too was called the Lord's "anointed" ten times. The oil of anointing, when used in worship, was a symbol of the divine Spirit; but in regal consecration it marked God's gift of His Spirit to aid the king of Israel in administering His rule. It marked David as the recipient and representative of the divine majesty. Saul too had received the "Spirit of God" (1 Sam. 11:6) as did the previous "judges" from Othniel to Samuel. But when Saul departed from the Lord after a brilliant beginning of delivering Israel from the Philistines (1 Sam. 9:16; 14:47), he became totally inept at governing the people due to a loss of the Spirit's gift of government.

Though this title of "the anointed one" was used twice by transference in Psalm 105:15 of the partiarchs and once of Cyrus, a divinely called ruler (Isa. 45:1; cf. 1 Kings 19:15), the title was only used absolutely of the king. Subsequently the word became the title for the great Davidite who was to come and to complete the ex-

---

[8]Eugene H. Maly, "The Jotham Fable—Anti-Monarchical?" *Catholic Biblical Quarterly* 22(1960): 299-305.

pected kingdom of God. All together, the noun "anointed" occurs thirty-nine times in the OT. Twenty-three times it is the title for the reigning king of Israel.[9]

This means that there were nine passages left where the "anointed one" denoted some coming person, usually in the line of David (1 Sam. 2:10; 2:35; Pss. 2:2; 20:6, 28:8; 84:9; Hab. 3:13; Dan. 9:25-26). He was Yahweh's king who would reign over His everlasting kingdom on earth; yet simultaneously He was that chosen Man in the line of election who was entitled to sit as God's representative on the throne of David. Though this term was by no means the clearest nor the most frequent in the OT, usage fixed it as the most fitting term, in preference to all other titles, to describe the expected King—the Messiah.

A PROMISED DYNASTY

More than a kingship was at stake, however. Next to the promise given to Abraham must rank the word of blessing poured out on David. The classical OT passage dealing with this new addition to the ever-expanding promise and plan of God was 2 Samuel 7 with its duplicate in 1 Chronicles 17 and commentary in Psalm 89.[10] It was the account of David's proposal to build a "house," or temple, for the Lord and the revelation Nathan received with God's counterproposal that he would not allow David to construct it. Instead, Yahweh would make a "house" out of David (2 Sam. 7:5-11)!

Historical and literary criticism have not always seen fit to treat 2 Samuel 7 in a uniform, much less kind way. Probably the most violent estimate of the text came from R. H. Pfeiffer,[11] who charged that the author's mind was "muddled," his text "obscure, involved," "badly written," full of "bad grammar and dreary style," filled with *"repetition ad nauseam"* and "monkish drivel." The whole chapter, he opined, was a late fourth century B.C. Jewish *midrash* based on Psalm 89, having no literary or historical value!

While others like Hermann Gunkel reversed the direction of literary dependence and declared Psalm 89 a free poetic expansion

---

[9]In addition to the above three exceptions, "anointed" was also used of the Levitical priests (Lev. 4:3,5,16; 6:22 [15]).

[10]For much of what follows and for greater detail, see W. C. Kaiser, Jr., "The Blessing of David: A Charter for Humanity," *The Law and the Prophets*, John Skilton, ed. (Philadelphia: Presbyterian and Reformed Publishing House, 1974), pp. 298-318.

[11]R. H. Pfeiffer, *Introduction to the Old Testament* (New York: Harper & Row, 1953), pp. 368-73.

of 2 Samuel 7, John L. McKenzie and C. J. Labuschagne[12] took the middle ground that both the historical book and psalm writers drew from an original common source. And contrary to those who would regard 2 Samuel 7:13 as a "deuteronomic addition," the verse is not only to be regarded as genuine, but it is precisely the point on which the theology of the whole passage pivots.

A House

It can be demonstrated that the role of building a temple was closely connected with the establishment of a kingdom in the ancient Near East. Such a connection was demonstrated in F. Willesen's fine study.[13] Thus, according to 2 Samuel 7:13, the "house" of David had to be first established by Yahweh before a temple could be built. Temple building could only be the completion and crowning effect of Yahweh's creation of a kingdom. This same emphasis on the necessity of God's work of establishing the kingdom taking priority over the construction of a house of worship can also be seen in 7:11c where the "you" is emphatically positioned in the Hebrew text: "And to *you* the Lord declares that the Lord will make *you* a house" (cf. "he," i.e., Solomon and the verb "to build" in 7:13a, 5b). The contrast, then, was between a kingdom established by men and one totally brought about by Yahweh.

God promised to make David a "house" (*bayit*). But what could this mean? *Bayit* referred to more than a residence; it was also a family: parents, children, and kin. For example, Noah went into the ark with his "whole house" (Gen. 7:1) and obviously not with the building of their residence; and Jacob ordered "his whole house" to get rid of their foreign gods (35:2). Later all the tribes could be subdivided into "houses" (larger family groupings, Josh. 7:14), and the posterity of a family, king, or dynasty would be called his "house" (Exod. 2:1; 1 Kings 11:38; 12:16; 13:2).

For 2 Samuel 7, the meaning of a "dynasty" was most fitting, especially since the expression "your house and your kingdom will be made sure forever" (v. 16) could only mean that David's "dynasty" would rule forever. This was the new addition to the promise plan: all that had been offered to the patriarchs and Moses

---

[12]John L. McKenzie, "The Dynastic Oracle: II Samuel 7," *Theological Studies* 8(1947): 195; C. J. Labuschagne, "Some Remarks on the Prayer of David in II Samuel 7," *Studies on the Book of Samuel* (Stellenbosch, South Africa: 1960), p. 29. For details on the synoptic problem in these texts, see our essay, "Blessing of David," pp. 300-303.

[13]F. Willesen, "The Cultic Situation of Psalm 74," *Vetus Testamentum* 2(1952): 289ff.

was now being offered to David's dynasty. Nor was that all; it was to last on into the future (v. 19).

Eight times in 2 Samuel 7 Yahweh promised to make David a house (vv. 11,13,16,19,25,26,27,29), not counting the instances of parallel ideas which use other terms. It was explained that David's "house" was a line of descendants (vv. 12,16,19,26,29) which the Lord would give to him in perpetuity. Usually monarchs worried, once they had succeeded in enforcing the peace after a long period of military gains, about the durability of their kingdom (cf. Nebuchadnezzar in Dan. 2). But David was relieved of this anxiety. His "dynasty," throne, and kingdom would be secure forever; it was established by the Lord.

A Seed

Even though the word "seed" is used only once in 2 Samuel 7:12, this promise of a dynasty which would have a long line of descendants was a reminder of a similar word to Abraham. "Seed" had a collective meaning of "posterity" even as it did in Genesis 3:15; 12:7; 13:15. But the seed simultaneously pointed to the one person who represented the whole group and was the earnest of a line of descendants yet to come. Thus David's "seed" would build the proposed temple (2 Sam. 7:13), meaning the single individual Solomon. But at the same time, the eternally enduring house would never lack a descendant to sit on the throne of David. In fact, in one expression in 2 Chronicles 22:10 Athaliah wanted to extirpate the "whole seed of the kingship" *(kol zera' hammamlākâh)*, i.e., the whole dynasty.

A Kingdom

As already noticed, one item in the promise during the era of the patriarchs and the Exodus was that Israel would have "kings" (Gen. 17:6,16; 35:11; cf. 36:31), including a "kingdom" (Exod. 19:6; Num. 24:7) and a "dominion" (Num. 24:19). Now that kingdom was being assigned to David and his family according to 2 Samuel 7:23-24,26,27.

It was not that God had abdicated His rule or that His reign had come to an end; for so closely linked was this newly announced reign of David with God's reign, that the Davidic throne and kingdom were later on called the Lord's own. Thus 1 Chronicles 28:5 speaks of Solomon sitting on "the throne of the kingdom of the Lord over Israel," 2 Chronicles 13:8 refers to "the kingdom of the Lord," and in 2 Chronicles 9:8 the king is placed by God "on His [God's] throne to be king for the Lord your God." Already in 1 Samuel 24:6

and 2 Samuel 19:21 he was called the "Lord's anointed." Accordingly, the theocracy and Davidic kingdom, by virtue of their special place in the covenant, were regarded as one. They were so inseparably linked together that in the future their destiny was identical.

More information on this kingdom can be gleaned from the royal psalms (2, 18, 20, 21, 45, 72, 89, 101, 110, 132, 144) and the eschatological psalms or enthronement psalms (47, 93-100). But for now, David was told in 2 Samuel 7 that the kingdom was irrevocable and eternal (v. 13, 16 bis, 24, 25, 26, 29 bis).

A Son of God

Particularly surprising was the divine announcement: "I will be to him a Father, and he shall be to Me a son" (2 Sam. 7:14). Now "Father" must have been a title David used naturally of God, for he had named one of his children Absalom, "my Father (God) is peace." Indeed, Moses had already taught Israel the same when he asked, "Is He not your Father, He who created you?" (Deut. 32:6).

Nor was the concept of sonship without its theological antecedents in times past. All the members of Israel were His sons, His firstborn (Exod. 4:22; 19:4). Interestingly enough, "the whole diplomatic vocabulary of the second millennium was rooted in the familial sphere."[14] Hence, it was most appropriate for this covenant with David.

What was new was that Yahweh should now treat David's son in a manner clearly reminiscent of the patriarchal and Mosaic promises. This was more than the Near Eastern titulary of divine sonship: "son of god-x"; it was a divine gift, not a proud human boast. It was also a particularization of the old word given to Israel (viz., His "firstborn") which now would be addressed to David's seed (Ps. 89:27). In a totally unique way David could now call Him "my Father" (v. 26), for each Davidite stood in this relation of son to his God. Yet it is not said that any single Davidite would ever realize purely or perfectly this lofty concept of divine sonship. But should any person qualify for this relationship, he would also need to be a son of David.

A CHARTER FOR HUMANITY

What God had promised David was no brand-new unrelated theme to His previous blessings. Already there had been in vogue a long development of theology which could inform, i.e., contribute to,

---

[14]Moshe Weinfeld, "The Covenant of Grant in the Old Testament and in the Ancient Near East," *Journal of American Oriental Society* 90(1970): 194.

David's covenant. Among the familiar themes already known to David in 2 Samuel 7, as they were again rehearsed in this word directed to him, were:

1. "I will make thee a great name" (2 Sam. 7:9; cf. Gen. 12:2, et al.).
2. "I will appoint a place for Israel and will plant them" (2 Sam. 7:10; cf. Gen. 15:18; Deut. 11:24-25; Josh. 1:4-5).
3. "I will set up thy seed after thee" (2 Sam. 7:12; cf. Gen. 17:7-10,19).
4. "He shall be My son" (2 Sam. 7:14; cf. Exod. 4:22).
5. "I will be to thee a God and you shall be to Me for a people" (2 Sam. 7:23-24; cf. Gen. 17:7-8; 28:21; Exod. 6:7; 29:45; Lev. 11:45; 22:33; 23:43; 25:38; 26:12,44-45; Num. 15:41; Deut. 4:20; 29:12-13; *passim*).
6. Yahweh's uniqueness (2 Sam. 7:22; cf. Exod. 8:10; 9:14; 15:11; Deut. 33:26; Pss. 18:31[32]; 89:6[7],8[9]; *passim*).
7. Israel's uniqueness (2 Sam. 7:22; cf. Exod. 1:9; Num. 14:12; Deut. 1:28-31; 5:26; 7:17-19; 9:14; 11:23, 20:1; 33:29; *passim*; and especially the plural verb in 2 Sam. 7:23: "Who are like thy people, like Israel, one nation in the earth whom God have gone [*sic*] to redeem," a deliberate quote of Deut. 4:7-8 with the same peculiar grammar).[15]
8. The exceptional use of "Adonai Yahweh" (2 Sam. 7:18-19 bis, 22, 28-29), which does not appear again in Samuel or Chronicles. Probably the special significance of this name, which appears only a total of five times prior to this, was caught by R. A. Carlson,[16] who noted that this was the name used when God promised Abraham a "seed" in Genesis 15:2,8. Its repeated use in 2 Samuel 7 is too striking to be accidental.

Thus the blessing of Abraham was continued in a blessing of David: "With Your blessing," prayed David, "let the house of your servant be blessed forever" (2 Sam. 7:29).

---

[15]For a list of twenty-four so-called deuteronomistic similarities to 2 Samuel 7, see Frank M. Cross, Jr., *Canaanite Myth and Hebrew Epic* (Cambridge: Harvard University Press, 1973), pp. 252-54.

[16]R. A. Carlson, *David the Chosen King: A Tradio-Historical Approach to the Second Book of Samuel*, trans. Eric Sharpe and Stanley Rudman (Stockholm: Almqvist and Wiksell, 1964), p. 127. The other five instances of "Adonai Yahweh" are Deuteronomy 3:24; 9:26; Joshua 7:7; Judges 6:22; 16:28. Note the promise content in each prayer. In Kings the double name occurs only in 1 Kings 2:26; 8:53 while "Adonai" appears in 1 Kings 3:10,15; 22:6; 2 Kings 7:6; 19:23.

But when David suddenly realized what had been given to him in this alternative proposal, he was completely overwhelmed. Sensing the solemnity and importance of the moment, he went into the presence of God and prayed a prayer which can be outlined as follows:

1. Thanksgiving for God's favor on him *now* (vv. 18-21)
2. Praise for God's work for Israel in the *past* (vv. 22-24)
3. Prayer for God's fulfillment of this promise in the *future* (vv. 25-29).

The highlight of the prayer came in 2 Samuel 7:19, after David had protested in verse 18 that he was personally unworthy of so singularly great an honor. In effect he asked, "What is so unique about me? And what is so special about my family?" The answer he expected was "Nothing!" He obviously felt that the blessing of God was incomparably greater than anything he deserved. Then he added in verse 19*a* his further amazement: "And as if this [present blessing on me and my family] were not enough in Your estimation, Lord God, You have also extended the promise concerning Your servant's dynasty far into the future."

Immediately in verse 19*b* came the words: "And this is the law for men" (*weᶻō't tôrat hā'ăḏām*). What type of sentence did these words form? Was it an interrogative sentence or an exclamation? Given the context and the parallel forms of *weᶻō't tôrat* plus a genitive in the OT,[17] it must be an ejaculatory type of sentence. Nothing else would fit the sequence as it joined with verses 20ff.

What then was the "this"? The antecedent will have to be the *substance* of the oracle and not the manner or way in which these great words came to David. The point was not that David was questioning, "Is this Your usual manner or custom in addressing men like myself?" Such an interpretation would make two mistakes: (1) it would prefer to view the words as a question; and more seriously, (2) it would insist on translating the word "law" (*tôrâh*) with such entirely anomalous meanings as "custom," "manner," or "estate" as does the Authorized Version, the New American Standard Bible, and the New English Bible. However, these English words translate such Hebrew words as *ḥōq*, *mišpāṭ*, and *gôrāl*.

As Willis J. Beecher concluded:

"This" ought logically to mean, from the context, the revelation spoken of in the passage concerning "the seed" of Abraham,

---

[17]See our article, "Blessing of David," p. 311.

Israel, and David, who is to exist and reign forever, Jehovah's son, Jehovah's king, Jehovah's channel of Blessing to all nations.[18]

C. F. D. Erdmann likewise urged that:

> It must be the *content* of the Lord's words about the future of his house that moves him, . . . not the fact *that* the Lord condescends to him . . . but *what* He has now *spoken* to him. . . . This is the divine *torah* or prescription . . . for poor human creatures.[19]

How then should *tôrâh* be understood? Usually *tôrâh* is "teaching"; it comes from the verbal root *yārâh*, "to direct," "teach," "instruct." Out of 220 OT examples of this noun, only in 17 cases is anything other than the law of God indicated.[20]

The "law of the man" cannot be translated "the law of *Adam*" since no reference to Adam or to a covenant being made with him appears elsewhere in the Davidic era. Nor can it be rendered "the law of *the Man*," i.e., the Lord God, since such a usage would be unknown up to this era. None of these translations will do.

Since the "this" of 2 Samuel 7:19*b* refers to *content* of the promise traced so patiently in the words of Nathan, and since that promise was knowingly extended to "all the nations of the earth" as early as in the patriarchal revelations, we conclude that the best translation is "This is the charter for humanity."

It is possible that Henri Cazelles[21] put his finger on the exact cognate expression to David's "Charter for Humanity" when in 1958 he pointed to the Akkadian term, *tērit niše*. As he translated the Akkadian phrase, it was an oracle: *"qui fixe le destin des hommes,"* or "the decree concerning humanity in general."

Precisely so in our passage! With the realization that he had just been granted an everlasting dynasty, dominion, and kingdom, David blurted out in uncontainable joy: "And this is the Charter for all mankind, O Lord God!"[22] Thus the ancient plan of God would continue, only now it would involve a king and a kingdom. Such a blessing would also involve the future of all mankind.

---

[18]Willis J. Beecher, "Three Notes," *Journal of Biblical Literature* 8(1887): 138.

[19]C. F. D. Erdmann, *The Books of Samuel* in J. P. Lange, *A Commentary on the Holy Scriptures*, 12 vols. (New York: Scribner, Armstrong & Co., 1877), III: 434.

[20]See our article, "Blessing of David," p. 313, nn. 48,49 for documentation.

[21]Henri Cazelles, "Review of Roland deVaux's *Les Institutiones de L'ancien Testament*," *Vetus Testamentum* 8(1958): 322; idem, "Shiloh, the Customary Laws and the Return of the Ancient Kings," *Proclamation and Presence*, John T. Durham and J. R. Porter, eds. (Richmond: John Knox Press, 1970), p. 250.

[22]For a treatment of the parallel 1 Chronicles 17:17, which has three dissimilarities, see W. C. Kaiser, Jr., "Blessing of David," pp. 315-16.

A PROMISED KINGDOM

Six times David's kingdom had been declared eternal (2 Sam. 7:13,16,24,25,26,29). But was this gift to David "a blank check of unlimited validity"?[23] M. Tsevat, along with a host of other commentators, cannot accept this stress of irrevocability or unconditionality as part of the original passage. Rather, they would prefer to treat as normative the theme of conditionality which stressed the "if" clause and the necessity of loyalty and fidelity as found in 2 Samuel 7:14-15; 1 Kings 2:4; 8:25; 9:4-5; Psalms 89:31-38[30-37]; 132:11-12.

Yet David himself reflected on this same promise in 2 Samuel 23:5 and called it an "everlasting covenant" *(berît 'ôlām)*. His exact words were: "Certainly my dynasty is established by God, for He has made with me an everlasting covenant, arranged in every detail[24] and guaranteed." The same thought is repeated in the royal psalm by David (21:6-7[7-8]) where he rejoiced that God had "made him most blessed forever" and that the "covenantal love of the Most High [to David] would not be moved."

Psalm 89:28-37 [29-38] also commented on the immutability of this eternal covenant. It would endure "forever" (28, 29, 36, 37, Eng.): "As the days of heaven" (29), "as the sun" (36) and "moon" (37). God "will not violate, nor alter the word that is gone out of [His] lips" (34); He has "sworn by [His] holiness; [He] will not lie to David" (35)!

Nevertheless, the argument for conditionality still rages. Could not this covenant be broken *(pārar)*? Indeed, even though the Abrahamic covenant was also "everlasting" (Gen. 17:7,13,19), yet "the uncircumcised man . . . has broken [it]" (v. 14). Even the later "everlasting covenant" would be broken by the inhabitants of the earth (Isa. 24:5), and an adulterous Israel despised "the oath of God" (the covenant) "to the extent of breaking *(lehāpēr)* the everlasting covenant" (Ezek. 16:59,63).[25]

The solution to these apparent breakings, frustrations, invalidations of the covenant was the same as it was for the "if" clauses which concerned Tsevat and others: "If your children will keep My covenant and My testimony that I shall teach them, their children

---

[23]Matitiahu Tsevat, "The Steadfast House: What was David Promised in 2 Samuel 7:11*b*-16?" *Hebrew Union College Annual* 34(1963): 73.

[24]Ibid., p. 74 for this translation of "every detail."

[25]For a review of the evidence and a contrary opinion, see Marten H. Woudstra, "The Everlasting Covenant in Ezekiel 16:59-63." *Calvin Theological Journal* 6(1971): 27-28,31-33.

shall also sit on your throne forevermore" (Ps. 132:12; cf. 2 Sam. 7:14*b*-15; 1 Kings 2:4; 8:25; 9:4-5; Ps. 89:30-33[Eng.]). The "breaking" or conditionality can only refer to *personal* and *individual* invalidation of the benefits of the covenant, but it cannot affect the transmission of," the promise to the lineal descendants. That is why God would staunchly affirm His fidelity and the perpetuity of the covenant to David in spite of succeeding rascals who would appear in his lineage. For in that case, He "finds fault with them" but not with His Abrahamic-Davidic-New covenant (cf. Jer. 31:32; Heb. 8:8).

This same state of affairs shows up from the new research on the promissory land grant treaties of the Hittites and neo-Assyrians. M. Weinfeld,[26] by linking the "royal grants" made to Abraham and David with the grants of "land" and "house" (dynasty) in Hittite-Syro-Palestinian politics, has demonstrated that the unconditional gift was also explicitly protected against any subsequent sins made by the recipients' descendants. In these treaties the grant of "land" or dynasty may be delayed or individually forfeited; however, it must still be passed on to the next in line instead of being granted to someone outside the specified family. So it was in David's situation: rascals there may be, but the blessing would never be revoked from the family; thus it was an "everlasting covenant."[27]

The Ark and the Kingdom

Nothing was more intimately connected with the presence and power of Yahweh than the ark of the covenant. This could be seen especially in the "history of the ark" in 1 Samuel 4:1-7:2. But 2 Samuel 6 also stressed its importance for the kingdom David was about to receive which is detailed in the next chapter. The introduction of the ark to Jerusalem, a politically neutral enclave near the border separating Judah and the northern tribes, was important to establishing the extent of the kingdom over all Israel.

Such a connection between David, the kingdom, and what most were pleased to call the cult was not an argument for sacral king-

---

[26]Weinfeld, "Covenant of Grant" pp. 189-96. Note his brilliant observations even on the alleged conditionality of the Mosaic covenant, p. 195.

[27]More recently H. Neil Richardson, "The Last Words of David: Some Notes on II Samuel 23:1-7," *Journal of Biblical Literature* 90(1971): 259,263, following F. M. Cross, Jr. (although both "with some hesitation"), he finds an epithet for El here in 2 Samuel 23. He translates it: "His covenant the Eternal has given me." But this is a most unlikely suggestion in light of the awkwardness of the expression and the absence of the divine name El as in Genesis 21:33.

ship.[28] This can best be seen by first tracing the development of the narrative about the ark.

Exodus 25:10-22 recorded the proposal for building the ark, and Exodus 37:1-9 narrated its actual construction by Bezaleel. During the wilderness wanderings, the ark of the covenant of the Lord went before Israel three day's journey to seek out resting places for the people (Num. 10:33-34). So important was this "box" (*'arôn*; cf. Joseph's "coffin" in Gen. 50:26 and Jehoiada's "chest" for contributions in 2 Kings 12:9ff. [10ff.] and 2 Chron. 24:8ff.) that the "Song of the Ark" equated its presence with Yahweh's presence:

> Whenever the ark set out, Moses said, "Arise, O Yahweh, and let thine enemies be scattered; and let those who hate You flee before You." And when it rested he said, "Return, O Yahweh, to the ten thousand thousands of Israel."
>
> —Numbers 10:35-36

On the other hand, when Israel presumed to launch an attack on her own without "the ark of the covenant of the Lord" being with her, she was soundly defeated (Num. 14:44). But when it accompanied Israel's march across the Jordan (Josh. 3-4) and around Jericho (Josh. 6), the nation was usually successful. Only Israel's own sinfulness could frustrate its effectiveness.

When the ark was removed from Shiloh and lost to the Philistines (1 Sam. 4-5), the only conclusion could be Ichabod—the glory of God had departed. But its presence was too powerful for the Philistines; so they transported it back to Beth Shemesh without any further judgment (1 Sam. 6), after a plague had visited every Philistine city where the ark had been placed in the interim. But Uzzah was rebuked when he impulsively lunged to catch the tottering ark as David began to bring the ark to Jerusalem (2 Sam. 6). In this case, these men were aware of the prescribed method of treating the holiness of God. Thereby they stood under greater condemnation than the Philistines who had touched the ark and had used a cart to transport it in their ignorance (1 Sam. 6).

The apex of the ark narratives is 2 Samuel 6 and Psalm 132 where its function and significance are closely connected with the presence of Yahweh, for in von Rad's words, "Wherever the Ark is, Jahweh is always present."[29] But in what sense was the presence of

---

[28]For a refutation of sacral kingship see Arthur E. Cundall, "Sacral Kingship—the Old Testament Background," *Vox Evangelica* 6(1969): 31-41.

[29]Gerhard von Rad, *Old Testament Theology*, 2 vols. (London: Oliver and Boyd, 1962), 1:237.

God intended? Was the ark (1) a witness to that presence, (2) a guarantee of Yahweh's presence, (3) a pledge or earnest of His presence, (4) a domicile of the Deity, (5) identical with Yahweh, or (6) an extension and representation of His presence?[30] Basically, it was a *pledge* of His presence, for that presence was not automatic nor mechanical. It was so only where this presence was "grasped believingly"[31] as Israel found out quickly in 1 Samuel 4:1-7:2. Nor was this mere thing-holiness. The Lord was not content with either mere "thingliness" nor inwardness. Both aspects were important: the internal and external.

Yahweh's enthronement was also associated with the ark and the place of atonement (*kappōret*). His very name was "Yahweh of Hosts who sits enthroned on the cherubim" (2 Sam. 6:2; cf. 1 Sam. 4:4; 2 Kings 19:15; 1 Chron. 13:6). Woudstra concludes that this name when used of the ark points to God's "omnipotence, majesty and glory."[32] It spoke at once of the nature of His condescension, the character of His indwelling, and the reality of His person.

Therefore, when David brought the ark into a tent-shrine in 2 Samuel 6:17, until he could build the temple, he moved to establish the kingdom given to him by God. The two topics, viz., the ark and the Davidic kingdom, are the subjects of Psalm 132, which celebrates the "oath" sworn to David and the signal shout or song of the ark. "Arise, O Yahweh, and go to thy resting place ... for your servant David's sake" (132:8-10).

The Royal Psalms[33] and the Kingdom

The royal psalms are steeped in the ideology of the Davidic dynasty and presuppose the promise and oath made to him. They formed a unity centering on the Davidic king who, as Yahweh's son, resided in Zion, the chosen city, ruled over Yahweh's people, and was heir to the promise.

---

[30]For documentation see, Henton Davis, "The Ark of the Covenant," *Annual of the Swedish Institute* 5(1966-67): 43-47. Also see R. E. Clements, *God and the Temple*, Philadelphia: Fortress Press, 1965), pp. 28-39 and Marten H. Woudstra, *The Ark of the Covenant From Conquest to Kingship* (Philadelphia: Presbyterian and Reformed Publishing House, 1965), pp. 13-57.

[31]The phrase is Woudstra's, ibid., p. 46.

[32]Ibid., p. 77.

[33]The earliest discussion of "Die Königspsalmen" appeared in 1914 by Hermann Gunkel. In 1933 Gunkel and Begrich published the most comprehensive study, *Einleitung in die Psalmen*, ed. J. Begrich (Gottingen: Vandenhoeck & Ruprecht, 1933), pp. 140-71. See now Keith R. Crim, *The Royal Psalms* (Richmond: John Knox Press, 1962).

Psalm 2 contrasted the hostility of the nations directed at the Lord *and* His Messiah over against God's answer to them in the form of the royal investiture of His son, the Davidic king.

> Yet have I established My king
> > on Zion My holy mountain.
> I will make announcement concerning Yahweh's decree:
> > He spake to me,
> > 'You are My son! Today I have begotten you.
> Ask of me, and I will give peoples to be your inheritance
> And the ends of the earth for your possession.'
> > > —Psalm 2:6-8

Thus, as God's son, he claimed rule over the world. It was not the eternal continuance of David's *house* that was in view here but the triumphant conclusion to the divinely established filial relationship of the *person* of the Davidite to God. This personal kingship was explained by von Orelli[34] as follows:

> In these words [v.7] He has acknowledged him as belonging most intimately to Himself, investing Him even with personal kingship to God. The 'I have begotten thee' suggests still more strongly than the simple 'My son art thou,' that the Messianic king has received a higher life from above. The conferring of this dignity was bound in the speaker's case to a definite point of time. The 'to-day' was his Messianic birthday, whether on this day he first entered outwardly on his office, or its inner greatness was then revealed to him by prophet's message or personal inspiration.

Centuries later Paul would mark that "to-day" in the life of the Messiah as the day of the resurrection (Acts 13:30-33). That was the day when He was "marked out" to be the Son of God with power (Rom. 1:3-4).

In a beautiful combination of the Sinaitic theophany (vv. 7-15) and an invincible King David (vv. 31-46), Psalm 18 and its verbal parallel in 2 Samuel 22 picture the victory and triumph of David. As a result, God's name was lauded in front of the nations, and the covenant was kept forever (Ps. 18:47-50).

Psalms 20 and 21 appear to be paired as petition (20:4) and answer (21:2). The prayer for victory of Psalm 20 was answered with joy and thanksgiving in the numerous blessings in Psalm 21. The enemy was so soundly defeated that the scale of events outstripped the power of any king and called once more for the Messiah (Ps. 21:9b-12).

---

[34]C. von Orelli, *The Old Testament Prophecy of the Consummation of God's Kingdom Traced in Its Historical Development*, trans. J. J. Banks (Edinburgh: T. & T. Clark, 1889), p. 161.

The Davidite was addressed as "Elohim" in Psalm 45:6. The judges of Israel represented God and also were called "Elohim" in that the solemnity of coming before a judge was comparable to coming before God (Exod. 21:6, 22:8,9,28; cf. Ps. 82:1,6). Yet Psalm 45:6 claimed even more than Exodus did for the judges:

> Thy throne, O God, endures for ever and ever;
>   a scepter of equity is the scepter of Your rule.

Thus not only was the office of the king identified with Deity, but the very person of the king and his dynasty would rule like God forever! (Note vv. 2,16-17.) Just as the Davidite was addressed in Psalm 89:26-27 as God's "son," His "firstborn" and "the Highest" (*'elyôn,* "Most High" when applied to God), so his throne by metonymy was now called Elohim in Psalm 45. Thus what God stood for in heaven, David was appointed to be as a symbol and pledge of God's kingdom on earth. Human language appeared to be on the brink of bursting all boundaries as it described this unique filial relationship of a man and God.

The Hebrew text refuses to be softened as most contemporary translations insist on doing (e.g., the RV, RSV, NEB, but not JB or NASB). Neither did the NT writers miss the impact of this verse in Hebrews 1:8-9.[35] The mystery of the passage is that the "God" whom the psalmist addressed is Himself appointed by God!

Psalm 72 emphasizes the righteousness, blessing, endlessness, and world-wide extent of the Davidic kingdom.[36] Prompted by the words of 2 Samuel 23:1-7, Psalm 72:6-7 pictured the righteous king as sun and rain to his subjects. While they flourished, so did the boundlessness of the realm. The concluding royal blessing of verses 16-17 brings to mind the theology of Genesis and the blessings of Moses in Leviticus 26 and Deuteronomy 28.

The most detailed commentary on 2 Samuel 7 was to be found in another royal psalm, Psalm 89. After commenting at length on the Davidic covenant in verses 3-4, 19-37; verses 38-51 lamented the downfall of the monarchy and pleaded that God would continue to be faithful to His promise to David. Likewise, Psalm 101, another royal psalm, prayed for guidance for God's chosen ruler.

One of the most-quoted psalms in the NT, however, is the royal psalm, Psalm 110. Here, the psalmist combined priesthood and roy-

---

[35]See the fine classic, Oswald T. Allis, "Thy Throne, O God, Is For Ever and Ever," *Princeton Theological Review* 21(1923): 236-66.

[36]See Roland E. Murphy, "A Study of Psalm 72(71)" (Ph.D. diss., Catholic University of America, 1948.)

alty in the Messiah. For just as the whole nation had been constituted a kingdom of priests, a holy nation, so now the Davidic monarch was made a priest-king after one named Melchizedek, whose history and life paralleled the older man of promise, Abraham. The conquering scepter in the hands of the new Davidite to come would resume the Balaamic prediction, viz., his conquering rule would dash in pieces all his enemies.

As David, no doubt, paused one day to reflect on the great victory God had given to that older man of promise, Abraham, when he took on four Mesopotamian kings (Gen. 14) and won, stopping only to pay tithes to the priest of Salem (Jerusalem?) on the way home, he too felt refreshed (Ps. 110:7), as if he had drunk deeply from a cool brook. That same promise was his; and thus the outcome of his battles, kingdom, and dynasty were as much a foregone conclusion as they had been for Abraham.

Psalm 132 combined the bringing of the ark into Jerusalem with the oath sworn to David about his dynasty. Second Chronicles 6:41-42, which quotes verses 8-10, shows that this psalm was in use in Solomon's time at the dedication of his temple and that the ark had ended its long journey. Now the kingdom was indeed established by God, for the temple was complete and the earnest of God's presence was in Solomon's temple.

The last royal psalm is Psalm 144, which is substantially like Psalm 18. Having recalled God's pattern of deliverance, David sang a "new song" in the new age to come (Pss. 96:1; 98:1; 149:1; cf. Rev. 5:9; 14:3).

Whether these psalms depict, as H. J. Krause thought, a royal festival in Zion with a procession representing the entry of Yahweh into Jerusalem to commemorate the transfer of the ark is doubtful. Likewise, the same could be said of the Uppsala school and Sigmund Mowinckel with their "enthronement psalms" which are mistranslated to read "Yahweh has *become* king" (Pss. 47, 93, 96-99) rather than the correct rendering "Yahweh reigns." Nevertheless, nothing substantial in these views affects the theology of these psalms.

More significant is the fact that what happened to the king happened to the people. Their lives were totally bound up with his. When he acted in faithfulness and righteousness, prosperity and blessing were the result (Pss. 18; 45:6-7; 101). But when the king was rejected, so were they. The king, then, became the channel of God's blessings and judgments. So it would be with the last David or the new David; only His realm would be boundless and His reign would be righteous, just, and full of every perfection.

The Succession Narrative and the Kingdom

As already indicated earlier in this chapter, Leonhard Rost convinced most scholars that 2 Samuel 9-20 and 1 Kings 1-2 form a "court history" in which the first two chapters of 1 Kings proved the key for the whole work. It was held that Solomon succeeded David rather than his older brothers Amnon, Absalom, and Adonijah because, unlike his brothers, he did not imitate David's sin with Bathsheba.[37]

Such a narrow purpose for the inclusion of this section into Israel's oracles of God (i.e., the justification of Solomon's reign) was faulted by Jackson[38] since 1 Kings 3-11 went on to detail so much failure in the life of Solomon. (Could the "final editor" [?] be so sloppy and naïve?) And while the text in its internal design does bring out a "delineation of character," to use Jackson's fine phrase, there is more here than a mere moralizing on the character of David's family.

It is "theological historiography," as von Rad puts it, and the initial "operation of the Nathan prophecy."[39] Even though the anointed one became ensnared in his own lusts, humiliated by revolts from his own lusts, embarrassed by revolts from his own family, and cursed by others, God's guarantee still held. It was not so much "how David maintained legitimate control over the kingdoms of Judah and Israel," as Flanagan argued with some interesting bracketing of the narratives,[40] but how Yahweh controlled human destiny for His own purpose. True, there were only three explicit statements of Yahweh's intervention:

> But the thing which David had done displeased Yahweh.
> — 2 Samuel 11:27

> She had bore him a son, and he called his name Solomon, and Yahweh loved him. — 2 Samuel 12:24

> For Yahweh had ordained to defeat the good counsel of Ahithophel so that Yahweh might bring evil on Absalom. (This is possibly the pivot verse of the whole document.)
> — 2 Samuel 17:14

---

[37]For some of the more important contributions to a huge bibliography, see Jared J. Jackson, "David's Throne: Patterns in the Succession Story," *Canadian Journal of Theology* 11 (1965): 183-95; R. N. Whybray, *The Succession Narrative* (Naperville: Allenson, Inc., 1968); James W. Flanagan, "Court History or Succession Document?" *Journal of Biblical Literature* 91(1972): 172-81.

[38]Jackson, ibid., p. 185.

[39]Von Rad, *Theology*, 1:316.

[40]J. W. Flanagan, "Court History," p. 173.

But as Ronald Hals had demonstrated for the book of Ruth, [41] so here the theology of God's intervention was often more implicitly real than explicit. And it all revolved around God's plan for the throne and kingdom of David. In the midst of human tragedy and failure, relentlessly, God's purpose and promise still went onward.

---

[41]Ronald Hals, *Theology of the Book of Ruth* (Philadelphia: Fortress Press, 1969), pp. 3-19.

Chapter 10

Life in the Promise:
Sapiential Era

Jewish and Protestant scholars usually regard only Job, Proverbs, Ecclesiastes, and Song of Solomon as wisdom books while Catholic scholarship adds the extracanonical books of Ecclesiasticus (Ben Sirach) and the Wisdom of Solomon. Both groups also add to these four (or six) books a number of psalms.

The criteria for distinguishing wisdom psalms may be divided into two categories: formal (literary style) and thematic (content). Using the studies of Roland E. Murphy,[1] Sigmund Mowinckel,[2] and R. B. Y. Scott,[3] the following distinct style of wisdom psalms may be assembled: (1) alphabetic structure such as acrostic psalms; (2) numerical sayings, e.g., "three yea four"; (3) "blessed" sayings (*'ašrê*); (4) "better" sayings; (5) comparisons, admonitions; (6) the address of

---

[1]Roland E. Murphy, "Psalms," *Jerome Biblical Commentary*, 1 vol., Raymond E. Brown, Joseph A. Fitzmyer, and Roland E. Murphy, eds. (Englewood Cliffs: Prentice-Hall, 1968), p. 574; idem, "The Classification of Wisdom Psalms," *Vetus Testamentum Supplement* 9(1963): 156-67.

[2]Sigmund Mowinckel, "Psalms and Wisdom," *Vetus Testamentum Supplement* 3(1955): 204-24.

[3]R. B. Y. Scott, *The Way of Wisdom* (New York: Macmillan Co., 1971), pp. 193-201.

father to son; (7) the use of wisdom vocabulary and turns of phrases; and (8) the employment of proverbs, similies, rhetorical questions, and words like "listen to me." Examples of wisdom themes are: (1) the problem of retribution; (2) the division between the righteous and the wicked; (3) exhortations to trust personally in the Lord; (4) the fear of the Lord; and (5) the meditation on the written law of God as a source of delight.

Using both the formal and thematic criteria, the following psalms easily may be classified as wisdom psalms: 1, 37, 49, and 112. To these may be added 32, 34, 111, 127, 128, and 133. If meditation on the law of God is also utilized, Psalms 119 and 19:7-14 also may be included. Perhaps Psalm 78 with its invitation to "give ear, my people, to my teaching" and its proverbial *(māšāl)* and riddle *(ḥîdôt)* forms (v. 2) also qualify it to be classed with the wisdom psalms. Thus we conclude that Psalms 1, 19*b*, 32, 34, 37, 49, 78, 111, 112, 119, 127, 128, and 133 belong in the wisdom category along with the four wisdom books.

In the past forty years, most of the research in wisdom literature has dealt with the relationship of Israel's sapiential writings to those of her Egyptian and Mesopotamian neighbors. However, another welcome development has come about. Some have undertaken the task of discovering the connections between wisdom and Creation,[4] between wisdom and Deuteronomy,[5] and between wisdom and the prophets.[6]

Wisdom literature was indeed the recipient of theological legacies from Mosaic times and the prophetic history of the earlier prophets. The best case made for a clear connection between these eras (albeit in a reversed order of dependence for which we are arguing here) was Moshe Weinfeld's study of "The Wisdom Substrata in Deuteronomy and Deuteronomic Literature."[7]

---

[4]Walther Zimmerli, "The Place and Limit of Wisdom in the Framework of the Old Testament Theology," *Scottish Journal of Theology* 17(1964): 146-58.

[5]Moshe Weinfeld, "Wisdom Substrata in Deuteronomy and Deuteronomic Literature," *Deuteronomy and the Deuteronomic School* (Oxford: Clarendon Press, 1972), pp. 244-74; see also Erhard Gerstenberger, "Covenant and Commandment," *Journal of Biblical Literature* 84(1965): 38-51, esp. 48-51.

[6]William McKane, *Prophets and Wise Men* (London: SCM, 1965); also see our chapter 4 for a further discussion of some of these issues.

[7]Weinfeld, "Wisdom Substrata," pp. 244-45. In our order, Deuteronomy is clearly a second millennium document exhibiting the same outline in its entirety as did the literary *gattung* of Hittite vassal treaties. Cf. M. Kline, *Treaty of the Great King* (Grand Rapids: Eerdmans, 1962); Kenneth Kitchen, *Ancient Orient and Old Testament* (Downers Grove: InterVarsity Press, 1964); R. K. Harrison, *Introduction*

For Weinfeld, the presence of leaders and magistrates who were "capable men who fear God, trustworthy men who spurn ill-gotten gain" (Exod. 18:21), "wise men of understanding and full of knowledge" (Deut. 1:13-17; cf. Num. 11:11-30) corresponded well with the qualities demanded of leaders in wisdom literature. Thus, in Proverbs 8:15-16 it was by wisdom that "kings reign and rulers decree what is just . . . princes rule and nobles govern." Weinfeld noted that even the phraseology found in the appointment of the judges in Deuteronomy 1:9-18; 16:18-20, viz., "to respect persons in judgment," is seen again only in Proverbs 24:23; 28:21.

Some of the principal parallels Weinfeld listed for Deuteronomy and wisdom were:

1. "You shall not add to the word which I command, nor take from it" (Deut. 4:2; cf. 12:32 [13:1]).
   "All the word of God proves true . . . Do not add to His words" (Prov. 30:5-6).
2. "You shall not move your neighbor's landmarks" (Deut. 19:14; cf. 27:17).
   "Move not the ancient landmark set up by your fathers" (Prov. 22:28; cf. 23:10).
3. "You shall not have in your bag alternate weights (*'eben wā'āben*) . . . alternate measures (*'êpâh we'êpâh*) . . . [but] a full and just weight (*'eben še lēmâh*) you shall have. For all who . . . act dishonestly are an abomination to the Lord[8] your God" (Deut. 25:13-16).
   "Alternate weights (*'eben wā'āben*) are an abomination to the Lord" (Prov. 20:10,23); "but a just weight (*'eben šelēmâh*) is His delight" (Prov. 11:1).
4. "When you make a vow to the Lord your God, you shall not be slack to pay it" (Deut. 23:22-24).
   "Do not be rash with your mouth . . . when you make a vow to God . . . Pay what you vow" (Eccl. 5:1-5).
5. "You shall not be partial in judgment" (Deut. 1:17; cf. 16:19).
   "Partiality in judging is not good" (Prov. 24:23; cf. 28:21).
6. "Justice and only justice you shall pursue that you may live" (Deut. 16:20).

---

to the Old Testament (Grand Rapids: Eerdmans, 1969). Other scholars who believed that Deuteronomy influenced biblical wisdom are given by Weinfeld, "Wisdom Substrata," p. 260, n. 4. He names among others, A. Robert, *"Les attaches littéraires bibliques de Prov. i-ix," Revue Biblique* 43(1934): 42-68,172-204,374-84; 44(1935): 344-65,502-25. O. E. Oesterley, *Wisdom of Egypt and the Old Testament* (London: Society for Promoting Christian Knowledge, 1927), p. 76f.

[8]The expression "abomination to the Lord" appears, according to Weinfeld, "Wisdom Substrata," p. 268, four times in *Teaching of Amenemope* (14, 2-3; 13. 15-16; 15. 20-21; 18. 21-19. 1. In Deuteronomy it appears at 7:25-26; 12:31; 17:1; 18:9-12; 22:5; 23:18; 24:4; 25:13-16; 27:15 and in Proverbs at 3:32; 11:1,20; 12:22; 15:8-9,26; 16:5; 17:15; 20:10,23.

"He who pursues justice will find life" (Prov. 21:21; cf. 10:2; 11:4,19; 12:28; 16:31).

These, of course, are only the beginning. But they do illustrate the point that wisdom was not cut off conceptually or theologically from materials which we have judged to be earlier than sapiential times. Wisdom's influence also extended beyond its day into the era of the prophets. This development has been traced in part already in chapter 4.

Regardless of how far or, for that matter, in what direction that influence spread, the key question is: What theological rubric or special term brought promise and law together with wisdom? We believe that concept was "the fear of God/Lord."

THE FEAR OF THE LORD

The fear of the Lord more than any other phrase linked together the patriarchal promise with law and wisdom. Hans Walter Wolff argued the same point,[9] at least for part of that revelation based on his view of the sources, when he observed:

> God's normative word from Mount Sinai to all Israel is directed towards the same goal that He had set for the patriarchs: fear of God, which produced obedience through trust in God's promise (Gen. 22).

Wolff goes on to trace through some of the patriarchal and Mosaic materials what he regarded as one of the dominant themes—the fear of God. It appeared in the patriarchal era as the response of Abraham's believing faith in Genesis 22:12 when he willingly offered his son Isaac to God; in Joseph's believing response (Gen. 42:18); and especially as the divinely approved quality of life evidenced in Job (1:1,8-9; 2:3).

In the Mosaic era, the visibility of the fear of God increased. The midwives were among those who feared God (Exod. 1:17). Accordingly, "the people multiplied and grew very strong" (v. 20), and the families of the midwives prospered—and again the text underscored the reason—"because they feared God" (v. 21). So did Israel fear God at the Exodus (Exod. 14:31); in fact, if that fear would remain ever before them, they would not sin (20:20). Since the Lord was Israel's God, she should always fear Him (Lev. 19:14,32; 25:17, 36,43) and thus live.

---

[9]Hans Walter Wolff, *The Vitality of Old Testament Traditions*, Walter Brueggemann and Hans W. Wolff, eds. (Atlanta: John Knox Press, 1975), p. 75.

But it was the book of Deuteronomy that had made the fear of the Lord a focal point of concern (4:10; 5:26; 6:2,13,24; 8:6; 10:12,20; 13:4; 14:23; 17:19; 28:58; 31:12-13). This fear was not a worked-up feeling of some numinous awe, but it was the result of hearing, learning, and responding to God's Word (4:10; 8:6). In Deuteronomy, the fear of the Lord went hand in hand with "keeping His commands," "walking after Him," "serving Him," "loving Him," and "cleaving to Him" (cf. esp. 10:12-13; 13:5). Thus to fear Him was to love Him, cleave to Him, and to serve Him (10:20; 13:4-5).

To fear Yahweh was to commit oneself to Yahweh in faith as did *some* of the Egyptians (Exod. 9:20,30; cf. the "mixed multitude" that left Egypt with Israel in 12:38). Had not Solomon also prayed for "all the peoples of the earth" who would come to "know [His] name and fear [Him]" in 1 Kings 8:43?

However, one also had to learn how to fear Yahweh (Deut. 4:10; 14:23; 17:19; 31:12-13; Ps. 34:11[12]). This fear was a guiding principle for every aspect of life and for "as long as one lives on the earth" (Deut. 4:10; 5:26; 14:23; 31:13; Prov. 23:17).[10] It included the believer's obedience, love, loyalty, and worship as R. N. Whybray concluded.[11] Thus Obadiah remarked to Elijah, "I, your servant, fear Yahweh from my youth" (1 Kings 18:12).

When we come to wisdom books and wisdom psalms, the fear of the Lord has become the essence of the knowledge and wisdom of God. Even though this phrase occurred just over two dozen times apart from the suffixial forms such as "thy fear" or the verbal statements, its locations are all extremely strategic and often served the whole purpose for writing some of these books. In Proverbs 1:7 it functioned as the motto for the whole book, while in Ecclesiastes 12:13-14 it functioned as the total summation of the argument of the whole book (cf. also Eccl. 7:18; 8:12). Likewise in Job 28:28 it dramatically climaxed the whole poem on wisdom, which in itself was located at the eye of the whole stormy debate. Rather than viewing Job 28 as an inserted interruption in the flow of the argument between Job and his friends, it was rather the writer's attempt to give his readers a revelatory perspective in the midst of so much talk which was devoid of divine wisdom. Thus in three of the four

---

[10]See Weinfeld's discussion of "the Fear of God," "Wisdom Substrata," pp. 274-81; Gerhard von Rad, *Wisdom in Israel* (Nashville: Abingdon, 1972), pp. 65-73; Bernard J. Bamberger, "Fear and Love of God in the Old Testament," *Hebrew Union College Annual* 6(1929): 39-53.

[11]R. N. Whybray, *Wisdom in Proverbs* (London: SCM, 1965), pp. 96-97.

wisdom books, the fear of God/Lord was critically important to their understanding.

In addition to its appearance as the motto for the book of Proverbs, the "fear of the Lord" occurs thirteen more times in that book: 1:29; 2:5; 8:13; 9:10; 10:27; 14:26-27; 15:16,33; 16:6; 19:23; 22:4; and 23:17. In addition to this, one should also consider the verbal forms in 3:7; 14:2; 24:21; and 31:30.

Such a fear was the "beginning" (*rē'šît*, Prov. 1:7) of knowledge, the "first principle" (*tᵉhillâh*, 9:10) of wisdom. When men were rightly related to God, then they were in a proper relationship to understand objects and the world itself.

When men feared the Lord, they also avoided evil (Ps. 34:11,14; Job 1:1,8; 2:3; 28:28). Indeed, they hated evil (Prov. 3:7; 16:6) and walked instead in uprightness (14:2) and not in wickedness (16:17). The results of this type of life were an increased life span (10:27), increased wealth and honor (22:4), and security and protection (14:26; 19:23). The connection of blessing and the quality of holy living with the fear of God was not accidental.

Believers who feared God were easily distinguished from their counterparts in the Psalms also. They were the committed and righteous persons in the congregation of the Lord (Pss. 34:7,9 [8,10]; also in nonwisdom psalms like 25:12,14; 33:18; 103:11,13,17; 145:19). He is the man who keeps the law of God and meditates on it day and night (19:7-14; 112:1; 119:33-38,57-64). He praises the name of Yahweh (22:22-23) and God's favor rests on him (33:18; 103:13; 147:11).

Ecclesiastes also joined in to make a similar point: God had so built man that apart from a personal knowledge of the living God, i.e., a fearing of Him, everything else would be vapid (Eccl. 3:14). But it would go well for those who feared God (8:12), and they would come forth victorious having taken hold of true wisdom while rejecting evil (7:18). Even the worship of these men would reflect their God-fearing status (5:1-7). In fact, this was the wholeness and totality of men and women: they would fear God and keep His commandments. That was the whole purpose for writing the book of Ecclesiastes (12:13).

It may be said with confidence, then, that the fear of the Lord was the dominating concept and organizing theological principle in wisdom literature. It was the response of faith to the divine word of promise and blessing just as it had functioned in the days of Abraham and Moses.

Yet there was much more here than just a response of faith, belief, obedience, and worship. It was the entreé into the understanding and enjoyment of created realm.[12] One of God's blessings was His work of creation; this too was part of His work in history! True, it had no direct relation to the redemptive process in Israel, but it was, nonetheless, one of His words and works of blessing—in every sense of the term, a gracious gift to mankind. And the very wisdom by which He had formed the world originally, He offered to men and women as His wisdom. Without that wisdom, humanity was destitute of effective leadership and bankrupt in its appreciation or apprehension of God, man, and things; in fact, life itself became meaningless and devoid of satisfaction and joy. But when the fear of the Lord led the way, then life was a blessing from God.

LIFE IN THE LORD

The connection between the fear of the Lord and life is explicitly affirmed in the following texts from Proverbs:

The fear of the Lord prolongs life,
but the years of the wicked will be short.
—10:27

The fear of the Lord is a fountain of life,
that one may avoid the snares of death.
—14:27

The fear of the Lord leads to life;
and he who has it rests satisfied;
he will not be visited by harm.
—19:23

The reward for humility and fear of the Lord
is riches and honor and life.
—22:4

Just as Leviticus 18:5 had counseled all whose God was the Lord, "Do these things and you shall live," so the wisdom books continued the theme. They point out that: (1) obedience is the "path [or way] to life" (Prov. 2:19; 5:6; 10:17; 15:24); (2) the teaching of the wise and the fear of the Lord are a "fountain of life" (13:14; 14:27); and (3) wisdom, righteousness, and a gentle tongue each are a "tree of life" (3:18; 11:30; 13:12; 15:4).

That had been the message of the law of Moses. Since Israel had received God's grace and redemption, the people were urged to "observe" and "do" all of their new Lord's commands "so that [they] might *live*" (Deut. 8:1). Such *life* was not just a materialistic thing,

---

[12]Zimmerli, "Place and Limit," pp. 146-58.

but it had spiritual roots and goals. Men could not *live* by bread alone but by every word that proceeded out of the mouth of God (v. 3). Thus Israel had set in front of them life and death: they were urged to choose life (30:15,19). This they could do by loving the Lord their God, obeying His voice, and "cleav[ing] to Him, for He [was] their life" (v. 20).

To solve the problem of Sinai's relationship to promise was to solve wisdom's relationship to promise.[13] As Roland E. Murphy observed, these wisdom themes of "the fear of the Lord," "justice," "understanding," and "honesty" would have been identified by the Jews of that era "with the moral ideals expressed in the Law."[14] Thus, putting one's personal trust in the promised one who was to come (as Abraham had done in Gen. 15) was equal to being among those who "feared the Lord." Included within this initial decision to commit oneself to the God who promised an heir (the "Seed"), an inheritance (the "land"), and a heritage ("in your seed all the nations of the earth shall be blessed") was the subsequent life style of obedience to the word and commands of God. The result or fruit of this trust and obedience could be summed up in one word: "life." By definition, then, to fear God was to turn away from evil and to choose the way of life. All pride, arrogance, perverted speech, and devious behavior were to be dropped from the life of the man who feared the Lord (Prov. 3:7; 8:13; 14:2; 16:6; 23:17).

INTEGRATION OF LIFE AND TRUTH IN THE LORD

The greatest case ever made for the unity of all truth, so-called secular and sacred, is to be found in the book of Ecclesiastes. Solomon's whole point was positive, not negative or a mere naturalistic point of view. Six times the theme of the fear of God appeared (3:14; 5:7; 7:18; 8:12 bis,13) before the grand finale to his whole argument

---

[13]See provisionally Walter C. Kaiser, Jr., "The Law of the Lord: Teaching the Paths of Life," *The Old Testament in Contemporary Preaching* (Grand Rapids: Baker Book House, 1973), pp. 49-69,118ff. Coert Rylaarsdam, *Revelation in Jewish Wisdom Literature* (Chicago: University of Chicago, 1946), p. 23, also pointed to the parents' instruction fastened around the neck (Prov. 6:20-22; 7:3) as being similar to the function of the law as a guide in Deuteronomy 6:4-9; similarly, "the upright" will possess the land as an inheritance (Prov. 2:21; 10:30; cf. Deut. 4:21,38; 15:4; 19:10; 21:23; 24:4; 25:19; 26:1). Alfred von Rohr Sauer incorrectly argued that wisdom and law were later joined together in Ezra; "Wisdom and Law in Old Testament Wisdom Literature," *Concordia Theological Monthly* (1972): 607.

[14]Roland E. Murphy, "The Kerygma of the Book of Proverbs," *Interpretation* 20(1966): 12.

climaxed in 12:13: "Let us hear the conclusion of the matter: Fear God, and keep His commandments: for this is the wholeness (*kol hā'āḏām*) of man."

No one has given a more programmatic essay on this book than J. Stafford Wright.[15] In his view, Ecclesiastes 3:11 was one of the key verses:

> [God] has made everything beautiful in its time: also He has set eternity [*hā'ōlām*] in their heart so that no man can find out the work that God does from the beginning to the end.

Man in and of himself, argued Canon Wright, was unable to put the pieces of the puzzle of life together—secular or sacred. Yet he hungered to know how to make it all fit because he had a God-created vacuum as large as eternity, craving satisfaction in that being which had been made in the image of God. The "vanity of vanities" of Ecclesiastes, then, was not that life was a bore, filled with futility, emptiness, or the frustrating conclusion that nothing was worth living for. No! Instead "vanity" [*heḇel*][16] was simply that life *in and of itself* could not supply the key to its own meaning, nor could it truly liberate the person. No part of God's otherwise good universe could provide any all-embracing solution that would integrate truth, learning, and living.

Only when one came to fear God did he begin to perceive the unification of truth, learning, and living (cf. Eccl. 7:14 and 8:14 as well). Life was deliberately sketched in such stark contrasts as life and death, joy and pain, poverty and wealth so that every man might realize that apart from a relationship of a total commitment ("fearing") to such a Lord, nothing would ever make sense—nor could it ever!

The charges of Epicureanism, atheism, and hedonism were met head-on by Otto Zöckler:

> In a time inclined to the abandonment of faith in God's holy and just government of the world, he [the writer of Ecclesiastes] clings to such a faith with a touching constancy, and defends the fact of

---

[15]J. Stafford Wright, "The Interpretation of Ecclesiastes," originally published in *Evangelical Quarterly* (1964) and now through his kind permission it is reproduced in an anthology which the writer of this paper compiled and is now conveniently available in *Classical Evangelical Essays in Old Testament Interpretation* (Grand Rapids: Baker Book House, 1972), pp. 133-50.

[16]Theophile J. Meek contends that "in this short book, *heḇel* would seem to be used in at least five different senses: 'futile' (most frequent, e.g., 1:2); 'empty' (e.g., 6:12); 'sorry' (e.g., 6:4); 'senseless' (e.g., 8:14); and 'transient' (e.g., 11:10)." See his article, "Translating the Hebrew Bible," *Journal of Biblical Literature* 79(1960): 331.

the wise rule of the Eternal and Omnipotent God against all the frivolous scoffs of fools (ii. 26; iii. 20sq., v.1; v. 17-19; viii. 14; ix. 1-3; compare ii. 13; iv. 5; x. 2 sq.; x. 13,14) . . . He is never weary of pointing out the righteous retributions of the future as a motive to the fear of God, the chief and all-comprehending virtue of the wise (iii. 14-17; v. 6; vi. 6,10; viii. 12sq.; x. 9; xii. 13,14) and of commending unwavering constancy in individual callings as the best prudence . . . (compare ii. 10; iii. 22; v. 17,18; viii. 15, etc.).[17]

Once again the connection with the law was obvious: fearing God and keeping His commandments were closely linked together. The counsel given in this book was applied to the more practical situations of life, but its aim was to commend the same standard of righteousness commanded in the law of Moses. Its own contribution to the unfolding expansion of that same core of truth was that the fear of the Lord was both the inception and essence of a truly integrated life. There was no hard divorce between the secular and sacred, faith and knowledge, learning and believing, faith and culture.

Gerhard von Rad also rightly chastised those like William McKane who would apply an evolutionary pattern to wisdom by suggesting that earlier wisdom was at first fundamentally secular and then it was "baptized" and theologized into the Yahwistic religion. Said von Rad with reference to a passage such as Proverbs 16:7-12, where "experiences of the world" alternated with "experiences of Yahweh": "It would be madness to presuppose some kind of separation, as if in one case the man of objective perception were speaking and in the other the believer in Yahweh."[18] Von Rad had yielded somewhat, however. For while noticing the call of wisdom was always a divine call even though it was uttered in a secular world and apart from the sacred, he stressed that this divine call did "not legitimate itself from the saving history, but from creation."[19] Thus he concluded that the wisdom teachers were not at all interested in

> . . . searching for a world order . . . One can in no sense speak of a world order as really existing between God and man . . . The

---

[17]Otto Zöckler, *Proverbs of Solomon* in J. P. Lange, *A Commentary on the Holy Scriptures*, 14 vols. (New York: Scribner, Armstrong & Co., 1877), 10:17.

[18]Gerhard von Rad, *Wisdom in Israel* (Nashville: Abingdon, 1972), p. 62. Cf. William McKane, *Prophets and Wise Men* (Naperville: Allenson, Inc., 1965), p. 47. H. Carl Shank made some of the same criticism of such nature-grace dichotomies as are found in the commentaries of Leupold, Delitzsch, Hengstenberg, or Scofield's notes. See his article, "Qoheleth's World and Life View as Seen in His Recurring Phrases," *Westminster Theological Journal* 37(1974): 57-73, esp. 60-65, where he proposes a faith-sight dichotomy instead.

[19]Gerhard von Rad, *Old Testament Theology*, 2 vols. (Edinburgh: Oliver and Boyd, 1962), 1:452.

teachers move in a dialectic which is fundamentally incapable of resolution, speaking on the one hand of valid rules and, on the other, of ad hoc divine actions.[20]

But this disclaimer rips wisdom away from the rest of the Old Testament and from its own stated objectives. For while it may be conceded that Creation plays a greater role than previously in theology,[21] it must simultaneously acknowledge the biblical writer's interest in integrating all of this.

To introduce the topic of the integration of truth, fact, and understanding is to appeal to the unity of truth made possible by the one God who created a *UNI*-verse. Thus the doctrinal base for any norms of truth and character are grounded ultimately in a doctrine of Creation and the person of the Creator. It must also respectfully be pointed out that wisdom has as much a place in history between God and Israel as does Mount Sinai and the Mosaic covenant. To have seen the place for one is to have found the function of the other. Israel, like all creatures here below, was to fear the one true God, Yahweh. The universal standards were to be those norms prescribed in the law of God (Pss. 19; 119; Eccl. 12:13) and those proverbs on "life," "knowledge," "understanding," and the "fear of God." Consequently, a comprehensive world view and a full enjoyment of life was impossible apart from a recognition of the Creator, the same God who had spoken His commandments. Remember, this same priority of "fearing Yahweh" was exactly what Deuteronomy had required; only there it was a prerequisite to keeping the law and authentic living. Wisdom and law both reflected proper responses of the authentic believer in the promise.

WISDOM FROM THE LORD

Wisdom cannot exist apart from the source of wisdom; accordingly, it cannot be known or applied apart from "the fear of the Lord."

> Wisdom is to be found with God, and nowhere else; and unless the quest for wisdom brings a man to his knees in awe and reverence, knowing his own helplessness to make himself wise, wisdom remains for him a closed book.[22]

---

[20]Von Rad, *Wisdom in Israel*, p. 107.

[21]See Zimmerli, "Place and Limit," p. 146-58. "Wisdom thinks resolutely within the framework of a theology of creation," p. 148.

[22]Lawrence E. Toombs, "Old Testament Theology and the Wisdom Literature," *Journal of Bible and Religion* 23(1952): 195.

At least five passages in Proverbs associate wisdom with the fear of the Lord (1:7,29; 2:5; 8:12-14; 15:33). The fear of the Lord makes a man delight in wisdom and instruction (1:7), receive counsel and reproof (vv. 29-30), and listen to wisdom, understanding, and the knowledge of God (2:1-6).

Undoubtedly, the key teaching passage on wisdom is Proverbs 8. This chapter may be outlined as follows:

A. Wisdom's Excellence (Prov. 8:1-21)
1. In Her Appeal (vv. 1-3)
2. In Her Truth (vv. 4-12)
3. In Her Loves and Hatreds (vv. 13-16)
4. In Her Gifts (vv. 17-21)
B. Wisdom's Origins (Prov. 8:22-31)
1. Her Antemundane Existence (vv. 22-26)
2. Her Active Participation in Creation (vv. 27-31)
C. Wisdom's Blessings (Prov. 8:32-36)
1. Concluding Admonition (vv. 32-33)
2. Promised Blessing (vv. 34-36).

Centrally located in this discussion is verse 13 with its assertion that "the fear of the Lord is to hate evil: pride and arrogance and an evil way and a deceitful mouth do I hate." But McKane could not accept verse 13a as it stood. He repeated in his commentary on Proverbs[23] the argument he had developed in his *Prophets and Wise Men*,[24] viz., that "the fear of Yahweh is not an original ingredient of old wisdom" but rather it was a "prophetic reinterpretation of wisdom" and "imposed" on the ancient sage to give it more of a Yahwistic flavor![25] In support of this attempt to reinterpret the Proverbs

---

[23]William McKane, *Proverbs: A New Approach* (Philadelphia: Westminster Press, 1970), p. 348. He argues that verse 13a "interrupts the smooth transition from v. 12 to v. 14."

[24]McKane, *Prophets*, p. 48f.

[25]Norman Habel, "The Symbolism of Wisdom in Proverbs 1-9," *Interpretation* 26(1972): 144, n. 24; 143-49, incorrectly argued for a similar but internal division between "old [empirical] wisdom materials" and "Yahwistic reinterpretations" as illustrated in Proverbs 2:1-19 where verses 9-11,12-15 illustrate the former and verses 5-8,16-19 the reinterpretive process. But the scheme appears to be thinly supported by exegesis and the pattern imposed and intruded over the text and text sequence without any evidence. It would appear that whereas biblical scholars have argued for decades that the historical position of wisdom literature had to follow the assumed literary development of all other nations—poem, narrative, and wisdom (coming after the prophetic literature and more precisely after Ezekiel because of the predominant factor of elements like personal recompense), now since 1924, with the discovery and publication of the ancient Egyptian wisdom texts, they have

passage, it was asserted that Proverbs 8:12-14 was dependent on Isaiah 11:1f., which spoke of a spirit *(rûaḥ)* of wisdom *(ḥokmâh)* and understanding *(bînâh)*, a *rûaḥ* of counsel *('ēṣâh)* and power *(geͨbûrâh)*. But if Proverbs can be shown to be largely Solomonic[26] and all evolutionary claims proved to be as unfounded as we have argued above, then the wisdom made available to mankind and kings in Proverbs was the same wisdom with accompanying qualities which was to be found in prophetic descriptions of the messianic king who was to come.

According to Proverbs 8:12, wisdom was at home with prudence and easily guided it. Her intellectual power included all carefully thought out plans. She offered counsel, understanding, and the energy to carry out the duties conferred on kings, nobles, princes, and rulers of the earth.

Her temporal priority was stressed by the use of these ten words: The "beginning" of His work, *rē'šît* (Prov. 8:22); the "first" of His works of "old," *qedem ... mē'āz* (v. 22); "from eternity," *mē'ôlām* (v. 23); "at the first," *mēro'š* (v. 23); "from the beginning," *miqqadmê* (v. 23); "when there was not," *beͨ'ên* (v. 24); "before the mountains were formed," *beͨterem* (v. 25); "before" the hills, *lipnê* (v. 25); " or the first" of the dust ... was made, *weͨrō'š* (v. 26). Three more verbs described the way she came into existence: the Lord "created me," *qānānî* (v. 22); "I was born," *nissaktî* (v. 23), or if from *nāsîk* ("prince"), "I was appointed"; and "I was brought forth" *ḥôlāltî* (v. 24).

Since Proverbs 8:22-31 was an expansion of Proverbs 3:19, which stated that "Yahweh founded the earth by wisdom; by understanding He established the heavens," the discussion on the term *'āmôn* in verse 30 need not be so difficult. Without revocalizing the text to *'āmûn* (qal passive participle of *'āman*, "to nurse," hence, "nursling, child"), we may translate it "I was beside Him, the *Master Craftsman*."[27] Wisdom then claimed to have been present at

---

pretty much abandoned that view. Scholars are retreating to a new line of defense which allows for ancient "empirical wisdom sayings" to be placed first in chronological order but which also restricts theological wisdom sayings to much later prophetic-like reinterpretations. Such desperation tactics should be obvious to all who control and work with the ancient Near Eastern data and the wisdom literature of the Bible.

[26]See internal claims and such discussions as R. K. Harrison, *Introduction to the Old Testament* (Grand Rapids: Eerdmans, 1969), pp. 1010-21; Gleason L. Archer, Jr., *A Survey of Old Testament Introduction*, rev. ed. (Chicago: Moody Press, 1974), pp. 465-74.

[27]So argues Mitchell Dahood, "Proverbs 8:22-31: Translation and Commentary," *Catholic Biblical Quarterly* 30(1968): 518-19.

Creation; indeed, she claimed to have functioned as one of the means by which Yahweh created the world. Therefore, *'āmôn* stood in apposition to the pronoun representing Yahweh; and wisdom appeared as one of the key character traits manifested in that creation.

All this suggested not a hypostatization[28] or a mythological[29] origin for wisdom. However, Whybray concluded the following:

> The terms used to describe wisdom's origin are metaphorical not mythological, and the single word which can be interpreted as speaking of her *activity* [*'āmôn*] at the creation does not essentially go beyond the statement of 3:19. Everything which is here said about her can be naturally interpreted as belonging properly to the poetical personification of an attribute of Yahweh.[30]

Thus the connection or association (not, however, the full equivalence) of "the fear of the Lord" with wisdom denoted the intrinsically religious nature of any and all wisdom. Once again we can see that arrogant man in and of himself could and never would understand or receive prudent counsel. This had to begin with a personal relationship to the Lord, the essence of which continued to "inform" all of that man's thinking, living, and acting. Hence just as the attribute of God's holiness supplied the yardstick or norm for Mosaic theology, so God's attribute of wisdom provided the norm for all who related to it in "the fear of Yahweh."

EUDAEMONISM AND THE LORD

Many of the wisdom sayings at first sight appear to betray a materialistic sort of base pragmatism; that is to say, they appear to inculcate moral obligations merely for the sake of the well-being or happiness of the person. But such a "profit motive" interpretation misses the author's truth-intention in statements such as the following:

> The righteousness of the upright shall deliver them, but they that deal treacherously shall be taken in their own mischief.
> — Proverbs 11:6

---

[28]Helmer Ringgren, *Word and Wisdom: Studies in the Hypostatization of Divine Qualities and Functions in the Ancient Near East* (Lund: Hakan Ohlssons Boktryckeri, 1947).

[29]So Mitchell Dahood, "Proverbs 8:22-31," p. 521; W. F. Albright, "Some Canaanite-Phoenician Sources of Hebrew Wisdom," *Wisdom in Israel, Vetus Testamentum Supplement 3* (Leiden: E. J. Brill, 1955), pp. 1-15.

[30]Whybray, *Wisdom*, p. 103.

> A slack hand causes poverty, but the hand of the diligent makes rich.
> — Proverbs 10:4

Instead, the wise man was the one who observed a divine plan and order established in all things. Thus prosperity and blessing were not sought as ends in themselves, as if the wise man were arbitrarily making success a new idol. On the contrary, in accordance with God's pronouncement of "good" in Genesis 1, wise men approved work, things, and righteousness itself as "good" and self-vindicating. Diligence, obedience to the laws of God, and honest labor were rewarded; but neither the goal nor the motive was to be found in the blessing and reward itself. Every event in life was embraced in the plan of God (Eccl. 3:1-5:20). It was God who had made everything beautiful in its time (3:11), each with its own appointment. While "the plans of the mind belong to man," according to Proverbs 16:1, "the answer . . . is from the Lord." Men may plan their ways, "but the Lord directs [their] steps" (16:9; 19:21; 20:24; 21:2). It is ultimately not man that is earning his own reward; it is God who requites[31] to every man according to his work (24:12)—and that based on the principles of His "good" work in Creation and His character.

True, outwardly there appeared to be inequities, and the divine order was not always transparently obvious. But adversity or affliction were not always nor necessarily an evil (Eccl. 7:1-15), just as prosperity and material success were not always nor necessarily a good either (6:1-12). Moreover that divine order and purpose may often remain hidden and unknown even though good men such as Job sought to discover it. Only in Elihu's addresses did it become plain that God was using suffering as a teaching device (*mûsār*)[32] and as a method by which to "open Job's ears" (Job 33:16; 36:10,15).

Meanwhile, the Preacher argued for the removal of discouragements which appeared to contravene the plan of God (Eccl. 9:1-12:8). Even the so-called mundane aspects of life like eating, drinking, and enjoying the benefits of one's paycheck were described as "gifts" of God (2:24; 3:13; 5:18-20; 8:15; 9:9). Yet there was nothing inherently good in man that he should be capable on his own of

---

[31]See the review of the recent literature on the idea of retribution in the OT with four aspects of retribution in the book of Deuteronomy by John G. Gammie, "The Theology of Retribution in the Book of Deuteronomy," *Catholic Biblical Quarterly* 32(1970): 1-12.

[32]Jim A. Sanders, "Suffering As Divine Discipline in the Old Testament and Post-Biblical Judaism," *Colgate Rochester Divinity School Bulletin* 28(1955): 28-31.

enjoying himself and even his mundane existence apart from God (2:24; 3:12). This capability to be happy, blessed, and enjoy even eating, drinking, riches, wealth, and one's wife was in the divine order a gift from above.

The Song of Solomon celebrated that last-mentioned gift by dedicating a whole book to that theme. Again, if Solomon is the author of this work (and so the text as we have it lays claims in S. of Sol. 1:1; 8:12), then the entreé to this work can be made through another piece by the same writer: Proverbs 5:15-21. There in an allegory on marital fidelity, he likened enjoyment of coital love in the marriage bond to drinking water from one's own cistern and well. Said he,

> Let your fountain be blessed
> and rejoice in the wife of your youth,
> a lovely hind, a graceful doe.
> Let her affection fill you at all times with delight;
> be infatuated always with her love . . .
> For a man's ways are before the eyes of the Lord,
> and He watches all his paths.
> —Proverbs 5:18-19,21

Thus when Song of Solomon 4:12,15 repeated,

> A garden locked is my sister, my bride,
> a garden locked, a fountain sealed . . .
> a garden fountain, a well of living water,

it continued many of the same metaphors and theology. But the purpose of the book is stated in Song of Solomon 8:6-7. Love was a "flame from Yah[weh]"; it could not be extinguished, exchanged, or tempted by other goods such as riches, position, or honor. Indeed, Solomon had tried to woo the Shulamite maiden away from her shepherd boyfriend back home, but it was all to no use. Solomon could keep his "vineyard of confusion" (8:11), indeed, "his thousand" wives (v. 12). But as for the shepherd, he had his one very "own vineyard" (wife) for himself (v. 12). The book then was intended as a commentary on Genesis 2:24 and a manual on the blessing and reward of intimate married love once Yahweh had lit the flame and given the capability of enjoyment. Otherwise, it could not be purchased for love nor money—as Solomon learned the hard way and wrote under divine direction.

And what of that good above all goods—immortality or even the resurrection of the body? No text made the point more clearly nor was more hotly contested on textual or hermeneutical grounds than Job 19:23-27. Clearly Job had lost all hope in this life (17:1,11-16);

thus he cried out that he would be vindicated post-mortem, not ante-mortem. And did he believe that it would include a resurrection of his body? Job 19:26 is difficult: Does "from my flesh" mean *apart* from his body or *from* inside his body he hoped to see God? Let verse 27 decide: "My eyes shall behold [him] and not another."

Such exegesis is still greeted with deep resentment. The idea is too advanced, so it is claimed, for even the Solomonic era much less the patriarchal times where it may correctly be located. Never mind, of course, ancient man's preoccupation with the question of death and immortality. Never mind that Egypt already had geared the whole economy of the state to meet this one question of man's personal corporeal existence after death. Forget also, if we can, the Babylonian myth of Adapa and the narrative about Enoch in the prepatriarchal era. But even if we discount all this hard evidence, then let Job 14:7 be faced:

> If [a tree] be cut down,
> There is hope for [it]
> That it will sprout again *(yaḥªlîp).*

For often around the base of a felled tree, one shoot after another will spring up as a continuation of the otherwise dead tree. So it is with man in Job 14:14:

> If a man die,
> Will he live again?
> All days of my drudgery I will wait
> Until my sprouting *(ḥªlîpātî)* will come.

There it is! Job 14:14 stated in terms analogous to what happened to felled trees! Very few commentators will connect the two verses, but the writer intended his audience to do so. He did it by using the same Hebrew root in the same context in Job 14:7,14.

Likewise, Ecclesiastes 3:17 argues that God would meet man as his judge in that future day of appointed judgment (cf. 12:14); for the spirit of man goes upward (note the *article* on the participle and not the interrogative) while the life of the beast goes into the ground (3:21-22). Accordingly, man had best do something while he had breath and do it to the glory of God. But any deed of any significance would have to begin in the atmosphere of trust in the promised divine order of things, that is to say, in the fear of God.

Chapter 11

Day of the Promise:
Ninth Century

Now that David's "house" and Solomon's temple had both been established, the promise of God had reached a provisional plateau in its development. Thus the Exodus narrative, which declared Israel to be Yahweh's son, his own people, a kingdom of priests, and a holy nation, was continued and renewed in the promise of a Davidic seed which would possess an everlasting dynasty, throne, and kingdom, all of which would be a charter for humanity. God's future ruler was now visible in the line of David.

THE PROPHETS AND THE PROMISE

The prophets could now turn their focus on God's world-wide plan and kingdom. Alas, however, Israel's sin claimed a significant portion of the prophets' attention. Nevertheless, mingled with these words of judgment were the bright prospects of God's everlasting kingdom as announced so long ago in the promise.

But there lies the genius of the promise doctrine. It had, as Willis J. Beecher noted, a twofold character: "It was a standing prediction of the time to come, and it was an available religious doctrine for the time being."[1]

Thus the prophetic promise was not a group of scattered predictions which only later made sense after Christ appeared and reinterpreted many of the old prophetic words. For if the prophets merely had been prognosticating or foretelling the future, then the focus of their message would have fallen only on two things: the word spoken before the event and the fulfilling event itself. While this view of prophecy may be proper and legitimate in itself, it fails to capture precisely that aspect which captivated the hearts and minds of the OT writers and saints the most. Again Beecher best described what that difference was. For him, the word *promise* was to be preferred over mere prediction because the promise of the prophets also embraced

> the means employed for that purpose. The promise and the means and the result are all in mind at once . . . If the promise involved a series of results, we might connect any one of the results with the foretelling clause as a fulfilled prediction. So far our thinking would be correct. But if we permanently confined our thought to these items in the fulfilled promise, we should be led to an inadequate and very likely a false idea of the promise and its fulfillment. To understand the predictive elements aright, we must see it in light of the other elements. Every fulfilled promise is a fulfilled prediction; but it is exceedingly important to look at it as a promise and not as mere prediction.[2]

Of equal importance was the inseparable connection between the prophetic word and the history and geography in which that word was located. The prophets' messages were not heterogeneous and disconnected predictions randomly announced throughout an otherwise dull drone of chastisements. Nor was prediction even the main feature of prophecy. Rather, the prophets were proclaimers of righteousness who preached both law and promise to motivate the people to repentance and a life of obedience in the will and plan of God. Their predictions were often given as incentives to their contemporaries for holy living in that day, seeing that the future belonged to their God and to His righteous reign.

More was to be found in these predictions, of course, than novel glimpses of the future scattered as bits of candy to whet the appetite

---

[1] Willis J. Beecher, *The Prophets and the Promise* (1905; reprint ed., Grand Rapids: Baker Book House, 1975), p. 242.
[2] Ibid., p. 376.

of a sensate or occult mentality. Instead of any such whimsical purpose as this, the prophets often deliberately cast their words about the future in the phraseology and conceptual patterns of past prophecies. There was a deliberate borrowing and supplementing of the Abrahamic-Davidic promise. Hence, for them, the future was part of God's single, cumulative promise. Thus the so-called messianic passages in the writing prophets were mostly repetitions, supplements, homiletical implications, and amplifications on the promise as originally given to Abraham, Israel, or David. Accordingly, these predictions were not disconnected or scattered predictions but shoots off the common stem of the promise doctrine.

But some will surely object to the persistent inclusions in that single promise plan about Israel's national career with its geographical holdings. To be sure, some Jewish and rationalistic scholars concluded that since Israel's political career and geographical holdings occupied such an obvious emphasis in the promise predictions that this is all that was meant: these predictions were simply the demographic and political aspirations of the nation Israel as envisioned by some of Israel's prophetic bards! Consequently, all other attempts to apply this promise to the church or to Jesus Christ were false and way beyond anything the prophets ever intended. However, such a conclusion failed to take the OT itself seriously, much less the historical realities.

On the other hand, many Christian interpreters erred in the same manner, only on the opposite side of the promise. They denied that the promise had anything left in it for national Israel now that the Christian era has arrived. However, Willis J. Beecher of the Princeton faculty at the turn of the century commented:

> If the Christian interpreter persists in excluding the ethnical Israel from his conception of the fulfillment, or in regarding Israel's part in the matter as merely preparatory and not eternal, then he comes into conflict with the plain witness of both testaments [and we might now add " with history as well"] . . . Rightly interpreted, the biblical statements include in the fulfillment both Israel, the race with whom the covenant is eternal, and also the personal Christ and his mission, with the whole spiritual Israel of the redeemed in all ages. The New Testament teaches this as Christian doctrine, for leading men to repentance and for edification; and the Old Testament teaches it as Messianic doctrine, for leading men to repentance and for edification . . . The exclusive Jewish interpretation and the exclusive Christian interpretation are equally wrong. Each is correct in what it affirms, and incorrect in what it denies.[3]

---

[3]Ibid., p. 383.

The promise then was national and cosmopolitan. Israel would yet receive what God had unconditionally promised: nationhood, Davidic king, land, and wealth. But so would the nations of the earth receive the promised blessing in Abraham's seed. Indeed, the very ends of the earth would turn to the Lord (Ps. 72:11,17). Such cosmopolitan implications of this great promise would later be the subject of the Jerusalem council in Acts 15, and Paul would make the whole topic part of his discussion of the redemptive plan of God in Romans 9-11.

Therefore we conclude that the promise of God in the prophets was a single unified plan which was eternal in its scope and fulfillment even though there were climacteric plateaus reached along the way in the history of its development. In its build-up, it was cumulative. In scope it was both national and cosmopolitan as Israel and all tribes, peoples, and nations were linked by faith in a single program. Such a doctrine of Messiah and many of its accompanying features was, according to E. Jenni,[4] without any real counterpart in ancient Near Eastern literature or ideology.

THE PROMISE IN THE NINTH CENTURY

The division of the kingdom after the days of David and Solomon was the first in a series of crises Israel would face as a result of the corrosive effects of sin. Inexorably the storm clouds of divine judgment would continue to gather as a host of prophetic seers pleaded with the northern ten tribes ("Ephraim" or often just "Israel") and the two southern tribes ("Benjamin" and most frequently just "Judah" to represent both) to repent and abandon the ruinous course they had chosen. But as the nation continued adamant and resolute in its preference for evil idolatry and rebellion against God, the prophets declared with increasing definiteness that the people of God must once again first experience the crucible of divine judgment before they were delivered and finally allowed to fulfill their true destiny. Thus the present form of the divine institution of the nation had to be judged, but this would be followed by another new day, new servant, new covenant, and new triumph from God.

The first signal of this new development appeared in Elijah and Elisha (1 Kings 17-2 Kings 9), whose direct involvements into the political arena of the northern kingdom were more pronounced in their actions than their speaking. In their persons they symbolized

---

[4]E. Jenni, "Messiah," *Interpreter's Dictionary of the Bible*, 4 vols. (Nashville: Abingdon, 1962), 3:361.

two aspects of the divine power toward the people: Elijah was the divine judicial power opposing a rebellious people and containing wholesale violence; Elisha was the dispensing of divine blessing when people repented.[5] But the extended word of God through a long line of writing prophets also came shortly, probably first in the ministries of Obadiah and Joel.

Now without pretending to claim finality, it may be argued with a reasonable degree of assurance that Obadiah and Joel were the first of the writing prophets.[6] And for both of these prophets, a future day of the Lord (*yôm YHWH*) was the theme of their message. This day was signaled by its partial presence already in the tragic events of Edom's malicious joy over witnessing her rival, Jerusalem, being humiliated by an invader (Obadiah) and also in a devastating locust plague and drought (Joel) in Israel.

But regardless of any *present* effects of that impending day, its final appearance would be a time of divine reckoning with Israel and all nations when the Lord personally returned and revealed His righteous character. It would be a time more marked by its contents than by the length of time or duration of that "day." Like the "latter days" or "last age" (*'aḥªrît hayyāmîm*) which began to be discussed in Genesis 49:1 and Numbers 24:14, the day of the Lord is that time of world judgment when God will make known His supremacy over all nations and nature itself.[7] Yahweh will vindicate Himself by His great works which all men will recognize as divine in origin. Judgment would be universal, inescapable, and retributive.

EDOM AND THE PROMISE: OBADIAH

For the first time in prophetic literature, we find the phrase "day of the Lord" in Obadiah. Because of Edom's pride (1-9) and her violent action against her brother Jacob (10-14), she would receive

---

[5]This symbolism I owe to C. von Orelli, *The Old Testament Prophecy of the Consummation of God's Kingdom Traced in Its Historical Development*, trans. J. J. Banks (Edinburgh: T. & T. Clark, 1889), p. 194.

[6]For a discussion of the history of this dating, see Leslie Allen, *The Books of Joel, Obadiah, Jonah and Micah* (Grand Rapids: Eerdmans, 1976), pp. 129-33. The detailed proofs set forth by Caspari in 1842 still seem to be preferable to a 586 B.C. or postexilic date. Thus the book may be placed in the reign of Jehoram (2 Chron. 21:8-10,16-17), 848-841 B.C.; cf. G. L. Archer, Jr., *A Survey of Old Testament Introduction*, rev. ed. (Chicago: Moody Press, 1974), pp. 299-303.

[7]While the two expressions are never formally linked together, nor does "latter days" have the idea of judgment in it, Deuteronomy 31:17-18 does connect God's judgment with "that day" to come.

the same treatment as the heathen nations in that day of the Lord (15-21). Just as the Amalekites had represented the counterpart to the kingdom of God by their savage rearguard action against the straggling, sick, and aged Israelites as they journeyed through the wilderness (Exod. 17:8-15; Deut. 25:17-19), so Edom also had come to represent the kingdom of man. Edom now was the "quintessence of heathenism"[8] (Obad. 15-16; cf. Isa. 34:2,5 and Ezek. 35:14; 36:5). Marten Woudstra stated it clearly as follows:

> By divine command and approval this enmity [and we might add, note that old Gen. 3:15 word, "enmity"] existed between the people of God and the nations, the latter viewed as representatives of the forces of unbelief . . . A look at Ex. 23:22 ["I will be an enemy unto thine enemies"] should make it clear that this enmity was real . . .
>
> This accounts for the note of ultimate seriousness that runs through some of the Psalms, such as Ps. 137 and Ps. 139:21-22. In these Psalms the believing Israelite identifies himself with God's cause. That cause cannot triumph unless that which opposes it is brought low.[9]

In this case to mock and rejoice over the "inheritance" of Yahweh, the house of Israel (e.g., Ezek. 35:15), was to mock and challenge Yahweh Himself, for He had attached Himself to one people and one country (Deut. 4:33ff.) for the purpose of saving all. Besides He was the Sovereign over all nations anyway (Deut. 32:8,9), hence all jesting about His work of blessing or judgment among Israel was strictly out of place. Thus Edom would not escape that imminent divine judgment which also would fall on all the nations.

However, in contrast to the destruction of these nations, there would be a remnant, a "group of escaped ones" ($p^e l \hat{e} t \hat{a} h$; cf. Joel 2:32 [3:5] and Isa. 37:32 where it is parallel to the more common word for "remnant," $\check{s}^e$'$\bar{e}r\hat{\imath}\underline{t}$), in Mount Zion (Obad. 17) who would emerge victorious again under the impetus of the divine energy bestowed once more on them. Then Israel would again extend her rule over ancient Canaan and the territories surrounding it, including the Negeb, the Philistine country, Gilead in east-Jordan and Syria, and as far north as Zarephath in Lebanon—all this as promised to the patriarch Jacob and to Joseph (Obad. 18-20). David and Solomon had partially ruled these lands but had afterward lost them. But they would all return in that day.

---

[8]Patrick Fairbairn, *The Interpretation of Prophecy* (London: Banner of Truth Trust, 1964), p. 222.

[9]Marten Woudstra, "Edom and Israel in Ezekiel," *Calvin Theological Journal* 3(1968): 24-25.

The method God would use to reestablish His rule would be through human "saviors" (*môši'îm*, v. 21) performing the office of "judging," "ruling" (*šōp^eṭîm*), just as they had in the days of the judges (Judg. 2:16,18). Zion, i.e., Jerusalem, would be their center, and "the kingdom would belong to the Lord" (Obad. 21).

As for the fulfillment of this prophecy, Obadiah combined in one picture what history split into different times and events. Indeed, Judas Maccabaeus, John Hyrcanus, Alexander Janneaeus, and the Zealot opposition to the Roman rule brought about the demise of the Edomites or Idumaeans.[10] But that was only a token pledge of the final triumph of God against all hostile kindred nations. Hence the day of the Lord ran throughout the history of the kingdom of God so that it occurred in each particular judgment as evidence of its complete fulfillment which was near and approaching.

THE DAY OF THE LORD: JOEL

The occasion[11] for Joel's prophecy was a dreadful plague of locusts followed by a distressing drought—both harbingers of the great and terrible day of the Lord. Even though the time was late, there still was opportunity to repent. Yet it must be a heartfelt genuine sorrow for their sin and an about-face in life (Joel 2:12-13).

When the people responded with fasting, weeping, and prayer (2:15-17), then "God was jealous for His land and had pity on His people; the Lord answered" their prayers (vv. 18-19). With verse 18 the tone of this book reversed. Whereas judgment had prevailed from 1:1-2:17, now blessing and hope would dominate the remainder of the book. Such a change could be attributed to two facts: (1) the Lord their God "was gracious and merciful, slow to anger, and abounding in steadfast love" (2:13*b*) and (2) the people repented by "tearing [their] hearts and not [their] garments" (v. 13*a*). In response to their repentance, God promised to bless them. The gifts of God fell into two groups: (1) the immediate blessing of a productive land (vv. 19-27) and (2) the promise of a future outpouring of the Spirit of God on all flesh (2:28-32 [3:1-5]). Blessing, then, was to be part of the contents of that "day."

Meanwhile, the rest of the description of the day of the Lord was much like Obadiah's. It was "destruction from the Almighty" (1:15-

---

[10]Flavius Josephus, *Antiquities of the Jews*, 12. 8.1; 13. 9.1; 13. 15.4; *Wars of the Jews*, 4. 9.7.

[11]Most conservative scholars date Joel ca. 830 B.C., during the minority of King Joash and the regency of Jehoiada the high priest; cf. Archer, *Survey*, pp. 304-7 and A. F. Kirkpatrick, *The Doctrine of the Prophets* (London: Macmillan, 1897).

16), "a day of darkness and gloom," "cloud and thick darkness" (2:2), an "exceedingly terrible" day; "who could bear it?" (v. 11).

But the day of the Lord was again more than judgment. It was a time of deliverance for all who would call on the name of the Lord (2:32), accompanied by cosmic signs heralding its arrival (vv. 30-31). And as already noted, it was characterized by the outpouring of the Spirit of God on all flesh (vv. 28-29).

The time set for the outpouring of the Spirit was left indefinite, "after this" (*'aḥªrê kēn*). Of course, the "after this" could refer back to 2:23b where the former and latter rains would come "as before" (*bāri'šôn*); then somewhat later "after this" would the Spirit be poured out. Note, however, 2:29 [3:2] repeated the opening phrase of 2:28 ("I will pour out My Spirit") with just one slight change: "in those days" (*bayyāmîm hāhēmmâh*). Therefore, the eschatological meaning the apostle Peter gave to these verses on the day of Pentecost is to be found in 2:29 if it is not in 2:28. This outpouring could not have been in the immediate future since verse 26 pictures a period of quiet prosperity preceding any world crisis introduced in verse 28.[12] When Peter quoted this passage on the day of Pentecost, he located this blessing "in the last days" (*en tais eschatais hēmerais*, Acts 2:17). Such a view of the duration of eschatological time beginning with the Christian era and stretching until the second advent is found in a number of NT passages (e.g., Heb. 1:1-2; 1 Peter 1:20; 2 Peter 3:3). Furthermore, the same phenomena of having near and distant events, or multiple fulfillments, all being part of the single truth-intention of the author, appeared in Obadiah's vision of the day of the Lord with its more immediate victory over Edom and the distant total victory of the kingdom of God. Thus Pentecost was part of the day of the Lord. There would, however, yet be another final day—if not many in between—when God would pour out His Spirit like rain "on all flesh" (cf. Joel 2:23).

How extensive then would this supernatural blessing of the Spirit be? Usually when the OT used "all flesh" (*kol bāsār*), it meant the whole of mankind (Gen. 6:12-13; Ps. 145:21, *passim*). In this present context the phrase "*your* sons and *your* daughters," according to some, would definitely limit it to all Jews.[13] This is not

---

[12]Von Orelli, *Old Testament Prophecy*, p. 205, n.

[13]As Allen, *Books*, p. 98, n. 10 commented, the translation of JB and NEB, "all mankind," was therefore incorrect, hence the amazement in Acts 10:45 of a Gentile Pentecost. In Ezekiel 39:29 God had specifically promised to "pour out [His] Spirit on the house of Israel." But are not the two expressions different without being mutually exclusive of each other? It is interesting to note that Paul applied our passage to the universal call of the gospel in Romans 10:12-13.

altogether certain. What is certain is that difference of age (young and old), sex (sons and daughters), or position (servants or hand-maidens) would not affect the universality of this gift of the Spirit. Thus, what Moses had once mentioned as only a wishful ideal for every Israelite in Numbers 11:29 would now actually be seen. Israel would in that day not only serve the Lord as a kingdom of priests (Exod. 19:6) but as prophets, also. Undoubtedly, this benefit would be extended beyond the Jews even as later on the apostle Paul saw its application in Romans 10:12-13 to all mankind.

Besides the shower of God's Spirit on all flesh, heaven and earth would convulse with mighty signs similar to that great deliverance from Egypt when God sent the plagues of blood and fire (Exod. 7:17; 9:24) and when He appeared on Mount Sinai in pillars of smoke (19:18). Thus the natural world would be brought into intimate connection with the judgment and salvation of God as He inter-vened in human history. The original judgment day of Joel 2:1ff., temporarily halted by Judah's repentance, must again appear in the future. But whoever would "call on the name of the Lord" during those days "would be delivered" (*yimmālēṭ*, "be slipped away"). In Mount Zion, the head of the kingdom of God, there would be "those who escape" (*pᵉlêṭâh*), "survivors" (*śᵉrîdîm*, 2:32 [3:5]). However, while nations escaped, Yahweh would judge and destroy all nations in the valley of Jehoshaphat (3:2 [4:2]).

Again, there was an antecedent theology that had informed this doctrine of the day of the Lord (Exod. 32:34; Deut. 31:17-18,29;cf. Gen. 49:1; Num. 24:14; Deut. 4:30). What had begun in Exodus 32:34 as a "day of My visiting" when "My angel" "will visit on them their sins" was now projected from that day and the nation Israel to the last age and all nations. The appointed "day of Yahweh's visit-ing" the sin of His people in judgment grew. It was not just "a day of His visiting" which might be any time of national chastisement; it was "*the* day of His visiting," one day that stood out as supreme when compared to other days. In that final conflict on the earth, King Yahweh would decisively defeat the assembled nations who rose up against the armies of God. Suddenly the sickle of judgment would begin, and the reaping and treading of the winepress would com-mence. Heaven and earth would quake and multitudes would charge into the battlefield of the valley of decision.

Joel 3:1-21 [4:1-21] became the classic passage for the rest of the OT on God's final judgment on all nations. It also became the classic statement of the blessed result for the people of God. They would possess an exceedingly fertile land enriched with fountains of running water and dripping with wine and milk. And to climax it all, Yahweh would personally dwell in Zion.

This day of the Lord was repeatedly said to be "near" (*qārôḇ*, Obad. 15; Joel 1:15; 2:1; 3:14 and later in Isa. 13:6; Zeph. 1:7,14; Ezek. 30:3; *passim*). Beecher cautioned:

> This representation is made by prophets who lived many generations apart, and therefore by prophets who knew that other prophets had made it generations before. Perhaps this indicates that the prophets thought of the day of Yahaweh [*sic*] as generic, not an occasion which would.occur once for all, but one which might be repeated as circumstances called for it.[14]

And, of course, that final time would be climactic and the sum of all the rest. Though the events of their own times fitted the pattern of God's future judgment, that final day was nevertheless immeasurably larger and more permanent in its salvific and judgmental effects.

---

[14]Beecher, *Prophets*, p. 311; idem, "The Day of the Lord in Joel," *Homiletical Review* 18(1889): 355-58; idem, "The Doctrine of the 'Day of the Lord' Before Joel's Time," *Homiletical Review* 18(1889): 440-51; idem, "The Doctrine of the 'Day of the Lord' in Obadiah and Amos," *Homiletical Review* 19(1890): 157-60.

Chapter 12

Servant of the Promise:
Eighth Century

A flurry of prophetic activity was divinely inaugurated in the eighth century B.C., mainly to warn the northern kingdom of an impending destruction if she did not repent and reverse her way of life. Unfortunately, except for minor responses similar to those given to the preaching of Micah, which Jeremiah 26:18-19 informed us had a momentary effect on Judah during Hezekiah's reign, the northern ten tribes plunged headlong into destruction. This eventually came in 722 B.C. when their capital, Samaria, fell shortly after Syria's leading city, Damascus, had fallen in 732 B.C.

Graciously God provided as much as four decades of prophetic preaching prior to this calamity during the eighth century, but it was all to no avail. Included in this group of proclaimers were Amos, Hosea, Jonah, Micah, and the greatest of them all, Isaiah. Some of them began their warnings and promises while the nation was still flushed with the success of Jeroboam II and the expanded territory, wealth, and luxury his reign had brought. The rich stalked the poor and favored the guilty of their own rank in the courts. And all alike lacked credibility when they tried to walk syncretistically with Baal and Yahweh. Religious practice became a cover for all sorts of sins of immorality, injustice, and lewdness. Judgment or repentance had to fall, or God would no longer be credible.

REBUILDING DAVID'S FALLEN HUT: AMOS

For such times as these, God had prepared a herdsman and a dresser of sycamore trees from the town Tekoa, southeast of Jerusalem in the "wild west" of Judah. This southerner was sent north sometime around 760-745 B.C. with an urgent message of judgment and salvation.

The record of Amos's ministry was neatly laid out in three sections: (1) in 1:1-2:16 he thundered against Israel and her neighbors for their lack of righteousness towards one another and towards God Himself; (2) in 3:1-6:14 he enjoined Israel to seek God (5:4,6,14) or to get ready for a face-to-face showdown (4:12); and (3) in 7:1-9:15 he received five visions offering at first some escape but then hardening into no way of escape except for God's eschatological offer of hope vis-à-vis the present certain doom.

Most clearly, Amos viewed God as sovereign Lord over all the earth. Not only was He the deliverer of Israel from Egypt and the Amorites (Amos 2:9-10), but He had conducted additional exodii (9:7): the Philistines from Caphtor, the Syrians from Kir; these together with the Ethiopians had been uniquely favored by Yahweh. Consequently, all nations had to meet His standard of righteousness. Each nation that failed to live up to that standard stood condemned, not by its own gods, but by the only God, Yahweh. The list of divine grievances against these nations was ticked off by Amos: barbarism in warfare by Damascus (1:3-5) and Ammon (vv. 13-15); slave raids and slave trading by Philistia (vv. 6-8) and Tyre (vv. 9-10); Edomite hostility against his brother Jacob (vv. 11-12); Moabite desecration of the bones of the pagan Edomite king (2:1-3); rejection of the law of God on the part of Judah (vv. 4-5); and moral deviations of the northern ten tribes (vv. 6-16). All nations had better learn as quickly as possible that the norm set by the character and law of Yahweh marked the standards by which the righteous rule of God would judge all nations universally.

This Lord of history was a sovereign Ruler by right of Creation. In three hymns Amos celebrated the greatness of the one "who formed the mountains and created the wind and declared to man what His thoughts were" (Amos 4:13; cf. 5:8-9; 9:5-6). Indeed, the Lord of Hosts was His name. Yet He was more than Creator. He also was the controller of history and the destinies of men. His use of famine, drought, blight, pestilence, and war could have a redemptive purpose if men would only listen; for when men failed to listen to the *precept* of the word of His servants the prophets, perhaps they would listen to His *penalty* left one on the other—not in retribution for their sins so much as a device to capture their attention. Note the series of five penalties in Amos 4:6-11 falling like the toll of a funeral dirge one after the other with the even sadder refrain after each blast of divine judgment, "Yet you did not return unto Me, says the Lord" (4:6*b*,8*b*,9*b*,10*b*,11*b*). And then came the final and most devastating stroke of all: "Therefore . . . prepare to meet your God, O Israel" (4:12). It was as if the referee had counted on the mat of the pinned wrestler, one—two—three—four—five—, and then had said, "You're out"—for that is what this "meeting" with God was: the end of the northern kingdom! Israel and Judah together had been warned that such was God's method of dealing with men and nations. They had been warned of such alternative prospects of compounded judgment or blessing depending on what their response was, as far back in the canon as Leviticus 26 and Deuteronomy 28. In fact, some of Amos's vocabulary was directly informed by these passages, as were many of his fellow prophets' expressions on this subject.

God did more than act in history. He spoke! And when He had spoken, Amos was compelled to prophesy (3:8). The nexus between that reception of God's estimates, meanings, interpretations, or announcements and the prophets' proclamation of them was set forth in a series of cause and effect statements in 3:2-8. For example, could the trumpet blow in a city (like our air-raid siren) and the people not be afraid? Could two meet together (especially in a crowded place) except by appointment? Therefore, could God speak and Amos not prophesy?

Repeatedly Amos stressed Israel's remarkable position in history. When Amos reminded Israel, "You only have I known of all the families of the earth" (3:2), he was not claiming favored status or a chauvinistic partisanship for Israel; he merely reminded them of God's election. The word to "know" in this covenantal context had nothing to do with recognition or acknowledgement of one's deeds; it had to do with God's gift of choice—an unmerited choice as Deuteronomy 7:8 *passim* had made plain.

Likewise, all supercilious indulgence in solemn assemblies, feasts, offerings, and melodies were offensive to the God who inspected the heart of men first. A more pertinent prerequisite to meaningful religious observances was righteousness and justice (5:21-24). Otherwise all religious practice was despised and rejected by Yahweh.

In the same class belonged all the talk about longing for the day of the Lord as a panacea for all the present ills of society—as if Israel knew what she was talking about (5:18-20). For those who were not prepared for the day of the Lord, it was a day of darkness. To make it even more graphic Amos could describe the unreality of these religious escapists. That day would be like a man who fled from a lion only to meet a bear; and when he had shrewdly escaped both disasters with the lion and the bear, he went into his house and leaned on the wall only to be bitten by a serpent. That day was not to be fooled with or desired if men were not living and walking in the truth.

No less dangerous was the peril of complacency in 6:1-8, with no compassion for the needs of others or for the threatening disaster about to fall on Samaria. While the prophet's prayer of intercession for Israel did rescue her from certain trouble on two occasions (7:1-3,4-6), when the plumb line of righteousness was dropped alongside the nation, she was out of line morally (7:7-9), and national calamity was now a foregone conclusion (8:1-3; 9:1-4).

Nevertheless, there was hope beyond this disaster of the fall of Samaria. With a grand theological climax to the book in 9:11-15, God promised to rebuild David's house, which in its current dilapidated condition could only be likened to a "fallen booth" or "hut" (*sukkâh*). What was normally styled "the house (*bêt*) of David" (2 Sam. 7:5,11; 1 Kings 11:38; Isa. 7:2,13), or dynasty of David, would shortly be in a collapsed state with "breaches" and "ruins" in it. The Hebrew active participle stressed either its *present* state, the "falling" house, or its impending state of ruin, the house "about to fall." Thus the dynasty of David would suffer, but God would bring it back from its ruined condition, for He had promised David that His was an eternal house.

The suffixes on the words in 9:11 have special interest for the theologian. C. F. Keil commented on this passage that the feminine plural suffix on "breaches *thereof*" (*pirṣêhen*) could only refer to the tragic division of the Davidic house (which symbolized the kingdom of God) into two kingdoms, north and south (cf. 6:2, "these kingdoms").[1] God would, however, "wall up their rents." Thus even before Ezekiel (37:15-28) had pictured the unification of the ten northern tribes with the two southern tribes, Amos had envisioned the same result. The masculine singular suffix on *"his* ruins" (*hᵃrisoṭāyw*) referred to David himself and not to the "hut" which is feminine. Thus under a new coming David, the destroyed house of that promised Messiah would rise from the ashes. God would also

---

[1]Carl Friedrich Keil, *The Twelve Minor Prophets*, 2 vols., in C. F. Keil and F. Delitzsch, *Biblical Commentary on the Old Testament*, 25 vols., trans. James Martin (Grand Rapids: Eerdmans, 1949), 1:303.

"rebuild *her* (*bᵉnîṯîhā*) as in the days of old." The suffix is feminine singular this time and naturally refers to the fallen hut which would be rebuilt. But the phrase "as in the days of old" clearly points back to the antecedent theology of 2 Samuel 7:11-12,16 where God had promised that He would raise up David's seed after him and give him a throne, a dynasty, and a kingdom that would endure forever.

The interpretation of the Davidic promise in 2 Samuel 7 as a "charter for humanity" (2 Sam. 7:19) was repeated here by Amos (9:12): "That they may possess the remnant of Edom, even all nations who are called by My name." For many, verse 12 is even more problematic than verse 11—especially with its "offensive" reference to "the remnant of Edom" (*šᵉ'ērîṯ 'ᵉdôm*). Gerhard Hasel[2] noted that Amos employed the remnant theme in a threefold usage: (1) to counter the proud claim that all Israel was the remnant (3:12; 4:1-3; 5:3; 6:9-10; 9:1-4); (2) to describe a true remnant from Israel (5:4-6,15), an eschatological sense; and (3) to include the "remnant of Edom" along with the other neighboring nations as benefactors of the Davidic promise (9:12). It was this representative role of Edom, which we saw in Obadiah, that is singled out again here. For the epexegetical note in verse 12, "and/even all the nations/Gentiles who are called by My name," surprisingly did not cast Edom in the role of being vanquished by David's or Israel's military machine; rather it speaks of its spiritual incorporation into the restored kingdom of David along with all those Gentiles who were likewise "called by His name."

The usage of the phrase "called by my name" in the OT always placed each of the objects so designated under divine ownership.[3] What God or man named, they owned and protected, whether they were cities (2 Sam. 12:28; Jer. 25:29; Dan. 9:18-19) or men and women (Isa. 4:1; Jer. 14:9; 15:16; 2 Chron. 7:14). Thus when Israel walked by faith, Moses promised, "All the peoples of the earth shall see that you are called by the name of the Lord" (Deut. 28:10). But when they refused to believe, they were "like those who [were] not called by Thy name" (Isa. 63:19). The phrase then is very much like Joel 2:32 [3:5]: "All who call upon the name of the Lord."

The verb "to take possession of" (*yîršû*) was likewise chosen because of the antecedent theology in Balaam's prophecy of Num-

---

[2]Gerhard Hasel, *The Remnant* (Berrien Springs: Andrews University Press, 1972), pp. 393-94.

[3]For a full study, see W. C. Kaiser, Jr., "Name," *Zondervan Pictorial Encyclopedia of the Bible*, 5 vols., ed. M. C. Tenney (Grand Rapids: Zondervan, 1975), 4:360-70.

bers 24:17-18 that had predicted that a "star" and a "scepter" would rise in Israel "to take possession of Edom ... while Israel did valiantly." This one from Jacob would exercise dominion over all, predicted Balaam, for his kingdom would spread over the representatives of the kingdom of men present already in that early day: Moab, Sheth, Edom, Amalek, and Asshur. Yet does not Amos now add to the ancient divine revelation that God would by divine plan "take possession" of a righteous and believing "remnant" from all nations including even bitter Edom? Thus some believing Edomites along with all others who called on the name of the Lord would, to use Paul's term, be "grafted" into Israel as part of the people of God.[4]

FREELY LOVING ISRAEL: HOSEA

In no prophet is the love of God more clearly demarcated and illustrated than in Hosea. His marital experience was the key to both his ministry and his theology. It was a picture of the holiness of God righteously standing firm while the heart of God tenderly loved that which was utterly abhorrent.

Hosea bore this message of the love of God in his life as well as in word. He had been commanded at the inception of his ministry to marry Gomer, Diblaim's daughter, for so the expression "go and take to yourself a woman" (1:2) meant.[5] Since her name and her father's name appear to lack any special meaning, and since everything appears to be in strict narrative prose, we have rejected the allegorical or vision interpretation. Rather in our understanding of the grammar of the passage, Gomer was not a harlot when Hosea married her just as her unborn children were not "children of harlotry" until after they had been born and received a stigma on their name from their mother's loose style of life. For the only children mentioned are those she bore to Hosea (note especially 1:3, "She bore him a son."); and since he named the children (1:4,6,9), they were in all probability his own.

The construction of Hosea 1:2*b* has proved troublesome to many: "Go, take to yourself a wife of harlotry and children of har-

---

[4]See my article, "The Davidic Promise and the Inclusion of the Gentiles (Amos 9:1-15 and Acts 15:13-18): A Test Passage for Theological Systems," *Journal of the Evangelical Theological Society* 20(1977): 97-111.

[5]Cf. elsewhere: Genesis 4:19; 6:2; 19:14; Exodus 21:10; 34:16; 1 Samuel 25:43. Note also the figure of speech, zeugma, where one verb joins two objects while it strictly only goes with one of them: "Take to thee a wife ... and children." Cf. Genesis 4:20: "Such as dwell in tents and cattle," also 1 Timothy 4:3.

lotry." This can signify result rather than purpose as it does in Isaiah 6:9-12 and Exodus 10:1; 11:10; 14:4. Thus it was a way of stating at once the divine command and the subsequent result and experience. And so it was in Hosea 2:2,5,7 that Gomer like Israel left the security of her marriage and chased other lovers. That pattern of marital fidelity followed by spiritual promiscuity was exactly what Jeremiah 2:2 would remind Israel of in a later time: "I remember your youth when you went after Me in the wilderness."

Therefore God will once more "allure her . . . into the wilderness and speak tenderly to her" (2:14 [16]) even as Hosea was commanded by God, "Go once more, love [such] a woman [Gomer] who is . . . an adulteress" (3:1). All this was simultaneously aimed at the physical and spiritual harlotry of Israel; for as God commanded, Hosea named his children Jezreel, "God will scatter," Lo-ruhamah, "not pitied," and Lo-ammi, "not my people." Only the unyielding love of Yahweh could reverse the judgment of that generation, for there was a day coming when in accordance with the ancient promise, the people would be as innumerable as the sand on the seashore (Hos. 1:10 [2:1]; cf. Gen. 22:17; 32:12). In that day Israel would "be sowed by God" (Jezreel) and be called "My people" (*'ammî*) "sons of the living God" (Hos. 1:10-11 [2:1-2]; 2:23 [25]). This vocabulary is very reminiscent of the Mosaic revelation (Exod. 4:22; 34:15-16; Deut. 31:16), though more extensively developed by Hosea. Yahweh's love would remain true in spite of Israel's unfaithfulness (3:1), for even after the appropriate discipline, she would be betrothed again to him (2:19 [21]). Such love went back to God's deliverance of the nation from Egypt (12:9 [10]; 13:4). The threat to symbolically return her to Egypt (8:13; 9:3; 11:5) is another reminder of the Mosaic warning in Deuteronomy 28:68. Nevertheless, His love will still triumph. Hosea presents Yahweh as a father watching his son take his first steps (11:1ff.), a physician helping Israel (7:1; 11:3; 14:4), and a shepherd (13:5).

Thus there is a dual emphasis in Hosea: the righteousness of God and the love of God. Because He is righteous (2:19 [21]; 10:12), men should "turn" (*šûḇ*) to the Lord (5:4; 6:1; 7:10; 11:5; 12:6 [7]; 14:2) and "seek" (*bāqaš* in 3:5; 5:6,15; 7:10; also *šāḥar* in 5:15; *dāraš* in 10:12). Some of the most gracious calls to repentance in all Scripture are found in 6:1-3 and 14:1-3. Thus judgment could not have the last word; God's grace would. "Afterwards the children of Israel will return and seek Yahweh their God and David their king . . . in the end of the days" (3:5). This would not be the deported Davidic king but that promised messianic descendant of David (2 Sam. 7; Amos 9:11f.).

God's *hesed*, the only word the prophet had to describe "the riches of God's grace in the heart of God,"[6] would be evident when He again betrothed Israel (2:19 [21]). Thus He would "keep covenant and covenantal love" as the older texts had promised (Deut. 7:9,12; 1 Kings 8:23; cf. later Neh. 1:5; 9:32; Dan. 9:4; 2 Chron. 6:14). He would do this "because He loved your father, therefore, He chose their seed after them" (Deut. 4:37). For her part, Israel owed the same "loyal love" (*hesed*) back to Yahweh (Hos. 4:1; 6:4,6; 10:12; 12:6 [7]). This was one of the three important catchwords in God's "controversy" (*rîb*) or court case with Israel (4:1). She had no "truth" (*'emet*), no "loving-kindness" or "loyal love" (*hesed*), and no "knowledge of God" (*da'at 'elohîm*).

Each of these three charges was then taken up in reverse order, and each section closed with a bright picture of a better future day when God's love broke through the barrier of Israel's persistent sin. Their lack of the "knowledge of God" (4:1,6; 5:4) was evident from their physical and spiritual harlotry. Usually the expression "knowledge of God" meant theology or doctrine; what Israel lacked was respect for the law of God—e.g., five of the Ten Commandments are given as samples in 4:2. But it also meant a personal experience (cf. 5:4; 6:2; 13:4) and relationship with the only true God.

Accordingly, God would "return to [His] place until they . . . sought [His] face" (5:15). The first section (4:2–5:15) ended with a beautiful promise in 6:1-3 of a day when God would heal the people after He had torn them; men would then know the Lord, for He would raise them up again.

The second charge of no *hesed* was preferred in 6:4-10:15 with the glowing promise of God's love in 11:1-11 to conclude that section. Yahweh's heart *recoiled* within Him when He thought of giving up the northern tribes (11:8; cf. Deut. 29:23 where the same verb "to overthrow" is used of the cities of Sodom, Gomorrah, Admah, and Zeboim); and His compassions were deeply stirred.

The third section in 11:12 [12:1] to 13:16 [14:1] took up the charge of a lack of "truth" (*'emet*) or "faithfulness" (*'emûnâh*) and ended with a most magnificent appeal and promise in 14:1-9 [2-10]. God's words and free love would be all that Israel would need. The promised blessing would be restored if Israel would return to the Lord and offer the sacrifice of her lips. Indeed, "From the hand of the grave I will deliver them, from death I will redeem them. Where are your plagues, O death? Where is your sting, O grave?" (13:14).

---

[6]George Farr, "The Concept of Grace in the Book of Hosea," *Zeitschrift für alttestamentliche Wissenschaft* 70(1958): 102.

Thus God would redeem His people at last, for any changing of His mind on this point was unthinkable (13:14*b*).

MISSION TO THE GENTILES: JONAH

God's grace was extended to the most hostile and aggressive of Israel's Gentile neighbors—the Assyrians. Surprisingly, they were even more responsive to God's messenger than was Israel, all to the chagrin of Jonah. He had enjoyed prophesying about the expansion of Israel's national borders (2 Kings 14:25) during the reign of Jeroboam II. But to announce God's judgment to Nineveh, a mere forty days hence, was to provide an opportunity for her repentance and for God's merciful reprieve of His judgment; this Jonah disliked with a passion.

The theology of the book[7] then revolves around the extension of the grace of God to Gentiles: It is another amplification of Genesis 12:3. Much of its teaching centered in the character of God as already revealed in Exodus 34:6. As Jonah was reminded in Jonah 4:2, the Lord is gracious, merciful, slow to anger, and abounding in grace (*ḥeseḏ*). Yahweh is Creator of all (1:9) and the Ruler of all affairs of life as shown in His control of the sea (v. 15) and in His special appointments of a great fish (v. 17), a plant (4:6), a worm (v. 7), and a sultry east wind (v. 8). His power was not limited at all; He was the Judge of all the earth (Gen. 18:25). He was the leading actor in this book; and His was the first word, according to Jonah 1:2, and the last word (4:11).

Nineveh had cost the only living God no end of toil and effort; therefore, why should He not have pity on it as Jonah had pity on the castor oil plant (*qîqāyôn*), which in contrast had cost him no effort and no labor? The elliptical form of these two verses is all the more graphic when viewed against the clear theology of the book: God will have Gentiles to share in His grace as well. Accordingly, as Jonah affirmed in his credal confession of 1:9: "I fear Yahweh," so the polytheistic mariners "feared the Lord exceedingly" and "offered a sacrifice to Yahweh and made vows" (1:16).

So did the Ninevites affirm God's sovereignty in 3:9, saying, "Who knows? God may yet repent and turn from His fierce anger." Nineveh was spared as Jonah himself had been delivered from drowning—the subject of his prayer of thanksgiving in Jonah 2, which was laden with quotes from the Psalter.

---

[7]For a good overall evaluation of the book, see John H. Stek, "The Message of the Book of Jonah," *Calvin Theological Journal* 4(1969): 23-50.

Saving Gentiles was not new to the divine plan. God had been doing so for a long time now in the case of Melchizedek, the multitude from Egypt, Jethro, Rahab, Ruth, and others of their kind. They too were objects of His mercy even as Amos 9:7 had claimed. Now Nineveh could also claim that same distinction.

RULER OF ISRAEL: MICAH

Like his contemporary Isaiah, Micah stressed God's incomparability. As if to anticipate his ministry, his name means "Who is like Yah[weh]?" His message also concluded with the same question: "Who is a God like Thee, pardoning iniquity?" (7:18). Yahweh was "the Lord of the whole earth" (4:13); and this was evident, as with most of the prophets, in the dual combination of divine works: judgment and salvation. In three messages, each beginning with "Hear ye" (1:2; 3:1; 6:1), Micah decried the sin of Israel and Jacob. Their sins ran the gamut of wickedness including idolatry (1:7a), harlotry (v. 7b), greed (2:1-2), perversion of true doctrine and religion (2:6-9; 6:2-7), false prophets (3:5-6), occult (v. 7), and presumption (vv. 9-11). They had repeatedly broken the Ten Commandments: the so-called second table (6:10-12) and the first table (vv. 13-15).

But God will intervene. The vocabulary of theophany, complete with the now familiar themes of earthquake and fire, opened the prophecy in 1:2-4. Yahweh would come to destroy the northern kingdom and its capital, Samaria. This local intervention was the start of God's judgment, which always began at the house of God; but that same anger and wrath would be worked on all "the nations that did not obey" Him (5:15).

Yet Micah was no more able to rest his case there than was any other prophet of judgment or doom. He too ended each of his three sections with those glimpses of bright hope that sparkled with the ancient threads of the promise. Thus Micah 2:12-13 was the first such word of hope. So sudden was this about-face that most cannot see how the same prophet could have shifted so quickly from his words of doom. But Leslie Allen[8] has shown how similiar this word was to one credited to Isaiah in 2 Kings 19:31. He also noted that the word "gate" in verse 13 harked back to "the gate of Jerusalem" in 1:12 and "the gate of my people" in verse 9. Therefore, it did fit the internal scheme and context of the writer.

---

[8]Leslie Allen, *The Books of Joel, Obadiah, Jonah and Micah* (Grand Rapids: Eerdmans, 1976), p. 301.

Its meaning was twofold: Yahweh would regather His sheep, the "remnant of Israel," in some unspecified future day and lead them through the gate as their "Head" and "King." Three times in verse 12 Jacob and Israel were promised the same deliverance they had had from Egypt (Exod. 13:21; Deut. 1:30,33). "All of you," promised Micah, will be assembled and led by the "breaker" (*happōrēṣ*, the bellwether, leading ram) through the gates of their enemies' cities. Just as Sennacherib's blockade on Hezekiah inside Jerusalem had been suddenly swept away overnight in a most decisive way, so it would be in that wonderful day when King Yahweh led His people's procession in their new return.

The heart of Micah's message of hope was set in chapters 4-5. Here he moved in three stages. He first assured Jerusalem that in spite of the fact that "Jerusalem would become a heap of ruins" (3:12), yet as Isaiah had said (Isa. 2:2-4), "The mountain of the house of the Lord would be established as the top of the mountains" (Mic. 4:1-5). The second stage (Mic. 4:6-13), resembling Amos 9:11ff., assured Zion that she would ultimately triumph over all the nations even though the "tower" of David would lose for a brief time its "former dominion" and "the daughter of Zion" would experience for a time the pangs of childbirth. But the grandest prediction saw all the travail of the years exchanged for a ruler named "Peace," who would be born in the little town of Bethlehem in fulfillment of the ancient promise (5:1-15).

These events would come to pass "in the latter days" (4:1), a phrase whose meaning already had been well established by antecedent theology: this was to be part of the day of the Lord. Jerusalem itself would have its fortunes reversed. It would now be central in the thoughts, importance, and journeys of the nations. From that center would go not only ethical and doctrinal teaching but arbitration for all the nations as well (4:3a)! The result of Messiah's reign in Zion would be an unprecedented and uninterrupted era of peace and secure prosperity (vv. 3b-4).

Again, Micah promised a "remnant" would be regathered (4:7a) when the Lord would reign over them in Mount Zion (v. 7b). The "tower of the flock" (v. 8, *migdal 'ēder*) probably was a place near Jerusalem (Gen. 35:21), about a mile from Bethlehem according to Jerome.[9] It therefore stood for David's birthplace by metonymy. The "hill" (4:8, *'ōpel*), or Ophel, was the conventional name for the southeast

---

[9]Charles L. Feinberg, *Jonah, Micah, Nahum* (New York: American Board of Missions to Jews, 1951), p. 87. Others refer to the "sheep-tower" on south end of the temple hill.

slope of temple hill in Jerusalem where King David had ruled. Both these places would be restored to their "former dominion" (v. 8). God was doing all things, including the temporary demise of glory and the travail of the nation, according to His "plan" and "thoughts" (v. 12). In the end, Zion's military power would be as if she had an "iron horn" and her hoofs as bronze as she triumphed over her enemies (4:13; cf. Micah's probable namesake, Micah ben Imlah in 1 Kings 22:9).

From these pains of childbirth would come fruit. From Bethlehem, or according to its ancient name, Ephrathah (cf. Ruth 1:2), would come the Davidic "Ruler" (*môšēl*). As von Orelli commented:

> Out of Bethlehem, with scarcely the rank of a country-town, will come forth One whose name is here mysteriously suppressed, only the dignity that awaits him being mentioned . . . Moreover, the next mysterious feature forms a significant contrast to the obscure birthplace of the Messiah: "His going forth from the gray foretime, from days immemorial." Does this only mean that His extraction is traceable to the earliest age, that He is thus of good race, as in fact (Ruth iv.11ff.) David's ancestors are traced back to Perez, son of Judah? Although it must be conceded that *'ôlām* in poetic-prophetic discourse has not always an unlimited range (cf. Amos ix.11), it would yield here a very tame sense, especially to the Hebrew, to think only of physical descent from Jesse the humble ancestor, or from Judah. The descent of every genuine Israelite even from Jacob-Abraham was understood as matters of course. Or does this weighty description, containing a twofold, far-reaching definition of time, teach the pre-temporal existence of the Messiah, so that we should have here as in John i.1ff., viii.58, an irrefutable testimony to Christ's pre-existence? The expressions *qeḏem*, *'ôlām*, and the general conceptions of the Israelites, are too little metaphysical to warrant such an inference. Moreover, strictly speaking, a premundane existence is not affirmed, but a coming from time immemorial. In Micah vii. 20, *qeḏem* is used in reference to the patriarchal promises. We therefore do most justice to the statement by taking it to mean that the future ruler from Bethlehem is he who has been in God's view in the development of things . . . His beginnings are rooted in God's primeval redeeming plan.[10]

The scope of this new Davidic ruler's powers would be world-wide. He would defend Israel (5:5-6), enable them to overcome their enemies (vv. 7-9), and personally obliterate all weapons of warfare

---

[10]C. von Orelli, *The Old Testament Prophecy of the Consummation of God's Kingdom Traced in Its Historical Development*, trans. J. J. Banks (Edinburgh: T. & T. Clark, 1889), pp. 307-8.

(vv. 10-15). The "Assyrian" of verse 5 is typical and representative of all of Israel's enemies in that future day when the nations shall attempt to deal once and for all with "the Jewish question." The result here is the same as that already traced in Joel 3. However, there will be adequate princes ("seven," yea "eight," v. 5) to meet every onslaught from the enemy. The "remnant of Jacob" would be like dew and showers (v. 7), like a lion or a young lion (v. 8), i.e., a source of blessing for the righteous and conquest against the wicked.

What God required of men in the meantime (6:6) was (1) fair and just dealings with their fellowmen and (2) a diligent life of faith lived in close communion with God (v. 8). That was the epitome and quintessence of the law. Ceremonial exactitude as an end in itself was as despised by God as it was worthless to its participants.

Micah concluded his message with his confident expectations for the future and his prayers for Israel (7:7-20). "I will wait for the God of my salvation" (v. 7), he prayed in a psalm of confidence (vv. 7-10). And after praying for the accomplishment of God's purpose for his land and people (vv. 14-17; cf. vv.11-13), he hymned a song of praise to God (vv. 18-20) for His incomparable forgiveness and "steadfast love" (*ḥeseḏ*) (v. 18), which again demonstrated just what He had sworn[11] to their fathers Jacob and Abraham. Their sins and iniquities, not their persons, would be "cast into the depths of the sea" (v. 19). Micah's theology does indeed shout the question of Isaiah 40, "To whom then will you liken God?"

THE PROMISE THEOLOGIAN: ISAIAH

Beyond all question, Isaiah was the greatest of all the OT prophets, for his thought and doctrine covered as wide a range of subjects as did the length of his ministry. While his writing can be divided into two parts, chapters 1-39 keyed mainly to judgment and chapters 40-66 primarily emphasizing comfort, the book stands as a unit with its own continuity features such as the unique and distinctive phrase "the Holy One of Israel," which occurs twelve times in the first part and fourteen times in the second part.[12]

---

[11]The oath of God receives special treatment in Psalm 105:8-11. There and in all of its other occurrences (Gen. 22:16; 26:3; 50:24; Exod. 13:5,11; 33:1; Num. 11:12; 14:16,23; 32:11; in Deuteronomy, Joshua, Judges, and Jer. 32:22) "the content of this oath is the gift of the land" according to James L. Mays, *Micah: A Commentary* (Philadelphia: Westminster Press, 1976), pp. 168-69.

[12]Conservatives have pointed to some forty additional phrases or sentences that appear in both parts of Isaiah as evidence for its unity, cf. Gleason L. Archer, Jr., *A Survey of Old Testament Introduction*, rev. ed. (Chicago: Moody Press, 1974), pp. 345ff.

The second part of Isaiah's work is a veritable OT biblical theology in itself. It might well be called the "Old Testament book of Romans" or the "New Testament within the Old Testament." Its twenty-seven chapters cover the same scope as the twenty-seven books of the NT. Chapter 40 begins with the predicted voice of John the Baptist crying in the wilderness as does the Gospels: chapters 65-66 climax with the same picture as the Apocalypse of John in Revelation 21-22 of the new heavens and the new earth. Sandwiched between these two end points is the midpoint, Isaiah 52:13-53:12, which is the greatest theological statement on the meaning of the atonement in all Scripture.

No less significant, however, is the first part of Isaiah's writing. Its successive "books," to use Franz Delitzsch's term,[13] are the books of Hardening (chaps. 1-6), Immanuel (7-12), Nations (13-23), the Little Apocalypse (24-27; 34-35), the Chief Cornerstone and Woes (28-33), and Hezekiah (36-39).

In our view, Isaiah must be called the theologian's theologian. And when the continuing promise of God was being considered, Isaiah excelled both in his use of the antecedent theology of the Abrahamic-Mosaic-Davidic promise and in his new contributions and development of that doctrine.

The Holy One of Israel

At the heart of Isaiah's theology was his call in chapter 6. While worshiping in the temple, he was given a vision of the Lord exalted on His throne with His glory—the skirts of His garments—filling the temple. Then he heard the angelic attendants chant the superlative holiness of God, and he saw the earth-filling glory of God.

This vision with its anthropomorphic but highly theological language is the key to Isaiah's theology. In these two central concepts, holiness and glory, Isaiah had set before him the themes for his prophecy and ministry.

Yahweh was the thrice holy God whose uniqueness, separateness, and transcendence were so immediately apparent even to the prophet that he cried out, "Woe is me; for I am undone; because I am a man of unclean lips" (Isa. 6:5). Like Moses of yesteryear, Isaiah learned that since the Lord God was holy, Israel should also be holy. God's holiness was to be seen in His moral perfection, His righteousness, and in His pure conduct.

---

[13]Franz Delitzsch, *The Prophecies of Isaiah,* 2 vols. in C. F. Keil and F. Delitzsch, *Biblical Commentary on the Old Testament,* 25 vols., trans. James Martin (Grand Rapids: Eerdmans, 1969), 1:v-vii; 2:v.

But not only was Isaiah unfit in comparison to the holiness of God; so was Israel: "I dwell in the midst of a people of unclean lips" (v. 5). That was the point of placing chapters 1-5 in front of the call of Isaiah in chapter 6. It spelled out the necessity of Isaiah's message to Israel to either repent or face judgment. Israel was more the rebel (1:2,4), hypocrite (vv. 10-15), and contemptuous breaker of the commandments (5:8-23) than she was God's "holy nation" or His "kingly priests."

Yahweh was holy or separate from His people in His being as well as His morality. The idols, the "work of men's hands" (2:8,20), were "nothings" and "nonentities" (*'elîlîm*, 2:8,18,20 bis). Beside Yahweh there was none other. Such transcendence and majestic sovereignty made the teaching of God's incomparability one of Isaiah's grandest doctrines, especially in the oft-repeated question of Isaiah 40: "To whom then will you liken me?"

Thus God's judgment had to fall when a stubborn populace hardened its heart as a result of Isaiah's ministry of this word of holiness (6:9-12). Apparently, too many in Judah had mistaken the royal theology with its unconditional promise to David as a blanket approval of everything the people did, good or bad. The people falsely assumed that God would never visit Zion with destruction—He would only devastate His promise and everlasting plan. Therefore, according to their ill-advised reasoning, God was stuck with them—for better or for worse—and at the moment it was admittedly worse. But the surprise was to be theirs. Isaiah announced that he would preach "until the cities lie waste without inhabitant, and houses without men, and the land was utterly desolate, and the Lord [had] removed [the] men far away" (Isa. 6:11-12).

Such talk sounded treasonous. It admittedly sounded like a rejection of the patriarchal promise about the land and the Mosaic election of a people. That is where the second motif of Isaiah's vision of the Lord in the temple played its part: the glory of God.

God's glory would yet fill the whole earth. There would indeed be a remnant, called here "a tenth" (*'ašîrîyyâh*, 6:13), which would remain like a stump after the tree is felled. And "the holy seed was its stump," said Isaiah with a triumphant and obvious backward glance at the Abrahamic and Edenic word about the "seed" of promise. This theme he developed in the Little Apocalypse of Isaiah 24-27 and in 40-66. The glorious final state "at the end of the days" of God's plan would see Jerusalem exalted as the center of the nations and the center for instruction in the paths of the Lord (2:2-4; cf. the discussion in Micah). Zion would be the center from which God's newly reconstituted people would come after catastrophic judgment

(30:15). Thus, fair interpreters who take this call chapter (6) seriously do not find the theme of triumph and glory to be any more of an intrusion or a detraction than the demand for holiness is such with its accompanying threat of judgment. The two are authentic motifs in Isaiah.

The Branch of Yahweh

Who is the "sprout" or "branch" (*ṣemaḥ*) of Isaiah 4:2-6? Very few doubt that the one who is afterward called "the Branch" is the Messiah. Nor do they doubt that later prophets directly depend on Isaiah 4:2 for that title. Those prophets who use this title for Messiah are:

"Branch of Yahweh" (Isa. 4:2)
"Branch of David" (Jer. 23:5-6)
"The Branch, My Servant" (Zech. 3:8)
"Branch, a man" (Zech. 6:12).

In Isaiah 4:2 the "Branch of Yahweh" is the Davidic dynasty in its human ("fruit of the land") nature as well as its divine ("of Yahweh"). In this case "Branch" would be an equivalent term for "Anointed" or "holy One."

But many object that "Branch" was not yet a fixed designation for Messiah; besides, its parallelism with "the fruit of the land" (4:2) favored a reference to the sprouting forth of the land under the beneficent influence of Yahweh. However, as the following chapters of Isaiah show, Messiah was the Mediator of these benefits and He Himself was the greatest of all the benefits.

Is it any wonder then that the later prophets applied this title to the living personal source of all these gifts in the last days? Some of those gifts found already in this passage are (1) the promise of the fruitfulness of the land; (2) the certainty of a remnant of "survivors"; (3) the holiness of the remnant; (4) the cleansing and purification of the moral filth of the people; and (5) the radiant glory of the personal presence of Yahweh dwelling in Zion with His people forever. The "holy nation" of Exodus 19:6 would finally be completely realized as would the permanent "dwelling" of Yahweh in their midst. Even the "cloud by day" and "fire by night" (4:5) were to be renewed. For just as they were the visible proofs of God's presence in the wilderness (Exod. 14:19ff.), so they would be a shade by day and illuminate the night to shield the city of God from all violence.

Immanuel

What the previous "Branch [or Sprout] of the Lord" passage left indefinite was now given personal shape and definition in the Immanuel prophecies of Isaiah 7-11. This word came against the background of the Syro-Ephraimitic War in which Pekah, king of Israel, made an alliance with Rezin, king of Syria, to advance against Ahaz, king of Judah, with a view to installing the son of Tabeal as king on David's throne. This threat to Jerusalem and Judah was countered by Isaiah's invitation to Ahaz to "believe" God in order that Ahaz himself might "be believed," i.e., established (7:9). In fact, God would validate His good offer in so improbable a situation by performing any sign (i.e., miracle) Ahaz might choose from Sheol or heaven.

But Ahaz, true unbeliever that he was, piously rejected Yahweh's help with an oblique reference to Deuteronomy 6:16 about not tempting the Lord his God. The truth of the matter was that he expected little from Yahweh; moreover, he had probably already secretly sought the support of Tiglath-pileser, king of Assyria (2 Kings 16:7ff.).

Nevertheless, the Lord proceeded to give a sign. It was: "Behold, [you] the virgin are pregnant and bearing a son; you shall call his name Immanuel" (7:14). Now it is important to note several things: (1) the word *'almâh* denotes a "virgin" in every case where its meaning can be determined;[14] (2) it has the definite article, "*the* virgin*"*; (3) the verb "to call" is second person feminine and not third person feminine; and (4) the wording of this verse made use of older biblical phraseology: at the birth of Ishmael (Gen. 16:11); at the birth of Isaac (Gen. 17:19); and at the birth of Samson (Judg. 13:5,7). Thus, the sign given to Ahaz consisted in repeating to him the familiar phrases used in promising the birth of a son.

But this passage dealt with the birth of three children, all three being signs in Israel (8:17-18). Each of the three was introduced and then was later the subject of an expanded prophecy as follows:

1. Shear-Jashub—"remnant shall return"
   7:3 → 10:20,21,22; 11:11,16)
2. Immanuel—"God with us"
   7:14 → 8:8,10)
3. Mahershalalhashbaz—"haste spoil, hurry prey"
   8:1,3,4 → 10:2,6).

In each of these passages we have the mention of a child born in fulfillment of the promise that had been made to David, to the

---

[14]Besides this text, it appears in the account of Rebekah (Gen. 24:43); the sister of Moses (Exod. 2:8); in the phrase "the way of a man with a maid" (Prov. 30:19); and in the plural in Psalm 68:25 [26]; Song of Solomon 1:3; 6:8; and the titles to Psalm 46 and 1 Chronicles 15:20.

effect that his seed should be eternal . . . In the second half of his discourse on the three children, Isaiah thus reiterates the promise that had been made to David, and insists upon it. He makes it the foundation of his rebuke to the people for their corruptions . . .

Those who heard him understood that when Ahaz refused to ask the offered sign, the prophet repeated to him, in a new form, Jehovah's promise concerning the seed of David, and made that to be a sign that Jehovah would both keep his present pledge and punish Ahaz for his faithlessness. It may be doubted whether any of them had in mind the idea of just such a person as Jesus, to be born of a virgin, in some future century; but they had in mind some birth in the unending line of David which would render the truth, "God with us," especially significant.[15]

Furthermore, before this son, the most recent birth in the line of David, was able to understand right from wrong (7:16-17), a political revolution of major proportions would remove both Pekah and Rezin from power. But several other facts must be borne in mind at once if one is rightly to identify this "son." According to 8:8,10, he is addressed as the prince of the land ("thy land, O Immanuel") and as the expected anointed one of David's house in 9:6-7 [5-6] ("There will be no end of the increase of his government and peace [as he rules] on the throne of David over his kingdom . . . forevermore.") Also Isaiah, like his contemporary Micah, everywhere presupposes that a period of judgment must precede the glorious messianic age. Therefore, whatever this sign and birth is, it cannot be the completion of the "last days."

Who then was this child? His messianic dignity totally excludes the notion that he may have been Isaiah's son born to some maiden newly married to the prophet after Shear-Jashub's mother supposedly died. Still less likely is it a reference to any marriageable maiden or some particular ideal maiden present at the time of the proclamation of this prophecy since the prophet has definitely said "*the* virgin." It is preferable to understand him to be a son of Ahaz himself, whose mother Abi, daughter of Zechariah, is mentioned in 2 Kings 18:2—namely, his son Hezekiah. It is well known that this was the older Jewish interpretation, but it is also supposed that Hezekiah could not be the predicted "sign" of 7:14 since on present chronologies he must have already been nine years old at that time (about 734 B.C.). That last point is to be thoroughly studied before it is adopted. The chronology of Israel and Judah has been well secured with only one minor exception—a ten year difficulty in the

---

[15]Willis J. Beecher, "The Prophecy of the Virgin Mother: Isa. vii:14," *Homiletical Review* 17 (1889): 357-58.

rule of Hezekiah. Without arguing the point at this time, I would like to boldly suggest that only Hezekiah meets all the demands of the text of Isaiah and yet demonstrates how he could be part and parcel of that climactic messianic person who would complete all that is predicted in this Immanuel prophecy. Only in this, the most recent installment in the Abrahamic-Davidic promise, could it be seen how God was still being "with" Israel in all His power and presence.

In Isaiah 9:6, a series of descriptive epithets are given to this newborn son who is to climax the line of David. He is "wonderful Counsellor," "mighty God," "Father of eternity,"[16] and "Prince of Peace." These four names, represent, respectively, (1) the victory due to His wise plans and great skill in battle; (2) the irresistible Conqueror (cf. 10:21); (3) the fatherly rule of Messiah and His divine attribute of eternality; and (4) the everlasting peaceful reign of Messiah. His government and the peace during His regime would know no boundaries, for He would establish His kingdom in justice and righteousness forevermore (Isa. 9:7). Unique among the descriptions of peace that will be observed during that era is the picture of all nature at rest and devoid of hostility (11:6-9). Again, there is a graphic prediction of the restoration of both the north and south to the land "in that day" (vv. 10-16). And from the stump of David's father, Jesse, would come that "shoot," even a "branch" (*nēzer*), upon whom the sevenfold gift of the Spirit of the Lord would rest as He ruled and reigned righteously and awesomely (vv. 1-5). The whole picture of the future person and work of the Messiah was cast in terms of the Davidic promise as a glowing encouragement for Israel.

The Lord of History

Yahweh's purpose and plan embraced the whole earth with all its nations. Nations rose and fell in accordance with that plan (Isa. 14:24-27). But when national pride became exalted and motivated by imperialistic aggression, these nations were reminded quickly that they could not continue on ruthlessly. Even when they were the God-ordained instruments of judgment aimed at Israel, they were not to burn, kill, and destroy at will whomever they wished; for in that case, Yahweh would again remind them that they were merely His axes. The axe must not pretend that it was equal to the one who chops with it any more than the saw was greater than the one who

---

[16]It is not "Father of booty," which does not match the permanent attribute of "Prince of Peace"; rather, the Hebrew *ʾᵃḇ ʿaḏ* is "Father of Eternity" as *ʿaḏ* means in Genesis 49:26, Isaiah 57:15, and Habakkuk 3:6.

sawed with it (Isa. 10:15). So Assyria would learn that she served at the pleasure of the living God and not her own.

The prophecies concerning some ten nations were compiled in Isaiah 13-23. The most amazing of all is Isaiah 19. It is a burden message against Egypt wherein the Lord Himself would bring judgment on Egypt's government (2-4), economy (5-10), and wisdom (11-13). As if to underline the source of these judgments, verse 14 again stresses that it was Yahweh who had mixed a spirit of confusion in Egypt.

However, there was to be another "day," part of that grand future "day." "In that day," Judah would terrify Egypt according to the plan of the Lord of Hosts (19:16-17). And a harsh ruler would oppress his own Egyptian subjects (v. 20); but Yahweh would miraculously deliver Egypt so that she along with Israel and Assyria should be thirds together in worshiping the Lord and in inheriting from the Lord (vv. 24-25). Thus, even though the Lord would smite Egypt, He would heal her by sending a judge or "savior" as He had done for Israel in the period of the judges. Then Egypt would worship the living God along with Israel (vv. 18-19; 21-22).

As Yahweh had dealt with Samaria and Damascus in the Syro-Ephraimitic War, so would He deal with all nations. He alone would be sovereign in spite of all their supposed sovereignty. He would also finally triumph over them all. This process of shaking the nations is dramatically told in the "Little Apocalypse" of Isaiah 24-27.

The Chief Cornerstone

Proud Samaria was still standing when the prophecy of Isaiah 28 announcing the end of this "fading flower" of Ephraim was uttered. Yet there was a rebuke for Jerusalem also, for as in chapter 7, Judah had turned to Assyria instead of the Lord for her help. The word of the prophets was disregarded as so much trivia, for the people fancied themselves quite secure against death and Sheol. But they too were doomed. Their lies and deceit would shelter nothing: they would be caught in the overwhelming flood.

Meanwhile, Adonai, the sovereign Lord, was laying in Zion a foundation stone. The basic passage which informed the theology of this text is Genesis 49:24 where the "mighty one of Jacob" was called the "stone of Israel." Likewise, Deuteronomy 32:4 had identified God as a Rock (*ṣûr*), and Isaiah 8:14 identified God as both a rock and stone. In contrast to the shaky shelter offered by lies, the stone stood firm and immovable.

Ever since the Davidic dynasty had been inaugurated, this stone had lain in Zion. It was therefore a "stone of testing," for men would be tested by it. Whereas in Isaiah 8:14 the Lord Himself is called a Stone of stumbling and Rock of offense, here the stone is His revelation and work in the world. That stone would be fixed in location and precious in value so that all who believed in Him would not be restless. They would be quiet and relaxed in contrast to the excited, agitated, and false refuge previously offered by their lies.

It had been said of Abraham that he "believed" (*he'emîn*, Gen. 15:6) and God added it up to him for "righteousness" (*sedaqâh*). That faith was a full inward surrender to the Lord; it was a trust in the divine promise which was later repeated to the other patriarchs and to David, Solomon, and their line. The divine promise was the object and content of their faith. Isaiah's demand for faith appeared for the first time using the verb *he'emîn* in 7:9; thereafter it was used in 11:5 and 28:16. It was a believing trust, a regarding God as a steadfast object of trust. The stem *bāṭaḥ* is used of belief in God in Isaiah 30:15, but it is used of false confidence in Isaiah 30:12; 31:1; 32:9-11. Other great words of faith or belief in Isaiah are "hope" (*qiwwâh*, 8:17; 40:31); "wait for" (*ḥikkâh*, 8:17; 30:18); and "rest" (*nûaḥ*, 28:12 bis; 30:15).

Short Theology of the Old Testament

One of the most remarkable sections of all the OT is Isaiah 40-66. In its general plan, it is laid out in three enneads: chapters 40-48, 49-57, and 58-66. In each of these three sets of nine messages the focus is directed to the particular aspect of the person and work of God. It is as close to being a systematic statement of OT theology as is the book of Romans in the NT. Its majestic movement begins with the announcement of the person and work of John the Baptist and spins to the dizzy heights of the suffering and triumphant serv-ant of the Lord by the time the middle of the second ennead is reached. But this climax is again superceded by the concluding message on the new heavens and the new earth.

In each of the three sections there is a central figure. In Isaiah 40-48 the key figure is a hero who would come from the East to redeem Israel from captivity, namely, "Cyrus." The revelation of this hero, coming as it did right in the middle of the addresses (44:28-45:10), served as a bold challenge to the idols or deities embraced in that day to do likewise for the people. However, their inability to speak anything about the future could only lead to one conclusion: Yahweh was indeed the only God, and they were noth-ing at all.

In Isaiah 49-57 the central figure is the "servant of the Lord," who combined in his person all the people Israel, the prophet and prophetic institution, and the Messiah in His role as Servant. Again the climactic description and his most important work was located at the middle point of this ennead: 52:13-53:12. The salvation effected by this servant had both objective and subjective aspects (54:1-56:9); indeed, its final and concluding work would involve the glorification of all nature.

The third ennead, 58-66, triumphantly announces the dawning of a new day of salvation for nature, nations, and individuals. At the center of this ennead was a new principle of life—the Spirit-filled Messiah (61:1-63:6) who bore the powers and dignities of the prophetic, priestly, and kingly officers.

Thus in each successive ennead another aspect of the Godhead and God's work was celebrated. In order, the emphases on the persons of the Godhead are Father, "Servant" [Son], and Holy Spirit. In work, they are Creator—Lord of history, Redeemer, and sovereign Ruler over all in the "eschaton." The five major forces in Isaiah's message are God, the people of Israel, the event of salvation, the prophet, and the word of God. Finally, this message even has several distinctive stylistic features. It has a plethora of divine self-asseverations such as "I am the first and the last," or "I am Yahweh"; a long series of participial phrases after the formula "Thus says the Lord" or "I am the Lord" which continue on to detail His special character; and a profuse number of appositional words appearing after the names of Yahweh or Israel as well as a great abundance of verbs to describe Yahweh's work of judgment or salvation. Such is the style of this most magnificent section of the OT. But let us treat each of these enneads in turn to examine that theology more closely.

1. *The God of All (Isa. 40-48).* The theme of Isaiah's call returns in this section as the holiness and righteousness of God are praised repeatedly. God is "the Holy One" (40:25; 41:14,16,20; 43:3,14; 47:4; 48:17; and it continues in the later sections in 49:7 bis; 54:5; 55:5). He also is righteous (*sedeq*), i.e., straight, right, and faithful to a norm, His own nature and character. His righteousness could best be seen in His work of salvation, for the prophet often joined His righteousness and His performance of the covenant promise together (e.g., 41:2; 42:6-7; 46:12-13; note later 51:1,5,6,8; 54:10; 55:3; 62:1-2). Only of God could it be said, "He is right" (41:26) or He is "a righteous God and Savior" (45:21), who declares "what is right" (v. 19) and who brings men near to His righteousness (46:13).

His nature is especially to be seen in His singleness and self-sufficiency. In Isaiah's famous set of six variations on the formula of self-predication, he set forth the incomparability[17] of Yahweh: Beside Him there was no other God (44:6,8; 45:5-6,21). Thus the question remained: "To whom then will you liken Me?" (40:18,25; 46:5). The forms of self-predication[18] are:

> "I am Yahweh" or "I am Yahweh your God"
> (41:13; 42:6,8; 43:3,11; 45:5,6,18)
> "I am the first and I am the last"
> (41:4; 44:6; 48:12)
> "I am He"
> (41:4; 43:10,25; 46:4; 48:12)
> "I am God"
> (43:13; 46:9)
> "I am your God"
> (41:10)

But God's works were likewise enumerated in this first ennead. He was Creator, Kinsman-Redeemer, Lord of history, King of all, and Discloser of the future.

Repeatedly Isaiah stressed the fact that God had "created" (*bārā'*); "made" (*'āśâh* or *pā'al*); "spread out" (*nāṭâh*), "stretched out" (*rāqa'*), "established" (*kûn*), and "founded" (*yāsaḏ*) the heavens and the earth. In this vocabulary, so reminiscent of Genesis 1-2, he established God's ability to create as part of His credentials as rightful Lord of man's present history and final destiny (40:15,17, 23-34; 42:5; 43:1-7; and later 54:15-16).

Yahweh was also a Kinsman-Redeemer (*gô'el*) as Boaz was to Ruth. The verb to redeem (*gā'al*) and its derivatives appear twenty-two times. Here Isaiah used the motif of the Exodus as his source (cf. Exod. 6:6; 15:13; Isa. 45:15,21). Involved in this redemption were (1) physical redemption from bondage (43:5-7; 45:13; 48:20; and later 49:9,11,14; 52:2-3; 55:12-13); (2) inward, personal and spiritual redemption with the removal of personal sin for Israel (43:25; 44:22; 54:8) and Gentiles (45:20-23; 49:6; 51:4-5); and (3) the eschatological redemption when Jerusalem and the land were rebuilt (40:9-10; 43:20; 44:26; 45:13; 49:16-17; 51:3; 52:1,9; 53:11-12). Yahweh was a Kinsman-Redeemer without equal.[19]

---

[17]For an excellent study on this concept, see C. J. Labuschagne, *The Incomparability of Yahweh in the Old Testament* (Leiden: E. J. Brill, 1966), esp. pp. 111-12, 123f., 142-53.

[18]See the discussion by Morgan L. Phillips, "Divine Self-Predication in Deutero-Isaiah," *Biblical Research* 16(1971): 32-51.

[19]See F. Holmgren, *The Concept of Yahweh as Gô'el in Second Isaiah* (Diss., Union Theological Seminary, New York: University Microfilms, 1963). Also Carroll Stuhlmueller, *Creative Redemption in Deutero-Isaiah* (Rome: Biblical Institute Press, 1970).

Currently, Yahweh was in charge of history itself, and the nations did not frighten Him at all (40:15,17). In fact, foreign leaders were raised up to do His bidding in history (as is so aptly illustrated by Cyrus in 41:1-4); and they were ransomed or conquered on His authority (43:3-14; 44:24-45:8; 47:5-9). No wonder He was called "King" on four occasions. He was "King of Jacob" (41:21); "your King," O Israel (43:15); "King of Israel" (44:6); and as 52:7 summarized, "Your God is King." Isaiah also used the additional royal titles of "Shepherd" (40:9-11), "Witness," "Commandment-Giver," and "Leader" in Isaiah 55:3.[20]

One more word must be added before leaving the theology of this ennead: Yahweh was the discloser of the future. Before things happened, the prophet was told about them (41:22-23,26; 42:9; 43:9-10; 44:7-8; 45:21; 46:10-11; 48:5). The challenge to the gods, who were poor rivals and actually nonentities at best, was to declare what was to come to pass in the future, be it good or bad. The most graphic of all the predictions was the naming of Cyrus and two of his greatest works for Israel almost two centuries before they took place (44:28). On such works as these Isaiah rested his case. Yahweh was God of gods, Lord of lords, King of kings and beyond all comparison. He was the God of all.

2. The Savior of All (Isa. 49-57). Two words would summarize the second plank in Isaiah's minitheology book: servant and salvation. But it was the figure of the servant of the Lord that captured the limelight in this section.

The advances in the portrayal of this corporate figure of "servant" are already observable in the use of the singular form twenty times in Isaiah 40-53 and in the plural form ten times in Isaiah 54-66.[21] To demonstrate that the servant is a collective term as well as an individual one representing the whole group can be done from two sets of data: (1) the servant is all Israel in twelve out of the twenty singular references (41:8-10; 43:8-13; 43:14-44:5; 44:6-8,21-23; 44:24-45:13; 48:1,7,10-12,17); (2) the four great servant songs of Isaiah 42:1-7; 49:1-6; 50:4-9; and 52:13-53:12 all present the servant as an individual who ministers to Israel. Therein lies one of the greatest puzzles for those scholars who reject the corporate solidarity of the servant.

---

[20]Carroll Stuhlmueller, "Yahweh-King and Deutero-Isaiah," *Biblical Research* 11(1970): 32-45.

[21]Isaiah 54:17; 56:6; 63:17; 65:8-9,13 ter,14-15; 66:14.

Israel, the servant, is the "seed of Abraham," the patriarchal "friend" of God (41:8). "Abraham . . . was called and blessed" when "he was but one" and was subsequently "made . . . many" (51:2; cf. 63:16). Now God had already called Abraham His servant in Genesis 26:24; and so had Moses referred to Abraham, Isaac, and Jacob as servants of the Lord (Exod. 32:13; Deut. 9:27). In fact, all Israel was regarded as His servants in Leviticus 25:42,55. Thus the seed was still the center of God's blessings (43:5; 44:3; 45:19,25; 48:19; 53:10; 54:3; 59:21; 61:9). "The seed shall be known among the nations . . . that they are a seed whom Yahweh has blessed" (65:9,23; 66:22). That seed was God's "servant," or as it regularly appears in Isaiah 54-66, His "servant*s*." As John Bright noted,

> The figure of the Servant oscillates between the individual and the group . . . He is the coming Redeemer of the true Israel who in his suffering makes the fulfillment of Israel's task possible; he is the central actor in the "new thing" that is about to take place.[22]

In the four servant songs, many of the individual's titles or descriptions are matched by identical ascriptions made of Israel in the Isaianic poems, for example:

An Individual		*All Israel*
42:1	"my chosen"	41:8-9
49:3	"my servant"	44:21
49:6	"a light to the nations"	42:6; 51:4
49:1	"called me from the womb"	44:2, 24; 43:1
49:1	"named my name"	43:1*b*

Yet, striking as this evidence might be, the servant of the songs has the task and mission "to bring Israel back" and "to gather" Israel to Himself, "to raise up the tribes of Jacob and restore the preserved of Israel" (49:5-6). Therefore, the servant of the Lord cannot be totally equated with Israel as the servant in all respects. The apparent ambivalence is the same type of oscillation found in all the collective terms previously observed in the promise doctrine. They were all-inclusive of all Israel, but they were simultaneously always focused on one representative who depicted the fortunes of the whole group for that present time and the climactic future. The connection was to be found not in some psychological theory of personality but in the "everlasting covenant," even the "sure loyal love for David" (Isa. 55:3; 61:8; cf. 2 Sam. 7). The servant of the Lord was the messianic person in the Davidic line then and finally that

---

[22]John Bright, *Kingdom of God* (Nashville: Abingdon, 1953), p. 150ff.

last new David who was to come and who was known as the Seed, the Holy One *(ḥāsîd)*, the Branch, etc.

The second ennead also detailed the salvation won by the Servant. In a real turn of events, the prophet Isaiah had God take the cup of God's wrath from Israel's lips and put it to her oppressor's mouth instead (51:22-23; cf. the seventh century prophet Nahum [1:11-14]). Furthermore, a new exodus and redemption were envisaged for the future (52:1-6). This "good news" *(mᵉbaśśēr)* to Zion. Then all the ends of the earth would see God's salvation (52:9-10; cf. 40:9).

This Servant who would personally rule, a fact that would startle all the kings of the earth (52:15), would also be the One who would suffer on behalf of all humanity so as to make God's atonement available. The first advent of this Servant would amaze many (vv. 13-14), but His second advent would catch the breath of even the kings of the earth (52:15)—therein lay the mystery of the Servant. His rejection followed: men would reject His message (53:1), His person (v. 2), and His mission (v. 3). But His vicarious suffering would effect an atonement between God and man (vv. 4-6); and though He would submit to suffering (v. 7), death (v. 8), and burial (v. 9), He would subsequently be exalted and richly rewarded (vv. 10-12). On the Servant of the Lord, then, was laid the iniquity of all humanity.

The result of the Servant's suffering was that the "seed" would "possess the nations"; for their tent would be enlarged, the ropes lengthened, and the pegs driven in deeper (54:2-3). Yahweh would then be "the God of the whole earth" (54:5; 49:6). Thus, as "it was in the days of Noah," so it would be when Yahweh returned to "gather Israel" and extended His "steadfast love" *(hesed)* and "covenant of peace" (54:5,9-10). Meanwhile, the free offer of salvation was extended to all nations through David's son (55:3-5; cf. 55:1-2,6-9; 49:6; and the NT comment in Acts 13:45-49; 26:22-23).

3. *The End of All History (Isa. 58-66).* The inauguration of the "eschaton" was sharply demarcated by the ending of the "former things"[23] (41:22; 42:9; 43:9,18; 44:8; 46:9; 48:3) and the introduction of God's "new thing." There would be a "new" sincere repentance (58-59), a "new" Jerusalem (60), and a "new" heavens and "new" earth (65:17-25; 66:10-24; cf. 2 Peter 3:13; Rev. 21:1-4).

---

[23]C. R. North, "The Former Things and the 'New Things' in Deutero-Isaiah," *Studies in Old Testament Prophecy*, ed. H. H. Rowley (Edinburgh: T. & T. Clark, 1950), pp. 111-26.

This would be the aeon of the Holy Spirit according to 63:7-14. A call would go forth for a new Moses to lead a new exodus (vv. 11-14) and give them that "rest" (*nûaḥ*) promised long ago to Joshua. As the servant was empowered by God's Spirit (42:1), so was this "anointed" Person. Indeed, He was equated with the servant in Isaiah 61:1—"The Spirit of the Lord God is on me because the Lord has anointed me." There He described the joy of His mission (vv. 1-3) and the content of His message (vv. 4-9) including:

1. "You shall be called priests of the Lord and ministers of our God" (v. 6; cf. Exod. 19:6).
2. The "everlasting covenant" will be carried out (v. 8).
3. Their "seed" would be known among the nations as those whom God had truly blessed (v. 9).

Even the equipment and character of this Spirit-filled messianic Servant were noted in 61:10-11. He would be clothed with the "garments of salvation" and "cause righteousness and praise to spring forth before all nations."

The Redeemer would come in the last day "for the sake of Zion" (Isa. 59:20). He would be dressed as a warrior (59:15*b*-19) and would wage war on all evil and sin, especially that type of hypocritical life style described in Isaiah 57-59:15*a*. He would be invested with God's words and His Spirit (59:21). Then Jerusalem would experience violence no longer, for the Lord of glory would be her greatest asset (60). The wealth of the nations would pour into Jerusalem as all humanity arrived to praise the Lord (60:4-16). Then the exalted city of Jerusalem would be at peace forever, and the presence of the Lord of everlasting light would make the need for the sun or moon obsolete (vv. 17-22).

While the "day of vengeance" (63:4-6) and "year of redemption" brought judgment on the nations when God trampled down the nations in His winepress, even as Obadiah and Joel had proclaimed, God's irrevocable purpose for a rebuilt city of Jerusalem which would be inhabited by the "holy people" of God would be realized (62). Even though the clothes of the Hero were sprinkled with the blood of the winepress (63:1-6; cf. Isa. 34; Joel 3:9-16; and later Zech. 14; Ezek. 38-39), He would be vindicated as this aeon drew to a close and the new aeon began.

Part of that renewed—for so the word "new" should be understood—world to come, where righteousness dwelt, included new heavens and new earth. Once again, Isaiah's paradisiacal pictures of peace in nature came to the fore (cf. Isa. 11 and 65:17-25; 66:10-

23). Death would be abolished (cf. Isa. 25:8), and the everlasting world-wide rule and reign of the new and final Davidic King would begin. Only the judgment of eternal torment on the wicked and finally unrepentant interrupted this picture, for they were perpetually in agony and forever apart from God.

So Isaiah ended his magnificent shorter theology. His dependence on antecedent theology was evident at almost every turn. While relating the "servant" to the earlier teaching about the "seed" (Isa. 41:8; 43:5; 44:3; 45:19,25; 48:19; 53:10; 54:3; 59:21; 61:9; 65:9,23; 66:22) and to the "covenant" already given (Isa. 42:6; 49:8; 54:10; 55:3; 56:4,6; 59:21; 61:8), not to mention "Abraham" (41:8; 51:2; 63:16) or "Jacob" (41:21; 44:5; 49:26; 60:16) or "David" and the "everlasting covenant" (55:3; 61:8), Isaiah carefully systematized to a large degree the total plan, person, and work of God in the short scope of twenty-seven chapters. No wonder his theology has so profoundly affected men over the centuries.

Chapter 13

Renewal of the Promise: Seventh Century

The seventh century marked one of the most critical periods in the whole history of the nation of Israel, for it then tottered on the threshold of national destruction and the long-predicted Babylonian captivity. Already, Judah's sister nation of the ten northern tribes had met disaster in the previous century after refusing to repent of her sin in spite of the battery of prophets who were graciously sent to her and warned her of the impending danger. Especially disastrous was the northern kingdom's introduction of idolatrous calf worship and its accompanying forms of apostasy. Finally in 722 B.C., Samaria fell to the Assyrian invaders (2 Kings 17); the end came suddenly, and the land was quiet again.

But Judah was none the wiser for the lesson. She too plunged headlong into disaster, courting God's judgment at every turn, with very few reprieves of justice and goodness toward God or man.

Once again God sent prophets, this time to warn Judah. Their theme was the imminent divine judgment. Nahum warned of God's judgment on Nineveh because of that city's wickedness and her ruthless destruction of Samaria in 722 B.C., which had exceeded the method and extent of the divinely authorized judgment on Samaria. Zephaniah reintroduced the message of Joel and Obadiah; however, for him the day of the Lord was both a day of world-wide judgment and a day when Judah would be punished. Habakkuk's message carried God's rebuke for Judah's sin and Babylon's haughty excess in administering that rebuke. But the greatest of all these spokesmen for God was Jeremiah. No prophet agonized more over the announcement of the bitter words of impending judgment than did that man. Yet to him was also given a most surprising word about another future day when God would fulfill His ancient word of promise made to the fathers and David. Thus, as remarkable as the times were, so were the words of the prophets. Instead of concluding that the old promise had now failed and God's everlasting plan had been prematurely terminated, they projected its continuity on into the future.

MISSION TO THE GENTILES REVISITED: NAHUM

Nahum's prophecy was the complement to Jonah, for whereas Jonah celebrated God's mercy, Nahum marked the relentless march of the judgment of God against all sinners world-wide. Jonah 3:10 had focused on God as merciful and forgiving, but Nahum 3:1-8 now demonstrated God's judicial wrath against all wickedness.

However even in this book of judgment, Yahweh's mercy was not altogether absent. Triumphantly Nahum announced that Yahweh was "slow to anger" (1:3a), "good" and "a stronghold in the day of trouble" (v. 7). Thus while He will not overlook or absolve the wicked (v. 3b) since He is "a zealous God" ('ēl qannô') and an avenger of wrongs (v. 2), neither is He without love and forgiveness.

"A zealous [or less appropriately, "jealous"] God . . . is Yahweh" began Nahum in a simple but formidable introduction. Popular misconceptions about this adjective qannô' or the related noun qin'âh must not be attached to Nahum's meaning,[1] i.e., a God who was suspicious, distrustful, and fearful of rivalry. When used of God, it denoted: (1) that attribute which demanded exclusive devotion (Exod. 20:5; 34:14; Deut. 4:24; 5:9; 6:15); (2) that attitude of anger directed against all who persisted in opposing Him (Num. 25:11; Deut. 29:20; Ps. 79:5; Ezek. 5:13; 16:38,42; 25:11; Zeph. 1:18); and (3) the energy He expended in vindicating His people (2 Kings 19:31; Isa. 9:7; 37:32; Joel 2:18; Zech. 1:14; 8:2). Thus His zeal was

---

[1]Walter A. Maier has provided the main substance of our definition here, *The Book of Nahum* (St. Louis: Concordia Publishing House, 1959), pp. 149-50. His defense of Nahum's doctrines on pp. 70-87 is excellent and unmatched in other works on Nahum.

the forerunner of His vindication or impending punishment (Deut. 4:24; Josh. 24:19). He was the Judge, the "Vindicator" (*nōqēm*,[2] not "avenger"); for after years of affliction meted out by the Assyrians, Yahweh would move to vindicate His people. Even the Assyrians would be forced to recognize the universal sovereignty of the Lord.

Three types of transgression committed by Assyria are mentioned. The first, in Nahum 1:11, is probably a reference to Sennacherib's unsuccessful attack on Jerusalem (2 Kings 18), when his generals taunted God's covenant people, the Judeans, with slurs on the impotency of Yahweh (2 Kings 18:22ff.). This transgression was the same type of religious fault committed by the Pharaoh of the Exodus. The second set of sins is in 3:1—the blood guilt of Nineveh as she conducted some of the most murderous and brutal wars known to the ancient Near East.[3] Furthermore, she was filled with deception and lies; she could not be counted on in any of her dealings. Even her plunder was a ready witness against her as she disregarded others' property rights. The third set of sins appears in 3:4 and consisted of a harlotry, which in this case was the sale of nations wherein diplomats bickered over the fate of other nations. Consequently, Nahum was no proud nationalist who evidenced a contemptuous disdain for the heathen. On the contrary, one of his complaints was that Nineveh sold "*nations* through her harlotries and *peoples* through her witchcrafts" (v. 4) so that her sins passed "continually" over all nations (v. 19). Moreover, when Nineveh's fall came, it would be a relief as well as a warning to other nations, for the Lord said, "I will show *nations* thy nakedness and *kingdoms* thy shame" (v. 5). All of Nineveh's robbery, plunder, harlotry, murder, and warmongering, in addition to being basic sins, were also against Yahweh and His plan for the nations (1:11).

A word of blessing or promise was also to be found in Nahum. God still "knew those who took refuge in Him," and He would be their "stronghold in the day of trouble" (1:7). In fact, F. C. Fensham,[4] following the lead of W. L. Moran, identified the word "good" (*tôḇ*) as a covenant term in Nahum 1:7. And following the study of H. W.

---

[2]George Mendenhall, "The 'Vengeance' of Yahweh," *The Tenth Generation* (Baltimore: Johns Hopkins Press, 1973), pp. 69-104.

[3]See the boasts of Ashurbanipal and Shalmaneser as collected in D. D. Luckenbill, *Ancient Records of Assyria and Babylon*, 1:146-48,213; 2:319,304, as quoted in Hobart Freeman, *Nahum, Zephaniah, and Habakkuk* (Chicago: Moody Press, 1973), pp. 36-38.

[4]F. C. Fensham, "Legal Activities of the Lord According to Nahum," *Biblical Essays: Proceedings of the Twelfth Meeting of "Die ou-Testamentiese Werkgemeenskap in Suid-Africa*," ed. A. H. van Zyl (Potchefstroom, 1969), p. 18.

Wolff on Hosea and Herbert B. Huffmon on Near Eastern materials, Fensham also connected the word "to know" (*yāḍaʿ*) with the covenant God had made between Himself and His people (v. 7). Thus while God's enemies would suffer the heat of His anger (vv. 6,8), His own covenant people would be safe in His stronghold.

The "good news" (*meḇaśśēr*) that Nineveh was to be destroyed (Nah. 1:15 [2:1]) was a reminder of God's justice and faithfulness even as it had been in the parallel wording of Isaiah 52:7. Even as the tables had been turned on someone who had gone out from Nineveh (Sennacherib) and had planned and spoken evil against Yahweh and His covenant people only to find that matters had turned out differently, so the cup of affliction had been taken from Israel and had been given to the afflicting nations in Isaiah 51:22-23. Isaiah 52:10-13 went on to point to the universal work of God's salvation and to His Servant who would be His instrument by which His total reign over all humanity would be effected. But so did Nahum 2:1-2 [2-3] place the "good news" about Nineveh's destruction along with Yahweh's work of restoring "the majesty of Jacob and the splendor of Israel." The whole of Israel ("Jacob" and "Israel") would be "restored" (*šûḇ*) while those who had stripped and plundered her vine branches (cf. Ps. 80:8-16) would go down in defeat.

THE DAY OF THE LORD: ZEPHANIAH

Zephaniah ministered during the days of that remarkable king, Josiah (1:1). Abruptly he commenced his prophecy with an announcement of a universal judgment over all the "ground" (v. 2) and "mankind" (v. 3). The terms and scope of this impending divine judgment were precisely those given by God prior to the Noachic flood (Gen. 6:7). The day of the Lord was "at hand" (Zeph. 1:7). It would be "the day of Yahweh's sacrifice" (v. 7), "the great day of Yahweh," " the day of Yahweh's wrath," "a day of terror and distress," "a day of desolation and destruction," "a day of darkness and gloom," "a day of clouds and smoke," "a day of trumpet blast and battle alarm" (vv. 14-16).

Obadiah, Joel, Amos, and Isaiah had all spoken of this day, but Zephaniah alone emphasized more strenuously than them all the universality of its judgment while also surprisingly predicting the conversion of the nations as one of its fruits. Therefore, he urged, "Be still before Yahweh, Lord [of all]! For the day of the Lord is near. The Lord has prepared a slain sacrifice and consecrated His invited ones" (1:7). Isaiah 13:3 had already alluded to that sacrificial feast and to the guests who were the wild foes whom the Lord would

223

summon against His people. Judgment would begin against Judah first (Zeph. 1:4), for so judgment always begins at the house of God. It would be a divine rebuke for Judah's introduction of the worship of Baal, the celestial bodies, and Milcom (vv. 4-6).

Instead, Judah should "seek" (*biqqeš*) and "inquire of" (*dāraš*) Yahweh (1:6). That seeking could be defined: it was an attitude of humility (*ᵃnāwâh*) which turned back to trust Yahweh and drew near to Him (2:3; 3:12). Such humble people of the land observed and did the commands of Yahweh, for the will of God was their own (2:3). They also were known as those who "feared" Him and accepted "discipline" (*mûsār*) in Zephaniah 3:7.[5]

All three of these terms linked the prophet's message to the wisdom literature: the humble, the God-fearers, and those who accepted correction. They would be part of that future "remnant" (*šᵉʾērît*, 2:7,9; cf. 3:13) or "flock" (*ṣōʾn*, 2:6) who would enjoy the promised blessing of God after Yahweh had triumphed over the nations.

Beyond the terrible and dreadful day of the Lord, Zephaniah saw a new era dawning. The gods of the earth would vanish; and from the distant countries of the earth ("isles," meaning those countries surrounding the Mediterranean Sea), all would pray to Yahweh (2:11). Such pedagogical significance to the judgment of the nations had been previously taught in Isaiah 24-27. Now "everyone from his place" (Zeph. 2:11), where they were at home, would pay homage to the Lord.

As Kapelrud summarized the order of the promises,[6] they were as follows: (1) believers would be hidden on the day of wrath (2:3); (2) the remnant would settle down peacefully along the seacoast (v. 7); (3) Israel would have her revenge on her enemies (v. 9); (4) foreigners would call on the name of the Lord (3:9); (5) shame and wickedness would have come to an end and cease forever (vv. 11-13). These promises were followed with a final and triumphant shout: "The King of Israel, the Lord, is in your midst; you shall fear evil no more" (v. 15).

The purification of the language ("lip") of the nations previously defiled by the names of strange gods was much as Isaiah had promised to Ethiopia (Isa. 18:7) and Egypt (Isa. 19:18). Then the poor and humble would rejoice as Isaiah had promised in 29:19 and as von Orelli so aptly cautioned:

---

[5]See the fine discussion of Zephaniah's terminology in Arvid S. Kapelrud, *The Message of the Prophet Zephaniah* (Oslo: Universitetsforlaget, 1975), pp. 55-102.
[6]Ibid., p. 91.

If Zephaniah has not spoken of the human mediator of the days of redemption, who was to spring from David's stem, he bears witness all the more powerfully to the divine aim, which even the Messiah must serve, viz., the future blessed rule of God, which according to him also will have its centre on Zion, while dispensing life and blessing throughout the world . . . The range of the divine plan, the universality of the judgment which must subserve that plan, [and] the universality of the redemption arrived at, are dwelt on by Zephaniah with special emphasis . . . His visions move around the summits of Isaiah's prophecy, illuminating them from fuller consciousness of the range they command.[7]

THE JUST SHALL LIVE BY FAITH: HABAKKUK

If Zephaniah stressed humility and poverty of spirit as prerequisites for entering into the benefits of the company of the believing, Habakkuk demanded faith as the most indispensable prerequisite. But these are all part of the same picture.

Whereas Zephaniah stressed Judah's idolatry and religious syncretism, Habakkuk was alarmed by the increase of lawlessness, injustice, wickedness, and rebellion. So sensitive was his own heart to these things that he cried to God for relief; he must either be changed or the people's sin had to be dealt with in judgment (1:2-4).

The divine solution was as straightforward as it was disturbing to this prophet: the Babylonians would invade Judah and punish her (1:5-11). This only increased the agony of the prophet, for how could God use a more wicked agent to punish a less wicked people (vv. 12-17)?

The answer to that last question was delayed until the fivefold woe was given in 2:6-20. Here Habakkuk reminded Babylon, as Assyria had already been warned in Isaiah 10, that God is the one who wielded the axe of judgment; therefore, nations had better be especially careful what methods and what persons they involved in their warfare.

No wonder Habakkuk called his message a "burden" (*maśśā'*, 1:1). *Maśśā'* occurred 67 times in the OT,[8] probably being derived from the root *nś'*, "to lift." The first reference where this word was

---

[7]C. von Orelli, *The Old Testament Prophecy of the Consummation of God's Kingdom Traced in Its Historical Development*, trans. J. J. Banks (Edinburgh: T. & T. Clark, 1889), p. 322.

[8]The most recent study is by J. A. Naudé, "*Maśśā'* in the Old Testament with Special Reference to the Prophets," *Biblical Essays*, pp. 91-100. Note also the study by P. A. H. de Boer, "The Meaning of *Maśśā'*," *Oudtestamentische Studiën* (Leiden: E. J. Brill, 1948), p. 214ff.

used of a prophecy whose contents were detailed is 2 Kings 9: 25-26. There Jehu reminded Bidkar, his officer, how the Lord had uttered this *maśśā'* against Ahab, his father: "As surely as I saw the blood of Naboth and the blood of his sons yesterday, says the Lord, I will requite you on this plot of ground." Thus Jehu referred to Elijah's prophecy in 1 Kings 21:19,29 and called it a burden. Thus *maśśā'* could be nothing less than God's "sentence" (as the Jerusalem Bible correctly translated it) passed on Ahab and his son for murdering Naboth in order to get his vineyard. In Isaiah, nine of his eleven oracles against foreign nations were designated *maśśā'* (Isa. 13:1; 14:28; 15:1; 17:1; 19:1; 21:1,11,13; 23:1). Nahum (1:1) and Habbakuk (1:1) both had categorized their messages by this name (cf. later Jer. 23:33-40 for the people's mocking use of *maśśā'* and Zech. 9 and 12). These prophecies all emphasized the grave and solemn note in their contents. The modern versions that translate *maśśā'* as an "utterance" or "oracle" miss the aspect of "verdict" or "sentence." Habakkuk obtained God's verdict for Judah's sin and Babylon's excessive cruelty in carrying out the divinely decreed judgment on Judah.

Again there was more, however, than divine judgment even in a *maśśā'*. The central oracle found in Habakkuk 2:4 was a word of hope and salvation. The importance of this remarkable word was indicated by the direction given along with it to engrave it on stone tables in plain letters so that all who passed could easily read it (v. 2). It was to bear witness in the latter days after it had come to pass that God was true to His word.

But this word did not move to a ready condemnation of Babylon as Habakkuk might have expected. That had, in a way, already been given in Habakkuk 1:11: "He is guilty whose strength is his god." What needed to be shown to Judah, Habakkuk, and future generations was the striking contrast between the character of the wicked and the righteous people of God. To point to one's character was pretty well to determine one's final destiny.

Habakkuk 2:4a described the character of Babylon: "Behold he is a puffed-up person, his soul is not upright in him." His inflated opinion of himself and of his accomplishments were the very opposite of Zephaniah's humble and poor-in-spirit believer. In contrast to the arrogance and conceit of this haughty leader of the kingdom of wickedness stood the description of the believer in verse 4b: "But a righteous man shall live by faith." Thus, the righteous "shall not die," even as Habakkuk 1:12b had promised, but they "shall live" (2:4) despite the horror of the impending judgment.

What did living "by his faith" (*be'emûnātô*) mean to Habakkuk and his hearers?[9] When used of physical things, it meant "firmness" (Exod. 17:12), but in the moral realm it meant "moral firmness" or "trustworthiness" as in daily living or commerce (Prov. 12:17). It also meant, when used of God, that His fidelity to His word could be trusted (Deut. 32:4). But in Habakkuk 2:4, faith was simply an unwavering trust in God's word. In contrast to the overbearing disposition of the wicked, the believer, like Abraham in Genesis 15:6 and Isaiah in Isaiah 28:16; 30:15 put an immovable confidence in the God who had promised His salvation and the coming Man of promise. It was a steadfast, undivided surrender to Yahweh, "a childlike, humble and sincere trust in the credibility of the divine message of salvation."[10]

Therefore, despite Babylon's aspirations of empire building, another power would possess the earth: "for the earth will be filled with knowledge of the glory of the Lord as the waters cover the sea" (Hab. 2:14). This is a clear use of the older Isaiah 11:9 with slight changes.

With this bold announcement, Habakkuk prayed that the triumphant advent of God would come soon. Whatever had to take place by way of judgment under the hands of the Babylonians, he prayed that it would have an advantageous effect on God's work, that the ancient plan would be renewed and thus mercy would be interspersed with the wrath that also had to come.

Then borrowing language from God's appearance on Sinai (3:3ff.) and His victory under Joshua when the sun ceased its shining and the moon was rebuked during a hailstorm (Josh. 10:12-14), Habakkuk portrayed another theophany yet to come. He was frankly frightened by the awesomeness of God's glory as it appeared on this "day of trouble"; yet his joy was found in the same Lord in whom he had learned to put his trust and faith. God's salvation of his people (3:13) would include the salvation of His Messiah who would "crush the head [i.e., kingdom or dynasty] of the wicked" (3:13). Because the kingdom of the ungodly had been crushed, it no longer would be able to protect its inhabitants. But the redemption of God's people was assured. With that the prophet was confident and full of joy (3:16,18-19).

---

[9]I am indebted to von Orelli, *Old Testament Prophecy*, p. 325, for this analysis of the word *'emûnâh*.

[10]Ibid., p. 326.

THE WORD OF THE LORD: JEREMIAH

Jeremiah was the prophet of the "word of the Lord" (1:2). According to J. G. S. S. Thomson,[11] Jeremiah used "Thus says the Lord" or similar phrases one hundred and fifty-seven times out of the total of three hundred and forty-nine times such phrases are used in the OT.

"Behold, I have put my words in your mouth" (Jer. 1:9; 5:14), Jeremiah would say as the basis of his authority to speak for God. But if pressed further on the mechanics of this reception of divine revelation, he would describe how he not only spoke but also wrote at God's command (36:1-2). Baruch, Jeremiah's secretary, volunteered that the prophet was *in the habit of* dictating (36:18, Hebrew imperfect) while Baruch was writing (active participle) it down. This took place over a long period of time. What Baruch wrote was "from [Jeremiah's] mouth," and what Jeremiah spoke was from the Lord.

That word was more than an objective revelation spoken for the benefit of others. It was food for the prophet's own soul (15:16; cf. 1:4ff.), the "joy and rejoicing of his heart." On the other hand, the word of the Lord became a reproach to him (20:8), for the ministry of that word often seemed to be fruitless (v. 7f.) and without any good results. Nevertheless, an inner compulsion drove Jeremiah to persist even when he had determined to cease from speaking in the name of the Lord. God put that word in his heart, and it burnt like a fire in his bones until it was released. Most of Jeremiah's so-called confessions (11:18-23; 12:1-6; 15:10-20; 17:14-18; 18:18-23; 20:7-11) were conflicts such as this one. In his personal communion with God, he laid bare the depths of his own agony of soul as he cried out "violence and destruction" (20:8), and the people mocked him in return. Jeremiah pleaded his case before his Lord and sought God's vindication.

Jeremiah's prophecies can be divided into three parts, not including an introductory call chapter and a concluding historical chapter: (1) his earlier messages to Judah (2-24); (2) his prophecies of judgment and comfort (25-45); and (3) his messages to the nations (46-51). Each had its own distinctive contribution to the theology of the OT.

The Vanity of External Religion

In his celebrated Temple Gate Message (Jer. 7-10; cf. 26), Jeremiah demonstrated both his style and the essence of his call to

---

[11]James G. S. S. Thomson, *The Old Testament View of Revelation* (Grand Rapids: Eerdmans, 1960), pp. 60-61.

prophesy in Judah. As the people made their way into the house of God, Jeremiah announced three main propositions. (1) Attendance at the house of God was no substitute for real repentance (7:4ff.). (2) Observance of religious acts was no substitute for obedience to the Lord (7:21ff.). (3) Possession of the word of God was no substitute for responding to what that word said (8:8ff.).

The people had come to place an unholy confidence in the outward form of the ceremonial law and the theocracy. They felt they were impervious to any threatened judgment of God as they rallied around the slogan "The temple of the Lord, the temple of the Lord, the temple of the Lord are these" (7:4). God could not and would not storm His own sanctuary and dwelling place—so Judah thought! In the meantime, Judah continued to steal, murder, commit adultery, swear falsely, burn incense to Baal, and walk after other gods only to then come and stand brazenly in the presence of God and say, "We are delivered in order to do all these abominations!" (v. 10).

On the contrary, Judah would see, cried Jeremiah. It was not that God looked for sacrifice per se so much as an obedience that preceded that sacrifice. He had not spoken "for the sake of" (*'al d^{e}bar*) burnt offerings but for the same thing Moses had emphasized in Deuteronomy: "Walk in all the ways that I have commanded you" (Jer. 7:22-23).

Likewise, that word should have made Judah blush, but she turned it into a salve to superficially heal the hurt of that people. There was an outright rejection of that word. But all these charades would take Judah nowhere. The emptiness of such heartless, noncommital religion would lead straight to the day of God's wrath against Judah and ultimately against the nations.

Jerusalem the Throne of Yahweh

In a most astonishing prediction, Jeremiah made the following announcement in 3:16-17:

> And it shall come to pass, when you shall be multiplied and fruitful in the land, in those days, says the Lord, they shall no longer say, "The ark of the covenant of Yahweh"; and it shall no longer come to mind, nor shall they remember it or ask after it, nor shall they prepare it. At that time they shall call Jerusalem: "Throne of Yahweh," and all nations shall assemble to it, for the name of Yahweh, for Jerusalem, and shall no longer follow the hardness of their evil heart.

The ancient blessings of Genesis 1:28 were still remembered as God's promise drew to a conclusion in that final day. Amazingly, no longer would that most central object of all in Israel's worship be significant, nor would it even come into anyone's mind; for no longer would God's presence need a symbol when He himself was plainly discernible.

In so saying, Jeremiah clearly passed sentence on the ceremonial institutions of the Mosaic legislation which had been given with a built-in obsolescence. They were only modeled after the real, which existed apart from these temporary copies of it. Repeatedly Moses had been warned that the tabernacle was to be built after a "pattern" (Exod. 25:9,40; 26:30; 27:8) or "plan" shown to him in the mountain. Jeremiah here added to that idea by declaring that they would one day be needed no longer. Instead of God's symbolic enthronement between the cherubim, He would be enthroned in Jerusalem. For a declaration of inwardness, immediacy of access to God, and self-revelation of God, this word could not be surpassed.

The nations would then be drawn to the glory of God (3:17; cf. Isa. 2:2-3; Mic. 4:1-2) and the stubborn heart of Judah and Israel would have been dealt with and changed by a work yet to be described in Jeremiah.

Yahweh Our Righteousness

The "righteous Branch" already announced in Isaiah 4:2 is the same Davidite foreseen in Jeremiah 23:5-7 and 33:14-22. The special name given to this messianic "Branch" or "Sprout" (*semah*) is "Yahweh our righteousness" (*YHWH ṣidqēnû*), a name which is reminiscent of Isaiah's "Immanuel," "God is with us."

This name was shared with Jerusalem since it was to be Yahweh's throne. Thus the rule and reign of this final new Davidite would be in the interests of righteousness. He would proceed wisely and the righteousness of the people of God would be grounded, not in any outward institution, law, or action, but in Yahweh's character. In that day Yahweh would establish and protect the righteousness of His people.

Especially significant in Jeremiah 33:14-22 was the work of the "Branch," which would be the culmination of several ancient promises: (1) the Noachic covenant on the perpetuity of the seasons; (2) the Abrahamic covenant on the innumerable seed; (3) the covenant with Phinehas on the perpetuity of the priesthood; and (4) the Davidic covenant on the everlasting reign of his seed. In every case these had been declared "everlasting" or "eternal," and so they were in Jeremiah's projections.

The New Covenant

The heart of OT theology and of the message of Jeremiah was his teaching on the New covenant in Jeremiah 31:31-34. Set in the context of the "Book of Comfort" (chaps. 30-33), the message of Jeremiah rose to the lofty peaks of an Isaiah (chaps. 40-66). Especially significant were the six strophes of chapters 30-31: (1) 30:1-11, the great distress of Jacob in the day of the Lord; (2) 30:12-31:6, the healing of Israel's incurable wound; (3) 31:7-14, God's firstborn restored to the land; (4) 31:15-22, Rachel weeping for her children in exile; (5) 31:23-34, the New covenant; and (6) 31:35-40, the inviolable covenant given to Israel.[12] Note that the whole context, chapters 30-33, meticulously connected this New covenant strophe with the restoration of the Jewish nation.

It is the fifth of these six strophes that constituted the largest teaching passage on the problem of continuity and discontinuity between the Old and New Testaments. Yet it is precisely at this point where the biblical theologian's perplexity rises to its greatest height: Why call this covenant a *"New* covenant" especially since most of the content adduced in the "New" is but a repetition of those promises already known from the Abrahamic-Davidic covenant already in existence? What were the essentially new items that were "not like" (Jer. 31:32) and "no longer" similar to the old covenant (v. 34 bis)?

1. *Its Name.* This is the only place in the OT where the expression "new covenant" (31:31) occurs; however, it would appear that the concept was much more widespread. Based on similar content and contexts, the following expressions may be equated with the New covenant: the "everlasting covenant" in seven passages (Isa. 24:5; 55:3; 61:8; Jer. 32:40; 50:5; and later in Ezek. 16:60; 37:26); a "new heart" and a "new spirit" in three or four texts (Jer. 32:39 [LXX]; and later in Ezek. 11:19; 18:31; 36:26); a "covenant of peace" in three passages (Isa. 54:10; and later in Ezek. 34:25; 37:26); and "a covenant" or "my covenant," which is placed in the context of "in that day" in three passages (Isa. 42:6; 49:8; 59:21; Hos. 2:18-20). That makes a total of sixteen or seventeen major passages on the "New covenant."

Still, Jeremiah 31:31-34 was the *locus classicus* on the subject, as may be seen from several lines of evidence. It was this passage that stimulated Origen to name the last twenty-seven books of the

---

[12]This outline was suggested by Charles A. Briggs, *Messianic Prophecy* (New York: Scribners, 1889), pp. 246-47. The essentially same outline is given by George H. Cramer, "Messianic Hope in Jeremiah," *Bibliotheca Sacra* (1958): 237-46.

Bible "the New Testament."[13] But it was also the largest piece of text to be quoted *in extenso* in the NT, viz., Hebrews 8:8-12 and partially repeated a few chapters later in Hebrews 10:16-17. Furthermore, it was the subject of nine other NT texts: four dealing with the Lord's Supper (Matt. 26:28; Mark 14:24; Luke 22:20; 1 Cor. 11:25); two Pauline references to "ministers of the new covenant" and the future forgiveness of Israel's sins (2 Cor. 3:6; Rom. 11:27); and three additional references in Hebrews (9:15; 10:16; 12:24; cf. the two large teaching passages mentioned above).

2. *Its Contrasts.* Jeremiah 31:32 explicitly contrasted this New covenant with an old covenant made with Israel during the era of the Exodus. Repeatedly Jeremiah had stressed this type of antithesis in his message: "They shall say no more this . . . but . . . ; not like this . . . but this" (Jer. 3:16; 23:7-8; 31:29; cf. 16:14-15). Thus Jeremiah was attempting to revise Israel's warped values and religious crutches. Ezekiel later used the same formula—"They shall no longer say" (18:2ff.)—to introduce current maxims used by the people as a form of oath or religious declaration which need balance and correction due to an exaggerated emphasis on only one aspect of the whole teaching.[14]

The truth of the matter was that Jeremiah found no fault with the Sinaitic covenant. Both Jeremiah and the later writer of Hebrews were emphatic in their assessment of the trouble with the covenant made in Moses' day. The problem was with the *people*, not with the covenant-making God nor with the moral law or promises reaffirmed from the patriarchs and included in that old covenant. The text of Jeremiah 31:32 explicitly pointed the finger when it said, "Which covenant of Mine *they* broke." So also did Hebrews 8:8-9: "He finding fault with *them* . . . because they continued not in [His] covenant" (italics ours).

The verb *hēpērû* ("they brake") was not unique to the Sinaitic or obligatory types of covenants as opposed to Abrahamic-Davidic promissory types, for the same verb occurred in the Abrahamic covenant (Gen. 17:14, "the uncircumcised man . . . shall be cut off;

---

[13]T. H. Horne, *Introduction to the Critical Study and Knowledge of the Holy Scriptures*, 2 vols. (New York: R. Carter and Brothers, 1858), 1:37. Also Geerhardus Vos, *Biblical Theology* (Grand Rapids: Eerdmans, 1954), p. 321. Albertus Pieters had the same assessment in *The Seed of Abraham* (Grand Rapids: Eerdmans, 1950), p. 61.

[14]Also note Ezekiel 12:22; cf. 12:27 and Jeremiah 12:23. For a discussion with different conclusions, see Moshe Weinfeld, "Jeremiah and the Spiritual Metamorphosis of Israel," *Zeitschrift für alttestamentliche Wissenschaft* 88(1976): 17-55.

he has broken [*hēpēr*] my covenant").[15] Even the eternal and irrevocable covenant of David contained some qualifications which provided for *individual* invalidation, frustration, or destruction of the benefits of that covenant (1 Chron. 22:13; 28:7; Ps. 132:12). Indeed, Jeremiah 31:35-37 had argued that the stars would drop out of the sky and the planets spin out of their orbits before God would abandon His total pledge to the nation of Israel.

3. *Its Continuity.* The structure for Jeremiah 31:31-34 was best analyzed by Bernhard W. Anderson.[16] The expression *nᵉ'um YHWH* ("says the Lord") appeared four times: twice in the first section, indicating its beginning (v. 31*a*), its conclusion (v. 32*b*); and twice in the second section, again marking its beginning (v. 33*a*) and its end (v. 34*b*). In the second section (v. 34), there were also two climactic *kî* ("indeed") clauses.

When the items of continuity found in the New covenant are tabulated in this passage, they are: (1) the same covenant-making God, "My covenant"; (2) the same law, My torah (note, not a different one than Sinai); (3) the same divine fellowship promised in the ancient tripartite formula, "I will be your God"; (4) the same "seed" and "people," "You shall be my people"; and (5) the same forgiveness, "I will forgive their iniquities."

Even the features of inwardness, fellowship, individualism, and forgiveness had been either hinted at or fully known in the covenant made with the fathers. Deuteronomy 6:6-7; 10:12; and 30:6 had urged that Israel place the words of the Sinaitic law upon her heart. Indeed, Psalms 37:31 and 40:8 did claim this was so for some already: "Thy law is within my heart." The Lord's forgiveness was also celebrated in that oft-repeated formula: "The Lord, a God merciful and gracious, slow to anger, and abounding in steadfast love and faithfulness, keeping steadfast love for thousands, forgiving iniquity and transgression and sin" (Exod. 34:6-7; Num. 14:18; Deut. 5:9-10; Ps. 86:15; Joel 2:13; Jonah 4:2; and later Neh. 9:17,31). In

---

[15]Note the crucial importance made between conditional and unconditional covenants in Charles Ryrie, *Dispensationalism Today* (Chicago: Moody Press, 1965), pp. 52-61, and the strong disavowal in O. T. Allis, *Prophecy and the Church* (Philadelphia: Presbyterian and Reformed Publishing House, 1945), pp. 31-48. See D. F. Payne, "The Everlasting Covenant," *Tyndale Bulletin* 7-8(1961): 10-17: "A New Covenant? Yes, but only the unimportant details of the 'Old' were obsolescent, and even the author of Hebrews apparently could not quite bring himself to call the Old Covenant 'obsolete.'"

[16]Bernhard W. Anderson, "The New Covenant and the Old," *The Old Testament and Christian Faith*, ed. Bernhard W. Anderson (New York: Harper and Row, 1963), p. 230, n. 11.

fact, he removed transgression "as far as the East is from the West" (Ps. 103:8-12).

Thus the word "new" in this context would mean the "renewed" or "restored" covenant (cf. Akkadian *edêšu* "to restore" ruined temples, altars, or cities; Hebrew *ḥdš* connected with the new moon and Ugaritic *ḥdt*, "to renew the moon"). We conclude then that this covenant was the old Abrahamic-Davidic promise renewed and enlarged.

4. *Its Brand-New Features.* There were items of discontinuity as well. If we were to use all seventeen passages noted above, some of these would be: (1) a universal knowledge of God (Jer. 31:34); (2) a universal peace in nature and the absence of military hardware (Isa. 2:4; Hos. 2:18; Ezek. 34:25; 37:26); (3) a universal material prosperity (Isa. 61:8; Hos. 2:22; Jer. 32:41; Ezek. 34:26-27); (4) a sanctuary lasting forever in the midst of Israel (Ezek. 37:26,28); and (5) a universal possession of the Spirit of God (Joel 2:32ff.).

In this list, the New covenant transcends all previous announcements of the blessings of God. Thus the New is more comprehensive, more effective, more spiritual, and more glorious than the old—in fact, so much so that *in comparison* it would appear as if it were totally unlike the old at all. Yet, in truth, it was nothing less than the progress of revelation.

The "new" began with the "old" promise made to Abraham, Moses, and David; and its renewal perpetuated all those promises and more.

5. *Its Addressees.* Just as the Abrahamic and Davidic promises were made directly with each of these men, so the New covenant was made with all the house of Israel and the whole house of Judah. Now if this address of Jeremiah 31:31 appears too restricted and therefore of limited usage in pre-Christian times, so was Abraham's and David's promise.

But therein lies the solution for all of these passages, for the "seed" who would benefit from the Abrahamic and Davidic promises included all believers of all ages. So were the benefits of the New covenant applicable to all believers for the same reasons. George N. H. Peters demonstrated that

> we have decided references to . . . [a] renewed Abrahamic covenant, conjoined with the Davidic [as] being a distinguishing characteristic of, and fundamental to, the Messianic period, e.g., Micah 7:19-20; Ezekiel 16:60-63; Isaiah 55:3.[17]

---

[17]George N. H. Peters, *The Theocratic Kingdom*, 3 vols. (Grand Rapids: Kregel, 1957), 1:322. See also Francis Goode, "God's Better Covenant with Israel in the Latter Day," *The Better Covenant*, 5th London ed. (Philadelphia: Smith, English & Co., 1868), pp. 239-71.

It need only be noted that the New covenant also was part of that messianic era! Here then was a new footing for an old stalemate. The New covenant was indeed addressed to a revived national Israel of the future; but nonetheless by virtue of its specific linkage with the Abrahamic and Davidic promises contained in them all, it was proper to speak of a Gentile participation then and in the future. The Gentiles would be adopted and grafted into God's covenant with national Israel.[18]

The seventh century was the greatest moment of impending destruction for the nation; yet in the midst of the faithful warnings of God's servants came one of the most spectacular series of promises of hope.

---

[18]For further discussion of the New Testament implications, see W. C. Kaiser, Jr., "The Old Promise and the New Covenant," *Journal of the Evangelical Theological Society* 15(1972): 11-23.

Chapter 14

Kingdom of the Promise:
Exilic Prophets

The worst had happened. Jerusalem had fallen in 586 B.C., and the greater part of her citizens had entered a seventy year captivity in Babylon. Now the ominous notes of threatening would soon come to a conclusion, and the new emphasis of the prophetic theology would be the deliverance and new birth of God's people Israel.

Jeremiah's younger contemporary Ezekiel had been deported with King Jehoiachin in 597 B.C., about a decade prior to Jerusalem's fall to Babylon. From that place of Exile he continued to warn Judah in the first section of his book (Ezek. 3:22-24:27). In his meticulously dated prophecies, he turned to warn the nations during the dark hours of Jerusalem's seige and fall (Ezek. 25-32). (Note the prediction of the fall in 24:21-23 and the report of its happening in 33:21 as a type of bracketing of the messages to the nations.) Thereafter, the oracles of hope and promise take over in Ezekiel 33-48. With the old Davidic order at an end, there was only one place to go: to the new David, His throne, and His kingdom. This became the sustaining hope for a people who had lost every outward symbol of hope; it was also the all-consuming focus of Ezekiel and Daniel.

THE GOOD SHEPHERD'S REIGN: EZEKIEL

Ezekiel, a priest by descent, was called to be a watchman for Israel. His ministry was filled with some of the most exotic of all symbolic actions performed by the prophets. He was fond of allegories and parables, and he used them more freely than his colleagues. In his hands, the use of apocalyptic language received new impetus, especially in the third section of his work. But above all, it was his inaugural vision that explained the theme of his work: the glory of God. Ezekiel's language also was often repetitive in style. One of the most frequent phrases was "That you might know that I am the Lord." This phrase appeared 54 times, not including 18 more expansions of the same phrase. God's holiness was also set off in contrast to Israel's sinfulness, especially in the parable of the fondling (16:1-63), the parable of the two sisters (23:1-49), and the historical review of 20:1-31 with its repeated phrase "I acted for the sake of my name, that it should not be profaned in the sight of the nations among whom they dwell" (20:9,14,22).

But right from the beginning, Ezekiel made it plain that in spite of Israel's deep sin, Yahweh would remember His covenant with that nation exactly as He had pledged to do in the days of her youth (Ezek. 16:60):

> Nevertheless, I will remember My covenant with thee in the days of thy youth, and I will *establish (hēqîm:* (1) to set up what does not yet stand or (2) to cause to stand, ratify, stabilize, resuscitate what is already there) with thee an everlasting covenant.

In this case, "to establish" is best understood by meaning number two: it was a ratification of what was already there. Naturally, it will be necessary to judge the nation for her sin as Ezekiel 16:59 noted:

> I will even deal with you as you have done, which have despised the oath even to the extent of (*lᵉhāpēr,* the *lᵉ* of attendant circumstances) breaking the covenant.

But the promise and its blessings would continue!

The Glory of Yahweh

Dominating every scene and word of the book of Ezekiel is the throne of God (Ezek. 1:4-28). The vision of this throne constituted Ezekiel's call as he sat by the "river" Chebar; and its magnificence was sufficient to assure the prophet that like that heavenly chariot of God's throne which could easily bring His presence east, west, north, or south, so would that same presence of God be with him.

237

The scene was much like that which John would experience on the isle of Patmos as he wrote the book of Revelation (4-5). For Ezekiel there was a crystal platform holding a sapphire throne with the one enthroned having the "likeness" and "appearance of a man" (1:26). The platform was supported by four living creatures which in turn were associated with wheels that apparently were much like modern desk furniture wheels; they were able to turn in any direction without the need of a steering mechanism. All this was punctuated with the splash of lightning, the roar of thunder, and the rainbow of color surrounding the whole scene. Obviously the central figure was none other than the One enthroned; an awesome personage whose appearance radiated fire and brightness.

As for the meaning of it all, Ezekiel was told it was "the likeness of the glory of Yahweh" (1:28). The connection between fire and the presence of the Lord was well known in Israel. Moses had experienced it in his call at the burning bush, Israel in the wilderness saw the pillar of fire, Elijah on Mount Carmel experienced the powerful consuming presence of God; in fact, only Daniel (7:9ff.) would describe in detail his meeting with the "Ancient of days." But one thing was certain, the sheer weight, gravity (*kābēd*, "to be heavy," then "to glorify") of His presence evoked an attitude of worship from Ezekiel (1:28*b*), for he felt he was in the immediate presence of God. This meeting with Yahweh would comfort and direct the prophet as well as give shape to his whole message. God would triumph despite Israel's most tragic failure. His promise would not die; it would go on.

God's presence would continue to be with His prophet, His promise, the remnant, and His kingdom to come; but His presence would leave its place of residence where He had dwelt since the days of Israel's wandering. When Ezekiel was transported in a vision to the temple in Jerusalem (8:2-4) and there witnessed firsthand the horrible sins of Judah done right in the house of God, it was clear that God's glory could stay there no longer. There were such unspeakable absurdities as "the image of jealousy" (goddess Asherah poles? cf. 2 Chron. 33:7,15) erected in the temple (8:3*b*); animal worship (vv. 7-13); women weeping in sympathetic magic for Tammuz, the Sumerian god of vegetation (vv. 14-15); and worship of the sun (vv. 16-18).

The only possible sequel to such confusion was that of Ezekiel 10:18: "Then the glory of the Lord departed from off the threshold of the house." Indeed, for Judah, her government, her religious pretense, and her religious institutions, it was Ichabod: "The glory had departed"!

Yahweh the Sanctuary

During those days of Exile, Yahweh Himself would be the real temple of the true believers (Ezek. 11:16-20): "Yes, I have removed them far off among the nations; and, yes, I have dispersed them in the lands and have become for them a sanctuary for a little while in the lands where they have gone."

Yahweh Himself, men would learn, was more important than buildings and all the trappings. What was more, He would one day restore the people to the land, bringing them from every country to which they had been dispersed (11:17). Only in that future day all the old abominations would have been removed and a new inner capacity would be implanted in the people—their inner man would be so changed that Ezekiel could only refer to it as a "new spirit," "one heart," and a "heart of flesh" (11:19). Such was the old vision of Isaiah 4:2-6 and Jeremiah 30-31.

The New Davidic Kingdom

Ezekiel 17 is an allegory of the cedar of Lebanon (i.e., David's house) with its indictment of the last Davidite, Zedekiah, who relied on Egypt rather than Yahweh. But all was not lost, for this history concluded in 17:22-24 with the promise of a sprig, a tender shoot from the top of this majestic cedar tree, that would grow to overtake all the other trees (kingdoms).

The Babylonian eagle would carry away the crown of the cedar tree into captivity, but God would exalt the lowly. Once more Yahweh would break off another twig, this time from the transplanted sprig, and this new piece of cedar He would replant on the mountain heights of Israel. There what would only appear to be insignificant would grow into a powerful tree under which all the birds of heaven would seek shelter. To that new tree, all the kingdoms of earth would come and acknowledge their inferiority and its superiority.

Once again the theme of God's new World Ruler coming from humble origins was the point (cf. Isa. 7:14ff.; 9:6ff.; 11:1ff.; Mic. 4:1ff.). While Zerubbabel was the next Davidic person to govern, and he was transplanted from Babylonian exile back to Zion, he clearly did not exhaust the universal terms of this passage.

The remnant would inherit all the ancient promises given to David and Abraham. And God's kingdom would triumph over all the nations; in fact, under the umbrella of that kingdom would dwell all sorts of nations (or as the oriental figure loved to put it, all the birds of heaven and beasts of every type would seek its shelter).

The Rightful King

One last installment in the developing doctrine of promise is to be found in the first section of Ezekiel, 21:26-27 [31-32]. As the prophet unleashed his message of destruction against Jerusalem, the temple, and the land of Israel (cf. Ezek. 20:45-21:17), he was instructed to mark the crossroads where the advancing king of Babylon would need to determine whether he was going to take the road southeast to the Ammonites or the road to Jerusalem. Even though Nebuchadnezzar would use divination (belomancy, necromancy, and hepatoscopy, 21:21), Yahweh had already (!) determined that the lot would be for him to proceed to Jerusalem (v. 22).

As for the wicked Davidic prince, Zedekiah, he should remove his "crown" (*miṣnepet*) and the high priest his "mitre" (tiara or turban, *ᵃṭārâh*, cf. Exod. 28:4,37,39; 29:6; 39:28,31; Lev. 8:9; 16:4). For the kingdom and the priesthood, as experienced up to that point in Israel's history, would be abolished and suffer an interruption for a time. They would remain in ruins until the advent of One appointed by Yahweh reclaimed them (21:27 [32], *ᶜaḏ bô' ᵃšer lô hammišpāṭ*, "until he comes whose right it is").

This passage is remarkably similar to Genesis 49:10. No doubt Ezekiel deliberately harked back to the messianic promise given to Judah as Judah's only hope in her hour of tragedy. When David and Aaron's lines had failed to carry out their divine mission, then the earnests of the promise must cease until the One to whom the kingship and priesthood *together* belonged would claim them. When He appeared, then crown and mitre would be given to this new and final King-Priest, the Messiah.

Meanwhile, His counterpart continued to manifest himself in a series of antimessiahs. There was the king of Babylon in Isaiah 14:12ff. and now the king of Tyre in Ezekiel 28:11ff. Each message was addressed not so much to an historical figure but to one who epitomized the final representative (Antichrist) of the Serpent's seed as promised in Genesis 3:15. History was not a contest between mere mortals; it was simultaneously a supernatural battle for dominion,[1] and Satan had his own succession of tyrants corresponding to God's Davidite line as well as his climactic person, the tyrant of all tyrants.

The Good Shepherd

If any passage was at the heart of Ezekiel's contribution to the ongoing promise, it was Ezekiel 34:11-31: "I myself will search for

---

[1]Anthony Williams, "The Mythological Background to Ezekiel 28:12-19," *Biblical Theology Bulletin* 6(1976): 49-61.

my sheep, . . . I will feed them in justice." No doubt this passage served as a background for Jesus' message on the "Good Shepherd" in John 10.

The picture of the shepherd, of course, points to the benevolent Ruler who can be trusted in the leadership role. Coming, as it does, on the heels of the fall of Jerusalem, it was good news indeed to learn that there was some Leader who would gather the smitten and scattered nation. This same figure of the tender Shepherd appears in Psalms 78:52-53; 79:13; 80:1; Isaiah 40:11; 49:9-10; Jeremiah 31:10; and later in Zechariah 11.

Relief for this battered flock was promised in an eschatological era, in "a day of clouds and thick darkness" (34:12; cf. Joel 2:2; Zeph. 1:15). Then Yahweh would destroy the oppressors ("fat and strong ones") who had pounced on the weak (34:16).

Just as Jeremiah 30:9 had pointed to a new David to come, so now Ezekiel 34:23-24 promised:

> I will raise up over them one shepherd to feed them, my servant David, who will feed them and be their shepherd. And I, Yahweh, will be their God, and my servant David a prince in their midst. I, Yahweh, have said it.

The themes are very familiar by now. God's Servant is that representative person promised to head up the whole group known as the "seed" of Abraham, Isaac, Jacob, and David. Part of the tripartite formula appears here as well: "I will be their God." This too was a piece of the old promise doctrine (note 34:30 for a fuller repetition of the formula). And when God pointed to David, the prediction of an everlasting dynasty, kingdom, and throne came easily to mind once again. Ezekiel loved to call that future Davidic King a "prince" (*nāśî'*). In fact, twenty out of his thirty-eight usages of this word "prince" refer to a coming Davidic King, the Messiah.

As if to make sure that the readers and listeners of this message connected this new word about the Good Shepherd with the old promise, Ezekiel was instructed to call this promise about a future Davidic "prince" and its paradisiacal effects on nature God's "covenant of peace" (34:25). That is only an alternative name for the New covenant, for its banishment of wild beasts and picture of safety, fertility, and productivity are similar to what Isaiah (11:6-9) and other prophets hoped for (Hos. 2:22; Joel 3:18; Amos 9:13-14; and later Zech. 8:12). The "peace" of that covenant is the restored *harmony* that exists in a world where things *work* as they were meant to operate without the negative intrusions or wasteful disappointment.

The New Cleansing and New Birth

There is a passage that comes close to matching the majesty and scope of Jeremiah's New covenant passage; it is Ezekiel 36:25-35. Here Ezekiel promised that Yahweh, "for the sake of [His] holy name" ("not for [Israel's] sake," 36:22*a*,32*a*; cf. 36:22*b*,32*b*), would vindicate Israel by regathering them to their own land from all the countries where they had been dispersed. Thus "through" Israel all the nations of the earth would acknowledge that God had performed what He had promised, and thus His holy reputation and character would remain untarnished.

But that was not the half of it. More importantly those who came under the New covenant by personal belief would experience what von Orelli has clearly stated as

> cleansing or justifying (ver. 25), and positive *new-birth* through the Spirit of God (ver. 26f.) in consequence of which the people will henceforth be able and willing to keep the divine commands. . . . The Lord himself must sprinkle this impure people . . . The human heart, the source of all volition and inclination (Deut. xxx.6), of all desire and effort, is unfit for God's service (Gen viii.21), as Israel's whole history shows . . . God will give His accepted people a new heart, related to the former one as flesh to stone, i.e., instead of a heart hard, stubborn, unreceptive, one sensitive to God's word and will, receptive to all good or as Jeremiah says, like a soft table on which God can write His holy law. And the new Spirit that is to fill these receptive hearts will be God's Spirit, who impels to the keeping of divine commands . . . Every individual member of it is *born again* of water and spirit. . . . Although the outward bliss, which is the fruit of this inner work of grace, is presented under O.T. limitation (xxxvi.28f), the act of grace itself, from which the peace with God springs, is seen with divine clearness.[2]

No wonder Jesus marveled that Nicodemus did not know about the new birth and the work of the Holy Spirit (John 3:10). As a teacher of the Jews, he should have been familiar with this passage and therefore the teaching on this subject. Men could be cleansed by the same Lord who would by the gift of the Spirit perform a heart transplant in them and give them a new birth. Related activities of the Spirit have already been enumerated in Joel 2:28-32 and Isaiah 42:1; 44:3; 59:21. Then a purified people would dwell once again in a purified land, like the Garden of Eden (36:35), where the Edenic blessing would once again reign unchallenged (vv. 37-38).

---

[2]C. von Orelli, *The Old Testament Prophecy of the Consummation of God's Kingdom Traced in Its Historical Development*, trans. J. J. Banks (Edinburgh: T. & T. Clark, 1889), p. 322 (italics his).

A Reunited Restored Israel

It is most likely that the valley where Ezekiel received his vision of the dry bones in Ezekiel 37:1 was the identical place where he received his first revelation of the imminent destruction of Jerusalem (3:22). If so, the book would be bracketed in a rather unique way.

The scattered dry bones were the whole house of Israel (37:11) to whom Ezekiel was given the frustrating command to "prophesy" (v. 4). As he obeyed, the miracle of reassembly took place through the medium of the preached word of God and the powerful work of God.

But these men, even though they had been restored, were still not revived; they were dead! Therefore Ezekiel was told to "prophesy" again, and breath and life came into those who had been slain (37:9).

The teaching was expressly given by Ezekiel in 37:12-14:

> Behold, I am about to open your graves and bring you up from your graves, my people; and bring you to the land of Israel . . . And I will put my Spirit within you and you shall live again and I will place you in your own land.

Thus as Adam had the breath of life breathed into his nostrils and he became "alive," so would a restored Israel. This chapter then does not deal with the doctrine of the personal bodily resurrection but with national resurrection.

Moreover, the two separated brethren, the ten northern tribes of Joseph or Ephraim and the two southern tribes of Judah and Benjamin, would be reunited under a new David in that day of national resurrection according to Ezekiel 37:15-28. In that passage Ezekiel was told to join the two sticks, marked Judah and Joseph, respectively, into *one* stick (vv. 16-19). Then they will once again, for the first time since 931 B.C., be "*one* nation" (v. 22*a*), under "*one* king" (v. 22*b*), with "*one* God" (v. 23), and "*one* shepherd, my servant David" (v. 24). And this state would last "forever" (v. 25) as part of God's "everlasting covenant" (v. 26). Yahweh's "dwelling place will be with them" (cf. the "rest" and "place" themes of the prophetic history of Joshua's era), and He "will be their God and they shall be [His] people: then the nations will know that the Lord has sanctified Israel, when [His] sanctuary is in the midst of them for evermore" (vv. 27-28).

With that keynote theme, Ezekiel proceeded to give a detailed description of the restored land of Israel after he had treated the battle with Gog and Magog in chapters 38-39. In that land a new temple would again be the dominating piece of architecture. From this temple would issue a stream of life which increased in depth and power as it made its way to the sea formerly known as the Dead Sea (cf. Ps. 46:4-5; Isa. 33:13-24; Joel 3:9-21). Along its banks were the trees of life yielding their healing leaves and monthly fruits in a restored paradise picture of the new Jerusalem.

But is Ezekiel 40-48 merely an ideal, symbolic description or a prophetic reality? Perhaps each of these categories is a little too simplistic for the depth of idea here. In our view, there is to be a real relocated temple in the midst of the land. There worship of the living God will continue as described here under those concomitant features of worship known in the day Ezekiel was writing. (Compare this to how the prophets described the armaments of future eschatological battles in terms of the implements of war known to that day, viz., bow and arrows, spears and horses.)

Certainly when Ezekiel described the river of life and the fruit, he was moving more to apocalyptic terminology such as we later meet in John's Apocalypse. But the reality of a restored heaven and restored earth, wherein the "Lord is there" (Ezek. 48:35) in the new Jerusalem of Israel, is secure. The conclusion of Ezekiel's prophecy, then, is an expansion and further elaboration of Isaiah 65 and 66, which speak of the new heavens and the new earth. Only here the accent falls on the Lord tabernacling in the midst of His worshiping people wherein nature is healed and restored to its original design and productivity.

THE PROMISED KINGDOM'S SUCCESS: DANIEL

The theology of Daniel is clearly the antithesis of the successive kingdoms of mankind. In contrast to these kingdoms is the abiding but finally triumphant kingdom of God. Daniel, another exile along with Ezekiel,[3] looked beyond the catastrophe of the collapse of Jerusalem and the Davidic line to that abiding promised kingdom of God.

The Stone and the Kingdom of God

The dream of Nebuchadnezzar recorded in Daniel 2 set the stage for this prophecy. There a colossal image is described which is

---

[3]We do not hesitate to defend a sixth century Daniel. The case for this date, though extremely unpopular with biblical scholars, must still be pressed on evidential, not doctrinal, grounds. See the arguments of my colleague Gleason L. Archer, Jr., *A Survey of Old Testament Introduction*, rev. ed. (Chicago: Moody Press, 1974), pp. 377-403, and the bibliography he cites there.

composed of four decreasingly valuable metals with increasing weakness and division as one proceeds from head to toes. This image represents the human alternative to that "Stone" which falls on the feet of the colossus and crushes the whole image to pieces. After this, the "Stone" becomes a great kingdom which fills the whole earth. The "Stone" calls to mind Isaiah's "Cornerstone" (Isa. 28:16) while the metals are clearly identified as the four kingdoms beginning with Babylon, followed by the split dominion of Medo-Persia, Graeco-Macedonia, and the Roman or Western empires.

The interpretation given in Daniel 2:44 was crystal clear:

> In the days of these kings the God of heaven will set up an eternal kingdom, which shall never be destroyed, and its dominion shall not be delivered to another people. It will crush and destroy all these kingdoms, but it shall last forever.

As in Obadiah 21, the kingdom was Yahweh's, and so it would be here.

The Ancient of Days

The parallel chapter of Nebuchadnezzar's dream of Daniel 2 is Daniel's vision of chapter 7. Again there were four kingdoms; and Nebuchadnezzar's head of gold, identified as Babylon in chapter 2, was Daniel's "lion" (7:4). The earthly monarch's silver breast and arms were Daniel's "bear" (v. 5), later identified with the ram with two horns in Daniel 8:20 as Media and Persia. The belly and thighs of brass or copper in Daniel 2 was in Daniel 7:6 a leopard with four heads and four wings. This is the same as Daniel's rough goat which grew four little horns in Daniel 8:21-22, which is Alexander the Great of Greece and the four generals who succeeded him. Nebuchadnezzar's iron-and-clay-legged image became a terrible and indescribably horrible beast in Daniel 7:7. This is a picture of a western or Roman empire which finally was divided among ten kings plus a boastful antichrist (vv. 24-25) who would subdue three of the ten kings and shout against the Most High and wear out the saints of God for a designated period of time until God's everlasting kingdom would arrive (vv. 25b-27).

In Daniel 7, then, the same four world empires appear, only this time in succession out of the storm-laden sea. But, again, when their time had expired and the ruler coming from among the ten horns of the fourth beast had done his worst against the God of heaven and His saints, the "Ancient of days" approached in judgment. Said Daniel in verses 13 and 14:

I beheld in visions of the night, and lo, one like the Son of man came with the clouds of heaven, and came to the Ancient of days and was brought before Him. And authority was given to Him, and glory and kingship, and all peoples and nations and tongues shall serve Him. His dominion is an everlasting dominion, which will not pass away and His kingdom one that will not be destroyed.

In contrast to the beastly nature of the empires of men, a *human* Mediator comes from the Most High God whose countenance and person immediately remind one of Ezekiel's and Isaiah's vision. Thus the coming Messiah would not only be the true David, but He would also be the true Son of man,[4] combining in His person the high calling of humanity and the position reserved alone for God. His heavenly origin was stressed in that He came "with the clouds of heaven" (7:13, which is more explicit than the falling stone of 2:34), and His divinity was underscored by the abiding and indestructible kingdom and dominion that was given to Him (7:14).

Those world powers governed by that mixture of savage, sensuous, and self-serving impulses grim with distorted features, horns, teeth, and carnivorous appetites would now confront God's judgment as the Ancient of days took His seat in Court. His garments were sparkling white and pure as snow, His head of hair was like pure wool, and His throne was like a fiery mass of flames. The judgment was in accordance with what was written in the books (7:10), and the judgment thrones were set up on earth (v. 9). The retinue of the Ancient of days was immense: ten thousand times ten thousand served Him and stood before Him (cf. the heavenly retinue of the judge in Zech. 14:5).

The Saints of the Most High

The "saints of the Most High" (7:18,22,27 in the Aramaic phrase, *qaddîšê 'elyônîn*),[5] to whom the kingdom and dominion were given after the judgment of nations, were in the same line of descent as the "holy nation" (*gôy qādôš*, Exod. 19:6) or the "holy people" (*'am qādôš*, Deut. 7:6; 26:19) of the Mosaic era or the "seed" promised to Eve and the patriarchs. Israel had been promised a great

---

[4]See E. J. Young, "Daniel's Vision of the Son of Man," *The Law and the Prophets,* ed. J. Skilton (Nutley, N.J.: Presbyterian and Reformed Publishing House, 1974), pp. 425-51.

[5]For the most recent defenders of the Israelite view and for the massive bibliography, see V. S. Poythress, "The Holy Ones of the Most High in Daniel vii," *Vetus Testamentum* 26(1976): 208-13; and Gerhard F. Hasel, "The Identity of the Saints of the Most High in Daniel 7," *Biblica* 56(1976): 173-92.

kingdom already in the OT (Num. 24:7; Isa. 60:12; Mic. 4:8), and this kingdom was to be ruled by the coming Davidic King. It is of more than passing interest that "the saints" belonged to God (note the possessive genitive) and that they formed a remnant even as Isaiah had spoken of a "holy seed" (*zera' qōdēš*, Isa. 6:13)[6] that would remain after the repeated destructions.

The Seventy Weeks

The future of Jerusalem and the nation of Israel was outlined for Daniel as he realized that the seventy years of captivity prophesied by Jeremiah (29:10) were almost over. That future involved seventy sevens or weeks (Dan. 9:20-27) arranged in three groups: (1) one set of seven weeks, (2) another of sixty-two weeks, and (3) a final set of one week. Hence 490 weeks (i.e., years) were to be divided into 49, 434, and 7 years respectively. The purpose of this further extension of time before the awaited consummation set in was described in the six infinitives of verse 24:

> to finish the transgression
> to abolish sin
> to atone for iniquity
> to bring in everlasting righteousness
> to seal vision and prophet
> to anoint the most holy [place].

The order of events before the full redemption arrived included the complete deliverance from sin and guilt, the conclusion of prophetic activity, and the introduction of the righteous kingdom with its anointed sanctuary in Zion as predicted in Ezekiel 40-48, Zechariah 3:9ff., and their predecessors.

Most commentators agree that the 490 years began with the decree of Artaxerxes in his twentieth year of reign in 445 B.C. (Neh. 2:1-8),[7] which allowed the city of Jerusalem to be rebuilt, and continued through 483 of those 490 years, until the first advent of Messiah. But commentators differ widely on whether there is a gap of undetermined length between the first 69 weeks or 483 years and the last week of 7 years or whether that week also did not expire

---

[6]A fact noticed by G. Hasel, ibid., p. 191.

[7]The word for "decree" is literally the "word." According to a recent paper read by Dr. A. MacRae at the 1976 annual meeting of the Evangelical Theological Society, that "word" was the one given by Jeremiah. Thus, he would favor two gaps of unspecified duration between the seventh week and sixty-two weeks and between the sixty-ninth and seventieth week, respectively.

during the first Christian century during the persecution of the early church as symbolized by Stephen's martyrdom. The former position points to the temporal notation of *"after* the sixty-two weeks [period]" (9:26) and the cutting off of Messiah (approx. A.D. 30) and the destruction of the temple (A.D. 70) while the latter group tends to equate the "anointed one" and the "prince" of verse 26 and to argue for the completion of the seventieth week during the first century A.D.

In our view, the "anointed One" (*Māšîaḥ*, 9:26), "the princely, kingly, Anointed One" (*māšîaḥ nāgîd*, v. 25) is the same one as the "Son of man" in 7:13 who will return to earth in triumph after He has suffered death on earth.

The Little Boastful Horn

Over against God's holy remnant in the final day will stand the "little horn" (7:8), "prince" (9:26*b*-27), or "king" who will "do according to his will," "magnify himself above every god," and "speak boastful things" (11:36).

Just as the king of Babylon in Isaiah 14 and the king of Tyre in Ezekiel 28 functioned as surrogates for the evil one in his challenge against God and His people, so Daniel envisioned the appearance of one who turned out to be Antiochus (Epiphanes) IV. His desecration of the altar of the sanctuary by offering on it a pig (11:31) and his breaking of his covenant were part and parcel with that final Antichrist who was to come as the "beast" (Rev. 13), the "man of sin" (2 Thess. 2), or the "little horn" and "prince" of Daniel. This did not mean that Daniel was undecided between a historical or eschatological personage for his meaning. Rather, the meaning was one and only one throughout. But as the later Antiochian school of interpretation explained it by their principle of *"Theoria,"* the prophet was given a vision of the future in which he saw not only the final fulfillment as the conclusion to the word he uttered, but he also often saw and spoke of one or more of the means and connecting personages who were so in tune with one or more aspects of that final fulfillment that they became a collective or corporate part of the single prediction. The apostle John similarly described his understanding of this person: "Antichrist is coming; even now there are many antichrists" (1 John 2:18). Together they embodied a whole "seed" (Gen. 3:15); however, they did have from time to time their representatives who were only earnests and harbingers of the final Antichrist even as each chosen child of the successive patriarchs and reigning Davidites were representatives yet one with the single meaning about the true Seed, Servant, and David who was to come.

The Future Resurrection

"At that time," "a time of trouble such as never was since there was a nation," God would deliver His people and introduce His everlasting kingdom (12:1). The projected completion of the promise with its kingdom, throne, and reign would come to fruition.

As in Isaiah 26:19, God would restore that godly band of believers to life by means of a bodily resurrection of the dead. One class would enjoy eternal life, for their names were written in the book (12:1-2). The other class would be resurrected to eternal shame, contempt, i.e., their doom (cf. Isa. 24:22; 66:24). Job had been assured that just as a tree would sprout again even if it were cut down, so would a man live again (Job 14:7,14). In fact, he longed for the opportunity to look on his Redeemer with his own eyes even after the worms had destroyed his body (19:25-27).

Thus as the colossus of human attempts to tyrannize men came to an end with the irruption of the kingdom of God and His King according to the ancient but renewed promise, there appeared one final all-powerful king who was the summation of all the power and kingdoms of men, the antimessiah. But God's Messiah easily would vanquish that evil one, introduce His kingdom, and give that new righteous and everlasting dominion to His "holy ones," many of whom He would resurrect bodily from the dust of the earth; and they would shine as stars forevermore.

Chapter 15

Triumph of the Promise: Postexilic Times

With the divinely predicted yet nevertheless surprising permission of the Persian king, Cyrus, a small portion of the exiled nation returned to Jerusalem under a representative of David's royal house, Zerubbabel, and the high priest Joshua. But everywhere the persistent reminders of their abysmal defeat under the Babylonians was all too evident.

Even when they strove to again lay the foundations of that most important symbol of the presence of God, their sanctuary, discouragement took its toll; and the whole project came to a complete stop for sixteen long years (Ezra 4:24). Everything was wrong: they lacked the means, then the inclination, and finally even the will to build the temple; for their every attempt met with constant opposition both from within the small group and from the outside (Ezra 3:12-13; 4:1-22). So it would have remained had not God graciously sent the prophets Haggai and Zechariah (Ezra 5:1).

GOD'S SIGNET RING: HAGGAI

The theological problem of this period was simply this: Where was the activity and presence of God to be found? Certainly it did not lie in the dilapidated political state or in the destroyed temple. Thus the circumstances of life had forced men to enlarge their thinking on the internal promise of God while its external fortunes seemed to flounder.

But those sixteen years of indifference toward the construction of the house of God had proven costly, not only to Israel's spiritual development, but also in her recent material reverses.

In the year 520 B.C., Haggai met the people's flippant excuse that the time was inopportune (a way of really blaming God for not having prospered them more so that they could erect the temple) by asking the people to apply the same logic to their own luxuriant dwellings (1:2-4).

In fact, so bothersome had the fact that the temple lay in "ruins" (*hārēb*, 1:4) become to Yahweh that He called for a "drought" (*hōreb*, v. 11) on their crops. Once again, where the *precept* of God had not been heeded, then the *penalty* of God was used to capture the people's attention. Thus the small group of returnees were sowing more and harvesting less, eating and drinking more and enjoying it less, wearing more and feeling its warming effects less, and earning more and able to buy less (v. 6). This was what they should take to heart and consider carefully (1:5,7; cf. 2:15,18). Not every single or isolated reverse was to be interpreted as an evidence of the discipline of God against the nation. But when these calamities began to come to them in a series and so increase in severity that the prestige and well-being of the whole nation was affected, then that nation should know that it was the hand of God, and men should return to Him. This principle was first announced in Leviticus 26:3-33 and used in most of the prophets, especially Amos 4:6-12.

Amazingly the people responded and "obeyed" the word of the Lord and the voice of Haggai the prophet (1:12). God added His ancient name and promise with the words, "I am with you" (1:13; 2:4) as His Spirit stirred up the leadership and the people to work on the house of the Lord (1:14).

The proof that God still dwelt with Israel, according to the ancient promise given in connection with the tabernacle (Exod. 29:45-46) and the tripartite formula, was to be seen in the fact that He made His Spirit abide among them (2:5). Furthermore, the small beginnings of that second temple were directly connected with the fortunes, glory, and honor to be received in the future temple of God described by Ezekiel and others; for Haggai pointedly asked in 2:3, "Who is left among you who saw the glory of *this* house [the second temple] in its former glory [Solomon's temple]?" Then he boldly proclaimed, "I will shake all nations so that the treasures[1] of all nations shall come in, and I will fill *this* house with splendor, says the Lord of Hosts." All three temples were one and the same as they participated in the splendor of the universal acknowledgment accorded to the temple of Yahweh in that final day. Indeed, the nations would pour their wealth into that house in recognition of Yahweh's sovereignty as had been envisioned by Isaiah 54:11-14; 60; Jeremiah 3:14-18; and Ezekiel 40-48. Thus men were not to despise the day of small things begun in the name, power, and plan of God.

But before such a day could come, there would be a world-wide convulsion in the physical, political, and social realms (2:7,21-22). This accorded well with the by-now-familiar prophetic theme of the day of the Lord. The judgments of God and His undisputed triumph were described by Haggai in terms used of past conquests when God had acted decisively for Israel, e.g., at the Red Sea when "the horses and their riders went down" or in Gideon's deliverance when every one fell by the "sword of his fellow." So Yahweh would shake the heavens and the earth and "overthrow" (cf. Sodom and Gommorah) the throne of kingdoms and destroy the power of the kingdoms of the nations (2:22).

The significance of this shake-up for David's royal house became clear in 2:23 when Haggai declared that "on that day" Yahweh would take Zerubbabel, a Davidite, God's "Servant," and make him a "signet ring" *(hôṭām)*. Therefore the overthrowal of the kingdoms was in order to exalt the coming Davidic person. Thus Zerubbabel, the current heir to the throne of David, had in his office and person a value that would be raised to an exceptionally glorious status when the projected world-wide catastrophe catapulted all competing empires into their final termination.

This "signet ring" was the seal of authority which had been taken abruptly from Jehoiachin (also named Jeconiah and Coniah) in Jeremiah 22:24, for God had rejected his leadership. The use of seals in marking property and documents was well known in the ancient Near East; therefore the signet ring was no doubt the royal insignia which was used in authorizations and authentications of the power and prestige of that government (cf. signet ring in S. of Sol. 8:6; Ecclus. 17:22). This new Davidite will be God's sign to the world

---

[1]The word "desire, treasure of all nations" *(hemdāṭ kol haggôyîm,* 2:7) is clearly plural and therefore is not a reference to the Messiah. However, Herbert Wolf, "The Desire of All Nations in Haggai 2:7: Messianic or Not?" *Journal of the Evangelical Theological Society* 19(1976): 97-102, pointed to other OT passages where the plural verb and noun clearly refer to an individual; thus the reference could be messianic.

that He intended to continue to fulfill His ancient promise. The "mercies of David" were "sure" or "unchangeable" (Isa. 55:3). Even His title of "My Servant" was more than polite court language. On the lips of Yahweh, it was a transparent reference to that corporate entity but final single individual who embodied the whole group as announced in the eighth century by Isaiah (eg., Isa. 42:1).

GOD'S CONQUERING HERO: ZECHARIAH

With eight night visions (1:7-6:8) and two burden messages (9-11; 12-14), the priest-prophet Zechariah traced the growth of God's kingdom from its humble beginnings to its triumphant victory over every opposing force. Working hand in hand with the prophet Haggai, Zechariah delivered the most intense call to repentance ever given by any OT prophet (Zech. 1:1-6) in November, 520 B.C. The evil that had "overtaken" *(hiśśîgû,* v. 6) the nation in the catastrophe of 586 B.C. and the seventy years of exile were exactly what Moses had warned with the very same vocabulary in Deuteronomy 28:15,45.

In the mutually complementary eight visions, Zechariah received a whole picture as God's answer to those who questioned the validity of the old promise and the future of Zion. In the first vision the report of the four horsemen was disheartening, for the nations of the earth remained at ease and comfort (1:11) despite the repeated threats of imminent destruction. But by the time of the eighth vision, the four chariots had completed their work of carrying out the judgment of God in every direction (6:1-8). How this was to be done was detailed in the second vision where the four horns (1:18-21 [2:1-4]), the same, no doubt, as Daniel's four successive world powers, were humbled and broken off by four smiths raised up by God. While judgment was to be ordered upon the nations, Jerusalem was to experience a rebuilding, enlargement, and exaltation (2:1ff. [2:5ff.]). Its most important feature was: "I will be to it, says Yahweh, a wall of fire round about, and I will be glory in its midst" (2:5 [9]; cf. Isa. 60:19; Rev. 21:23); and "Lo, I will come and take up My abode in your midst, says Yahweh. And many heathen nations shall join themselves to Yahweh on that day, and they shall be My people; and I will dwell in your midst, and you shall learn that Yahweh of Hosts has sent Me to you" (2:10-11 [14-15]).

My Servant Branch, the Stone

The outward establishment of the city of God as the personal residence of Yahweh must be preceded by a divine work of inner cleansing. For in Zechariah's fourth vision, he saw the high priest Joshua wearing dung-spattered clothes and standing in the presence of the angel of the Lord with the accusations of Satan being hurled at him. For the accuser, the Lord ordered silence; but for the be-smirched high priest, He ordered the removal of his filthy garments and the new clothing of rich clean apparel. The guilt of the whole nation was resting on the high priest, and thus it had made them all unclean (cf. Hag. 2:11-14). But it also promised the reestablishment of the office of high priest after a long interruption (Zech. 3:7). "The iniquity" of the land "will be removed," promised Yahweh, "in one day" (v. 9). Thus Joshua as representative of that "kingdom of priests" (Exod. 19:6) was a "sign" (*môpēṭ*, 3:8).

It was a "wonder" that the high priesthood even existed after the long interruption of the Exile; yet it too was a sign of the future. The advent of God's true and only adequate representative was the Messiah who here is called by three titles.

The "Branch" or "Sprout" of 3:8 and 6:12 was another proper name for the last Davidite, who would arise out of obscurity, already known from Isaiah 4:2 and Jeremiah 23:5-6. The fact that He appears as the "Servant" in connection with the priesthood cannot be a mere coincidence. It is here made plain that the "Branch" or "Servant" will not only be David's successor but also Joshua's. As Isaiah had declared that the Servant would give His life as an atonement for others and thereby remove their iniquity, so Zechariah 3:9 promised that the Messiah would do so in "one day."

But if the "Servant-Branch" represented Messiah's first advent, then the "Stone" as in Daniel 2:34-35 represented Messiah's second advent. Thus in the fuller passage of Zechariah 6:9-15, Zechariah was directed to make "crowns" from silver and gold brought from Babylon. This event summarized the eight night visions and their scope in one act—princely gifts coming from the far-off Babylon were but a harbinger and precursor of the wealth of the nations that would pour into Jerusalem when Messiah the Branch was received as King of kings and Lord of lords. These gifts were made into a crown for the King-Priest, the "Man" whose name was "Branch" who would "build the temple of the Lord," "sit and rule on His throne," and "be a Priest on His throne" (6:12-13). The same Lord who helped complete the building of that second temple would rule as Priest and King—both offices in one Person! That numerous peoples would come to seek the Lord resident in Jerusalem in that day and that ten men would cling to the skirts of one Jew, saying, "We will go with you, for we have heard that the Lord is with you," was the prospect outlined by Zechariah in 8:20-23.

The same Priest-King was the theme of Psalm 110, only there He was a conquering King; here in Zechariah 6 He is enthroned in peaceful dominion.

The King of Humility and Righteousness

As Zechariah began the first of his two burden messages, he predicted the victorious progress of Alexander the Great (Zech. 9:1ff.). The theme was already set: there was to be a judgment coming in which God would destroy the Gentile world powers that had also held sway over Israel. Israel's true King was coming and His inauguration into office would be symbolized by His riding on the ass (9:9, cf. Judg. 5:10; 10:4; 12:14).

His character was "righteous," the same description used by Isaiah (9:7; 11:4-5; 32:1). Yet He had also been "delivered" and was therefore victorious as a mark of the grace of God to Him. He was "humble," or even "afflicted," the same concept attributed to the "Servant of the Lord" in Isaiah 53:7. Yet this was Israel's new King. He was meek and yet He was victorious; He would destroy the implements of war (Zech. 9:10*a*), and yet He would reign in peace over the whole earth (v. 10*b*). The later picture was identical with that of Isaiah 9:1-7; 11:1-9; and Micah 5:2-5. "His dominion will be from sea to sea and from the Euphrates to the ends of the earth" as Psalm 72:8 had proclaimed (cf. Zech. 9:10*b*).

Yet even after Israel had been restored to the land after the Babylonian exile, the prospect of a regathered, reunified nation still appeared in Zechariah 10:9-12. The importance of this passage and its late postexilic date should not be lost by those who interpret the promise of the land spiritually or as a temporal blessing which has since been forfeited by a rebellious nation due to her failure to keep her part of the conditional (?) covenant. On the contrary, this hope burned brighter as Israel became more and more hopelessly scattered.

The Smitten Shepherd

Israel had had evil rulers (shepherds) who had taken advantage of their flock, but the Good Shepherd was at first accepted and then rejected and sold for thirty pieces of silver (Zech. 11:7-14). As long as He ruled them in the past, He had used two staves named "delight" and "union" *(no'am, hoblîm);* but when these two staves were broken, the power this brother-kingdom wielded in God's name was snapped. Thus the Lord was dismissed from the nation in His Davidic representative. Then as a reward or as their estimate of His service, they weighed out the sum paid for a slave (Exod. 21:32):

thirty pieces of silver! Thus the Shepherd became the Martyr-Shepherd (Zech. 13:7-9) for the sheep who had rejected His leadership.

But in another section (Zech. 12:10-13:1), the people would mourn for the One whom they had pierced as one mourned for his only son. The Shepherd was not personally deserving of this suffering, but He suffered on behalf of the sins of His people.

But the Spirit would be poured out on the people in that day, the divine Spirit of grace and supplication, for mercy and the cry of true penitence of heart and genuine sorrow for rejection of the Messiah. And as Ezekiel had predicted that the Spirit of God would give the knowledge of Yahweh and of the Savior, so that same Spirit would open conviction and repentance in the hearts of Israel.

That Final Day of Victory

One decisive battle remained yet to be fought by Yahweh. In that day, He would bring the nations of the earth together as they attempted to deal decisively and conclusively with the "Jewish question" (Zech. 14:1-2). But that was the very day selected by the Lord of Hosts in which He would go forth and fight against those nations (v. 3). With great convulsions in nature, the Lord of Glory shall descend with clouds (Dan. 7:13) along with all His saints (Zech. 14:5) and plant His feet on the Mount of Olives (vv. 4-5). Then history and the first aspect of the grand plan of God's salvific promise would be wrapped up in the most decisive triumph ever witnessed. He also would remain victor over all men, nations, and nature (v. 9ff.). Holiness to the Lord would be the dominant motif from that day onward (v. 20f.) as the wealth of the nations is gathered in worship of the present King, the promised "Seed" (v. 14ff.). Seventeen times in this second "burden" message of Zechariah 12-14, Zechariah had proclaimed, "In that day"; and twenty-two times he had pointed to "Jerusalem" and thirteen times to the "nations." These statistics alone can correctly identify the time, themes, and participants stressed in these chapters: it was earth's finest hour as her Creator, Redeemer, and now-ruling King returned to complete what He had promised to do so long ago.

GOD'S MESSENGER OF THE COVENANT: MALACHI

One more prophet, now later in the fifth century, answered the incredulous and blasphemous taunts of a people immersed in their own miseries and who complained, "Where is the God of justice?" (Mal. 2:17).

Malachi's response was simple: "The Lord whom you seek will come" (3:1). However, before He would come, Yahweh would send a forerunner to prepare the way ahead of Him (v. 1), just as Isaiah had predicted (40:1ff.), for it was necessary that mankind be morally prepared for such an advent. But when the Messenger of the covenant (*mal'ak habberît*, 3:1) would come to His temple, He would be none other than the promised Messiah, for the day of His coming was also the day of the Lord so frequently mentioned by the prophets (v. 2).

"The Lord" (*hā'āḏôn*, note the article and singular form) will come to "His temple"; thus He was Yahweh (cf. Isa. 1:24; 3:1; 10:16,33). This "angel [or messenger] of the covenant" was the Mediator through whom the Lord Himself would take up His abode in His temple. This new residence in the temple was partially realized in God's gracious presence in the temple built in response to the preaching of Haggai and Zechariah, and thus ended the self-imposed absence of the glory of God mentioned in Ezekiel 11:23.

But Malachi now also saw a personal abode of this "angel of the covenant," the coming Messiah, in His temple. Furthermore, so intense was His presence that it would contain a dreadful danger for all sinners. Asked Malachi, "Who can endure the day of His coming and who can stand when He appears?" (3:2). Accordingly, this was but a repetition of the promise made at the time of the Exodus: Yahweh would signally manifest Himself in the person of the theophanic Angel. That is what He promised in Exodus 23:20-21:

> Behold, I will send an Angel before you . . .
> for My name is in Him

(cf. Exod. 23:23; 32:34; 33:2).

Hence, Malachi's generation, like the eighth century audience of Amos (Amos 5:18,20), was mistaken in longing for the day of the Lord as if that day would be a cure-all for an unprepared people. The presence of the Lord could mean that they would all be consumed, for His holiness and their stiff-necked ways could not mix (cf. Exod. 33:3).

It was necessary that the hearts of men be sifted as in a furnace or as by soap so that the filth or dross of sin could be purged. Such a judgment would fall particularly on the priests (3:3) who would need to be cleansed before they could be used in his service.

The forerunner is first presented as a "messenger" (3:1) and then as "Elijah the prophet" (4:5). Probably we are not to think of Elijah the Tishbite, a fact sometimes encouraged by Elijah's translation into heaven without experiencing death. But after the analogy of that new or second David, so there was to be a new or second Elijah. He would be a man in the "spirit and power" of Elijah even as Jesus pointed to John the Baptist and said that he was Elijah, for he came in the "spirit and power of Elijah" (Matt. 11:14; 17:11; Luke 1:17). Thus the work of the second Elijah was also to turn the hearts of the fathers to the children and the children to the fathers in reconciliation. For if men would not voluntarily dedicate themselves wholeheartedly to the Lord, then He would be forced ultimately and finally to come and visit the earth with a "curse" (*ḥērem*, 4:6 [3:24]). This "curse" was a "ban" or an "involuntary dedication" of everything to the Lord by which He finally took what rightfully belonged to Him as a rebuke for steadfast resistance to giving any part to Him.

But Malachi was certain that all would not end in gloom and despair:

> For from the rising of the sun to its setting, My name shall be great among the Gentiles, and in every place incense shall be offered to My name, even pure offerings, for My name shall be great among the Gentiles, says the Lord of Hosts.
>
> —Malachi 1:11

Yahweh's success was as extensive geographically as was the circuit of the sun, and His places of worship were to be located not just in Jerusalem but "in *every* place" men and women would offer "pure offerings," i.e., worship unspoiled by soiled hands or hearts. God's name would be "great" and highly exalted among the Gentiles. Thus the Mosaic discussion of "place" and offerings is climaxed by a universality and a purity unknown in history past or present but surely a real part of the future.

THE KINGDOM IS THE LORD'S:
CHRONICLES, EZRA-NEHEMIAH, ESTHER

At the end of Israel's long historical climb from nonexistence into nationhood and from destruction into a weakened state in the postexilic period, the chronicler (perhaps one or more writers of Ezra, Nehemiah, Esther, 1 and 2 Chronicles) selected those historical events and words from the Davidic and Solomonic kingdom which could be used to project the image of the anticipated eschatological consummation of the promise in the new David. His awaited reign would be the climax to the old promise, and this prospect would rekindle hope amid the encircling gloom of the meager growth during the postexilic period.

The People of the Promise

The chronicler had a vision of a reunited Israel in a future day with its capital at Jerusalem along the lines of the glorious days of David and Solomon. Forty-one times in Chronicles and eight times in Ezra-Nehemiah he referred to "all Israel" besides such additional phrases as "all the house of Israel" or "all the tribes of Israel." This "all Israel" theme definitely underscored the prophets' description of the future reunification of the divided kingdom into one united kingdom (e.g., Isa. 11:13; Hos. 1:11 [2:2]; Jer. 3:18; Ezek. 37:15).

The people would be God's people, a united congregation (*'ēḏâh*) of Israel as they lived, loved, and worshiped Yahweh with a "whole [or perfect] heart" (*lᵉḇāḇ šālēm*). This expression occurs nine times in Chronicles out of a total of thirty times in the whole OT, but altogether there are thirty references in Chronicles to "heart" in the sense of right or wrong relationship. As Hanani the prophet said to King Asa:

> For the eyes of the Lord run to and fro throughout the whole earth to show Himself strong on behalf of those whose heart is perfect toward Him.
>
> —2 Chronicles 16:9

Life in the Promise

The Torah or law of God was the standard by which the people of God received their instruction. Thirty-one times the chronicler referred to the name of Moses as compared to twelve times in Samuel-Kings; and almost forty times "Torah" was used in Chronicles as compared to a mere twelve times in Samuel-Kings. Fourteen times the law was designated "the Torah of the Lord," or "of God" or "of the Lord God."[2]

In Nehemiah 8 there is an account of how Ezra brought the Word of God with him and read it to the people as they listened intently (vv. 8-9). As he read, Ezra "gave the sense" (v. 8, *śôm śeḵel*).

---

[2]These statistics come from Jacob M. Myers, "The Theology of the Chronicler," *The Anchor Bible: 1 Chronicles* (Garden City: Doubleday, 1974), pp. lxxviii f. The bibliography on the chronicler's theology grows constantly in recent days. Some of the more recent contributions with good bibliography are Roddy L. Braun, "The Message of Chronicles: Rally Round the Temple," *Concordia Theological Monthly* 42(1971): 502-14; P. Ackroyd, "The Theology of the Chronicler," *Lexington Theological Quarterly* 8(1973): 108-16; Phillip Roberts, "An Evaluation of the Chronicler's Theology of Eschatology Based on Synoptic Studies Between Samuel-Kings and Chronicles," (M.A. thesis, Trinity Evangelical Divinity School, 1974); John Goldingay, "The Chronicler as a Theologian," *Biblical Theology Bulletin* 5(1975): 99-126; H. G. M. Williamson, "The Accession of Solomon in the Books of Chronicles," *Vetus Testamentum* 26(1976): 351-61.

Thus as King Jehoshaphat had earlier sent out a group of men to instruct the people of Judah from the Torah of the Lord (2 Chron. 17:9), so Ezra now in these postexilic times had

> made up his mind to study the law of the Lord, and to do it and to teach its statutes and ordinances in Israel.
>
> —Ezra 7:10

Just as Solomon had been promised the blessing of the benefits of God's unconditional promise to the house of David "if" he was careful to observe all that the Lord had commanded Moses (1 Chron. 22:12; 28:7), so "all Israel" was urged to walk with their "whole heart" in accordance with all that God had commanded in the law of Moses. That would be the pathway of life and blessing. The eternal plan of God was part and parcel of this balance between divine sovereignty and human responsibility.

While it is true that the chronicler more frequently than not stressed the aspect of divine agency in human events in contrast to the parallel account recorded in Samuel-Kings which focused on the human agency, there was a message in the book that emphasized both aspects of divine sovereignty and human responsibility. In cases where men were clearly at fault, God still allowed the cause or situation to stand, "for this thing is done of Me," said Yahweh. For example, in the case of Rehoboam's rejection of the sagacious advice to cut taxes, he refused and thereby split the kingdom but "the cause was of God as Ahijah had predicted" (2 Chron. 10:15; cf. 11:4).[3]

This dual presentation of the events of Israel's history during the postexilic days also led to the technique of indirect references to God in writing such histories as the book of Esther. Ronald M. Hals[4] made an excellent case for God's all-causality even though His name was absent: the oblique but telling references to "another quarter" (*māqôm*, Esth. 4:14), the passive form in Esther 9:22, "the month *had been turned* for them from sorrow into gladness," and the timely coincidences (?) of the king's insomnia (6:1) or the reading of Mordecai's earlier favors done for the king (v. 2). Even the question "Who knows?" of Esther 4:14*b* is not one of despair or frustration but a rhetorical device which has its own answer for any who reflect with any care on what was happening.

---

[3]For additional passages, see 1 Chronicles 10:13; 11:9; 21:7; 2 Chronicles 12:2; 13:18; 14:11-12; 16:7; 17:3,5; 18:31; 20:30; 21:10; 22:7; 24:18,24; 25:20; 26:5,7,20; 27:6.

[4]Ronald M. Hals, "Comparison with the Book of Esther," in *The Theology of the Book of Ruth* (Philadelphia: Fortress Press, 1969), pp. 47-53.

The Kingdom of the Promise

God's promise to David was repeated in 1 Chronicles 17:14. "I will set him over My house and My kingdom forever." So David blessed Yahweh in his prayer of thanksgiving for the freewill gifts so abundantly and generously provided by Israel in response to the need for a temple to be built by Solomon.

> Yours, O Lord, is the greatness,
> the power, and the glory,
> and the victory, and the majesty;
> for all that is in heaven and in earth is Yours;
> *Yours is the kingdom,* O Lord,
> and you are exalted as head over all.
> Both riches and honor come from You
> and You *rule over all;*
> in Your hand are power and might
> and in Your hand it is to make great and to give strength to all.
> —1Chronicles 29:11-12

This "kingdom of Yahweh" which was "in the hands of the sons of David" (2 Chron. 13:8) belonged to the Lord. The king of Israel was merely God's vicegerent who owed his office to God and who symbolically continued that reign as an earnest of God's triumphal occupation of that throne. Thus to aid the sagging spirits of a downtrodden people, the chronicler revived the image of the kingdom at the height of its greatest power in order to set forth the glories of Messiah's kingdom.

Therefore the focus on the temple, the ordinances connected with the temple, and the emphasis on music and prayer in times of revival and worship were a fitting doxology to the one to whom the kingdom belonged and whose reign had already begun in believers but was yet to have its total sway over heaven and earth. That ancient prophetic word of promise had not failed, nor would it.

This message had a larger audience in mind than the Israelites themselves, for the total purpose of the genealogical lists in 1 Chronicles 1-9 was not satisfied when it served merely to authenticate those uncertain about their lineage and who wished to be included in the priesthood of Zerubbabel's day. It also exhibited the connection of the nation with the whole human race and thus addressed all descendants of "Adam." The word was not as direct as Genesis 12:3, "In your seed [Abraham] all the nations of the earth shall be blessed." However, the inference of the genealogy and the explicit claim of the promise made with David as unfolded in the kingdom theology of the chronicler made it clear that all mankind was affected by the enormity of God's eschatological work.

PART III
THE CONNECTION WITH
NEW TESTAMENT THEOLOGY

Chapter 16

The Old Testament
and
The New Testament

There is no finer summary of the connection that exists between the Old and New Testaments than that given by Willis J. Beecher in his Stone lectures delivered at Princeton just after the turn of this century:

> The proposition that the Old Testament contains a large number of predictions concerning the Messiah to come, and that these are fulfilled in Jesus Christ, may be Scriptural in substance, but it is hardly so in form. The Bible offers very few predictions save in the form of promises or threatenings. It differs from the systemized theologies in its [refusal to disconnect] prediction from promise or threatening ... [and] in emphasizing one promise rather than many predictions. This is the prevailing note in both testaments—a multitude of specifications unfolding a single promise, the promise serving as a central religious doctrine.

> This biblical generalization of the matter may be thus formulated: *God gave a promise to Abraham, and through him to all mankind; a promise eternally fulfilled and fulfilling in the history of Israel; and chiefly fulfilled in Jesus Christ, he being that which is principal in the history of Israel* (italics his).[1]

---

[1]Willis J. Beecher, *The Prophets and the Promise* (1905; reprint ed., Grand Rapids: Baker Book House, 1975), p. 178. Note that I am heavily indebted to Beecher for the outline and much of the substance that follows in the definition of the promise.

THE NEW TESTAMENT CATCHWORD
FOR THE OLD TESTAMENT

The NT writers named this single plan or development the "promise" *(epangelia)*. About forty passages may be cited from almost every part of the NT which contain this word "promise" as the quintessence of the OT teaching. Moreover, there is only *one* promise; it is a single plan. Paul, in the dock, affirmed:

> And now I stand to be judged for the hope of *the promise* made of God to our fathers; unto which our twelve tribe nation . . . hopes to attain.
> —Acts 26:6-7

His confidence, then, rested on a single promise, not a prediction, nor a number of scattered prognostications. It was a definite singular plan of God to benefit one man and through him to bless the whole world.

This one promise can be identified as that which was given to Abraham and repeated to Isaac, Jacob, and David. The writer of Hebrews said that God "made promise to Abraham"; yet Abraham also "having patiently endured, obtained the promise" (Heb. 6:13-15,17). Further, Isaac and Jacob were "heirs with him [Abraham] of the same promise," but they "received not the promise, God having provided some better thing concerning us" (11:9,39-40). Rather than posing a contradiction, the text distinguishes between receiving the *word* of promise, its partial samples of the total fulfillment, and receiving the climactic *fulfillment* itself in all its aspects. Obviously they did not receive that last aspect, but they did have the promise itself along with an earnest of it as well; they "received the promises," "not what was promised" (vv. 33,39). Likewise, Paul identified "the promise" made "to Abraham and his descendants" as the one which rested on grace and "guaranteed to all his descendants" that "they would inherit the world" (Rom. 4:13,16).

The single promise was made up of many specifications; thus it was possible for the NT writers to speak of promise*s*, using the plural. Oftentimes the writer used the article with the plural: "The promises [given] to the fathers" (Rom. 15:8-9; cf. 9:4); "inherit the promises" (Heb. 6:12) or Abraham who had "the promises" (Heb. 7:6; cf. 11:13,17). But the use of the plural did not weaken the concept of a single all-embracing doctrine of promise that included threatening and blessing, Israel and the nations, Messiah and all the believing community of all times; rather, it pointed to its multifaceted nature and breadth of scope.

For the NT writers, this one promise of God epitomized all that

God had begun to do and say in the OT and that He continued doing in their own new era. Among the variant features embraced by this single promise were the word of the blessing of the gospel for Gentiles (Gal. 3:8,14,29; Eph. 1:13; 2:12; 3:6-7); the doctrine of the resurrection from the dead (Acts 26:6-8; 2 Tim. 1:1; Heb. 9:15; 10:36; 2 Peter 3:4,9; 1 John 2:24-25); the promise of the Holy Spirit in a new fullness (Luke 24:49; Acts 2:33-39; Gal. 3:14); the doctrine of redemption from sin and its consequences (Rom. 4:2-5,9-10; James 2:21-23); and the greatest of all, the promise of Jesus the Messiah (Luke 1:69-70,72-73; Acts 2:38-39; 3:25-26; 7:2,17-18; 13:23,32-33; Gal. 3:12).

The promise was continually fulfilled in the OT; yet it awaited some climactic fulfillments in connection with the two advents of the Servant-Messiah. Still, the promise went on beyond these two advents and remained eternally operative and irrevocable (Gal. 3:15-18; Heb. 6:13,17-18). The generation of the first century believers, according to Hebrews 6:18 (note the *"we"* and *"us"*), were given the same two unshakable and immutable signs that the promise was just as unchangeable and irrevocable for them (and hence the succeeding generations) as it was for the patriarch: The divine word of promise (Gen. 12,15) and the divine oath (Gen. 22). God thereby bound Himself eternally.

The very phraseology adopted by the NT writers likewise showed a strong predilection on their part to employ the identical technical terms and metaphors used in the OT. For example, there are numerous references to my Son, my Holy One, Servant, Elect or Chosen One, Messiah, Kingdom, Branch, Shoot, Lamp of David, Seed, Root of Jesse, Horn, Lion, Star, etc.[2] In their view, they were contributing to one continuous doctrine.

THE UNITY OF THE OLD TESTAMENT AND THE NEW TESTAMENT

Cheap and facile contrasts between the two testaments are as abundant as they are wrong-headed.[3] Marcion's well-known attempt

---

[2]For a detailed list of the Davidic list of references in the New Testament, see Dennis Duling, "The Promises to David and Their Entrance into Christianity— Nailing Down a Likely Hypothesis," *New Testament Studies* 20(1974): 55-77.

[3]Robert Gordis, *Judaism in a Christian World* (New York: McGraw-Hill, 1966), pp. 136-37, quotes Claude G. Montefiore's *(Synoptic Gospels*, 2:326) brilliant response to such contrived contrasts by giving a series of contrived retrogressions from the Old to the New Testament as a proper rebuttal to those who painfully and artificially do the opposite.

to excise the OT from the church's canon was a clear failure. Unfortunately, as Marcion himself recognized all too well, such a move must also carry with it the necessary corollary that a good part of the NT text be likewise excised since it too often pictured God in much the same way and used much of the OT doctrine and Jewish culture. To greater or lesser degrees others followed Marcion's lead. For Schleiermacher, Harnack, Kierkegaard, and the younger Delitzsch, the OT was a waste or just a pagan religion.

Nor was Origen's solution any better. His way out of the problem of the amount and type of continuity and discontinuity between the two testaments was to change the obvious meaning of many OT passages into allegories. In his *De Principus*, 4:9, he proposed this remedy:

> Now the reason for the erroneous apprehension of all these points
> . . . is no other than this, that holy Scripture is not understood by
> them according to its spiritual, but according to its literal meaning
> . . . All narrative portions, relating either to the marriages or to the
> begetting of the children, or to battles of different kinds, or to any
> other histories whatever, what else can they be supposed to be,
> save the forms of hidden and sacred things.

Recently, David Leslie Baker has attempted to classify the modern solutions to the problem of the relationship between the two testaments.[4] Basically, Baker found three different solutions: (1) Arnold A. van Ruler and Kornelis H. Miskotte represented an OT solution in which the OT was the essential and real Bible with the NT being its sequel or merely its glossary of terms. (2) On the other hand, Rudolf Bultmann and Friedrich Baumgartel took the NT as the church's essential Bible and the OT was regarded as its non-Christian presupposition or preliminary witness. (3) There are a variety of solutions which Baker grouped under the rubric "biblical solutions." These included Wilhelm Vischer's christological approach, where every (!) OT text pointed to some aspect of Christ's person, work, or ministry; the typological approach, where the OT was investigated for its historical and theological similarities or correspondences to the NT; and the salvation-history approach, in which the OT was "actualized" in the NT. Others, within this grouping of "biblical solutions," suggested a continuous tension along the lines of continuity and discontinuity between the testaments, e.g.,

---

[4]David L. Baker, "The Theological Problem of the Relationship Between the Old Testament and the New Testament: A Study of Some Modern Solutions," (Doctoral thesis, University of Sheffield, August 1975); now published as *Two Testaments: One Bible* (Downers Grove, Ill.: InterVarsity Press, 1976).

Th. C. Vriezen, H. H. Rowley, C. H. Dodd, John Bright, and Brevard S. Childs.

Our solution does not appear to fit easily into any single one of these three categories. The imposition of external grids over the biblical materials must always be rejected. Thus the selection of one part of the canon of the testament over the other is just as arbitrary and deduced *ab extra* as is the application of some such principle as a christological, typological, or salvation-history approach. Where the text, as it now exists, does not validate such an organizing principle, then it is to be laid aside in favor of one that can be inductively validated. The object of the discipline of biblical theology is to discern what flow of continuity, if any, the writers betrayed in their works. Were they aware of any antecedent contributions to their subject or related subjects? And did they ever indicate that these could be grouped together or were to be differentiated from what the people of previous generations had been told?

The evidence already culled from the OT canon in part II of our work clearly argues that these OT men strongly believed that they were part of a single tradition. But, by the same token, NT connections were more than historical-chronological continuities, textual citations of previous writers, or shared ethnic and cultural heritages. The connection of subject matter and terminology was even more obvious and pointed than those of history, literature, and culture. It would be impossible to describe the message of a NT writer without referring to the Seed, the people of God, the kingdom of God, the blessing of God to all nations, and the day of the Lord, etc. Moreover, these shared subjects gave way to shared vocabulary which tended to become technical terms because of frequent appearance at critical junctures in the argument.

Moreover, history had a certain compelling force within it, for as the writers of the gospel frequently expressed it, the Messiah "must" (*dei*)[5] suffer and then rise gloriously. Likewise the apostles took comfort in times of persecution against the early church that this was nothing more or less than what had been foretold by the OT writers and the expected antipathy that had already occurred historically against God's Anointed (Acts 4:25-30). It was all predestined in the "plan" of God, to use the word of Peter and John.

This was not a "casual" and "free" use of the OT. In contradis-

---

[5]Mark 8:31; Luke 17:25; 22:37; 24:7,26; Acts 17:3. See W. Grundmann, *"Dei," Theological Dictionary of the New Testament*, 9 vols., Gerhard Kittel, ed., and G. W. Bromiley, trans. (Grand Rapids: Eerdmans, 1965), 2:21ff.

tinction to the opinions of most modern assessments of the NT use of the OT, the writers appealed to the OT in a very sober and measured way. On rare occasions, they did refer to the OT only for illustrative purposes (e.g., "which things [*hatina*] can be put in another way [*allēgoroumena*]," Gal. 4:24). But when they cited the OT for doctrine or in disquisition aimed at impressing the Jewish part of their audiences with the obvious continuities in this new religion, they had better not have been wide of the mark established by the original truth-intention of the OT writers, nor were they in our view.

THE BETTER COVENANT

The key to understanding the "better covenant" of Hebrews 8:6 is to observe the equation made between the Abrahamic promise (Heb. 6:13; 7:19,22) and the New covenant (8:6-13). Since the Mosaic covenant was the first to be completely actualized and experienced by the nation, the Abrahamic is not the first according to that writer's numbering. The Mosaic did have its faults (v. 7), but it was not because of any inadequacies on the part of the covenant-making God; rather, many of the provisions had a deliberately built-in planned obsolescence. This was indicated from the beginning when the ceremonial and civil institutions were expressly called "copies" or "patterns" made after the real (Exod. 25:9; Heb. 9:23). Many were temporary teaching devices until the "surety" of the "better covenant" arrived (Heb. 7:22). The superiority came from the progress of revelation and not from the errors or deliberate misinformation of the former covenants.

Of course, the Sinaitic or Mosaic covenant was, as we have argued above, an outgrowth of the Abrahamic; yet many of its provisions were merely preparatory. Thus when God *renewed* the ancient patriarchal promise, which continued to appear in the Sinaitic and Davidic promises, nothing was deleted, abrogated, jettisoned, or replaced except that which was clearly so delimited from its first appearance. Thus Jesus by His death renewed the covenant, but He did not institute an entirely "new" covenant.

Our contention is not that the New covenant only fulfilled the spiritual promises made to Abraham's seed. True, the middle wall of partition had been broken down between believing Jews and Gentiles (Eph. 2:13-18); but this again did not imply or explicitly teach that national identities or promises were likewise obviated any more than maleness and femaleness were dropped. Paul's claim is that Gentile believers have been "grafted into" the Jewish olive tree

(Rom. 11:17-25)[6] and made "fellowheirs of the same body and par-takers of his *promise* in Christ by the gospel" (Eph. 3:6). Since "salvation is of the Jews" (John 4:22), and since there is only one fold, one Shepherd, and yet "other . . . sheep . . . which [were] not of this fold" (John 10:16), it should not be too surprising to see the NT writers add to the emerging thesis of the OT that there was just one people of God and one program of God even though there are several aspects to that single people and single program.

Paul made the Gentile believers part of the "household of God" (Eph. 2:19) and part of "Abraham's seed" (Gal. 3:16-19). Further-more, he called them "heirs" according to the promise (Gal. 3:19), which "inheritance" was part of "the hope of their calling" (Eph. 1:18) and part of the "eternal inheritance" given to Abraham (Heb. 9:15). Thus Gentiles, who were "aliens from the state of Israel" (Eph. 2:12) and "strangers and foreigners" (v. 19) to "the covenants of promise" (v. 12), have been made to share in part of the blessing of God to Israel.

However, in the midst of this unity of the "people of God" and the "household of faith" there yet remains an expectation of a future inheritance which will also conclude God's promise with a revived nation of Israel, the kingdom of God, and the renewed heavens and earth. Again, it is evident that we share already in some of the benefits of the age to come; yet the greater part of that same unified plan still awaits a future and everlasting fulfillment.

---

[6]See the superb analysis of this passage by Bruce Corley, "The Jews, the Future, and God: Romans 9-11," *Southwestern Journal of Theology* 19(1976): 42-56.

Bibliography

I. *Major Works From 1787 to 1963*

Denton, Robert C. *Preface to Old Testament Theology.* New York: Seabury, 1963. (See especially the bibliography on Old Testament theology from before 1787 to 1963 on pp. 126-44.)

II. *A Short Selected Bibliography From 1963 to 1977*

Alonso-Schökel, Luis. "Old Testament Theology." *Sacramentum Mundi.* Edited by Karl Rahner. Vol. 4. London: Herder and Herder, 1969. Pp. 286-90.

Anderson, B. W. "Crisis in Biblical Theology." *Theology Today* 28(1971): 321-27.

Baird, William. "The Significance of Biblical Theology for the Life of the Church." *Lexington Theological Quarterly* 11(1976): 37-48.

Baker, D. L. *Two Testaments: One Bible.* Downers Grove, Ill.: InterVarsity, 1976. (See extensive bibliography on pp. 393-535.)

Barr, James. "Story and History in Biblical Theology." *Journal of Religion* 56 (1976):1-17.

————. "Trends and Prospects in Biblical Theology." *Journal of Theological Studies* 25(1974): 265-82.

Becker, J. C. "Biblical Theology in a Time of Confusion." *Theology Today* 25(1968): 185-94.

————. "Biblical Theology Today." *Princeton Seminary Bulletin* 61(1968): 13-18.

————. "Reflections on Biblical Theology." *Interpretation* 24(1970): 303-20.

Childs, Brevard S. *Biblical Theology in Crisis.* Philadelphia: Westminster, 1970.

————. "The Canonical Shape of the Prophetic Literature." *Interpretation* 32(1978): 46-55.

Clavies, H. "Remarques sur la méthode en théologie biblique." *Novum Testamentum* 14(1972): 161-90.

Clements, R. E. "Problem of Old Testament Theology." *London Quarterly and Holborn Review* 190(1965): 11-17.

Deissler, Alfons. *Die Grundbotschaft des alten Testaments.* Freiburg i Breisgau: Herder, 1972.

Fohrer, Georg. *Theologische Grundstrukturen des alten Testaments.* Berlin: Walter de Gruyter, 1972.

Bibliography

Gaffin, Richard B., Jr. "Systematic Theology and Biblical Theology." *Westminster Theological Journal* 38(1976): 281-99.

Harvey, Julien. "The New Diachronic Biblical Theology of the Old Testament." *Biblical Theology Bulletin* 1(1971): 7-29.

Hasel, Gerhard. *Old Testament Theology: Basic Issues in the Current Debate.* Rev. ed., Grand Rapids: Eerdmans, 1975. (See his selected bibliography on pp. 145-55.)

Hefner, P. "Theology's Task in a Time of Change: The Limitations of Biblical Theology." *Una Sancta* 24(1967): 39-44.

Hughes, Dale. "Salvation-History as Hermeneutics." *Evangelical Quarterly* 48(1976): 79-89.

Jansen, John F. "The Biblical Theology of Geerhardus Vos." *Princeton Seminary Bulletin* 66(1974): 23-34.

_____. "The Old Testament in 'Process' Perspective: Proposal for a Way Forward in Biblical Theology." *Magnalia Dei: The Mighty Acts of God.* Edited by Frank Cross *et al.* Garden City, N.Y.: Doubleday, 1976. Pp. 480-509.

Jasper, F. N. "The Relation of the Old Testament to the New." *Expository Times* 78(1967-68): 228-32, 267-70.

Landes, G. M. "Biblical Exegesis in Crisis: What Is the Exegetical Task in a Theological Context?" *Union Seminary Quarterly Review* 26(1971): 273-98.

Laurin, Robert B. *Contemporary Old Testament Theologians.* Valley Forge: Judson, 1970.

Lehman, Chester K. *Biblical Theology: Old Testament.* Vol. 1., Scottdale, Pa.: Herald, 1971.

McCullagh, C. B. "Possibility of an Historical Basis for Christian Theology." *Theology* 74(1971): 513-22.

McKenzie, John. *A Theology of the Old Testament.* Garden City, N.Y.: Doubleday, 1974.

Martens, Elmer. "Motivations for the Promise of Israel's Restoration to the Land in Jeremiah and Ezekiel." Ann Arbor: University Microfilms, 1972.

_____. "Tackling Old Testament Theology." *Journal of Evangelical Theological Society* 20(1977): 123-32.

Martin-Achard, Robert. "La theologie de l'ancien Testament apres les travaux de G. von Rad." *Etudes théologiques et religieuses* 47(1972): 219-26.

Murphy, R. E. "Christian Understanding of the Old Testament." *Theology Digest* 18(1970): 321-32.

Ogden, Schubert. "The Authority of Scripture for Theology." *Interpretation* 30(1976): 242-61.

Polley, Max E. "H. Wheeler Robinson and the Problem of Organizing Old Testament Theology." *The Use of the Old Testament in the New and Other Essays.* Edited by James M. Efird. Durham, North Carolina: Duke University Press, 1972. Pp. 149-69.

Robertson, Palmer. "The Outlook for Biblical Theology." *Toward a Theology For the Future.* Edited by David F. Wells and Clark H. Pinnock. Carol Stream, Ill.: Creation, 1971. Pp. 65-91.

Ruler, A. A. van. *The Christian Church and the Old Testament.* Grand Rapids: Eerdmans, 1971.

Rylaarsdam, J. C. "Of Old Testament Theology." *Criterion* 11(1971): 24-31.

Sanders, J. A. "Major Book Review: *Biblical Theology in Crisis* by Brevard Childs." *Union Seminary Quarterly Review* 26(1970): 299-304.

Scullion, John J. "Recent Old Testament Theology: Three Contributions." *Australian Biblical Review* 24(1976): 6-17.

Tate Marvin E. "Old Testament Theology: The Current Situation." *Review and Expositor* 74(1977): 279-300. (See that entire issue with articles by Terence E. Fretheim [on the theology of Gen-Numb, pp. 301-20], John D. W. Watts [on Deuteronomic theology, pp. 321-53], James L. Crenshaw [on Wisdom theology,

Bibliography

pp. 353-69], and Wayne Ward ["Towards a Biblical Theology," pp. 371-87]).

Vaux, Roland de. "Is It Possible to Write a 'Theology' of the Old Testament?" *The Bible and the Ancient Near East.* Translated by Damian McHugh. London: Darton, Longman and Todd, 1971. Pp. 47-62.

Verhoef, P. A. "Some Thoughts on the Present-Day Situation in Biblical Theology." *Westminster Theological Journal* 33(1970): 1-19.

Walther, James Arthur. "The Significance of Methodology for Biblical Theology." *Perspective* 10(1969): 217-33.

Wright, George Ernest. *The Old Testament and Theology.* New York: Harper and Row, 1970.

_____. "Reflections Concerning Old Testament Theology." *Studia Biblica et Semitica: Festschrift Th. C. Vriezen.* Wageningen: 1966. Pp. 376-88.

Youngblood, Ronald. *The Heart of the Old Testament.* Grand Rapids: Baker, 1971.

Zimmerli, W. *Grundriss der alttestamentlichen Theologie.* Stuttgart: W. Kohlhammer, 1972. (Soon to be released in English translation as *An Outline of Old Testament Theology.*)

Zyl, A. A. van. "The Relation Between Old Testament and New Testment," *Hermeneutica* (1970), pp. 9-22.

Index of Authors

275

Index of Authors

Index of Authors

Index of Subjects

Index of Subjects

Faith   67, 89, 91, 92, 93, 94, 173, 226-27
Fall   71, 72, 77, 78, 83
Fallen hut of David   48, 195-97
Father   101, 102, 152, 198
Fear of God/Lord   46, 50, 67, 68, 89, 104,
   110, 167, 168-71, 172, 173, 175, 176, 178,
   181, 200
Fellowship   63, 75, 116, 233
Finger of God   103
Firstborn   34, 50, 60, 101-103, 105, 107,
   109, 110, 152, 161, 231
Forgiveness   14, 114, 116-18, 233.
Form Criticism   7

Gathered to his people   99
Glory of God/Lord   83, 119, 120, 133, 205,
   206, 227, 230, 237-38, 253, 256, 257
God of the father(s)   58, 60
Good Shepherd   48, 198, 240-41, 255-56
Gospel (or Good News)   91, 113, 217, 223,
   266, 269
Grace   63, 72, 80, 83, 92, 100, 104, 109, 113,
   114, 171, 198, 199, 200, 256, 264

Heart, perfect   259-60
History of religions   4, 5, 10, 11, 15, 17, 22
History of tradition   7, 26, 55n, 58
Historicism   4, 5
Holiness   44, 109, 111, 116, 118, 158, 178,
   197, 205, 207, 213, 237, 256, 257
Holy nation   44, 50, 105, 108, 110, 162, 182,
   206, 207, 246
Holy One   217, 266
Holy Spirit   213, 218, 242, 265
Holy war   123, 134-36
House of David   46, 49, 50, 139, 142, 149,
   150-51, 157, 160, 195, 209, 250, 252

Image of God   74, 75, 76, 115
Immanuel   205, 207-210, 230
Incomparability of God   201, 206, 214
Interpreter's One-Volume Commentary   3
Interpretation   2

Judgment   78, 79, 81, 83, 139, 181, 182, 185,
   186, 187, 188, 189, 190, 192, 193, 194, 198,
   200, 201, 204, 205, 206, 207, 213, 218, 219,
   220, 221, 223, 224, 225, 226, 229, 246, 252,
   253, 255, 257

King   46, 49, 69, 108, 130, 141, 144-48,
   149, 155, 159, 160, 161, 162, 184, 198, 214,
   215, 243, 256
Kingdom   14, 46, 48, 49, 50, 108, 145, 146,
   147, 149, 150, 151-52, 155, 156-64, 182,
   188, 196, 208, 209, 210, 236, 239, 244-46,
   249, 253, 258, 261, 262, 265, 267, 269
Kingdom of priests   44, 50, 107-108, 162,
   182, 190, 206, 254

Kinsman-Redeemer   214
Knowledge of God   199, 234, 256

Lamp (of David)   147, 265
Land, the   14, 33, 39, 50, 58, 59, 60, 65, 86,
   89, 90, 91, 108, 123, 124, 125, 126, 127,
   132, 139, 141, 157, 172, 184, 204, 207, 214,
   224, 243, 244, 254, 255
Law (of God)   46, 51, 56, 59, 61, 62, 63, 65,
   66, 67, 94, 112-13, 114-19, 123, 132, 145,
   155, 168, 170, 171, 172, 174, 175, 179, 183,
   193, 204, 232, 233, 259, 260
Liberalism   2
Life   67, 91, 112, 130, 139, 168, 170, 171-72
Little book of comfort   48
Love of God   197-99

Mighty acts of God   2

Name (Divine)   45, 46, 63, 65, 106-107, 120,
   121, 133, 170, 196, 251, 255, 257, 258
Name (human reputation)   80, 86, 91, 153,
   189
Nation   103, 107, 110, 111
New birth   242
New covenant   35, 48, 50, 113n, 143, 157,
   185, 231-35, 242, 268
New heavens and new earth   205, 212, 217,
   218-19, 244, 269
New song   162
Normative theology   6, 11, 12, 14, 17, 33,
   40, 168

Oath   12, 33, 34, 159, 162, 204n, 265
Obsolescence   8, 268

Passover   104, 105
People (of God)   103, 105, 106, 111, 125,
   145, 146, 182, 185, 186, 190, 198, 204, 213,
   218, 221, 230, 232, 233, 236, 243, 253, 259,
   267, 269
Place for (the Divine) Name   65, 123, 124,
   130-33, 136, 141, 153, 243
Plagues   103-104
Plan (or purpose) of God   14, 24, 28, 29, 30,
   32, 39, 46, 50, 51, 69, 89, 98, 109, 129, 140,
   144, 149, 150, 164, 179, 182, 183, 184, 197,
   201, 203, 206, 210, 218, 221, 225, 252, 256,
   260, 267, 269
Positivism   9, 27
Post von Rad era   3, 27
Process theology   4
Progressive revelation   8, 34, 39, 49, 85, 88,
   268
Promise   12, 14, 24, 33, 41, 43, 44, 45, 46,
   47, 48, 49, 50, 51, 52, 56, 57, 58, 59, 61, 62,
   65, 66, 68, 69, 80, 82, 83, 86, 87, 90, 91, 93,
   94, 95, 99, 100, 101, 107, 110, 111, 113,
   124, 126, 127, 129, 136, 139, 140, 143, 145,
   146, 150, 154, 155, 157, 159, 162, 168, 170,
   172, 182, 183, 184, 196, 197, 199, 201, 202,
   205, 206, 208, 210, 221, 222, 227, 232, 235,

280

Index of Subjects

Index of Scripture References

(This index of Scriptures was provided by my Graduate Assistant, Mr. Dennis Magary, and all the indices were typed by my secretary, Mrs. Mark (Jan) Olander. Their labors have contributed immensely to making this volume more useful, and for this I am most appreciative.)

OLD TESTAMENT

289

Index of Hebrew Words

Index of Hebrew Words

Index of Hebrew Words